D0164328

FIBERGLASS BOATS

Other titles of interest

Sailboat Hull & Deck Repair
Don Casey
Everyone knows that fiberglass is durable, malleable, and easy to maintain, but what is not generally known is that it is also easy to repair. With a bit of fiberglass cloth, some resin, and these clear step-by-illustrated-step explanations, readers will be amazed at the wonders they can work. Among the repairs covered are rebedding deck hardware, replacing portlights, fixing leaky hull-deck joints, and repairing cracks, holes, blisters, and gouges. Part of the International Marine Sailboat Library.
Hardbound, 128 fully illustrated pages, $19.95. Item number 013369–7.

Sailboat Refinishing
Don Casey
Of all the improvements to a tired-looking boat, none will have a more dramatic impact than refinishing. Few boat tasks are easier – made even more so here by the step-by-step directions accompanied by detailed illustrations so clear that nothing is left to the imagination. Focuses on the hulls, decks, cabins, spars, and wood trim of fiberglass boats, and covers painting, varnishing, repairing gelcoat, and applying hull graphics.
Hardbound, 144 fully illustrated pages, $19.95. Item No. 013225–9

Spurr's Boatbook: Upgrading the Cruising Sailboat
Second Edition
Dan Spurr
A revised and expanded edition of the best-selling stem-to-stern, project-by-project approach to improving any sailboat for safe and comfortable coastal or offshore cruising. 'Its crisp style, clarity of detail and excellent source references should ensure it a place in any nautical library.' – *Sailing*
Paperbound, 352 pages, 422 illustrations, $24.95. Item No. 060554–8

Boatowner's Mechanical and Electrical Manual:
How to Maintain, Repair, and Improve Your Boat's Essential Systems
Second Edition
Nigel Calder
This best-selling, seagoing equivalent of a homeowner's fix-it-yourself manual covers everything in a power- or sailboat that has bolts, screws, moving parts, wires, or grease, and can break.
'This book should be standard equipment with every boat.' – *SAIL*
'An impressive compilation of advice on boat equipment and systems – one of the best we've seen . . . Much of the information cannot be found anywhere else.' – *Practical Sailor*
Hardbound, 592 pages, hundreds of illustrations, $49.95.
Item No. 009618–X

FIBERGLASS BOATS

3RD EDITION

HUGO DU PLESSIS

INTERNATIONAL MARINE
Camden, Maine

Published by International Marine, a Division of The McGraw-Hill Companies.

Third Edition published in 1996 in Great Britain by Adlard Coles Nautical, an imprint of A&C Black (Publishers) Ltd., London.

First Edition published by Adlard Coles Ltd. 1964; reprinted 1966; Second Edition 1973; reprinted 1974; Second Edition revised 1976; Reprinted 1978, 1979.

Copyright © Hugo du Plessis 1964, 1973, 1996

A CIP catalog record for this book is available from the Library of Congress.
ISBN 0–07–050317–6

Questions regarding the ordering of this book should be addressed to:

The McGraw-Hill Companies
Customer Service Department
P.O. Box 547
Blacklick, OH 43004
Retail customers: 1–800–262–4729
Bookstores: 1–800–722–4726

Typeset in 10¹⁄₂ on 12pt Goudy Old Style
by Falcon Oast Graphic Art
Printed and bound in Great Britain by
Hillman Printers (Frome) Ltd, Frome, Somerset.

Dedication
To my grandchildren, Nichola, Simon, Sam and Hayley. In the hope that helped by this book, builders can be inspired to make good fiberglass boats which will last long enough for them, one day, to buy cheaply and go adventuring; as I did with my beloved old *Crimson Rambler*, built long before I was born and to which I owe much. For no boat, however grand or fast, will ever bring as much fun and adventure as one's first, cheaply bought, old cruiser.

Author's note
Except where stated all photographs are my own but I am indebted to the companies who, over many years, have allowed me to take them, in particular and most recently the help given by Tony Brewer of Bondicell Ltd, Lymington. My thanks also to the many owners whose boats, with or without their permission, I have photographed – usually the nasty parts, as these most interest a surveyor. Some have been my own.

Contents

Introduction   vi

Section A • General principles

1 Principles of fiberglass boatbuilding   1
2 Materials   11
3 Tools and working conditions   24
4 Health and safety   27

Section B • Understanding how fiberglass can fail   34

5 Physical failure   35
6 Destructive influences   41
7 Fatigue   47
8 Factors of safety   49
9 Effects of heat   53
10 Fire   55

Section C • Turning a bare moulding into a boat

11 Glassing-in   63
12 Joins   68
13 Stiffening   75
14 Bulkheads   94
15 Attaching fittings   98
16 Sealants   107
17 Hardspots and stress concentrations   113
18 Double shell mouldings   121
19 Sandwich mouldings   125
20 Wood and fiberglass   145
21 Fiberglass and other materials   149
22 Sheathing   151
23 Access   157

Section D • The gel coat – that shiny fiberglass look

24 Gel coat   159
25 Weathering   167
26 Nasty little lumps   169
27 Replacing a gel coat   194

Section E • In the beginning – moulding

28 Conditions for moulding   201
29 Moulding   204
30 Moulding faults   210
31 Mouldless construction   214
32 Thickness   217
33 Mechanisation   226
34 Inspection and quality   229

Section F • Maintenance and use

35 Design for low maintenance   234
36 Maintenance and cleaning   247
37 Overloading   251
38 Painting   256

Section G • Repair

39 Temporary repair   259
40 Minor repair   264
41 Major repair   267
42 Every crack tells a story   270
43 Testing   274

Appendix Technical terms & equivalents   280

Index   283

Introduction

*'Knowledge discloses to wise men and disguises
from fools how little they know'*

This is a completely new and rewritten edition of *Fibreglass Boats*, and is confined to general principles and good practice. It does not go into detail like some other books which are a tale of how one amateur built one boat, but is applicable to all fibreglass boats. Or indeed to anything made of fibreglass, from kitchen sinks to church steeples. It also covers the little known basic theory of fibreglass, the way it fails, what it will do, and even more what it will not do, much of it never published before.

It is written in language the average boat owner or boatyard worker can understand. Frightening formulae and equations are reduced to the minimum and simplified, inserted for interest rather than essential reading. No knowledge of chemistry or mathematics is required.

Into the book have gone my forty years' experience of fibreglass boats, principally as a surveyor specialising almost exclusively in fibreglass. Consequently I have far wider experience of the good and bad points of fibreglass, what happens to it over the years, the silly mistakes and even gross blunders that are made, than a builder with his own limited range for a particular market niche.

As before, the book covers how to turn a bare moulding into a strong and seaworthy boat. Then we examine how to keep it that way for our children and grandchildren. Most wooden boats sailing today were built before fibreglass was thought of; it would be a sad reflection on our times if fibreglass boats did not last as long.

Like many other young men without much money my first small cruiser was built in my grandfather's day (and cost less than my present yacht's modest little dinghy! And half the price of the liferaft – despite needing it a lot more!). Will there be boats like that for my grandsons? I hope so, and I pray this book may help. Incidentally that old boat is still sailing and giving adventure to another generation who have not attained the affluence so widely assumed essential to own a boat.

The first edition of *Fibreglass Boats* was written when my daughter was a baby. Now I have grandchildren that age. Fibreglass boats too have grown up and are currently going through a period of development as radical as any in their history. Gone is the optimistic over-confidence of early years. As in life, time and experience bring wisdom. At last we are beginning to realise how little we know. Moreover what *is* known is not known widely enough or else is ignored. Fibreglass is not the slapdash, foolproof process it was thought to be in the early years of boundless enthusiasm, but a very complex material which undergoes subtle changes throughout its life. Until recently, this view would have been regarded as heresy.

Fibreglass has become widely accepted and is now not only the conventional building material for boats but is actually respectable – something which even the most optimistic would hardly have believed possible forty years ago. Unknown millions of fibreglass boats have been built, from dinghies and canoes through to yachts and fishing boats of every size, up to warships of almost a thousand tons.

Owners should never take a fibreglass boat for granted simply because it is made of fibreglass, especially a new boat that has not had enough use to reveal its faults. Moreover they should not assume the boat is automatically suitable for their purpose. Increased lightness of construction and sophistication under the competitive pressures of higher speed at lower cost may mean that it cannot take treatment that would never be questioned on an older, sturdier fibreglass boat.

Most attention nowadays is directed towards current production, new developments and wonder materials. That is of academic interest to the vast majority of owners whose boats are older. They are concerned with what they have now. It is largely for that majority that this book is written.

I am one of the few remaining who can remember the way boats were built ten, twenty, thirty years ago, even the exciting pioneering days forty years ago. Therefore I frequently describe how boats used to be built because that is what is relevant to many of today's owners, as well as boat repairers and surveyors. If you know how boats were made then, the limited state of the art, what was common practice, the often primitive and, by modern standards, unsatisfactory conditions, untrained workers and other problems builders faced, you can understand better what is happening to those boats now.

Some things will be regarded as heretical. But I have been so labelled before. I was one of the first to suggest, in the days of wild claims for 'no maintenance', that fibreglass boats *did* need maintenance and that they would one day have to be painted.

The previous editions of *Fibreglass Boats* were in print for over twenty years with separate editions in Britain, the USA and Russia (during the Cold War too). Wherever I go in my modest cruising style I find boatyard managers with a copy on their shelves, and boats with a copy on board. On desert islands I have met people who said they built their yachts with the aid of my book. May this edition be as useful to as many.

Hugo du Plessis
Yacht Samharcín
Royal Cruising Club

Terminology

Fibreglass is the registered trade name of Fibreglass Ltd in Britain, and Fiberglas, the trade name of Owens-Corning Fiberglas Corporation in the USA (both now under the same ownership) for glass fibres supplied by those particular companies.

In Britain 'fibreglass' has been adopted as the popular generic term for glass reinforced plastics also called GRP. With the increasing use of other reinforcements such as carbon fibre and Kevlar, the term FRP, fibre reinforced plastics, is more correct. But 'fibreglass' (with a small f) is the term which has stuck, whether technically correct or not.

So bowing to general use, I refer to the moulded material as fibreglass and thank Fibreglass Ltd for permission to use the term.

Where the context refers to the actual glass fibre reinforcement I use the term glass fibre because those companies are not the only makers.

In a lifetime of sailing, and in particular the world of liveaboard cruising folk in which I now spend most of my time, I have met many lady sailors and lady skippers, including singlehanders. Most have been competent seamen and when it came to boat work good handymen too. Or to use an old term, good ship's husbands.

The use of 'he' or '-man' is in no way meant to be discriminatory. It is common usage in the English language. Therefore unless obvious from the context, 'he' may be taken as referring to both sexes. We are all members of the *human* race.

Acknowledgements

I am indebted to many people over the last forty years, whose names are lost in the mists of time. Also those hundreds of trusting owners who asked me to examine their boats. I have learnt something from every boat.

For this edition I thank the many companies who have given help and information despite being of little commercial benefit. In particular Mr A J Horton of Scott Bader Ltd, Michael Taylor of Tyler Boat Company, Patrick Mouligné of R P Associates, Damien Jacquinet of Nidacore, Tony Brewer of Bondicell. Sovereign Chemicals kindly lent me their latest moisture meter for evaluation.

Finally the late Adlard Coles who persuaded me to set one finger to typewriter for the first edition of *Fibreglass Boats* in 1959 when fibreglass was fresh, young and exciting. Also my faithful helpers in those days, Leonard Pilgrim, Kathleen Rixon and Ada Chapman working in the stables of my old family home at Newtown Park.

General principles

Fibreglass is not like traditional materials. Anyone working on a fibreglass boat must have a general idea of how the boat was moulded and the particular characteristics of the material, especially its limitations. This applies whether fitting out a bare shell, making alterations in later years, fitting equipment to a new boat, or effecting a repair.

It is also something the owner should know if he is to maintain and use the boat properly and keep within its limitations – a most important point frequently overlooked. Unlike a sturdy old wooden boat, it cannot be taken for granted that a fibreglass boat can sail anywhere, especially the popular cruiser/racer built to sail faster at lower cost in a competitive market.

A basic familiarity with the techniques of moulding is assumed, just as books on building wooden boats do not go into simple carpentry.

CHAPTER

1

Principles of fibreglass boatbuilding

People talk about the 'fibreglass revolution' as if the material caused the revolution. Not so. The revolution has been in factory production. The demise of the local, waterfront boatbuilder, building one-off boats to order, went hand in hand with the change to boatbuilding factories in industrial areas with a range of standard boats, often subsidiaries of large companies in unrelated industries. Boatbuilding has become big business and the market international.

This development was inevitable to satisfy the booming demand of an affluent society. It had already started with wooden boats. There were redundant wartime factories with the expertise to make aluminium or steel boats, but they missed the opportunity. Fibreglass just came along at the right moment and proved the most suitable material for the new scale of production, while itself requiring that scale to be economic. Now it has ousted wood, the traditional material since the dugout canoe, and has become conventional itself. Technically it is not greatly superior to wood, steel or aluminium and in some respects is worse.

The individually designed, one-off yacht has gone, except for top flight racing machines. Production boatbuilders must sell one design to as many buyers as possible. Builders need to think in hundreds, even thousands, because large capital investment is involved.

Designs must have wide appeal, be fashionable and 'safe'. Consequently they tend to follow similar lines and look alike, strongly influenced by racing and rating rules even for cruising yachts. The market is very competitive and is dominated by the need for performance and comfort. Other types of boats are still built, but outside this fashionable mainstream the choice is limited.

The industry is governed by what can be sold at greatest profit in greatest number, and yet is critically dependent on selling in those numbers. Factory builders cannot fall back on repairs and fitting out as a waterfront boatyard can. Like an aircraft which loses flying speed they will crash. Boats are a luxury market, the first to be hit by any recession. The survivors have generally been those with the best business management and not necessarily the best boatbuilders.

Construction is dominated more by production convenience than best boat practice. In particular, little consideration is given to what can be maintained, modified or repaired conveniently and cheaply in later years. Yachts are no longer built to last, as they were in our grandfathers' day. Now they are consumer durables.

Speed sells. In seeking ever more competitive performance even ordinary boats become lighter and flimsier, as computerised design refines the parameters.

Comfort is the other selling point. Many 'luxury' yachts stuffed with creature comforts have hulls of poor quality. Price is no guide to the integrity of the hull, yet no part of the boat is more important. Since marketing and economics dominate factory boatbuilding we must view fibreglass boats in this light.

What is 'fibreglass'?

What is this stuff, fibreglass, which fills marinas? It consists of two principal components. A thermoset plastics resin, generally polyester but sometimes epoxy, and glass fibre reinforcement. Despite the popular name it is typically about 80% resin and only 20% glass fibre.

The resin is always the major part. Fibreglass boats are really plastics boats. They look, feel and behave like plastics, which gave rise to much contempt in the early days, and scathing remarks about soap dishes, which was not helped by some novel designs. In theory it is possible to make a boat out of polyester resin alone and it would look exactly like a fibreglass boat – as long as it held together. But it is not possible to make a boat out of glass fibre alone. It would be as watertight as a woolly jumper and as shapeless as a wet blanket. Neither material by itself can make a

Photos 1.1 (a) A typical modern scene. Row after row of production cruisers, fast, fun to sail but mostly lightly built, designed for performance and comfort below. **(b)** At the other extreme are sturdy, hard working fishing boats handling heavy gear in all weathers. Note the close spaced, massive frames (Photo: Aqua-star Ltd, Guernsey).

boat, but together they form a very versatile and strong material.

The role of the polyester is underestimated. It makes the boat watertight, binds the fibres together without which their strength cannot be captured, and gives the shiny colourful finish we recognise as 'fibreglass'. A more accurate term would be a polyester boat as the French and Germans refer to them. Yet despite being the minor component the glass fibres are still vital. Buried within the moulding they provide strength and toughness, reinforcing the brittle polyester. They are not dissolved, as is sometimes thought when the fibres become almost invisible; as everyone knows glass is transparent.

Composite materials are common. Reinforced concrete and motor tyres are two everyday examples. Most materials in nature are composites too. Wood is a far more complicated composite than anything made by man, who is himself a bone-reinforced chunk of flesh.

Why glass?

Glass is a very inert material. It does not absorb water and thereby swell or rot, it has high heat resistance, and does not burn. Only the strongest chemicals attack glass. It virtually lasts for ever. On the face of it, an ideal material for marine use. Yet, as is well known, glass is very easily broken. So how could glass make anything strong? A very good question.

Glass breaks because it does not bend, as we learn when we are young and try to 'bend' a window with a ball. Yet if it can be prevented from bending, or rather from bending sharply, it is a remarkably strong material in both tension and compression. When embedded in resin, glass fibres cannot bend, so their strength can be captured without their fragility.

You are probably reading this by electric light, brought to you along wires suspended on strong glass insulators dangling from great pylons. But it is as very fine fibres that glass shows its most remarkable strength, 500,000 lb/in^2 or 35,000 kg/cm^2 – many times more than the strongest steel. However, it has never been possible to capture such high strength in practice, principally because the fibres are very sensitive to notch effect, just as a glazier uses a diamond cutter on window glass. Even touching a fibre is enough to damage it, so the effective strength is only a tenth of the highest theoretically attainable.

There are a few fibres stronger than glass, such as sapphire whiskers (but not Kevlar or carbon) in the realm of aerospace, where the sky is the limit in cost. Yet there is one fibre not only stronger but so common that it is in every household: a spider's web. Scientists are attempting to train spiders to produce webs in commercial quantities and one day the boast for a super racing machine may not be Kevlar and carbon fibre but some exotic cobweb. My house should be worth a fortune!

Making fibreglass

Fibreglass is a man-made material. But so are all others. Even wood, a product of nature, has to be carefully selected, sawn and shaped. The difference is the way these materials are made

Table 1.1 Comparative fibre strength – tensile

	E glass	S glass	Kevlar 49	Carbon	Dyneema Polythene
Tensile strength					
lb/in^2 x 10^3	450	600	525	490–700	390
MPa	3100	4140	3620	3400–4900	2700
Tensile modulus E					
lb/in^2 x 10^6	10.5	12.4	18	33–75	12.5
GPa	72	85	124	230–540	87
Elongation to break %	4.3	4.8	2.5	1.5	
SG	2.55	2.49	1.44	1.80	0.97

Note: *Quoted figures can vary considerably according to grade and source, particularly carbon fibre. (Ref: Du Pont, Kevlar User Guide); Anchor Reinforcements data.*

into a boat. Wood is bought in planks or sheets of factory-made plywood. Steel is supplied in plates or sections of precisely known strength and quality. Screws and nuts and bolts are bought in boxes. But fibreglass is 'made' on the spot by the user, from polyester resin and glass fibre. It can be compared with making a cake. Moreover, just as there are good and bad cooks, so there are good and bad moulders.

Regardless of how carefully the suppliers of the resin and glass control these basic materials (and nowadays that is pretty reliable) the strength and quality of the end product are entirely in the hands of the moulder who uses them. This cannot be emphasised too strongly.

Polyester resin is supplied in drums in liquid form. The glass fibre comes in rolls. In simple terms the technique is to saturate the glass fibre with resin in a mould so that when the resin solidifies, which it does quite quickly by the addition of peroxide catalyst without heat or pressure, a hard, strong material is formed. Moreover this does not have to be formed to shape afterwards like wood or steel; it is at once in the shape of the mould, and substantially in one piece, not built up from many separate pieces held together with innumerable fastenings. But an absolutely essential requirement is some form of mould or support until it has set.

Although basically easy, the process is so unlike any other that if you have not used these materials before do some trials before tackling anything important. That includes the repair kit you picked up in the chandlery in case it was ever needed. When up the creek is not the time to find out how to use it.

Lamination

A fibreglass moulding is built up layer by layer in a series of laminations, similar to plywood. Each layer of fibreglass is strong but is bonded to other layers by lines of unreinforced polyester resin. There is little intermeshing of the fibres. Considered as a whole, the strength is adequate. But unlike the resorcinol of plywood, polyester is not a strong glue. Therefore the boat's design, especially detail design and

Table 1.2   Comparative strength of materials

| | Fibreglass | | | | Steel | Aluminium | Ply-wood |
	Mat	Woven rovings	Design Mat/WR	Uni-directional			
SG	1.5	1.7	1.6	1.8	7.1	2.7	0.8
Weight lb/ft³	94	106	100	112	443	168	50
Glass content % Gc	30	50	40	60	–	–	–
Strength x 10³							
Tensile lb/in²	12	27	18	40	35	20	8.5
N/mm²	85	187	123	277	240	140	59
Compressive lb/in²	17	21	19	24	35	20	4
N/mm²	117	147	132	162	240	140	28
Modulus x 10⁶ E							
Tensile E lb/in²	0.9	2.0	1.4	2.5	30	10	1.2
N/mm²	6.4	13.7	10.0	17.5	206	69	8.3

Note: Figures quoted for the various forms of fibreglass vary greatly, as do the moulding tolerances. These are typical only for comparison. Nowadays the practice is to calculate for the particular lay up and combination of mat and rovings. These values are based on formulae specified in the EEC draft proposals for GRP boats as follows:

Ultimate tensile strength	$1278\ G_c^2 - 510 G_c + 123$ N/mm²
Tensile Modulus E	$(370\ G_c - 4.25) \times 10^3$ N/mm²
Compressive strength	$150\ G_c + 72$ N/mm²

Other authorities use different formulae. There is no general agreement.

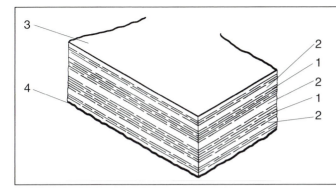

Figure 1.1 Laminates
A fibreglass moulding is made up of layers of glass reinforcement, 1, bonded together with layers of weaker unreinforced polyester resin, 2.

The side that was laid up against the mould with the gel coat, 3, is smooth. The opposite side, 4, uncontrolled by the mould face is uneven.

attachments, must not induce delamination.

When applied 'wet-on-wet' there is good chemical bond and with glass mat some intermeshing. With a largish moulding, however, all layers cannot be made like this because of the time involved. Workers like to eat and sleep. So much of the moulding must inevitably be wet-on-dry, ie new layers on top of fibreglass that is already hard. When newly set, fibreglass is still chemically receptive to fresh resin, but later the bond becomes purely adhesive.

Resin/glass ratio

It is commonly quoted and assumed that the glass provides the strength and the resin just keeps the water out. Therefore the more glass the stronger the moulding. While true in theory, it neglects elementary engineering principles. Stiffness, ie resistance to bending, is proportional to the cube of thickness (Chapter 18). The principal requirement in boatbuilding is rigidity, not high strength, the figures most often quoted. Generally when a boat is stiff enough a boat is strong enough.

Within reasonable limits, for a given weight of glass fibre and therefore strength, a high resin content moulding will be stiffer than a low one. It will also be more damage resistant – a valuable practical characteristic which gets little consideration. The boat will of course be more expensive, heavier and, crime of crimes, slower.

Moulding

A fibreglass boat cannot be moulded in thin air in the way that a wooden boat can be made where only lines on paper existed before. The first stage is to create the shape – a pattern. In effect you have to make two boats in order to get one, although in terms of practical economics it is one boat to get hundreds. The initial shape can be made of anything. It does not need to float. It can be just a shape, a master pattern. Yet as every moulding depends on the accuracy of that pattern, it must be absolutely right. Unlike building wooden boats there is no second chance with fibreglass. Mistakes will be locked in. If wrong, all will be wrong.

The surface finish will be reproduced in exact detail too. Any blemish will be copied by every boat. So a great deal of time, trouble and expense will go into giving the pattern a superb finish.

Traditionalists bemoan the passing of the skills which go into building a wooden boat compared with what they decry as the crude 'bucket and brush' way fibreglass boats are moulded. They overlook the skill required to make the pattern and mould, which is far higher than for building a wooden boat. Paint and putty can cover bad work on wood. But when making the pattern for a production run of hundreds of fibreglass boats there is only one standard: perfection.

From this master pattern is made the female mould, nowadays always fibreglass too. This is a negative mould – the shape of the moulding in reverse; the boat inside out. Obviously the moulding has to come out of the mould and the easier the original shape allows this, the better.

If the finish of the mould is good, every moulding will come out of the mould needing virtually no further surface treatment. This is a great saving in labour compared with the careful preparation, painting and making good required with other materials.

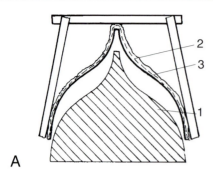 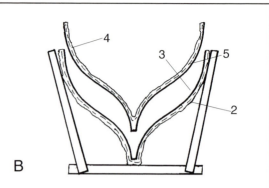

Figure 1.2 Moulding: pattern – mould – moulding

A First is made the shape, the pattern, 1, accurate in size and detail and as nearly perfectly finished as possible.

Over this is moulded the fibreglass mould, 2, the exact negative of the pattern. The gel coat, 3, picks up the perfect finish of the pattern.

B The mould is inverted and in this negative shape is made the moulding, 4, with the exact shape and surface finish of the pattern. Note that the gel coat, 5, is now the outside.

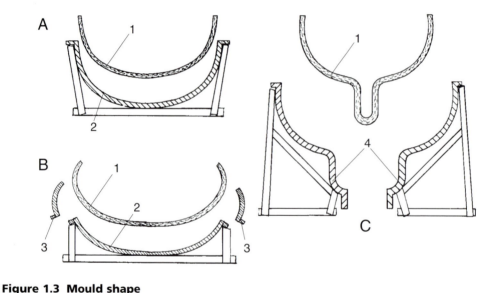

Figure 1.3 Mould shape

A A simple shape, 1, will release from the mould, 2, easily as it is a straight draw.
B If there are undercuts a straight draw is impossible. So the portion causing the undercut, 3, must be detachable.

C Deep shapes are also difficult to release and often made in a mould split along the centreline, 4. This makes moulding easier too.

Seldom realised, by enthusiasts starting off, is the capital cost to make a set of moulds. The shapes are often complicated and parts must fit accurately. A substantial production run is essential to amortise the cost. The price of the boat must be based on a guess of future sales. Then it is sink or swim, which is why a reces-

sion sinks so many boatbuilders who guessed wrongly at the state of the economic climate several years ahead. Fibreglass boatbuilding is a risky business.

Mouldless construction, used for one-off boats or backyard building, is a misnomer. A former of some kind is still essential but in this

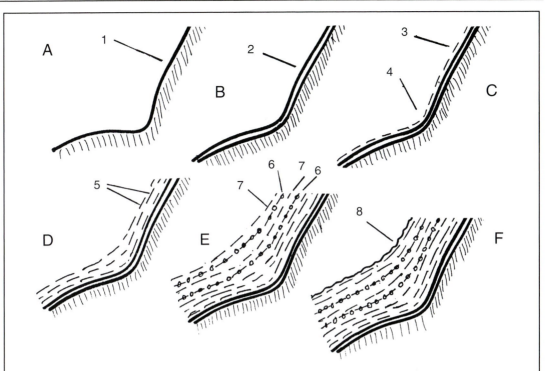

Figure 1.4 Sequence of moulding
A The mould is carefully polished so its own gel coat, 1, will impart a good finish to the moulding. Release agent is applied if necessary.
B The first step is applying the gel coat, 2.
C As soon as possible the first layer, 3, is moulded very carefully. This is the most critical of all. It should be thin mat and must be worked perfectly into features, 4.
D When the first layer has set sufficiently that it cannot be disturbed one or two further layers of mat, 5, are moulded. These may be thicker. Note how the feature is rounding off and becoming easier to mould.
E Now the main structural layers can be built up using alternate layers of woven rovings, 6, and mat; as many as required. The last layer should be mat, 7.
F The final stage is a thick coat of finishing resin, 8. Note how this inner surface is uneven because it is not controlled by the smooth mould face.

case it is a cheap, simple, expendable male mould (Chapter 31).

Fabrication cost

No comparison with other materials is valid unless it considers the cost and trouble of fabrication. Wood and steel may be cheaper but they have to be bought in sheets, sections or planks, made in sizes and thicknesses to suit the supplier not the user. Before they are boat shaped and carefully fitted a lot has to be cut away by various means, all laborious, intensive and energy consuming. Then the many separate pieces have to be joined with innumerable expensive fastenings. Wastage is very high simply because the material is the wrong shape in the first place. Fibreglass, on the other hand, is moulded to size, shape and thickness by the user and needs little more material than is required for the job. There is very little waste, a virtue in a world where conservation is a rising hymn.

As fibreglass is the right shape first time and is in one piece, it means an enormous reduction in the labour cost. In principle it is no more trouble to mould a complicated shape than a simple one.

Gel coat

When moulding a fibreglass boat the finish is put on first. That may sound nonsense, yet it is quite simple. Consider a boat being made in a female mould. What is to be outside must obviously go into the mould first. This is the gel coat (Chapter 24), a thick layer of specially formulated unreinforced resin, which takes up the smooth, highly polished surface of the mould. After this the strength-giving fibreglass layers are built up.

Unlike paint, a different material applied last of all in conventional construction of almost everything else, the gel coat is an integral part of the moulding. It is polyester resin and so melds into the rest of the moulding as it sets and cures.

The gel coat is the only part of the boat which is seen, the familiar appearance of fibreglass – the sales appeal. So it has to be good. Less appreciated is its important role of protecting the structural fibres from minor damage. It is also supposed to keep water out, but of that more later (Chapter 26).

Inside finish

The inside or natural finish of fibreglass is quite different because there is no mould to form a smooth polished surface. Consequently it is uneven and often shows fibres or weave. The inside follows the general shape of the mould but not the detail and thus tends to round off features. Nowadays it is considered ugly and has to be hidden from view. Yet the inside of a wooden boat, with its untidy frames and seams, was considered 'boaty' and rather nice.

Although uneven the surface should be solid and glossy with resin, like 'a summer sea ruffled by a catspaw of a breeze', and reflects the skill and care of the moulder. Bad mould-

Photo 1.2 Not being controlled by the smooth mould surface, the inside is rough with a fibre pattern. Nevertheless it must be solid with plenty of resin, never fibrous, whiskery or full of pinholes. A glossy resin rich surface is even better. Note the nuts, not glassed over and accessible.

ings are resin starved, the mat has a prominent fibre pattern, even whiskers, and the weave of woven rovings is conspicuous, often with multiple pinholes. Perhaps this is why some builders are so anxious to hide it.

'No maintenance'

In the exciting pioneering days it was claimed that fibreglass boats required no maintenance whatever. That shiny finish would last for ever. (Fortunately this was before the Trades Descriptions Act.) It was probably the main factor making fibreglass popular, or indeed surviving at all in the face of widespread prejudice.

The aura still lingers, although it is more correct to say low maintenance. Certainly the colourful finish is durable compared with most in a marine atmosphere. After ten years or so the owner may consider painting the surface but for appearance only. The gel coat itself lasts the life of the boat.

That at least is the theory and for the topsides and deck is generally true. Unfortunately it has been discovered that gel coats have a tendency to blister underwater; the dreaded osmosis or 'boat pox' (Chapter 26). The fashionable and frequently unnecessary cure is to strip off the gel coat and replace it with something not much better. Yet in most cases the fault lies not in the gel coat, which may be the soundest part of the boat, but in the moulding beneath.

A wooden boat, painted every year, appears each spring in pristine freshness. But a fibreglass boat, denied this annual beauty treatment, must display the accumulated scars of previous years with nothing to hide its shame. That is what the magic slogan 'no maintenance' really means.

Other materials

Because it is easy to mould to shape there is a tendency to regard fibreglass as suitable for every part of the boat. This is bad practice. For many purposes metal and wood are better.

For good design one must think fibreglass, and not slavishly copy other materials. It may be cheaper or more convenient for production to make a part in fibreglass. But will it do the job as well? Will it stand up to wear? First and foremost a fibreglass boat must be a strong, seaworthy, practical, trouble free boat, not just a pretty, easily made, boat shaped fibreglass moulding.

Skill

Despite having become a factory industry, fibreglass boatbuilding has always been labour intensive. Only recently has it been more widely accepted that good moulding can be done only by good workers. Early on it was considered a crude bucket and brush job, on a par with pouring concrete. Being all done in a mould nothing could go wrong. Or so it was thought. Not like the skilled craft of building a wooden or steel boat. It was seldom appreciated that skilled or not, the moulders working in the mould were actually building the boat. Their workmanship was just as crucial as when building a wooden boat.

Tin cans v plastic bottles

It is often claimed that for serious cruising one must have a steel boat. Fibreglass is not strong enough. This is not true of fibreglass in general. What it does reflect is that most current fibreglass yacht design and building is not strong enough. It is unrealistic to compare a steel yacht purpose built for sailing round the world with a popular fibreglass fun-to-sail cruiser/racer made for weekend sailing.

A fibreglass cruiser can be made as strong and tough as you like. Moreover it would be lighter and faster than an equivalent steel boat, but inevitably uncompetitive with popular cruisers. As few moulders would interrupt their production cycle to make a specially strengthened boat, and would charge outrageously if they did, it is generally cheaper to order a one-off steel or wooden boat.

Strong fibreglass boats do exist – yachts as well as work and fishing boats – but inevitably in the upper price range. To add to the confusion, most expensive fibreglass yachts are no stronger than cheap ones.

Because one boat of a particular class has made a spectacular voyage, it does not follow that any other boat of that class can do the same. It may have been specially strengthened for publicity or by an owner later.

I have long been impressed by the way nearly all wooden boats, especially older ones, are considerably stronger and tougher than most fibreglass boats. This is not to imply that fibreglass as such is weaker. Far from it. But its nature allows a very different, lighter, cheaper construction, and its high material cost encourages the minimum in a competitive market. Fashion also demands ever faster boats. The scene is entirely different from when those wooden boats were built.

Existing boats

There is a huge and growing fleet of earlier boats, ten, twenty, even thirty years old. Unlike steel and wood, which have been

a   b

Photo 1.3 (a) The biggest fibreglass ships, the 470 ton minehunter, *H.M.S. Sandown*, built by Vosper Thorneycroft, Southampton, England (Photo: Vosper Thorneycroft Ltd).   **(b)** The first large motor yacht, *Bebe Grand*, 55 ft (17 m), built by Halmatic Ltd in 1955 and still in service. Even after 30 years there were no blisters. To make a yacht of this size in those days needed much courage and faith at a time when most builders were making only dinghies – and people said even *they* had more faith than sense (Photo: Scott Bader Ltd).

around for generations. Millions of boats have been made without anyone knowing what is going to happen to them, or even how to get rid of them. To add to the difficulty there has been continual development. New boats will still give trouble but in different ways.

Many good boats have been made, conscientiously moulded to the state of the art at the time. One cannot do better, even though it is found later to have been not good enough. But there were also an awful lot of builders in the early boom years moulding hulls with unskilled, untrained labourers working on a speed related bonus. Quality control meant expense. These builders included many of the largest and best known.

Energy

Fibreglass is a low energy material. It takes comparatively little to make polyester resin, which is a by-product of the oil industry, described by those living near a refinery as the stink, and would otherwise be burnt as waste. Glass fibre needs a furnace to melt the raw glass but the energy required is not as great as for metal. After that, all the fibreglass moulding and subsequent work is done without heat or pressure. The only energy used is to heat the workshop.

Steel takes a vast amount of energy to dig it from the ground, ship the ore, melt and roll it into usable form. All fabrication, cutting, shaping and welding requires high energy. Throughout its life it needs more energy to shift the greater weight. Smelting aluminium needs even higher energy. Wood requires energy to fell and transform the tree into usable form and then power tools or human energy to shape it. It takes more oil to make a ton of steel, which is not made from oil, than a ton of plastics which is. And being lighter, a ton of plastics is a lot more material.

Simple chemistry

Like all organic chemistry the reactions are far more complex than simple school chemistry. However, one need not be a chemist to use the materials. A simple analogy can explain what happens.

Polyester resin in the liquid state consists of long chains of molecules, hundreds of groups long, like a centipede with hundreds of hands. When the whistle blows, in the form of adding catalyst, the centipedes join hands and form a solid lump. This is polymerising or hardening.

Centipedes are mere flesh and can be pulled apart quite easily. But imagine them crawling through a roll of wire netting. Now when they hold hands the wires stop them being pulled apart and the linked centipedes turn the flexible netting into a rigid, strong mass. If you see some similarity with reinforced concrete or a ferro-cement boat you are right. Similarity to a wooden boat is coincidental, the fact that both are boats.

Fitting out

The fibreglass moulding comes out of the mould more or less in the shape of a boat. How can that shape be turned into a sound, safe and seaworthy boat? The following chapters describe the basic principles.

These apply also to all work done later when making additions, alterations or repairs. As the boat ages and moves down the social scale owners become more impecunious and tend to do more of their own work. They often spoil their boats through ignorance. Obsolescence requires the addition of things unheard of when the boat was built.

Earlier boats were simpler and more easily altered. Modern boats with their sophisticated internal mouldings and fancy glued woodwork are often impossible to change. This, however, is a social problem. Yet a boat with a short life because it cannot be updated is a crime against nature.

Materials

Polyester resin and glass fibre come in various forms for many applications. It is essential to use materials approved for marine use; avoid job lots.

Polyester resin

Polyester is a wide family of chemicals. As you read this you may be sitting in an armchair upholstered with soft polyurethane foam, a form of polyester, and wearing trousers or a skirt made of polyester fibre more often known by trade names like Terylene or Dacron. There are polyester ropes and sails and polyurethane paints too.

For some unscientific reason polyester has been accepted internationally as the term for the particular form used for making reinforced plastics mouldings, some of which become fibreglass boats. Even so there is no one type of polyester. They are all blends of several resins. The principal properties have to meet the hundreds of national, industrial and military specifications, but can vary in the secondary properties relevant for boats.

Polyester resin, as supplied, is a thick almost colourless liquid which resembles golden syrup in appearance and is just as horribly sticky. It is a two-part resin. To make it harden a peroxide catalyst must be added. The amount required is small, about 1–2%. Setting time depends on the temperature, normally about 15 minutes and should not be longer than an hour. It can be adjusted by varying the amount of catalyst.

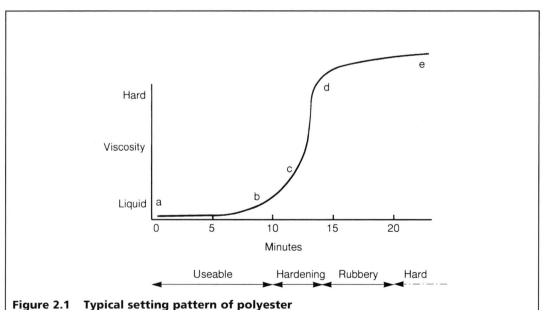

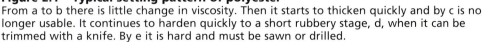

Figure 2.1   Typical setting pattern of polyester
From a to b there is little change in viscosity. Then it starts to thicken quickly and by c is no longer usable. It continues to harden quickly to a short rubbery stage, d, when it can be trimmed with a knife. By e it is hard and must be sawn or drilled.
   Note: the actual time will vary according to catalyst and temperature.

A peculiar feature is that after adding catalyst the resin remains liquid and usable for a time with no apparent change, then begins to harden quite suddenly. Within minutes it becomes too stiff to work and soon after is solid. The liquid resin is just an intermediate phase. The chemical reaction in the manufacturer's cauldron was halted while still incomplete by introducing an inhibitor. The first action of the catalyst is to gobble up this inhibitor. Only then can the hardening start and the reaction be completed (Fig 2.1).

Polyester resin is destined to be solid sooner or later even without a catalyst. The inhibitor cannot hold it in check indefinitely. Consequently liquid resin has a limited shelf life. A tin will often have gone hard when you want to use it.

This rapid setting after the initial period of no apparent change is apt to catch out the inexperienced. A basic rule is never to mix more than can be used during a short working time. Interruptions are fatal. Lock the door, take the telephone off the hook and let the tea get cold. Resin waits for no man once catalyst has been added.

Factors affecting setting time	
Extending	*Decreasing*
Cool temperatures	High temperatures
Cold resin	Warm resin
Conductive surface, eg metal	Low conductivity surface, eg fibreglass or wood
Wind and draughts, open air	Direct sunlight, fluorescent lights, ultraviolet light
Most fillers	
Thin mouldings	Thick mouldings, bulk fillings
Moisture	
Low reactivity resins	Contact with newly set resin
Reduced catalyst or accelerator	High reactivity resins
	Increased catalyst or accelerator

Polyester requires a third component to make it set at room temperature, an accelerator, generally purple cobalt napthenate. Nowadays resin is usually supplied pre-accelerated, ie it is already mixed in, but always check. (It is often coded PA.) If not, then the resin will not set unless accelerator is added separately. This can be dangerous (Chapter 4). For safety buy pre-accelerated resins.

Styrene is a constituent of most polyester resins and gives the familiar smell. It is not only the solvent to make them fluid but is also an essential part of the chemical reaction. Being a volatile liquid it evaporates and is now considered mildly toxic. To reduce styrene emission environmentally friendly resins have been developed (Chapter 4).

Working conditions are also important. Resins are sensitive to temperature and damp during the critical working, setting and curing time. Serious work demands controlled temperature and dry conditions (Chapter 28). Nowadays a production moulder should have a specially built or adapted building. The days have gone when a polythene tent at one end of a dusty factory was considered adequate, although that is how most earlier boats were moulded.

It is possible to work outside these limits, such as for emergency repairs (Chapter 39) but quality will suffer. In extreme conditions of near freezing damp weather, the resin may not set at all, or only very slowly and will have poor strength and water resistance.

Manufacturers do not make special boat resins, although some of the resins they do make are approved for boats by the appropriate authorities, and are quite adequate. Boats are not the largest use. An amateur or small business buying quantities less than tons will have to take what they can get, probably a general purpose resin, which may not be the best for marine use. A specialist fibreglass supplier should be able to supply the specifications but a chandler or hardware store will know nothing more than it says on the can, which will probably claim to do everything.

Comparing data can be difficult. Manufacturers give the principal properties such as strength and moduli, but for a technical product the information is often scrappy. It is difficult to compare secondary properties as they quote different ones, if at all, and often in different units. Few mention those relevant to boatbuilding, in particular wet strength and weathering, elongation to break and the length of the 'green' or uncured stage.

The resin should be matched to the elongation to break of glass fibre, normally 2.25%. Therefore the resin should be at least 2.5% so that it does not crack until the glass fails. However, the strongest polyesters tend to be brittle with lower elongation. Consequently a lower strength but more flexible resin makes a better, more resilient moulding than a theoretically stronger one – especially in the long term, when use and natural stress relief cause breakdown.

General purpose resins are usually the cheaper orthophthalic polyesters but the tin will seldom say this. To reduce water absorption, the major cause of blistering, it is now common practice for the gel coat and outer layers of hulls to be moulded with more water resistant but dearer isophthalic polyesters (Chapter 24). The terms refer to the acid from which the resins are made. There is no difference in appearance or use. Being more difficult to make, hence more expensive, few moulders use isophthalic throughout. Older boats would have been moulded with orthophthalic. Blistering had not then become a problem and anyway nobody knew why.

Polyester Resin

Polyester resin is made from oil and coal, via the complex knitting that is the modern petrochemical industry. It was discovered by the Swedish chemist Berzelius in 1847, almost a hundred years before going into production as a wartime electrical insulation to replace natural varnishes cut off by Japanese conquests.

It is made by the reaction of a dibasic acid with glycol, a dihydride alcohol. The acid is unsaturated maleic anhydride modified with saturated orthophthalic or isophthalic acid. The glycol is ethylene or propylene glycol. To crosslink these long chain molecules styrene is used as a reactive monomer. Other acids, glycols or monomers may be used or blended for special properties.

A manufacturer may claim a resin is isophthalic by adding a modest quantity. This is not as good as one consisting entirely of isophthalic but it is cheaper. Even moulders may be deceived, let alone an owner who has no idea what it means but assumes it must be better.

There are other grades of polyester, such as self-extinguishing, heat resistant, food quality or chemical resistant. The only ones usually of interest are self-extinguishing (Chapter 10).

The low flashpoint of 90°F, 32°C, means that liquid polyester is classified as highly inflammable. This does not imply that it is dangerous like petrol (gasolene), but it is rated as hazardous for transport and may not be sent by post or air. In Britain it comes under the 'Highly Inflammable Liquids and Petroleum Gases Regulations', so always take sensible precautions.

Gel coat

This is the visible part of the boat where defects show (Section D). Gel coats are polyester resins specially formulated to be applied on the mould face. They are a blend designed to give good appearance, colour, water and weather resistance, freedom from crazing and cracking, abrasion resistance and any other properties according to what the suppliers think most important. The primary properties meet required standards but secondary ones can vary.

Gel coats are not paint but an integral part of the moulding, all melding together, and to cure properly depend on the mass of moulding which lies behind curing at the same time. If the timing is wrong they will not cure properly. They should not be used separately, though this is often wrongly specified.

Finishing resins

Polyester resins are air inhibited. Once in contact with air solvents and styrene evaporate so the resin does not cure properly and remains tacky. Finishing resin, sometimes called flow coat or top coat, contains wax which migrates to the surface and shields it. But this hinders subsequent bonding unless it is sanded.

Finishing resin may need to be improvised to finish off a repair. A recommended method is to dissolve 10% of paraffin wax in styrene heated to 140°F, 60°C (just too hot to touch), and add to the resin to reduce the proportion of wax to 0.4%. If styrene is not available use polyester. Candle shavings are a substitute for wax.

(**Note: styrene and polyester are inflammable. Heat with caution in a water bath, and not over a naked flame.**)

Thixotropic resins

On a sloping surface like a boat hull, resin will tend to drain to the bottom before it sets.

Therefore most general purpose resins are supplied thixotropic, ie the resin flows readily when pushed, as when brushed or rolled, but reluctantly when not.

Resins can be made thixotropic by adding colloidal silica, a very fine, fluffy, white powder, such as Aerosil or Cab-O-Sil, also wood flour, or mixed with Pregel which is a very thick polyester paste. Highly thixotropic resins make good putties.

In very early days, large amounts of chalk were used. However, quality was very poor, mouldings weathered badly and few boats lasted long. But the way chalk reduced the cost of expensive resin had irresistible attraction for some moulders, although the original purpose was not cheapness but to make moulding possible. Although never used now, fear of fillers lingers.

Cure

Polyester resins set quickly to a rubbery state which soon becomes hard, but do not develop full hardness, strength and water resistance until much later: a matter of months rather than hours. This is the curing period. Epoxy behaves in a similar manner.

During the curing period it is still somewhat flexible, or 'green', although hardening steadily. The most critical stage lasts a few weeks only. Some specifications require the hull to stay in the mould for a stipulated time to harden, but most production moulders want it out as soon as possible.

Until the stiffening and accommodation are built in and the deck fitted, the hull will be floppy. If it cures and hardens while distorted this will become its permanent natural shape regardless of how it was moulded. Forcing it back into the shape it is supposed to be will stress it just as much as by deliberately distorting a moulding of the right shape. Therefore it is very important that the moulding is properly supported in the *correct* shape, preferably by a fitting jig, during those critical first few weeks.

Cure is temperature dependent and mouldings should be maintained at room temperature. If halted by low temperature it will continue when the temperature rises again, but because there may have been subtle changes or evaporation of constituents cure will never be as complete as if maintained at correct temperature throughout. The more cured a moulding is at the time of the interruption the less damage any pause will do, so early stages are most critical. Newly moulded hulls are often transported elsewhere in wintery weather for fitting out, and so they undergo an important part of the cure in outdoor temperatures.

If a major part like a hull, deck or internal moulding does cure distorted it will be difficult, even impossible, to make it fit when assembled. Forcing it to fit will pre-stress and damage one or both mouldings. Since major units are expensive to scrap, especially if a lot of equipment and weeks of work have gone into fitting out separately, any distortion should be avoided.

The boat can still distort for the first year. It will not be fully cured when it leaves the factory or even when it starts sailing. Yachts are often distorted by rigging forces and if sustained this will become permanent. For the first season rigging should be slackened off when not in use. Many modern yachts bend like a banana under hard tightened rigging even at the best of times.

Evaporation of styrene will affect cure. It is an essential part of the crosslinked reaction. When spraying or working in hot conditions, some resin manufacturers recommend adding 15% extra styrene to compensate for evaporation. A small amount still evaporates even after setting. Environmental resins (Chapter 4) improve cure as well as reducing styrene fumes to legal limits.

Polyester and epoxy resins contract during cure, another common cause of distortion as well as print through or telegraphing, which causes a fibre pattern on the polished surface. In free space contraction can be 10%, but as a moulding the glass fibres, which do not change, prevent this. Therefore a fibreglass moulding always has locked-in internal stresses. A lot of defects which occur later – especially breakdown of the resin/glass bond – are due to relief of these stresses.

Resins which cure quickly with a short 'green' stage are unsuitable for boat sized mouldings where it is impossible to lay up every layer wet-on-wet and intervals of overnight or longer occur. If it cures too quickly the chemical action bonding layers together will be lost and interlaminar strength will be poor. Different contraction during cure will cause interlaminar stress and distortion. The larger the moulding the slower and more closely controlled the cure should be.

It is probable that no moulding made under production conditions is ever theoretically fully cured. The best that can be hoped is to be adequate. Even now that is vague. Undercure is a major cause of trouble on older boats today. Conditions then were almost universally more primitive, by modern standards often downright unsuitable. There was little appreciation of the need for careful day and night temperature and humidity control, still less the will or the capital to build the special workshop needed. Cure, such as it was, just happened.

Post-cure

Post-curing is sometimes specified. By heating the moulding to about 175°F, 80°C, soon after release, full and better cure can be obtained in a day. At somewhat lower temperatures it may take several days. However, it is seldom practicable to 'cook' a boat sized moulding. Owing to greater contraction there is a risk of critical distortion. In theory a boat going into a tropical climate will post-cure itself. However, this will generally be too late to do the job properly. Quoted properties are based on post-cured laboratory samples, always more favourable than practical boat mouldings.

Exotherm

The chemical reaction when a polyester or epoxy resin sets is exothermic, ie it gives out heat. How hot it gets depends on how quickly the heat can escape. As conductivity is low, the hotter it becomes, the faster the reaction and the more heat is generated. Thin sections do not become as hot as thick ones or a lump. The often quoted theory is that exotherm is essential for proper setting and cure. In practice, when spread in a mould the heat is conducted away through the mould or air so quickly that temperature rise is negligible.

A thick lump is different. Heat cannot escape as quickly as it is generated so it really does get hot, sufficient to crack the resin and damage fibreglass in contact or even to catch fire. Often this happens with dregs in a pot and does no real harm other than to someone's nerves when they see smoke and hear resin crackling. But it can be structurally damaging when bulk infilling.

Exotherm can be reduced by using a retarder. Where strength is not important water can be used for this purpose, and special water thinnable polyesters are available.

Catalyst

Peroxide catalysts are hazardous (Chapter 4), and a fire risk because their oxygen content feeds a fire.

The commonest catalyst is liquid Methylethylketone peroxide, MEKP. A paste, Cyclohexanone peroxide, is more convenient for small kits and comes in tubes like toothpaste. Occasionally Benzoyl peroxide is used.

The peroxide is dispersed in a carrier, di-methyl or di-butyl phthalate. This takes no part in the reaction and, being a plasticiser, should be minimal. The proportion of peroxide varies and should be as strong as practicable. Being an initiator and not part of the reaction, the proportion may be varied to control setting time. A normal proportion is 1–2%. It should not be less than 0.5% but in poor conditions can be boosted to 7%.

Relative to the resin the catalyst measurement needs to be within about 0.5%. However, if using separate, smaller scale measures the accuracy required is much less,

Approximate measurements

	Resin		Catalyst
1lb = 500g	= 0.4 litres	10 cc	= 1% of 1 kg
	= 0.75 pints	5 cc	= 1% of 1 lb
1 litre	= 1.25 kg	10 drops	= 1% of 1oz
	= 2.5 lbs	10 drops	= 1% of 25 g
		1 fluid oz	= 29 cc

Note: These are *approximate* measurements, but sufficiently accurate for practical work. As a crude measure, baked beans and most canned food weigh about the same as resin, so tins can be used as measures. Polyester will dissolve cheap polystyrene measures.

eg relative to a nominal 2% of catalyst the same tolerable accuracy is 25%. Most jobs in this book require working with quantities of about 1 lb, 0.5 kg, or less of resin. A medicine glass or cheap, graduated syringe is adequate for the catalyst. With smaller amounts use an eye dropper or dropper bottle, counting the drops.

Catalyst must never be forgotten, although very easy to do in the confusion of working. Uncatalysed resin will set eventually through migration from subsequent moulding but only very slowly, and will never cure properly or develop full strength or, in particular, water resistance. Once covered by further moulding it is very difficult to detect later, and the error is responsible for many elusive defects.

Regardless of the quantity, once catalyst has been added polyester will always set. Accuracy is needed only to control setting time and avoid being caught unawares.

Colour

Polyester and epoxy resins are almost colourless. It would be feasible to make fibreglass boats translucent, and underwater some moulders consider this good practice. Some very early dinghies were translucent. (One was nicknamed the 'Pig's Stomach' by its owner!) But although people knew the water was there the makers found they got frightened if they could see it through the bottom.

Since then gel coats, where visible, have always been coloured – the familiar fibreglass boat appearance. In the early days most boats were moulded with coloured resins right through. It was considered the logical way to get a solid opaque colour but is responsible for many faults which occur years later. Good practice today is to colour the gel coat only, while the structural moulding is done with clear resin. Quality is inevitably worse with opaque resin because the worker cannot see what he is doing and work out bubbles, air pockets and patches of dry glass. Neither can the foreman or surveyor.

Heat resistance

Polyester and epoxy resins are thermosetting, ie setting is an irreversible, once only chemical reaction. (In contrast thermoplastics like polythene and PVC can be melted and reformed indefinitely as can steel and lead.) Although they never melt they can be softened, degraded and so lose strength. Damage depends on the time and degree of exposure, and is permanent if excessive or prolonged (Chapter 9).

Two temperatures are quoted, often vaguely, and can be misleading:

- Heat resistance (HRT) is the safe temperature for prolonged exposure without loss of strength.
- Heat distortion (HDT) about 20°C higher is the temperature at which an arbitrary reduction in strength occurs.

All polyester and epoxy resins have low heat resistance compared with metals.

Storage life

Officially the shelf life of polyester is six months. Normally in a closed can at average temperatures it will last at least a year, perhaps even two. But that is since it left the factory. It may have been on the chandler's shelf for months. Life is longer in metal cans than plastics containers. Plastics containers expose the resin to light and are vapour permeable. Ageing polyester solidifies slowly. If it pours it can be used although thick resin makes bad mouldings.

Storage life will be less at higher temperatures. In early days my company was the major supplier of kits. For shipment to or through the tropics we obtained resin with added inhibitor, otherwise it arrived solid. It is feasible to add inhibitor, usually hydroquinone.

Do not put unused resin back in the drum. Temporary exposure to sunlight or fluorescent tubes can initiate polymerisation even if not catalysed. Once that starts a small amount can trigger the rest. A drum full will get very hot and may even explode.

Peroxide catalysts do not solidify but lose strength. A weak 30% concentration may be useless before the resin. Test old catalyst before use, otherwise you may find the resin does not set, or takes a long time. Solid resin is obvious to the eye but dead catalyst looks no different.

Accelerator will last indefinitely dispersed in resin but if separate it will solidify like polyester.

Although glass fibre does not age the binder

and coupling agent dissolve in atmospheric moisture. Old glass mat becomes fluffy and difficult to handle and the resin bond will be poor.

Failure to set

Polyester resin should set within an hour. If appreciably longer loss of volatiles will affect the strength and degree of cure.

Provided catalyst has not been forgotten and not stale, and the temperature is reasonable there is little to go wrong. Poisoning is rare but possible, most often from phenol in plywood glues or sawdust and some wood preservatives. Also to a lesser extent, from copper, bronze and zinc.

Vinylester resins

Vinylesters are similar to polyesters but with superior toughness, elasticity and lower permeability. They use the same moulding methods and catalysts. Naturally the price is higher. In conjunction with the stronger reinforcements they are preferred for high performance mouldings, especially where the design requires some flexibility, because they have a higher threshold of damage. They should not be used alone as surface coatings.

Styrene emission is higher and foaming causes some moulding problems.

Epoxy resins

Epoxies are a different family of resins although similar in appearance and behaviour. They are more expensive but being stronger adhesives they are often used for repairs or attachments and sometimes for high performance moulding. However, unless post-cured their strength is little better than polyester. They are also more affected by sunlight.

When used properly under the right conditions epoxies have better water resistance, and are the approved replacement for gel coats, or as a sealer. But they are not the wonder materials so often claimed. Better does not mean complete water resistance. At best they are three times better. Even then it assumes ideal application and complete cure.

Good polyester is better than mediocre epoxy. The controlled moulding shop conditions under which a gel coat is applied are nearer ideal than the average uncontrolled

shed or breezy open air when applying epoxy later. This reduces theoretical superiority.

Like polyesters epoxies are two-part mixtures which require a hardener to make them set. But the hardener is part of the reaction, not an initiator as with polyester. The amount, 10% to 50% depending on the hardener, cannot be altered. So there is no control over setting time which is just as temperature dependent. Exotherm starts sooner than with polyesters so setting time is more influenced by thickness or mass. However, they are less affected by low temperatures and damp. With special hardeners some epoxies will set in freezing temperatures or underwater, but they will not cure properly under such conditions: a point usually glossed over.

Unlike polyester, epoxy is a specific chemical, rather than a family. There is some blending – mainly added solvents as raw epoxy is too thick to use. The main variation of properties is achieved by different hardeners. Correct choice of hardener is essential.

Flash point is 310°F, 154°C. For transport epoxy is classified as non-hazardous. But this is little help as the hardeners are classified as poisonous chemicals.

Even when cured, epoxies still contain active amine hardeners which neutralise peroxide catalysts. Therefore although epoxy may be used over hard polyester, polyester cannot be used over epoxy whether cured or not. These amines may also affect paint and antifouling. Epoxy itself is affected by the styrene in polyester.

Epoxy Resins

Epoxy resins were discovered in Britain by W.H. Moss in 1937. They are made by condensing diphenylolpropane with epichlorhydrin. The aliphatic polyamine hardener reacts with the epoxy groups to crosslink the long chain molecules.

Phenolic resins

In 1944 phenolic resins were used for lightweight aircraft radomes, the first fibreglass mouldings. But they were hot setting. Only recently have they become available for hand lay-up, although cold casting, two-part resins were sold for art work before polyesters. They are cheap but their principal advantage is good fire resistance. The disadvantage is that phenols poison liquid and uncured polyester, even by their fumes, so they must be kept well apart.

Glass fibre

Glass fibres used for reinforcement are very fine, much finer than the coarse, itchy insulation grade. They are a tenth of the thickness of a human hair (0.0002–0.0004 in, 5–10 microns [1 micron is 0.001 mm]), and therefore almost invisible.

Why are they white when everybody knows glass is normally clear? Glass fibres appear white because in the dry state there is multiple refraction of light. Actually they are clear which shows up when the fibres are wetted with resin.

There are many kinds of glass. The standard grade for boats is 'E' glass or electrical grade, a borosilicate glass, with good water and chemical resistance. The cheaper 'A' or alkali glass is not approved. It was sometimes used on early boats or by mistake since then. Job lots are often 'A' glass and looks the same as 'E' glass. 'S' glass is a stronger, more expensive grade. 'R' glass has better fatigue resistance.

Composition of 'E' glass	
Silicon dioxide	52%
Calcium oxide	16.7%
Aluminium oxide	14.4%
Boron oxide	10.6%
Magnesium oxide	4.7%
Sodium and potassium oxide	0.8%

It might be considered odd that 'A' glass which is used for bottles and windows does not have a good enough water resistance for boats. It is a matter of degree. Erosion which may be hardly noticeable on a glass bottle will eat away a fine glass fibre completely in just a few years. Actually failure will occur far sooner because fibres are very sensitive to notch effect from the slightest surface roughness; hence the importance of protecting fibres from erosion.

Chopped strand mat

This is the general purpose reinforcement, commonly referred to as mat or just glass. It

---

Glass fibre

Glass fibre is made using a direct melt furnace. The materials are dry blended and charged into a furnace where they are heated to 1600°C. The molten glass is run into a platinum alloy trough which has small holes measuring approximately 1 mm diameter. As the glass comes out it is drawn down to micron size at high speed and coated with a coupling agent to promote good adhesion between the glass and resin. Being too delicate to handle they are immediately combined into the familiar strands.

In the British Museum there are some vases made of glass fibre in ancient Egypt, about 1400 BC. Roman and Venetian glass makers used it for decoration. Two hundred years ago it was used in France to make dress fabrics but found to be embarrassingly delicate. Beautiful German-made Victorian Christmas tree decorations had silky glass fibre tails.

Commercial production was started in the late 1930s by Owens Corning Fiberglas in the USA and Fibreglass Ltd in Britain mainly for insulation purposes. As with polyester resin boatbuilding was never the original idea.

---

looks like a squashed white doormat, a mat of random short fibres, about 2 in, 50 mm, long, held together with a binder for ease of handling. It is the easiest form to use. The binder dissolves in resin so the mat breaks up readily and when 'wet' can be worked easily into any shape.

The binder can be a polyester powder or polyvinyl acetate emulsion. In Europe only powder binder is now approved for boats. Belated research into blistering showed that emulsion binder reacted with seawater, but most boats moulded before about 1980-82 would have been made with emulsion bound mat. It was not only fully approved then but preferred for easier moulding.

(**Note**: the ordinary binder does not dissolve in epoxy. A different mat must be used.)

The strength of mat is less than with woven materials but adequate for most purposes. When wet-on-wet there is some intermeshing of fibres giving good interlamina bond. Early boats were all mat, as are most small boats still. Bulk to provide stiffness, not highest strength, is the main requirement for most mouldings.

Glass mat is measured in grams per square metre, usually 300, 450 or 600 g/m^2, equivalent to 1, 1^1/$_2$ and 2 oz/ft^2 in earlier measurement and still used in the USA. These figures are nominal. The manufacturer's tolerance is ±10%.

Gauze

Surfacing gauze, also called tissue or veil, is a gossamer-like mat used to give marginal reinforcement to a thick layer of resin or gel coat, or prevent print-through and telegraphing from a fibre pattern behind.

Rovings

Rovings are a thick, loose bunch of parallel strands, typically $1/8$–$1/4$ in, 3–6 mm, diameter. It is the reinforcement used for spray up or chop where a string of rovings are fed into a chopper gun and sprayed on to the mould together with a stream of resin. The end product is similar to mat but faster to apply and eliminates binder problems.

Woven rovings

This is a bulky, loose fabric, and is the other commonly used reinforcement. Having long continuous strands it is stronger than mat or spray up yet loose enough to wet out fairly readily and build bulk quickly and cheaply. It is cohesive and does not break up like mat. Consequently it is more difficult to work into difficult places and tends to bridge angles.

Being woven, the long fibres do not intermesh so interlamina bond is weak. Good practice is to interlayer with mat. The final layer should always be mat to give a more solid and resin rich surface.

Woven rovings is measured in g/m^2, or oz/yd^2. Moulders often use the heaviest weight, such as 1000 g/m^2, 24 oz/yd^2, to build bulk more quickly. Thick fabrics are harder to wet out and consequently are usually done badly with dry strands and voids in the interstices. Two thinner layers are better than one thick one. It is bad practice to use a single layer of heavy woven rovings as can often be seen on light boats and sandwich moulding.

Cloth

Cloth is a much tighter, thinner fabric made from single strands not bulky rovings. (Moulders often call woven rovings cloth too.) There is wide choice of weights and weaves, mostly unsuitable for hand lay up.

The fewer crimps or cross overs the stronger the cloth and the better it drapes, eg satin weave and knitted fabrics (Fig 2.2).

It is a high strength, high cost reinforcement, uneconomic for building bulk. However, it is right for sheathing provided a suitable weave is used (Chapter 22).

Special finishes are applied by the manufacturer to suit the resin. Some are unsuitable for polyester and epoxy is different again. It is important to select the right finish and be wary of anything unknown. The very first fibreglass boats were moulded entirely with cloth because no other form of glass fibre was available. As the resins were expensive too, and required hot moulding, the cost of cloth was less important. Since then only light weight racing machines have been moulded with cloth.

Scrim cloth

Scrim is a very low strength, loosely woven, open weave cloth. A lot of resin is needed to fill the gaping interstices, about 10/1 compared with around 1/1 for strong cloths, and even the top 3/1 for mat. If resin is stinted the surface is a mass of pinholes, a serious matter if used for sheathing to make a hull or deck waterproof. Some misguided people buy it because it is cheap, convinced that because it is 'fibreglass' it must be strong. But of all reinforcements scrim is the most useless.

Tape

This can be used for binding, eg repairs to oars, spars or tools, and in taped join construction with plywood. The selvedge edges do not fray like cut pieces of cloth. Tape comes in various widths, weights and weaves and must also be chosen with care.

Tight weaves can be difficult to wet out although being cohesive they can be pulled tight when binding, so squeezing the resin through. Unfortunately the commonest available is weak scrim.

Knitted fabrics

Recently more sophisticated fabrics have been developed, based on knitting or stitching several layers and types of fabric together. As fibres are not crimped at crossovers the strength is increased. Unlike the rectangular

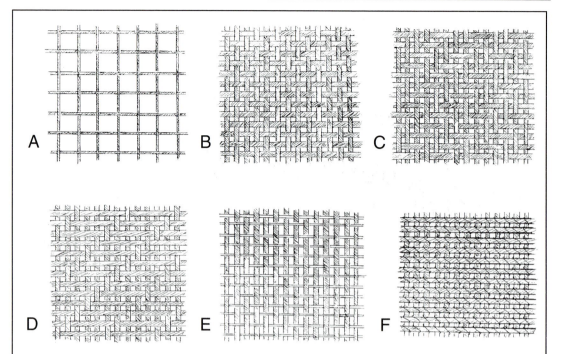

Figure 2.2 Weaves of cloth
A Scrim cloth. A very open loose plain weave. Note the large interstices compared with strand thickness.
B Plain weave. Simple over/under. The commonest.
C Twill. Over two, under two.
D Satin weave. Over four, under one. (Five shaft.) The number can vary. Gives greater flexibility and easier drape.
E Uni-directional. More fibres in one direction to give greater strength.
F Knitted fabric. To avoid weakening crimping, strands are superimposed, not woven and lightly stitched together.

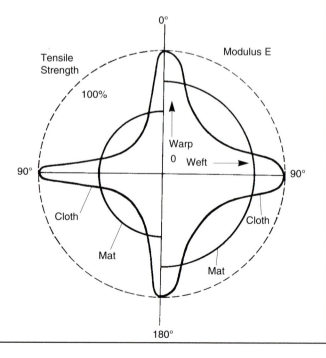

Figure 2.3 Orientation
Glass mat has equal strength and modulus (stiffness) in all directions. Woven materials are strongly orientated in the direction of warp and weft, and fall to a much lower value at 45°. At this angle mat is actually stronger.

pattern of a woven fabric strands can be at any angle so strength is better orientated. However, they tend to be thick and harder to wet out well.

Composites

The commonest combination is woven rovings and glass mat. More exotic composites combine glass fibre with Kevlar or carbon fibre or polythene.

Orientation

With glass mat the fibres lie in random directions so the strength is the same in all directions in the plane of the laminate. But with woven material the strength lies in the 90° orientations of warp and weft. Being the most favourable these figures are quoted. In between, at 45°, both strength and stiffness fall off dramatically and are less than supposedly weaker glass mat. Sophisticated designs now lay woven rovings at different angles, or use orientation to optimise strength in a required direction (see Fig 2.3).

Unidirectional fabric

Cloth, woven rovings and tapes can be woven with more or thicker strands in the warp or weft than the other. This increases the strength and stiffness in that direction. In the extreme case all fibres run in one direction.

Wet strength

The figures nearly always quoted are for dry strength, despite a boat's natural element being water. Wet strength is always less and largely unpredictable but should be assumed to be no more than 90%. Moreover it will not remain constant, decreasing with use and prolonged periods afloat, which is perhaps one of the terminal factors.

A hull will not have uniform water absorption right through so wet strength will not be the same everywhere. Wet strength and water absorption go together.

High strength materials

Lowered costs and fierce technical competition for space-age racing yachts has encouraged greater use of high strength reinforcements. Claims for super strength are often wild

and deliberately distorted, eg to claim that carbon fibre is ten times stronger than steel fails to say that this is specific strength, meaning weight for weight. There is always a price and not just the sky high cost to be considered. Improvements in one direction always mean loss in another; they must be used to solve the right problem.

Kevlar and carbon fibre both have greater stiffness than glass, but not appreciably greater strength. However, in boat construction stiffness is the higher requirement. They are normally used as composites with glass fibre. Being more expensive, it is good practice to put them only where their superior stiffness can be used to greatest effect.

Moreover, the resin, lay up and other reinforcements have more overall influence. Unless a superior quality resin like epoxy or vinyl ester is used as well, the full benefit cannot be obtained. The boat must be designed for these materials, and not just upgraded.

Composites are difficult to calculate because of different moduli and co-efficients. There are plenty of disastrous examples where designers have got the sums wrong. Unlike aircraft, for which these high tech systems were developed, yacht design is based on materials of uncertain strength, moulding of untested quality, operating in an environment of unpredictable forces and never backed by an apparently bottomless budget of taxpayer funded research.

Stronger materials allow a thinner moulding, so the higher cost is offset by using less, and fewer layers mean lower labour cost. Or so the suppliers claim. In fact these fabrics are more difficult to mould and because of the low margin of error, they require a higher level of skill, inspection and expensive testing than ordinary boatbuilding. These factors offset the savings.

These materials are like an Olympic runner compared with a round-the-park jogger. Mat and woven rovings are adequate for ordinary boats. High strength materials are for the athlete who demands that final edge of perfection and will pay anything to get it.

A few builders of ordinary boats try to obtain maximum sales value from the minimum of expensive Kevlar or carbon fibre. Saving weight is the usual advantage claimed.

Yet on the weight of the boat as a whole the saving is small.

'S' glass

'S' glass is a stronger, stiffer, more expensive fibre made from a different blend of glass. It has little advantage over Kevlar and carbon fibre although it may be used in composites instead of 'E' glass.

Kevlar

Kevlar is the trade name for Du Pont de Nemour's para-aramid fiber, a synthetic fibre similar to nylon. The grade used is Kevlar 49.

It is lighter than glass fibre and is tough, has good stiffness, fatigue strength, dimensional stability and impact resistance (one much publicised use is bullet proof vests). Abrasion resistance is good. As protection for fibreglass, eg against ice, it is lighter than metal.

Kevlar is a thermoset so does not melt and can withstand any temperature the resins will. It is self-extinguishing with low smoke emission (not that anyone would notice with the resin smoking like a wet bonfire). Compressive strength is less than glass fibre, so it must be used in tension. Strength is considerably reduced when wet.

The thermal coefficient of expansion is zero or slightly negative. Although hailed as being stable that creates stress when embedded in a resin that is not.

Kevlar is more difficult to mould. It does not wet out and become transparent like glass so the worker cannot see and work out air bubbles beneath. Neither can the foreman or inspector. A lot more skill and care is needed, adding to the cost and risk of failure. Fabrication is also difficult; cutting needs special shears and it fluffs up when trimmed or sanded.

Fibre treatment must be right for bonding. Job lots may be ballistic grade, specially treated for the poor bonding necessary for that application.

Carbon fibre

Carbon fibre was developed in Britain at the Royal Aeronautical Establishment. It is the stiffest fibre commonly available but tensile and compressive strengths are comparable to glass fibre. The fibres are about as fine but more delicate and brittle and their impact strength is low. Being soft it needs physical protection and if exposed must be painted because it is degraded by sunshine. It is seldom used alone except for spars. Carbon fibre too requires moulding skill.

Unlike all other fibres and resins, carbon fibre is a fair electrical conductor. Dust in electric tools can cause short circuits or earth leakage. It should not be used underwater because of electrolysis problems. Even above water aluminium in contact will corrode. A carbon fibre mast needs a lightning conductor to prevent it exploding if struck.

Just specifying carbon fibre is not enough – some cheap grades are little better than glass fibre. Being used for stiffness, only high modulus types are worth considering. (Table 1.1 quotes standard grade.) Although tensile strength does not vary dramatically the high modulus grades can have twice the stiffness of standard, and even standard is twice that of Kevlar.

High performance polythene

A recent development is super polythene fibre, Spectra or Dyneema, as stiff as the best glass and so light it floats. It has the best impact strength and ductility but to capture that advantage it must be used with more resilient resins like vinyl ester. It has a tendency to creep, and bonding to polythene is difficult (it makes a good release agent) so the fibres require special treatment.

Other fibres

Stone Age man used natural fibres and resins for various purposes and some underdeveloped countries still do so. At one time sisal was tried. Although cheap it was stiff to handle and absorbed resin. Using intermediate technology there may still be scope for other natural fibres, and natural resins too, applying conventional moulding techniques.

Resin putties

Resin putties are commonly available but most are made for car body or domestic use and do not have good water and weather resistance. However, they are easy to make oneself by mixing filler into polyester or epoxy resin.

Talc has fair water resistance and also, being a lubricant, is easy to sand, a desirable feature for cosmetic repairs. Most other fillers clog badly. Toilet quality talcum powder is expensive however; baby powder is cheaper and purer. It is better to buy it in bulk, as it is less likely to contain starch. Some thixotropic agent improves workability.

Other fillers impart special properties, to resins as well: graphite gives wear resistance; iron or aluminium powder compatibility with metals; slate flour, carborundum, fine sand, solid glass Ballotini, wear resistance (but are almost impossible to sand or file); microballons (phenolic bubbles) and hollow glass Ballotini, ceramic or silica spheres, pumice and fuel ash give light weight; lead, slag and spent nuclear fuel heavy weight.

Graphite fillers also make plastics conductive. Underwater there may be electrolysis problems.

Avoid chalk, kaolin (china clay), coconut flour, wood flour and other water absorbent fillers in wet situations.

Short or milled glass fibres impart strength. But the amount which can be worked in is small, about 10% only. The strength is insignificant compared with mat.

Sawdust is often used for bulk filling but be careful it has not come from plywood. The glue dust contains phenol and will poison polyester. Make sure it will set first. A sawdust filling holds a screw well and can be used for inserts. Woodflour is thixotropic and light.

Thixotropic agents alone will thicken a resin to putty consistency. Whatever is used a putty should be stiff, like cake mix (the Gougeon Brothers say peanut butter), but allow for reduced viscosity after adding catalyst, and even more with the higher proportion of epoxy hardener.

Putty and fairing have lower elongation than fibreglass and very often crack or break away.

Release agent
Fibreglass mouldings are made with a resin which sticks to everything in sight. So why does it not stick to the mould? The reason is because a release agent is used to prevent this, usually a wax. Other kinds, like PVA, form a thin barrier film. 'Breaking in' a mould, building the waxy surface, is an important part of moulding. Moulds are expensive, often irreplaceable, a master pattern even more so. A stuck moulding is therefore a disaster. Many early enthusiasts got no further.

When making attachments the usual requirement is a good bond but sometimes a part must be detachable. As well as release agent anything compatible can be used to prevent sticking: wax polish, polythene, oil, candle grease, but not soap.

References
RINA Symposium on GRP Ship construction, Oct 1972.

Professional Boatbuilder, No 28, April/May 1994.

Glass Reinforced Plastics, edited by Brian Parkyn.

Tools and working conditions

Like concrete, once the resin has hardened the shape cannot be altered; right or wrong you are stuck with it. Otherwise it is as easy to work as a soft metal using ordinary metal rather than wood working tools, although until cured it is sticky and clogs. The glass content is abrasive and blunts cutting edges; this is not a great problem in small scale use but for production, diamond tools are needed.

Polyester and epoxy are thermosets. They do not melt but can soften and get sticky when heated by friction.

Care is needed to avoid chipping or scratching the conspicuous gel coat.

Drilling

Use ordinary twist drills or, for large holes, a hole saw. Keep speed low to avoid heating. Preferably one should drill from the gel coat face to prevent chipping, or back the gel coat with wood.

Sawing

Use a fine tooth hacksaw, padsaw or jigsaw. Be particularly careful with a sandwich or cored moulding as it is very easy to cause delamination, especially if using a coarse tooth saw for a plywood core. Blunt saws will heat the resin.

Avoid cutting towards the gel coat. When using a jigsaw from the gel coat side use a laminate blade, which cuts on the downstroke, not an ordinary blade cutting on the upstroke.

Sawn edges should be sealed, preferably with resin. This is important where exposed to the weather or water, otherwise the moulding will erode from the bare edge.

Filing

An open pattern file is less liable to clog particularly when the resin is still 'green'. Thin steel files are easily cleaned. The cutting stroke must be away from the gel coat.

Avoid sawing or filing steel on board. The filings will not be noticed at the time but soon tiny rust stains will appear, even from stainless steel. These etch into the gel coat.

Hammering

The shape cannot be altered and hammering will shatter the resin. If a moulding does have to be hammered, when forcing to fit, use a soft faced mallet and tap gently. Be careful when hammering anything nearby, eg riveting, and avoid using fibreglass as a working surface. Hammering inside can cause star cracks in the gel coat outside, which may not become apparent until later (Chapter 42).

Chiselling

To hack away fibreglass use a wood chisel but not a good one.

Sanding

The heat from friction softens the resin and it becomes sticky, even when fully cured. Dry glasspaper will clog badly. Use 'wet and dry' with plenty of water. Very open grade discs clog less, but may be difficult to obtain as they are usually stocked only by specialist tool stores. Flexible lacework discs are also good. Both are resistant to water and solvent. Cheap paper discs used on popular electric drills are useless – they clog and tear in no time. Resin bonded discs are usually available only in larger sizes – 7 in, 175 mm – and intended for high speed grinders. In an ordinary electric drill the speed is lower but they still work quite well.

A high speed disc sander must be used with caution. In unskilled hands it is devastating. A few seconds' carelessness will cut deep into the moulding. An orbital sander is suitable only for fine sanding and finishing.

When it is known that extensive sanding will be required, mix a small amount of talc into the final layers. It will have little effect on other properties but reduces clogging.

The dust is abrasive and itchy, therefore a mask and goggles are essential (Chapter 4).

Kevlar

Kevlar behaves differently from fibreglass and carbon fibre. Ordinary tools can be used if really sharp but for best results special sickle shaped drills are needed and a different saw tooth set. This is complicated when Kevlar is a composite with fibreglass.

Sawn Kevlar has a fuzzy edge. On composites Kevlar should be tailored to end short of a sawn edge. Smooth sanding is impossible; shaving the fuzz raised with a razor has been suggested.

Trimming

New mouldings have a ragged edge. Soon after setting, the fibreglass will be rubbery and can be trimmed with a sharp knife. When hard it must be sawn. Timing is critical. If too soon, the moulding may be lifted and not go back to shape.

Welding

If attached metal is welded or brazed, the intense conducted heat will damage the fibreglass. Fittings to be repaired by welding must be removed. Sparks and droplets will burn fibreglass, including from welding nearby.

When used in a minor role on a steel boat, eg lining a fish hold, welding or cutting on one side can ignite unseen fibreglass near the other.

Vice

For serious cruising a vice is essential. The problem is where to fit it. Some owners mount the vice on a heavy piece of wood which can be moved around in which case the bottom should be padded so it does not scratch. Hard clamps will damage a gel coat or crush a thin moulding. Do not use a vacuum base even though the smooth gel coat looks ideal, because it would be delaminating.

Paint brushes

For casual use, as well as most professional fit-ting out, no better or cheaper way to apply resin has yet been found than a paint brush. But it is a shovel not a craftsman's tool, a way to slosh on quantities of resin that would disgust a painter, and then crudely stipple it in.

Brushes must be cleaned before the resin sets hard, otherwise consumption will be formidable. (They make good firelighters.) Brushes have a short life anyway so you need only buy the cheapest.

Rollers

Consolidation is an essential part of moulding. The resin has to be worked into the mat or weave, right into every strand and around every fibre, all millions of miles of them. This is done with rollers. To avoid picking up a bird's nest of sticky fibres contact is minimised by using a row of nylon or metal discs, which a farmer would recognise as a miniature disc harrow. Others have longitudinal grooves, like a Mississippi stern wheeler. Single discs are used for angles and difficult places. Like brushes they must be cleaned regularly.

Some moulders use mohair rollers but these cannot apply as much pressure or consolidate as thoroughly as disc rollers.

Cleaners

Acetone is generally used for cleaning tools. It is cheap, readily available and efficient. Traces left in brushes are not actively harmful to polyester. But it is inflammable and dangerous, and for industrial use now it is unpopular because of the fumes and VOC emission.

Unfortunately there are few alternative solvents which are environmentally acceptable, cheap, not carcinogenic and not harmful to polyester. Strong detergents and emulsifiers have been used but are not as effective and, being water based, greater care is needed to dry tools or spray before reuse. DBE (dibasic ester) is a less volatile organic solvent.

None of these are any use after polyester sets. Anything which dissolves hard resin will be strong, nasty and dangerous to handle. Hard epoxy is even tougher.

Cleaning and keeping clean

For personal cleanliness and skin protection when working with resins apply a barrier cream before starting to work. Afterwards a good hand cleaner should take off resins easily and painlessly.

To prevent build-up during work, dust the hands frequently with talcum powder to absorb stickiness. Have an unlimited supply of non-fluffy rags because paper towels stick and disintegrate.

Do not use solvents on your skin, especially for regular use. These degrease the skin and destroy its natural self-cleansing action which will slough off resin in a few days. The painful part is the way it sticks to hairs. It is advisable to wear a hat when working overhead, although a beard will still be a problem. Resin also sticks particularly tenaciously on fingernails.

The box above gives a recipe for a simple hand cleaner recommended by the Gougeon Brothers for epoxy but it is also good for polyester. It is cheap and works better than most expensive kinds.

Resin sticks well on boat surfaces too and gets transferred anywhere possible (even impossible) by drips, feet, fingers and clothes. Fibreglass moulding is a messy business. No wonder traditional boatbuilders scorned it.

What does not get dirty does not have to be cleaned. When working below, especially during repair or alterations, take elaborate precautions. Remove everything vulnerable like upholstery and protect what has to be left. Sanding dust too will get everywhere, so cover openings and seal lockers with masking tape.

Feet are particularly good at transferring resin from drips to deck via every clean surface in between. Newspaper follows sticky feet like a fat dog waddling after its master. Cardboard is less devoted. Put plenty of polish wherever hands may touch; overalls print sticky resin anywhere they brush against.

Liquid resin can be cleaned off clothes with acetone but be cautious: the colour may alter or the garment dissolve instantly. Peroxide catalyst too is a powerful bleach. Once hard there is no way to remove resin from clothes. Warn any smartly dressed visitors.

Animals have a tender skin beneath their fur. My spaniel frequently visited the workshop and sat to scratch in a puddle of resin. And did the same on the carpet when he got home. Carpet or hairy dog, out came the bottle of strong solvent cleaner. It made little difference to the carpet (fortunately patterned) but the poor dog would run howling round the garden.

Health and safety

The following instructions are taken from manufacturers' literature and other sources, and may not represent the latest medical opinion or conform to current national or local legislation.

Moulding
Fibreglass is a reasonably safe material to use provided common sense precautions are taken. It is not foolproof, however, still less clever person proof. The greatest danger is becoming careless and complacent. If using fibreglass for the first time remember it is an unfamiliar material. *Read the instructions.* Do not think you know better.

Children
The usual warnings apply about keeping curious little hands and mouths well out of the way; and hair too if you value your hearing!

Medical
In case of trouble seek medical advice immediately. It is not sufficient to tell the doctor what you have been using. It will probably mean nothing to him. Take the instructions and first aid advice, even the can. The label, if readable, will generally give advice.

Know *beforehand* what immediate first aid is required. There may be little time.

The general advice is to wash the skin if it has been in contact. In particular, guard against getting anything in the eyes. If any material is swallowed the usual advice is do not induce vomiting and drink a lot of water, but this varies according to the substance.

Production moulding
Production moulding is now closely controlled by burgeoning Factory Acts, EU directives, national, federal state and other legal require-

ments. Anyone starting production must study this jungle; it seems that small moulders are in danger of being regulated out of existence, entrepreneurs doomed, and only large companies able to afford to start.

In the early days of fibreglass, when the world was a freer place and we could set up moulding anywhere we could find a roof, nobody knew what the hazards were, or indeed that there were any.

Since then various harmful effects, mostly mild, have been attributed to the materials and moulding process. Some have been proved true and are now the subject of regulations. Others have been disproved or still not proven.

Styrene fumes
The principal problem nowadays is VOCs, volatile organic compounds, in particular the problem of styrene emission. Styrene is a major constituent of polyester resins, giving them their characteristic smell.

Although not dangerously toxic it is now recognised that prolonged exposure to styrene fumes is a health hazard. In Britain the present Threshold Limit Value (TLV) is 100 parts per million (ppm) averaged over eight hours. With hand lay up using ordinary moulding resins the levels are well above this, and considerably more when spraying (Fig 4.1).

In most other European countries, 50 ppm is the norm with 20 ppm, as in Sweden, the aim. 20 ppm is a convenient level since it is the threshold at which the smell is said to become noticeable. The levels are being steadily lowered and 20 ppm seems likely to become universal.

The situation in the USA (1995) is confusing with different state, federal and regulatory bodies producing their own standards, some

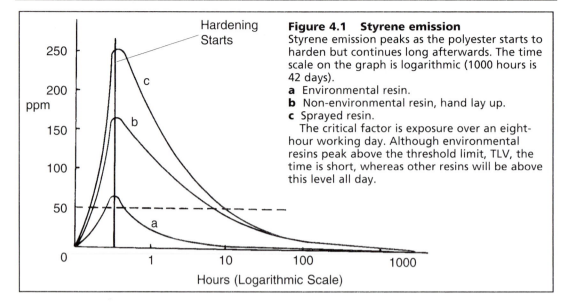

Figure 4.1   Styrene emission
Styrene emission peaks as the polyester starts to harden but continues long afterwards. The time scale on the graph is logarithmic (1000 hours is 42 days).
a Environmental resin.
b Non-environmental resin, hand lay up.
c Sprayed resin.
   The critical factor is exposure over an eight-hour working day. Although environmental resins peak above the threshold limit, TLV, the time is short, whereas other resins will be above this level all day.

(as in California) very tight. They are fiercely contested by powerful lobbies. Politics and legal interpretation add confusion and eminent researchers publish conflicting reports. The gist is that nobody really knows what is safe.

The threshold levels are for prolonged exposure, applicable to those workers using polyester every day, head down in an open mould. Short periods during repair or fitting out, even at considerably higher concentration, are not a serious hazard, although some people do find styrene fumes more unpleasant than others.

At a continuous concentration of 200–400 ppm there is irritation to the nasal passages; at 400–1000 ppm increasing dizziness, nausea and headache. 800 ppm and over becomes intolerable to mucous membranes, while 10,000 ppm may cause death in less than one hour, but for that you would have to put your head in the drum.

The Environmental Protection Agency, EPA, in the USA intends to classify styrene as a carcinogen although evidence for this is still scanty. Other countries seem unlikely to follow at the present time.

Styrene fumes are heavier than air and will collect inside a boat mould. Long handled rollers keep the worker's head in clearer air. With biggish mouldings the whole workshop may exceed the limits. High concentrations build up inside during repairs or fitting out. Worst of all is working in a closed space like a locker. A mask is no use unless it is a gas mask to absorb fumes and not just filter dust. The alternative is a clumsy, air fed, spaceman helmet.

A major problem is measuring the styrene vapour because it will vary as work progresses. The recommendation is to average measurements over a five minute period. Even that is misleading, however. Spray moulding will have high peaks while actually spraying. Moreover present measuring instruments may have a 20% error.

Styrene will still be given off during cure. Some precautions are needed inside a newly moulded hull. In an extreme case a badly undercured boat could be hazardous to occupy. This is more likely after repairs, often done hurriedly and not under good enough conditions for proper cure. Sleepers would not wake up dead (what a plot for a thriller), but they could have a headache not due to a hangover. The distinctive smell can linger for a very long time, but is not itself hazardous. The concentration has to be high and prolonged, months or years not days, for it to be dangerous.

Vinyl ester resins produce more fumes than ordinary polyester. Epoxy gives off little and is an alternative where controls are strict.

To meet stricter regulations, 'environmental resins' have been developed. These contain an additive which migrates to the surface, and reduces styrene emission to a safe level but does not eliminate it completely.

Volatile Organic Compounds

As well as concern about workers' health there are now strict controls on the release of Volatile Organic Compounds (VOC) into the atmosphere, particularly in the USA. Styrene, therefore polyester, and acetone are among the offenders. Styrene fumes end up in the atmosphere whether rising from the mould or blown out of a ventilator. Many foams are a source of ozone depleting CFCs and are also controlled.

The ghosts of those boatbuilders who scorned fibreglass because it was messy must now be laughing at the way it has become classed as a 'dirty' industry. Back to wood? Yet there are worries about the forests too.

Ventilation

As well as general ventilation special care is needed at the worksite, with ducts to reduce the fumes near the worker's head. The closer they are the more effective but inevitably the worker must move about.

Having got rid of fumes from the worksite what do you do with them? There are increasingly strict controls about exhausting into the air, as well as possible complaints from neighbours, and perhaps even litigation.

Good ventilation is expensive. As well as a capital cost a major problem is heat loss. Expensively warmed air is blown out and incoming cold damp air must be heated and dried. To be economic there must be an efficient heat exchanger; alternatively a closed circuit with air scrubber may be used. Both are expensive.

The practical implication is that fibreglass moulding now requires a purpose built factory and large capital investment. Even an amateur in his backyard can expect a visit from the council inspector.

Drugs

Drugs have a synergistic effect with styrene fumes, causing hallucination, and this has been responsible for some dangerous hull moulding. Anyone suspected of being a drug addict should not be allowed to mould anything important. Some medicinal drugs may have a similar effect. Management must therefore be alert to the effect of drugs, legal or illegal.

Styrene fumes aggravate the effects of alcohol too. A newly repaired boat stinking of styrene could affect a crew's judgement if the 'sun is over the yardarm'.

No smoking

There must be a strict no smoking rule. Resins, catalysts and solvents are all inflammable and have inflammable vapours. Styrene fumes become poisonous when inhaled through a lighted cigarette.

Repair

An owner or boatyard doing repairs is unlikely to bother about the regulations and precautions which a production builder is bound to observe. Neither will an amateur fitting out a bare hull. On a single repair, fumes are unlikely to be more than mildly unpleasant even if well above the toxic threshold. A boatyard doing frequent repairs or an amateur on prolonged fitting out needs to take more precautions. For comfort alone contrive ventilation below, such as a simple fan or vacuum cleaner.

Store inflammable materials outside the boat. Be careful with heaters and lights. Electrical tools should be flameproof but a small user will almost certainly ignore that recommendation. Unfortunately, many a fine ship has been destroyed by fire due to carelessness when under repair.

Polyester resin

Polyester is reasonably safe to use provided common sense precautions are observed. If swallowed, *do not induce vomiting*. It will certainly cause irritation of the alimentary tract, but more likely to be lethal through solidifying internally, especially if catalysed, and causing total constipation.

A more likely and milder problem is eating with sticky hands, so clean your hands before eating and do not eat on the job.

Catalyst

Catalysts are moderately powerful peroxides, also not for internal consumption but a lot easier to swallow. MEKP could be mistaken for gin! If ingested, wash out the mouth with water but do not swallow. Then drink a large quantity of water. If there is delay in obtaining medical assistance, induce vomiting and give Milk of Magnesia.

Splashes on the skin should be wiped off quickly. In the eyes it can be serious as well as painful. Wash copiously with water immediately.

Peroxides are a strong source of oxygen and will feed a fire. Consequently they are a far more serious hazard than is suggested by their moderate inflammability.

Heat, metals and other contaminants can cause the peroxide to decompose vigorously. Do not store in metal containers or close to heat.

Accelerator

To make polyester resin set at room temperature requires an accelerator, usually purple cobalt napthanate. At first it was common to supply separate accelerator. This was dangerous in unskilled hands, as all were in those early days, because if mixed with catalyst direct there will be a vigorous reaction. A salesman's way of playing down an explosion which could, and sometimes did, blow the roof off!

I was the first to supply safe kits with the accelerator already dispersed in the resin. Nowadays pre-accelerated resins (PA) are usual, even in bulk. But not always. If forced to buy accelerator separately, mix it into the whole drum, then keep accelerator, measures, stirrers, rags and everything connected with it far away from catalyst. Never use the same for both. Even traces can cause a 'vigorous reaction'.

Epoxy

The resin itself is less hazardous but the amine hardeners are the most toxic materials likely to be encountered. Most cause dermatitis. Avoid breathing the fumes; if heated they are poisonous, and their effects can be delayed.

Like polyester epoxy will cause more than indigestion if taken internally. Do not induce vomiting and see a doctor immediately.

Spraying epoxy is highly dangerous. The fumes can cause burns to the respiratory tract, sensitisation, chemical pneumonia, eye injury and other serious complications. If it must be sprayed, spaceman protection is essential.

Solvents

Most effective solvents are powerful and must be treated with the same precautions as other industrial solvents. Generally they are highly inflammable and Class B fires. Non-inflammable substitutes are available but not all are as effective or cheap.

Solvent fumes can make you light headed, therefore be cautious about using a ladder, operating machinery or driving.

Do not use solvents to clean your skin. They remove the oils which provide natural protection against bacteria, as well as roughening the skin. Persistent use will lead to serious skin trouble.

Normal solvents like acetone are effective only on liquid resin. Anything which dissolves hard polyester or epoxy will be too dangerous for ordinary users. Always be careful with unfamiliar solvents or 'something we use at work'. It is important to know what is in the can.

Other materials

Some plastics foams are based on isocyanate. This may be liberated during foaming and also when heated by sawing or sanding. Flexible foams may disintegrate into dust with age, warm temperatures, or bacteria. This dust is not only dirty and unpleasant but explosive, and reputed to be carcinogenic.

Dermatitis

Polyester resin and particularly amine epoxy hardeners can cause dermatitis. Most people are unaffected; generally trouble occurs only with workers using resins every day, but once sensitised there is no cure and even fumes can cause a rash. On no account should anyone already suffering from dermatitis use polyester or epoxy resins. Removing resin from the hands will open up the sores.

If you are allergic or have a sensitive skin

avoid working with polyester and epoxy resins altogether. Get somebody else to do your dirty work. There is no sure protection.

Barrier cream is a wise precaution for everyone and makes it much easier to clean hands afterwards. Rubber gloves are often recommended but many people find them clumsy and uncomfortable and resin always seems to get inside the wrists. They soon become stiff as a mailed fist. Gloves should be industrial quality, not domestic, and elbow length. Perspiration due to wearing impervious gloves every day can cause skin infection so cotton inner gloves are recommended. Disposable polythene gloves may be preferred.

Asthma

Fumes from polyester and epoxy can affect asthma sufferers. Keep out of the workshop altogether.

Eyes

All these materials will be harmful and painful if they get into one's eyes and may cause serious damage. Wear goggles whenever there is a chance of splashes.

Resin drips are a serious risk when working overhead. One difficulty is the way they smear lenses when wiped off. Once hard they can be difficult to remove without scratching; solvents may craze plastics lenses.

The greatest danger is splashes from catalysts or hardeners. Solvent is painful rather than serious and soon passes.

The general first aid treatment is immediate and copious washing with water. The first aid kit must contain an eyebath. Resins, however, are not water soluble. Once set it can be removed from the eye like a foreign body but requires medical attention. Never wash it out with solvent. Be careful not to get anything into the eyes through rubbing with hands or gloves, and do not rub the eyes if anything has got into them. Dust from sanding is abrasive and painful. It is particularly painful with contact lenses which many workers find they cannot use. Always wear goggles.

Personal protection

It now seems common, particularly in the USA, for moulding workers to wear overalls,

hoods, masks and goggles. As moulding requires a warm temperature this must be uncomfortable. Whether such protection is really necessary is a moot point; it was never so in the past, and moulding is no more hazardous now.

Uncomfortable jobs do not attract good labour.

Fire

In the liquid state all the materials are inflammable. Ordinary precautions are required. When hard they are as safe as wood (Chapter 10).

Transport

Because of the low flashpoint polyester resin cannot be sent by post or air. Even stricter restrictions apply to peroxide catalysts. Fibreglass repair kits are specifically mentioned. Acetone and most solvents are also banned.

Epoxy resin is not subject to restrictions, other than precautions against leakage, but hardeners are classified as poisonous chemicals, as well as having a lower flashpoint.

Storage

Polyester resin and catalyst must be stored in cool conditions, away from heaters and not exposed to hot sunshine. Storage should be secure and kept locked. Resins, catalysts and hardeners are dangerous in the wrong hands.

Glass fibres

It has been suggested that glass fibres could cause lung cancer. They float in the air and can be inhaled, but at present there seems no proof of this. Only lifelong moulders are likely to be affected. However it is still under investigation, with manufacturers employing consultants to prove there is no risk, while unions call equally eminent consultants to claim there is, and health authorities say they do not know.

The risk has been likened to asbestos. But there is an important difference. Glass breaks across the fibre so the fragments are 0.005–0.01 mm in diameter. Asbestos fibres splinter. Those which cause cancer and lung diseases are thinner than one micron,

0.001 mm. Glass is also more soluble in water and tends to dissolve in the lungs whereas asbestos does not. Boats made of asbestos might last longer than fibreglass but what builder would dare to use it nowadays?

Coarse insulation glass fibre is horribly itchy to handle. Moulding grade is much finer and seldom causes irritation except to people with unusually sensitive skin.

Sanding

Sanding and grinding hard fibreglass creates a lot of dust with larger and sharper particles than the fibres. This dust really is itchy and uncomfortable with a particular ability to work its way up sleeves and down one's neck which may cause a minor rash. A good filter mask and goggles are essential. This dust, more than the fibres, is considered a possible cause of silicosis but only with prolonged exposure. Like most dust from an inflammable substance, there is danger of explosion or flash fire.

Dust from self-extinguishing resins containing antimony is toxic, an insidious danger because a repairer is unlikely to know. Be cautious when sanding in an engine or tank space, especially on any boat built to a military or government specification, or the stringent new regulations for sail training and charter yachts.

A small user is unlikely to have a grinder with continuous extraction, too clumsy anyway in an awkward space. Instead remove the dust frequently while working with a vacuum cleaner.

Needles

A painful but not poisonous hazard are needles – upstanding resinated fibres – often left in lockers and other obscure places difficult to mould. These fibres break off easily and are as painful as wood splinters or cactus thorns. Grope with care where you cannot see, or wear gloves.

Water tanks

There have been scare stories that styrene is a deadly poison, therefore fibreglass should not be used for water tanks because it will leach into the water. (That argument could be used to ban fibreglass boats altogether, like TBT antifouling.) As with most bar rumours and letters to yachting journals this claim is exaggerated. Styrene is toxic but not a deadly poison. If it was, imagine the regulations there would be about moulding!

Ordinary polyester resins are approved for water tanks, either separate or built-in, if well cured and ideally post-cured. Built-in tanks can be steam cured, even with a simple pipe from a kettle.

Separately moulded tanks should have the gel coat inside. When built-in they need a thick finishing coat over sound moulding with no pinholes, porosity or exposed fibres to trap dirt and algae.

When I have investigated complaints that water tanks were tainted it has always been due to something else – oil based putty, fittings green with corrosion, algae in plastics pipes, or just foul water – never the distinctive taste and smell of polyester.

Like a hull kept in fresh water fibreglass tanks are prone to blister and, being difficult to see, far more common than realised. (Few owners look inside!) Broken blisters harbour dirt and the 'blister juice' may well taint the water. Usually the frequent turnover of water will prevent a dangerous concentration, but when left for months, as during lay up, the water could become tainted. Tanks should therefore be drained and dried during lay up.

If a tank does blister, treatment recommended for a hull will be impossible. You cannot remove a gel coat working through a one-hand handhole, with most of it out of sight and beyond reach.

Waste disposal

All materials used in fibreglass boatbuilding are now regarded as pollutants. With some factories producing thousands of boats a year, waste disposal has become a serious problem. Although mainly aimed at big builders the stringent regulations will inevitably affect small producers too, and even repair yards and amateurs.

In Britain polyester resins and peroxides come under the Deposit of Poisonous Wastes Act. Other countries have similar regulations plus state and municipal controls, particularly in California. Substantial disposal requires approval by the appropriate authorities, or the expense of a specialist contractor. As most boatbuilders are now located in industrial estates, on-site disposal is not practicable.

The amount of liquid resin will be small because little is wasted. If poured on to a dump it will soak in and once the styrene evaporates will go hard and be no more of a fire or pollution hazard than mouldings. Waste resin must never be poured down drains. If catalysed it will set and cause a blockage. As it sinks and does not mix it will build up in a bend even if it is not catalysed.

Solidified resin and trimmings are not hazardous. They can be burnt but not near habitation as a lot of black acrid smoke is produced. Waste liquid resin burns more fiercely and smokily because of the styrene.

Even small quantities of dirty solvent will contaminate water. Some contractors will clean and recycle it or turn it into fuel.

Anything soaked in catalyst can ignite or explode spontaneously in a bin and must be disposed of safely without delay. Peroxide can also decompose violently through heat or contact with metals, acids, alkalis, reducing agents and many organic materials. Before discarding, containers should be washed out and catalyst well diluted.

Spillages of resin must be mopped up promptly and rags disposed of safely. Large quantities can be soaked up with sand, earth or other inert material but not with anything inflammable like sawdust. Clean the residue with hot soapy water.

Trimmings and especially dust from sanding should not be discarded near a watercourse or drain. Being finely divided, constituents will leach out readily. In particular they should not be dumped or used as landfill near a marina. Leached constituents would be as potent as 'blister juice' and could affect boats in the stagnant waters of the marina.

Small users should not dump waste in the dustbin indiscriminately; even used containers containing dregs can explode.

Burning old or scrap mouldings still leaves the glass fibre intact. There is environmental opposition in the USA to using this for groundfill, claiming constituents may leach out. How to dispose of millions of old fibreglass boats is one of the formidable problems we are leaving our children.

Under MARPOL, the international regulations controlling marine pollution, it is an offence to dispose of plastics at sea. So when the lifeboat lands you on shore after your fibreglass boat has sunk you may be arrested for 'disposing of plastics at sea'!

References

Material Safety Data Sheet, Scott Bader Ltd based on a report by the British Resin Manufacturer's Association.

Product Development Report: Low styrene emission polyester resins, Scott Bader Ltd.

BIP environmental resins.

British Safety Council: *Safety Code for Using Synthetic Resins*.

Threshold Limit Values, Guidance Note EH15/80, Health and Safety Executive (revised annually).

Health and Safety at Work, No 18 – Industrial Dermatitis Precaution Measures, HMSO.

The Protection of Eyes Regulations, 1974. Statutory Instrument 1681, HMSO.

EPA/CERI Publications Unit. EPA/625/7–91/014.

US Department of Commerce, National Technical Information Service, PB No 93–164127.

State of California, SCAQMD Rule 1162 on VOC emissions in polyester resin operations (1988).

West system instruction books.

Epoxyworks (Gougeon Brothers Inc), No 4, Spring 1994.

Understanding how fibreglass can fail

One of the first things an engineering student learns is the way steel fails and for the rest of his career that dominates what he makes.

Fibreglass behaves in a very different way, and many professionals fail to appreciate that even now. Part of the difficulty is because, unlike most metals, there is no one material, fibreglass, supplied to exact specifications. The properties can vary widely according to the lay up, the precise materials used and in particular the care and skill of the individual worker. No two pieces of fibreglass are exactly the same. Timber can be selected, but nobody can tell what fibreglass will be like until it comes out of the mould, and by then it is all or nothing. A really bad moulding should be obvious. Even so few builders have the courage to scrap an expensive moulding. The majority of troubles in later life arise because the mouldings are just plain mediocre.

Moulding is like making a cake. The ingredients are known. But how it turns out depends on the cook, and even the cook does not really know until someone eats it.

Engineers accustomed to precise specifications regard fibreglass with contempt. To them it is not an engineering material.

A great deal of this book concerns older boats. That more is known now, and the state of the art improved, is no help to the owner of a boat built to earlier standards, and very few were built even to them.

What anyway is state of the art? The highest quality, most seaworthy and durable, or what can be produced most economically?

Physical failure

This chapter may look technical, although it is written in non-technical language. However, it is one of the most important. Unless you understand the nature of fibreglass and the unusual way it fails nothing else can be done properly.

Fibreglass boats are not as forgiving as wooden or steel boats, and the popular, go-fast, cruiser/racer or planing motor cruiser even less so. This includes the way they are used.

Failure

Fibreglass does not fail in the way wood or steel does. Such differences might be considered deficiencies. But wood and steel also have deficiencies. Yet since earliest times boats and ships have evolved, making allowance for them.

There are no bad materials, only materials used in the wrong way in the wrong place for the wrong purpose. Not by fools but by clever people acting foolishly.

Fibreglass mouldings can fail in the following ways:

Breakdown of the resin/fibre bond
Failure of the glass/resin coupling agent
Fracture of the glass fibres
Cracking of the resin
Delamination
Degradation of the resin
Hydrolysis of the resin
Erosion of the glass fibres

This can be caused by:

Abrasion	Bad moulding
Pulverising	Water absorption
Splitting	Chemical attack
Overstrain	Age
Stress relief	Heat
Creep	Sunlight
Decay	Extreme cold

Comparison with metal

Steel is made under carefully controlled conditions to a high degree of precision. Its ultimate strength and other properties are known exactly. Within the range of fatigue it can be stressed almost to its limit repeatedly without loss of strength. It is ductile, meaning when that limit is reached steel yields before it breaks, ie it bends or dents. Even that does not seriously reduce its strength. Aluminium and most other metals are similar.

Composites like fibreglass do not fail at a predetermined and accurately known stress level, to which they can be stressed repeatedly, but progressively starting at a vague threshold well below the ultimate strength. Every excursion over that threshold will cause irreversible damage. Eventually it will fail well below its original full strength.

Uncertainty

No boatbuilder makes steel or wood. He buys sheets or planks and cuts and bends them to shape. But a moulder actually makes fibreglass in the mould, like a jobbing builder lays a concrete floor from bags of cement and a heap of gravel and sand.

Unlike the precise control in a steel mill, or the careful selection of timber by a master boatbuilder, there is little control on the quality of fibreglass. Everybody assumes that it will turn out all right. But nobody really knows.

Moulders' standards vary, and being labour intensive can also vary from day to day and between workers. Suppliers' data state what the properties ought to be if everything turns out right. But nobody can guarantee just what the moulder will actually do. Or, what is more relevant, actually did. Yet it works well enough – usually.

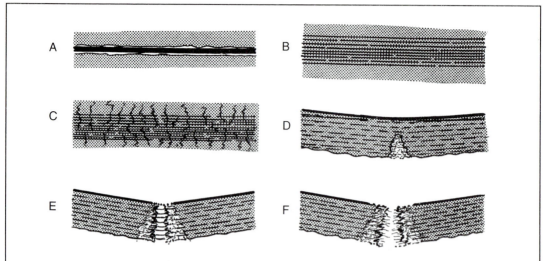

Figure 5.1   Sequence of failure
Dimensions show the approximate scale at each stage.
A Stage one: The resin/glass bond fails allowing the fibre to slide within a tunnel of resin.
B Stage two: Being no longer firmly embedded the stress on the fibres is not equally distributed. One fails throwing more stress on neighbours so they too break one by one, like Tom Kitten's buttons.
C Stage three: Without the fibres to reinforce it the resin cracks which in turn throws more stress on the fibres.
D This builds until parts of the moulding are just a mass of broken fibres and shattered resin.
E Soon the resin cracks away entirely but some fibres remain, like the steel reinforcement of a bomb shattered building, although they have little strength and no rigidity.
F Final stage: The moulding splits apart completely leaving a wide fringe of shattered resin and broken fibres.

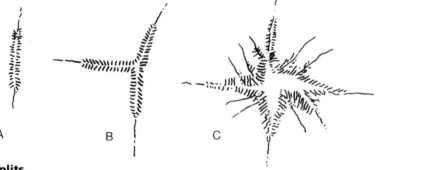

Figure 5.2   Splits
A Under impact fibreglass will normally fail by splitting not shattering.
B Splitting may be multiple, like torn trousers.
C Only if damage is severe will splits link to form holes, generally associated with severe abrasion.

The current trend is to build boats closer to the theoretical limits of strength regardless of whether, under production conditions, it is possible to mould to such standards with 100% reliability. Even a somewhat lower figure would require the expertise and quality control available on aircraft production but not boats. There is not the money.

Sequence of failure

Moulded fibreglass is not a homogeneous material, the same right through like metal, but a composite of comparatively weak brittle resin and strong fibres. Acting together they are complementary. But like a team of individuals, each will act differently under stress.

The main component is the resin which,

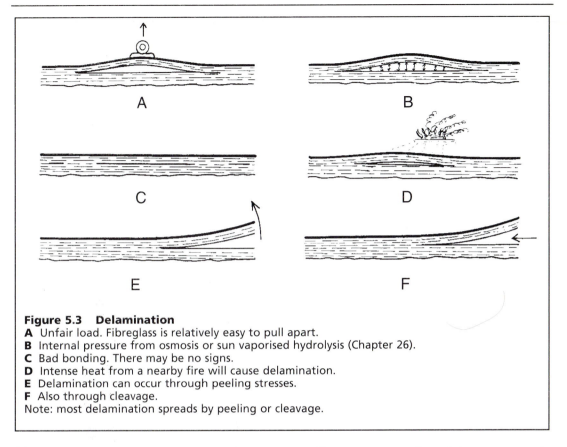

Figure 5.3 Delamination
A Unfair load. Fibreglass is relatively easy to pull apart.
B Internal pressure from osmosis or sun vaporised hydrolysis (Chapter 26).
C Bad bonding. There may be no signs.
D Intense heat from a nearby fire will cause delamination.
E Delamination can occur through peeling stresses.
F Also through cleavage.
Note: most delamination spreads by peeling or cleavage.

like concrete, is quite strong in compression but weak in tension. The tensile strength is primarily in the glass fibres. Obviously to do their job they must be firmly embedded, each one bonding throughout its length. In practice this bond is not perfect. It is a tall order to expect a worker to wet out a thousand miles of fibre every minute, which is the order of things. (A ton of fibreglass contains about a million miles of fibre.) Nevertheless there is a high degree of mechanical grip and tangling.

However, this applies only to the threshold of local failure. Fig 5.1 shows the sequence of failure after that. It is common sense that a composite of very different materials must fail progressively.

Every stage is irreversible. There can never be recovery or self-healing as with a ductile material, nor stress relief by yielding. A broken fibre is broken for ever. Shattered resin remains shattered. Bond failure is as permanent as divorce.

All three stages happen at once according to the local stress level. They may all escalate rapidly to catastrophic failure, or reach equilibrium.

Threshold and overstrain

It is very important to understand this concept of progressive damage or overstrain above a threshold well below the breaking strength. From the sequence of failure it is clear this must be so. There cannot be a sharp, breaking point as with steel. Every excursion above this threshold causes a little more damage. At low levels each is insignificant but always cumulative. Nearer the breaking point the moulding will not fail immediately but be so weakened that it fails after a few further stresses at that level, perhaps the next time. Moreover the threshold itself is progressively lowered so that a given level of stress moves increasingly up the scale of damage. It is like trying to break something with a hammer. The first blow may be unsuccessful; the second or third does it (Fig 5.4).

The threshold at which damage starts is vague and impossible to define, but in general

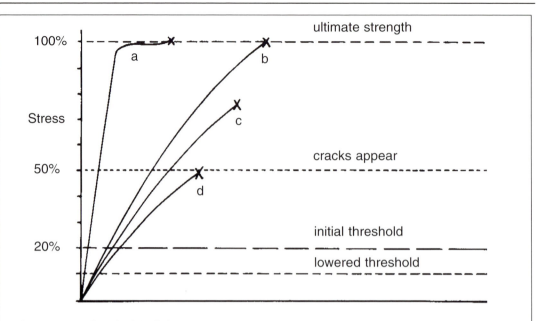

Figure 5.4 Threshold of damage
Every excursion over the threshold level of stress lowers the ultimate strength or level of failure.
a For comparison the typical stress/strain curve for steel, familiar to all engineers. Note the yield point at which steel becomes ductile before breaking.
b The theoretical curve for fibreglass. This is the single straight pull. Note the absence of a ductile stage.

c Repeated excursions above the threshold but below the theoretical ultimate strength will cause failure at a lower level.
d The failure level is progressively lowered. Note the threshold too is lowered. Every excursion over this becomes increasingly more damaging.
Note: cracks do not appear until 50% stress level. There can be considerable hidden damage without any visible signs.

will be as low as 20–25% of the ultimate strength. Note this is not the quoted theoretical strength but the *actual strength as moulded*, at that spot. This too is uncertain.

Woven rovings has the lowest threshold; glass mat somewhat higher. Many factors are involved: the type of lay up, materials, degree of cure, amount of use, history, age and, as always, quality of moulding.

Such a low threshold, or even the existence of a threshold at all, is frequently disputed by well qualified people. Yet this is generally a result of ignorance of the nature of fibreglass and obsession with the behaviour of steel and other materials. Professional pride, embarrassment, inconvenience or economic pressure may be involved too. In fairness hidden damage is very difficult to prove. At low levels there are no signs. Even telltale cracks do not appear until about the 50% level, and with flexible gel coats perhaps not at all. Often it

has to be assumed from the pattern of damage and, above all, knowledge and experience of fibreglass. That is why it is important to consult a specialist in fibreglass before agreeing to any repairs. Never be afraid to get a second opinion.

Quoted theoretical figures are based on laboratory tests using a single steadily increasing test to destruction. In real life this is equivalent to one good wallop. These are the most favourable conditions however. They do not reflect the progressively lowered strength due to repeated stress above the threshold. Progressive damage is closely linked to fatigue especially at higher levels. Figures for fatigue are seldom quoted in suppliers' literature, and never this low threshold.

Obviously abuse and damage will create stresses dangerously above the threshold. Yet ordinary hard use can also exceed the threshold albeit at a lower level. Being cumulative these stresses too can build up to a dangerous level. Owners, especially hard driving skippers, need to be aware of this.

Coupling agent

The theory that the glass fibres provide strength and the resin binds them together is too simple. A key factor must be the resin/glass bond. Unless firmly bonded the fibres will slide within the resin instead of acting together as theory says they do.

Smooth glass, as is well known, is a difficult material to bond to and polyester resin is not a good adhesive. They seem a poor choice. On the other hand both are cheaper than anything more suitable – always a powerful incentive. And it works.

To improve this bond the glass fibres are coated during manufacture with a coupling agent, generally a silane. This bonds to the glass fibre and crosslinks with the resin. Yet the bond is not perfect and still the weakest link.

At the start glass mat has a binder which is supposed to dissolve in the resin. Woven materials need a size during weaving, removed later. Inevitably a little binder or size remains. So although the fibre may be covered all round with resin these traces prevent perfect contact.

What happens later is complicated because many factors cause bond failure, any could predominate and probably all occur together to some degree. Water, as usual, is the main culprit. The resin is slightly permeable. As it absorbs moisture, it swells and breaks away from the glass. Moisture creeps along the fibre by capillary attraction. The coupling agent is not water resistant anyway and is hydrolysed, opening further capillary paths. One thing leads to another.

Relief of locked in stresses set up as the resin tries to contract during cure (see page 40) will cause bond failure as the boat ages. Being the weakest part, use, let alone occasional misuse, will also add to bond failure over the years.

All old boats show a distinct white fibre pattern. Whether this is original due to poor moulding as many assume, or natural ageing, or stress relief, or widespread hydrolysis of the coupling agent or hard use, seems to depend largely on which hobby horse the person is riding and probably all are in the race.

Each boat may well be different. In most cases until the gel coat is taken off nobody can see anyway, and that is never done until the moulding is already in a poor state! What is certain is that fibreglass boats get weaker with age.

Bending

Most damage to fibreglass is caused by bending. The sharper the bending, the greater the stress. Often the sharpest bending does not occur at the point of impact or pressure, but where the smooth pattern is distorted by a bulkhead or hardspot nearby (Chapter 17).

Impact is generally inwards. This puts the inside of the hull in tension and the gel coat in compression. Resin is strong in compression so failure will usually start at the inside face. It is common to find fracture of the inner face or delamination without apparent structural damage outside.

Splits

Impact generally causes a split not a hole, often running in several directions, like torn trousers. Only with multiple impact will splits join to form holes (Fig 5.2).

Abrasion

Fibreglass is soft compared with metal and therefore particularly vulnerable to wear or abrasion, one of its major disadvantages. Most damage, other than single impact, is accompanied by abrasion over a wider area. The gel coat and then the fibreglass beneath are ground away. When hammered by pounding it is pulverised.

Delamination

Basically a moulding consists of layers of glass fibre orientated in the plane of the moulding with little or no intermeshing and held together only by the comparatively weak resin. It works well enough, provided nothing is done to pull or force the laminations apart (Fig 5.3).

The best bond is obtained between layers laid up wet-on-wet, which allows some intermeshing and chemical combination. If wet-on-dry, ie the underlying layer has set, the bond is purely adhesive, although if 'green' there will still be chemical interaction. The older it is the less receptive and the more likely the surface will be contaminated.

The earlier environmental low styrene emission resins used wax which gave a poor interlaminar bond. This has been superseded by other additives but a lot of boats built around 1990 would have been moulded with those resins.

Delamination occurs most readily along a woven rovings or cloth interface. Because of the long woven fibres there is never inter-meshing as with glass mat. Once started delamination will spread by peeling. Sandwich or cored mouldings are particularly prone to delaminate along the core interface.

Thermal stress

Glass and resins have different co-efficients of thermal expansion. Temperature changes cause internal stress and failure of the resin/glass bond. Being a poor conductor of heat there can be a temperature gradient through a moulding, stressing the interlaminar bond and sometimes causing delamination.

Stability is at moulding temperature. Unless exposed to fire temperatures go down further than up. The range is greatest where winters are very cold; air temperatures vary much more than those of water. Boats are most vulnerable when ashore.

Residual stress

During cure resin contracts but glass fibres, being in a stable state, do not. Without reinforcement contraction would be 5–10%. Therefore residual stresses are set up in the resin because it is prevented from contracting by the fibres. Corresponding stresses are set up in the glass.

At boat scale cure tends to pre-stress parts of the moulding that are of different strength, eg the hull/deck join, or different ages. The shape often alters subtly. Most boats have a sink or slight hollow at the bows. Telegraphing – the appearance of a fibre pattern in the gel coat – is common. So is 'bond burn' where anything has been glassed on.

Creep

Within moderate limits fibreglass will bend and spring back. But this is time dependent. If maintained, distortion will become permanent due to internal stress relief. But having no ductility this can happen only by local failure of the fibres and resin. Therefore creep must weaken the moulding in the same way as overstrain.

Fatigue

Fibreglass is vulnerable to fatigue. The effect is similar to overstrain and lowers the threshold. Fatigue life is fairly high at low levels of stress but very short at high stress (Chapter 7).

Hidden damage

Splits, holes and abrasion are obvious and cannot be disputed. Cracks, although often hard to see, are another indication, yet they do not occur until about the 50% stress level, well above the threshold and into significant internal damage. Surrounding all obvious damage there must be hidden internal damage where the moulding has been stressed above the threshold and thereby weakened.

Many surveyors scoff at this idea. Insurance surveyors in particular like to see something tangible. Yet from knowledge of the way fibreglass fails it must be so.

Most repairers think that because the split or hole has been patched the boat will be as sound as before. They do not realise that until the weakness around it has been reinforced the repair cannot be as strong.

The trend to more flexible gel coats, mandatory with some authorities with the object of preventing gel coat cracks, does nothing to stop the moulding beneath suffering hidden damage. They just make sure nobody knows about it. Cracks do give valuable warning.

References

M J Owen and T R Smith, *Plastics & Polymers*, Nottingham University, Feb 1968.
Paper from Southampton University on crack development.

Destructive influences

As might be expected the major destructive influences, apart from the owner and other boats, are weather, water and sunlight.

Weather

Weather affects only the exposed gel coat above water. But this is the part seen. Although durable as marine finishes go, the pristine, shiny appearance does not last for ever. However, protected by paint or polish its life should be indefinite, ie as far as we know it should last as long as the boat, but not without that rude word: maintenance. Quality is crucial. A bad gel coat, whether due to material or application, will soon give trouble.

Water absorption

Water is the key factor behind most troubles with fibreglass, which should not surprise anyone. All plastics are permeable to some extent due to their long chain molecular structure, and no claims for a super coating will overcome that inherent property. The important thing is what happens when it gets there.

Fibreglass is a complicated mixture of materials, much more so than simpler plastics like a polythene bottle, and we must also consider a far longer time scale. Some of the constituents are slowly soluble or significantly altered by water (Chapter 26). There are also passengers which take no part in the basic reactions and remain as impurities.

Unlike wood, which can soak up its weight of water, the amount absorbed by fibreglass is about 2–3%, and even then only the part underwater and mostly the surface layers. On a 30 ft, 10 m, boat the amount is about a bucketful, not the absurd figures quoted by makers of dehumidifiers. Not having wood's cellular storage tanks there is nowhere to put it. So the resin swells. This initiates breakdown of the resin/glass bond, opening up capillary paths and erosion of fibres normally buried within the moulding.

Water absorption depends on the quality of moulding, not the gel coat. A good moulding hardly needs a waterproof gel coat. But if the moulding is poor, the most impermeable gel coat will only delay water absorption.

Hydrolysis

Fibreglass is not just pure polyester resin and glass but a witch's brew of many things of varying slow solubility in water (Chapter 26). Most depend on the quality of moulding. If water permeates into the moulding, as it will in time regardless of claims for wonder coatings, it will dissolve some constituents and alter the properties.

Little research has been done into this, or indeed into the long term properties of second class moulding at all. Sometimes it will even reduce the moulding to a spongy mass of little strength, but this is generally because of poor moulding in the first place. As always, moulding quality is the crucial factor. A major problem is that twenty years later, the builders are generally long out of business and there are no detailed records of exactly how the boat was made, without which the complex reasons can only be guessed.

However, some tests in laboratories and on naval vessels suggest that on drying, the fibreglass regains much of the lost strength. But as these would be better quality mouldings it cannot be taken as general. On boats of average quality it is more likely loss of strength could be a terminal factor.

Voids

Every fibreglass moulding, no matter how well moulded, will have millions of voids. These

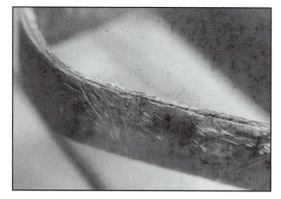

Photo 6.1   Erosion at a trimmed edge where unprotected. Time scale about eight years.

range from gel coat cavities as big as coins, through the millions of champagne sized air bubbles in the resin, to microvoids along fibres, and even between the long chain molecules. Water permeating into voids forms nuclei for attack and decay. High void content is a major feature of poor moulding (I have found voids ten feet long). Early boats, even good ones, also have more voids because the materials were harder to mould and the technique less understood.

Wicking

It is impossible to wet out every fibre perfectly, and the bond breaks down with use and age anyway. There are innumerable capillary paths along the fibres, often wide channels where whole strands are dry.

Moisture will wick along these, eroding further paths and connecting up voids. Bare fibres near the surface undermine the gel coat as well as being pipelines into the moulding.

Heat

All chemical and physical actions which cause breakdown are temperature dependent and speeded by heat. As a rough figure they double with every 10°C rise. Boats in tropical waters are likely to have a shorter life and experience more troubles than those in Northern waters; so will boats moored near power stations and industrial outfalls.

Sunlight

Polyester, like most plastics, is degraded by ultra-violet light. Obviously this is confined to

the gel coat, where it is most noticeable as faded colour.

Physical degradation is very slow, usually revealed by isolated cracks. The decks of some boats now have close spaced crazing. Whether this has occurred through materials or moulding is impossible to say with records long gone. It is reasonable to suppose it may become general in time unless the deck is protected by paint. Some early gel coats had low heat resistance and so do undercured gel coats.

Cold

Blistering, osmosis, permeability and other chemical and physical processes are slowed in cold temperatures. Very cold weather can crack and craze the gel coat due to contraction when most brittle. As temperatures go down further than up, extreme cold causes more trouble from different thermal co-efficients and aggravation of locked in stresses than extreme heat. Moreover it lasts longer.

The highest quality, longest lasting polyesters have lower resiliency and are more inclined to crack in winter cold. The best is not necessarily best for the job.

Ice

Ice will cause multiple scratches and gouges along the waterline. A lightly built boat would be holed by hitting ice at speed. Sometimes the ice not the boat is moving. Boats have been sunk, even in Britain, by tide borne ice floes.

Water freezing in gel coat cavities, or the tiny flaws common in non-slip deck patterns, will break up the gel coat around them. Ice in unsuspected pockets inside causes a lot of serious damage, eg to internal keels, moulded scuppers, embedding and sandwich mouldings. If water has got in through damage it will be difficult to make a further insurance claim or even to prove it.

Decay

To say fibreglass can decay may seem heresy. Yet why not? Everything decays; it is a fundamental law of nature. However, decay in fibreglass is chemical and physical erosion, not biological or bacteriological.

Belated research into blistering has shown that fibreglass contains water soluble molecules,

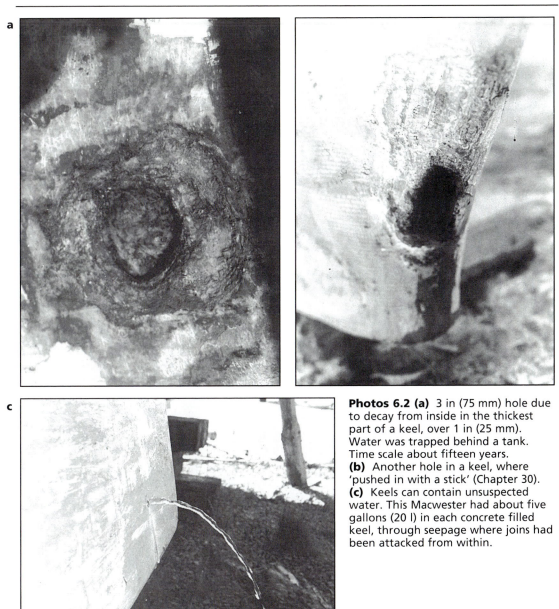

Photos 6.2 (a) 3 in (75 mm) hole due to decay from inside in the thickest part of a keel, over 1 in (25 mm). Water was trapped behind a tank. Time scale about fifteen years.
(b) Another hole in a keel, where 'pushed in with a stick' (Chapter 30).
(c) Keels can contain unsuspected water. This Macwester had about five gallons (20 l) in each concrete filled keel, through seepage where joins had been attacked from within.

WSMs, which form a predominantly acid solution. With free circulation of water this is carried away. But where trapped the concentration will become strong and aggressive 'blister juice'. Decay is then self-accelerating (Chapter 26).

A bottle or window glass might seem as water resistant as anything. But glass fibres are so fine, with such a relatively large surface area, that little erosion is needed to destroy them. Moreover they are so notch sensitive the least surface roughness will snap them like a glazier's dia-

mond cutter. Normally they are protected, buried in the resin which, although less resistant and eroded faster, is a very much larger mass.

Unrepaired minor damage can be a starting point for decay. Deep gouges bypass the protection of the gel coat. Unsealed edges and holes, already roughened and shattered by sawing, expose the heart of the moulding.

Just as pockets of rot are commoner on a wooden boat than rampant rot everywhere, so fibreglass will decay locally before general

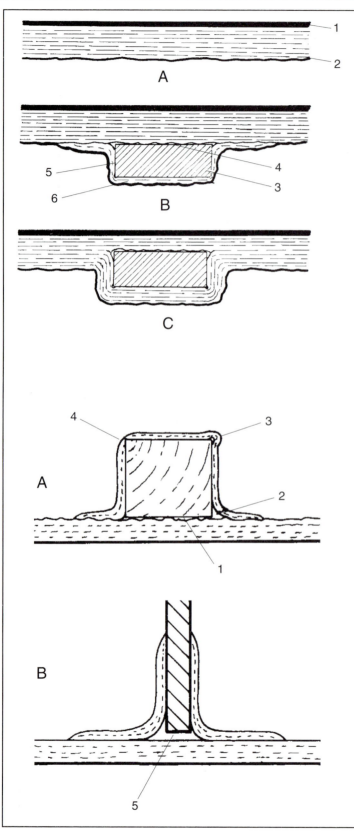

Figure 6.1   Decay inside embedding

A An ordinary moulding will be protected by a thick gel coat, 1, on the outside and a good coat of finishing resin, 2, on the uneven inside.

B When a block of wood, 3, is embedded this is generally before the finishing resin. It sits on the uneven inside surface, 4, so unless well bedded there will be gaps and waterways. It is secured by moulding but the inside face of this, 5, has no gel coat like the main moulding and therefore no protective resin. The finishing resin, 6, is applied overall at the end.

If water gets in, as at some time it probably will, the fibreglass around the embedding has no protection. Fibres are thinly covered or exposed: ideal conditions for decay.

C If embedded within the lay up decay will not be in an attachment but deep inside the main structural moulding, which is much more serious.

Figure 6.2   Waterways

A Intimate moulding over an embedding is almost impossible. Most embedding will have waterways, eg between the rough inside of the moulding and the straight sided insert, 1. Bridging at root angles, 2. On sharp corners the fibreglass will either ruck, 3, or pull thin and porous, 4.

B Bulkheads and partitions seldom fit closely so there is a gap, 5. Glass angles may bridge.

disintegration. The average boat has numerous potential troublespots. Few production boatbuilders seem to care, however; unlike wooden boats there is no long tradition of experience. What is known is sacrificed on the altar of production convenience.

Internal decay

Some places are impossible to protect with gel coat or finishing resin, eg inside embedding, stiffeners, inserts and, largest and most important, sandwich decks and hulls (Chapter 19). The inside face, laid up 'wet', will be raw with fibres exposed and unprotected, like the inside of any moulding before built up with finishing resin (Fig 6.1).

Does this matter? They are sealed so cannot possibly get wet. Do not believe it. That notorious American, Mr Murphy, has nothing on water when achieving the impossible. Any fastening is a potential leak and damage is always possible.

Embedding perfectly is difficult. Nearly always there will be gaps and poor bonding forming waterways so water can collect far from the point of entry. Moreover once water does get in it cannot be dried out. Trapped in a closed space with an unprotected face and thinly covered fibres the water will attack the soluble constituents and become aggressive 'blister juice' as described in Chapter 26. The decay will be hidden and unsuspected, the first indication probably a weep where it has eaten right through. More likely it will be somewhere difficult to see (Figs 6.1 and 6.2).

What is embedded may also rot or decompose, thus adding to the brew. Wood can swell and burst thin fibreglass, and so can rusting steel.

Rot

Fibreglass itself cannot rot. But down below there is a lot of wood which can and does. The sound old rule of wooden boatbuilding – avoid unventilated spaces – is often ignored. I have seen more toadstools growing inside fibreglass boats than on wooden ones, and rampant dry rot too.

Out-of-sight, out-of-mind. Behind those exotic veneers can be found cheap deal. Pretensions to quality often go no further than the eye can see.

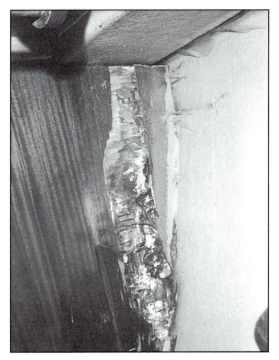

Photo 6.3 Dry rot on a fibreglass boat? Oh yes. Woodwork below can rot as readily as on a wooden boat.

Worm attack

Fibreglass is not attacked by teredo worm or gribble, a very important advantage in warm waters. But wooden keels or rudders are just as vulnerable as on a wooden boat. Even when sheathed with fibreglass they can be exposed by damage.

Internal woodwork, structural parts, bulkheads and sandwich cores can also be exposed by damage. If not salvaged promptly teredo may get to a wreck first; there have been stories of only fibreglass left. Termites and ants can do the same to a boat stored on land.

Ageing

Fibreglass will lose strength naturally with age, largely caused by breakdown of the resin/glass bond. Polyester will slowly break down into simpler groups. Water absorption and use speed this process.

Chemical attack

Pollution is a regrettable feature of modern life. Water is seldom pure, especially that kind misnamed fresh. (Actually pure distilled water is more damaging than river water.) Polyester is pretty chemical resistant but can be attacked by strong alkalis. I cannot imagine anyone wanting to sail in waters so polluted the boat was dissolved! But that is science fiction. The likely effect, even after long exposure, is gel coat blistering or etching.

Some of the earliest fibreglass boats were used on the Houston river where steel workboats were soon eaten through. Fibreglass boats lasted until replaced through obsolescence twenty years later.

Decks can be etched by fall out, and not only from big dirty industries or nearby power stations. The owner's central heating chimney can be as bad. (Also one's neighbour's!)

Most damage from chemicals will come through unwise use of cleaning solvents, paint removers, illegal fire extinguishers and spillages in lockers.

Fibreglassium masticus

Fibreglassium masticus – a thing which eats fibreglass – has already been named, but the world still eagerly awaits its discovery. Marine biologists suggest that, like some vile substances applied to the bottom of ships in Good Queen Bess's reign, fibreglass 'Twysteth their Dygestyons'.

While such a louse has not infrequently been claimed the lousy part has always been the moulding for which it had been quoted as an excuse. I have sometimes seen signs which by a stretch of imagination could have been caused by worms, but were more likely due to other reasons.

Bacteria and other organisms have shown they can evolve quickly. One soon developed a taste for plastics swimming pools. Polyester is an organic material. Why should it not be edible? With millions of fibreglass boats afloat in close packed marinas it could be only a matter of time.

Enough marine things flourish on the bottom of a fibreglass boat for a PhD thesis. They do no harm except minor physical damage when the squatters resist eviction. There are shellfish like piddock which can bore into rock so a soft gel coat should present no difficulty. I have yet to hear of such a case, even in tropical waters, and unless a plague occurs they should be no problem. They want a home not dinner!

Bad moulding

Most of these destructive influences stem from, or are aggravated by, less than perfect moulding, and the worst from plain bad moulding. I have found serious decay on boats only two years old.

Time and time again we come back to the importance of good quality moulding, as should be self-evident. It is the only way to minimise troubles later and is the principal lesson to be learnt from the past forty years of fibreglass boats. It would be nice to say the lesson has been learnt. But many well known builders would still get low marks.

Fatigue

Compared with most structural metals the fatigue strength of fibreglass is mediocre especially at high levels of stress. Instead of maintaining roughly constant strength until near failure fibreglass gets progressively weaker and the effect more serious. It is inseparable from overstrain and the damage threshold (Chapter 5).

Fatigue in fibreglass is very difficult to predict. As well as the usual variables of lay-up, materials and moulding, fatigue depends on the level of stress, compressive or tensile, and speed of application. Even in closely controlled laboratory conditions there is a wide scatter of results.

Therefore an essential part of good design and construction is to ensure that fibreglass is never stressed above the 25% threshold of damage. Above this safe zone one can only talk in general terms because overstrain and the progressively lowered threshold reduce fatigue life. One hefty excursion into the overstrain level will do damage equivalent to thousands of fatigue cycles.

The danger is that computerised design to tighter parameters may not make allowance

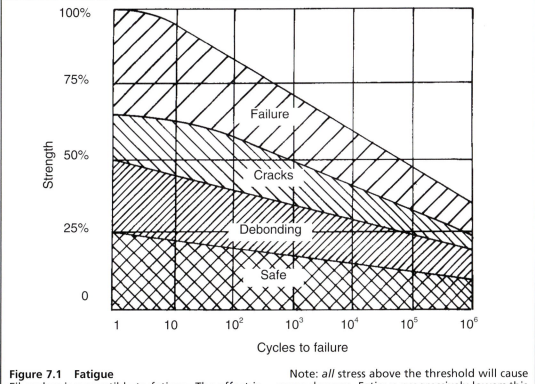

Figure 7.1 Fatigue
Fibreglass is susceptible to fatigue. The effect is similar to overstrain, especially at high stress levels.

Note: *all* stress above the threshold will cause some damage. Fatigue progressively lowers this safe level.

for unpredictable excursions into higher stress levels.

Practical relevance

What does a million cycles mean in practice?

A sailing yacht bashing to windward, or a motor cruiser driving into a head sea will have a pitching time of, say, once every four seconds. The box opposite shows what this means.

Fig 7.1 shows that after one thousand cycles failure may occur at 50% of the ultimate strength, and after one million at 25%. One thousand cycles could be just one leg of a tough round the buoys race. A hundred thousand, the first leg across Biscay of an ocean crossing. A million cycles might not occur for many years and the effects be indistinguishable from normal ageing or hydrolysis.

The stresses need not be continuous, and unlike a laboratory test obviously vary enormously. But everything is cumulative. They can build up over a season or several years or the boat's lifetime. These figures show critical stages can be reached in normal sailing times. They are based on the reduction in tensile strength, the property most often quoted. But stiffness, which is more important for a boat, will be reduced even faster.

All figures relate to the *actual* strength and stiffness of that particular part of that particular moulding, not the design figure. It could be less; locally a lot less. The boat will not fail all over but only at points of highest stress or greatest weakness. It is particularly important to avoid hard spots where the stress can be magnified many times (Chapter 17).

Failure, when it does come, will be rapid and probably catastrophic.

Wet strength

General figures for fatigue, when obtainable at all, assume dry conditions. Wet strength is lower and it has been reported that the safe level is only 15%. However a boat is unlikely to be wet right through like laboratory samples, or be in pure distilled water. Obviously the wettest part will be the outer layers yet, whether from sea or bilge water, it is these outer layers which carry greatest stress. Moreover progressive breakdown from fatigue

Time	Cycles
1 minute	15
1 hour	900
1 day	21,600
1 week	151,200
1 month	604,800
1 year	7,862,400

or

10^3	(one thousand)	approx	1 hour
10^4	(ten thousand)	"	10 hours
10^5	(hundred thousand)	"	5 days
10^6	(one million)	"	2 months

will increase the extent and depth of water absorption.

Pattern of failure

At high levels of stress, fatigue failure will generally occur in tension and at lower levels in compression. High glass content reduces failure in the short term. In the long term the resin has greater influence. In both cases, failure is similar to overstrain with the resin/glass bond the first to fail.

Factor of safety

The boat may be strong enough to start with. But if the designer has not made sufficient allowance for fatigue on a high tech design to tight parameters, or has made a mistake, a few hours racing could render the boat dangerously weak. Moreover the builder may not have achieved the standard expected. It can also be dangerous to use any boat for purposes for which it was not designed (Chapter 37).

Until it becomes serious fatigue is almost impossible to detect. Cracks will not show until failure is well advanced, unusual flexibility even later. This emphasises the importance of designing fibreglass with an adequate factor of safety. Fig 7.1 shows that below 25% stress, which is also the approximate threshold for overstrain, there is a safe zone with little damage from fatigue.

References

M J Owen and T R Smith, *Plastics & Polymers*, Nottingham University, Feb 1968.

S.N.A.M.E. Technical Bulletin 2.12.

Practical Boat Owner March 1995

Factors of safety

No engineering structure is designed to the limit. Always a factor of safety is applied to allow for the unpredictable, miscalculations and other factors, ie it is stronger than strictly necessary.

This assumes the strength of the material is known accurately in the first place; with fibreglass it is not.

What is the strength of fibreglass?

The first problem is to define the strength. Do we take the ultimate strength as with other materials, the catastrophic failure level? What else say the pundits? But all properties of fibreglass are time dependent. So should it be the single quick stress, simulating damage; or the considerably lower slow, sustained stress; or repeated stress as would happen in use? Or the even lower 25% threshold above which irreversible damage starts? Even then it has to be assumed the fibreglass has actually turned out as strong as it was supposed to be.

Such uncertainty is enough to turn a serious engineer pale.

Fibreglass is used for many things and suppliers like to quote favourable figures like super strength using aero-space reinforcements. These are irrelevant. Most important boat mouldings nowadays are a combination of ordinary glass mat and woven rovings. As the properties of each are different the strength depends on the particular combination and there are thousands. Yet the biggest variable is moulding expertise (or lack of it).

It would probably be asking too much to expect more realistic properties like stiffness using ordinary glass mat when moulded by an inexperienced, untrained builder's labourer straight off the dole queue; or bond strength after being walked over for three weeks and having alternate layers of stale spilt tea and

Factors affecting the strength of fibreglass	
Initial	*With use and age*
Imprecise data	Water absorption
Tolerance on materials	Chemical change
Moulding quality	Breakdown of resin/glass bond
Degree of cure	Hydrolysis
Wet strength	Stress relief
Moulding conditions	Fatigue and overstrain
	Hard use
	Damage

sawdust trodden in; or the degree of cure after someone turned off the heating one frosty night by mistake or the head office accountant questioned the heating bill.

Of course we fondly imagine, and every builder will swear with hand on heart, that fibreglass boats are never made that way. But it is no wild flight of fancy to say that to some extent at least half of all fibreglass boats were, certainly in earlier years.

Standards of the better moulders have improved and become more professional. Yet there are still second class boatbuilders working under economic pressure. At all levels the emphasis is on commercial expediency. But that is business, the law of the jungle, survival. And very few have survived.

There is endless research to get stronger materials, a spin-off of the huge 'better-ways-to-kill-people' industry. We should know everything about fibreglass by now. Yet we still have a great deal to learn. There is little information about what *really* happens to the strength and other properties of fibreglass boats as they get older; even good ones. We need information based not on unrealistic laboratory samples but on real boats as built. Especially as they used to be built. But nobody is interested – except the vast majority of boat owners who cannot afford new boats.

We know from generations of experience everything that happens to wood and steel boats from builder to abandoned hulk. But nobody knows how long fibreglass boats will last or what will happen to them. Except that bad ones do not last long and good ones probably longer than anyone wants.

Competent authorities quote figures, generally conservative, as the minimum design figures acceptable to them. Good moulders should attain them reliably. Middling class moulders will hope they do and usually will but sometimes not. Bad moulders did not care as long as the boats looked shiny enough to fool buyers.

Go-fast designers often exceed the conservative rule figures. By burning enough computer power to put forward convincing calculations an authority may be persuaded to accept them. But can the moulder achieve that higher target with absolute reliability? And how long will the boat retain that strength?

EU directives will require all boats to be certified, but that does not cover the millions already built. Some countries have minimal standards of construction but strict regulations about safety equipment. Strange how the bureaucratic mind thinks it better to save someone from drowning when the boat sinks than prevent it sinking in the first place!

Comparing the values quoted by different authorities and suppliers the spread is confusingly wide. Laboratory tests too show a wide spread; even then inconvenient figures are dis-

carded, a luxury not available to a practical boatbuilder.

This uncertainty emphasises the importance of a high factor of safety.

Tolerance

Do not assume tolerances and errors will cancel out. They are far more likely to add. In addition to quoted manufacturers' tolerances fibreglass moulding is not a precision process. The short and long term variables are unpredictable.

Commercial tolerance on weight of glass is ±10%. Over a boat moulding it is claimed this should average out to a lower figure. But as much of the boat will be moulded from one batch it will tend to be one way or the other. Analysis could show what the tolerance actually is but few moulders would adjust the lay-up.

Moulding quality is the widest tolerance of all, entirely under management's control but not the designer's.

No practical moulding will be as fully cured as laboratory samples, which are usually post-cured and unrealistic. Good moulders will try to get close, but due to unsuitable conditions many early boats fell well short.

With age polyester slowly breaks down into simpler components. Properties are also reduced by leaching of soluble constituents, WSMs, and hydrolysis.

A fibreglass moulding is born in stress. The resin contracts whereas the glass fibres, being unchanged, do not. Relief of stress tends to break the resin/glass bond.

Any stress above the threshold of damage (Chapter 5) will cause progressive and irreversible damage whether occasional or contin-

Table 8.1   Comparison of ultimate strength

	SG	Tensile strength		Compressive strength		Modulus E	
		lb/in² x10³	kN/m²	lb/in² x10³	kN/m²	lb/in² x10⁶	kN/m² x10³
Moulded fibreglass (average boat)	1.6	25	170	23	160	1.8	12
Steel	7.8	35	240	35	240	30	200
Aluminium	2.7	20	140	20	140	10	70
Plywood	0.8	8	60	4	20	1.2	8

uous. In the long term, even low levels of stress will cause fatigue.

High tech design to low factors of safety will specify certain materials. If in short supply it is dangerous to substitute others.

The designer's idea of normal use may not be the same as the owner's, or even common practice. Risk of damage is ever present. With a delicate racing machine which will be sailed to the limit failure is regarded as excusable. An ocean cruiser on the other hand must withstand the unpredictable, like pounding on a coral reef or weathering a hurricane. Failure far away from repair facilities spells disaster.

In between these extremes any ordinary boat should be able to bump against others, come off best in a moderate collision and not be damaged if it runs aground, a most obvious and foreseeable hazard which does not seem to occur to modern builders, designers or rule makers.

Reduced factor of safety with age

Factors of safety should apply throughout the life of the boat which, it is reasonable to suppose, should be at least fifty years. But they are not reduced equally. Chemical changes and internal stress relief are largely age and temperature dependent. Others are a function of how hard the boat is used or abused.

There is some excuse for a short life with a crack racing machine. It will be outclassed in a couple of years. By then the wealthy, one-track-mind owner will have bought an even more race winning boat and everyone except subsequent owners will have lost interest. But factors of safety are being cut on run-of-the-mill family cruisers too. Admittedly with rule-of-thumb design they were generous, and inconsistent with fashionable demand for ever higher performance, just as every modest family car must now be faster than a sports car a generation ago. It has not been lost on builders that reducing factors of safety reduces cost of production and increases profit.

On some of the most popular and widely sold production cruiser/racers built in recent years the factors of safety based on average use will be exhausted in about ten years. After that the boat is on borrowed time.

This is very little known, and the builders are never going to say so.

Wet strength

Water absorption reduces strength, and particularly stiffness, by 10–20%. Yet figures for wet strength are seldom quoted, even by suppliers of fully approved boatbuilding resins. Some people forget boats are used in nasty wet water.

Yachts regularly laid up ashore have a chance to dry out and the water absorption remains low. But the modern trend of laying up in a marina berth does not give the hull a chance to dry out. In tropical waters absorption is faster, and boats are usually afloat all year round.

Laboratory tests

A common test for water absorption is the two-hour boil, claimed to be equivalent to two years' actual immersion. But this is a trivial time for a boat and of doubtful relevance. Boats do not generally get boiled. The high temperature will post-cure the resin, making it unnaturally good, while susceptible constituents will be leached out making it unnaturally bad.

Accelerated weathering tests over a longer period are more realistic, yet also too aggressive to simulate real life. Being expensive to run, tests are not long enough to be equivalent to many years' use, more comparable to the guarantee period than the life of the boat!

The only real method, exposing samples for years, is slow. By the time useful information is obtained it is of historic more than practical interest. Few builders are even still in business.

Laboratory tests are made on samples carefully made by technicians under controlled and clean conditions. Moreover they are generally thin, small and have no gel coat. They are not representative of thick boats with a gel coat and water one side only. Therefore on properties like water absorption boats ought to fare better. On the other hand samples do not get the misuse and simultaneous stress that a boat receives.

Empirical design

The simplest course is to burn all the brochures and follow the empirical values and rules, at present all different, laid down by Lloyd's, Det Norske Veritas, Bureau Veritas, ABS, EU and others. But that is heretical in the computer age.

However, in some countries and soon throughout the EU all new production boats, even if imported, must be submitted to the national authority for approval. Despite the outcry, in most other fields of our free society designers are so hedged with mandatory rules, laws, bylaws, building codes, safety regulations, environmental concern, plus voluntary codes of practice, that most play safe and go by the book anyway.

For years past most eminent designers of racing yachts have made their name by skill at cheating the complicated rating rules, although being now done by computer they like to call it optimisation. It is hard to imagine they will not apply their ingenuity to optimise official rules too, and if there is advantage to be gained you may be sure factors of safety will be pared to the bone.

Effects of heat

Glass fibres have a high enough melting point to be unaffected by any temperature boats normally encounter. (Technically glass is a super-cooled liquid but to the ordinary mind solid enough. Any fool knows you cannot cut your finger on a sharp piece of water!)

Polyester and epoxy resins are thermosets. They undergo an irreversible chemical change when they polymerise from sticky liquid into hard solid and, like a boiled egg, nothing will turn them back again. However, although they do not melt they do soften and suffer permanent damage at temperatures which are low compared with metals (little above ambient temperature range). They also burn.

Heat distortion temperature (HDT)

There is no sharp transition. The HDT is the temperature at which the resin has lost an arbitrary proportion of stiffness, but it will gradually soften and get sticky below this.

Some fully approved early resins had an HDT as low as 95°F, 35°C. Nowadays for average boatbuilding resins it is likely to be 140–160°F, 60–70°C. The HDT of gel coats is generally a few degrees less. Higher quality resins may be over 100°C but tend to have less resilience and are unsuitable for boats.

No hull will encounter such temperatures while afloat, but they are close to a deck or upturned bottom in hot sunshine. Usual design figures for tropical conditions are 158°F, 70°C and can be exceeded. So structural weakening is possible, especially if a dark colour. In comparison the threshold of pain, eg a hot bath, is around 120°F, 50°C. Even in the British Isles a deck can occasionally get painfully hot to walk on. In the tropics my fibreglass deck is seldom too painful for bare feet, although a concrete dock certainly is, and attached metal can make a cat jump.

These metal fittings, and hence the surrounding fibreglass, are often highly stressed.

Generally low thermal conductivity limits the highest temperatures to the surface. Most of the moulding and internal stiffening will be at a less critical temperature. But the core of a sandwich moulding acts as an insulator, one of the virtues claimed, so the whole outer skin will be at high temperature. Some cores soften too.

Heat can also come from engine rooms and galleys below. A hot engine room and a tropic sun-warmed deck will weaken the moulding right through. Surface temperatures of fibreglass near exhaust runs and stove pipes must not exceed 150°F, 65°C. As a crude guide, if it smells it is too hot.

The resin will harden on cooling although the surface may remain tacky. However, damage is time dependent and cumulative. If prolonged, bond failure or delamination is probable. Therefore regular heating to a level where the resin becomes softened and sticky must be avoided. Overheating when drying a hull during treatment for osmosis has caused serious damage and permanent distortion.

Some authorities claim the resin actually gains strength due to post-curing, but this will be negligible when the boat becomes aged. Also it ignores internal damage. Most hobby-horse riders forget fibreglass is a composite.

Figures for epoxy depend on the hardener, which is probably unknown. With general purpose hardeners they are lower than for average marine polyesters, about 110–120°F, 40–50°C.

Heat resistance temperature (HRT)

This is the safe temperature which, in theory, can be maintained indefinitely without the resin degrading, losing strength or cracking, generally 35–55°F, 20–30°C, lower than the HDT. But it assumes the resin is perfect and probably post-cured. With practical moulding, design should allow a prudent margin. Moreover it refers to the resin only. There may still be accelerated physical failure.

The poorer the quality of moulding, especially cure and resin related factors, the lower both HRT and HDT. Then even British sunshine may be too strong.

Delamination

Because of the low thermal conductivity substantial temperature differences can exist through the thickness of the moulding, eg when the upper side of the deck is in hot sunshine and the under side shaded. Then the thermal expansion can cause sufficient stress to initiate delamination. This has been known, even in Britain, on the wide expanse of a multi-hull. Also after exposure to fire.

Thermal co-efficient of expansion

The co-efficients of glass and resin are different. The resin/glass bond is already pre-stressed by contraction during cure. In theory thermal expansion in warm conditions will reduce that because it is greater for resin than glass, but in cold weather the opposite. In practice the resin and fibres are so jumbled the theory is meaningless. Either way it contributes to progressive breakdown.

Co-efficients of thermal expansion		
	per °F x 10^{-6}	*per °C x 10^{-6}*
Polyester resin	50	90
Epoxy resin	50	90
Glass fibre	3.1	5.5
Fibreglass (mat)	15	28
Fibreglass (woven rovings)	8	14
Carbon fibre	-1.3	-2.4
Kevlar	-2.8	-5.2
Steel	6.1	11
Stainless steel	5.8	10.4
Bronze	10	18
Copper	11	20
Aluminium	13	23
Lead	16	29

Most boats nowadays are made from alternate layers of glass mat and woven rovings. These too have different co-efficients which will cause stress along the resin interfaces.

With Kevlar and carbon fibre the difference between fibre and resin is aggravated by their higher stiffness. Also with carbon fibre the thermal conductivity is high, comparable to metals. Heat is carried deep into the moulding, whereas the conductivity of glass is on a par with polyester. Fibreglass is a moderate insulator.

Gel coat

Near the HDT the gel coat will indent and mark. At still higher temperatures it will craze and blister.

Hot fat will craze fibreglass sinks and the constituents are leached by boiling water. They are generally integral with a large interior moulding and irreplaceable. While possibly adequate for careful use on weekend sailing they should not be fitted on serious cruising yachts, especially charter boats. This is a place for stainless steel.

Cigarettes must never be stubbed out on fibreglass or left burning on an edge. The scars burn deep.

Chemical activity

All chemical and physical activity is speeded up by heat at the approximate rate of doubling with every increase in temperature of 18°F, 10°C. This includes almost everything causing the deterioration of fibreglass. In practical terms it represents sailing from Northern waters to the Caribbean, Florida or summer Mediterranean.

Polyester resin polymerises by a complex chemical reaction and over the rest of its life that is very slowly being reversed. It will never revert to the liquid state, which was an unstable intermediate phase, but it will tend to break down into the simpler basic groups from which it was formed at a rate that depends on the temperature.

Fire

Fibreglass burns. Therefore it is dangerous. Therefore we must make lots of regulations. So runs the bureaucratic mind. Apparently they have never heard of wood, or that it has been used for building boats and ships since the dawn of time.

Steel does not burn. Yet there have been terrible fire disasters with steel ships. I saw the 120,000 ton *Betelgeuse* burning in Bantry Bay. None survived.

What are the facts?

Although fibreglass in the solid state will burn, it is not dangerously inflammable, much the same as wood, and certain features such as charring and natural fire barriers formed by the incombustible glass fibre actually make it safer.

In any case fires do not start with the structure of the boat but with the contents. In Britain, following numerous fire casualties, there are now strict regulations covering furnishings, bedding, clothes and upholstery for domestic use, especially the use of plastics foams. These do not yet (1995) apply to boats, other than sail training ships and charter yachts (an important point to note if intending to use an existing boat for *any* form of charter or hire, even day sailing).

Despite endless regulations about fuel, gas and engines, furnishings remain a little appreciated but major fire danger on most private boats, especially older ones built before the hazards of plastics foams were realised.

Effect of glass fibre

I have seen many fibreglass boats damaged or destroyed by fire. The resin burns away leaving a vaguely boat shaped mass of blackened non-inflammable glass fibre. But without resin to hold it together it has no strength and is no longer watertight.

Generally it does not get as far as that. The resin tends to form a thick layer of sticky, black, almost incombustible char which prevents fire reaching the still unburnt material beneath. In addition, layers of high glass content like woven rovings form a fire barrier. After a fire it is usual to see woven rovings hanging loose like dead skin. Glass mat is not so effective which is why older boats, built entirely of glass mat, burn better than later ones. Woven materials also retain their integrity better than mat. The Royal Navy claims a superstructure made entirely of woven rovings or cloth will withstand fire better than aluminium.

Because of this fire barrier fibreglass generally burns from an edge such as a gunwale, hatch or window. It does not readily burn through the face of a hull or deck. An inside face does not burn so readily as a gel coat, an important safety feature because all fires at sea, the most dangerous and frightening time, will start inside.

Flammability

The important thing is not whether a substance burns but how readily it catches fire. Put a match to fibreglass when properly hardened and it is difficult to ignite. But do not try that with petrol! There must be a good blaze going already before the fibreglass will catch fire.

Technically ordinary polyester mouldings will have a BS 476 Part 7 Class 3 Spread of Flame. That is not good for a structural material but far from dangerous. Average fire retardant resins can get to about Class 2, perhaps Class 1. Some claim class 0 but only with a high glass content. This emphasises that although quoted as if nothing else mattered, the resin is not the only factor. Also important

a

b

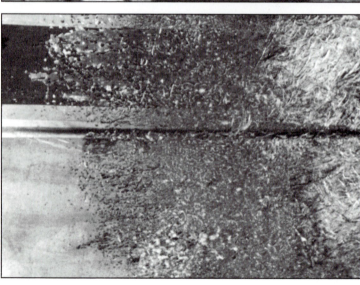

Photos 10.1 (a) Outside of a hull set on fire by a nearby building. Note how layers of woven rovings acted as a fire barrier. The inside was not even scorched.
(b) Burning spreads progressively along the gel coat. Unburnt portion at left, then blistered and charred, until at right it has burnt away to the glass mat beneath.

Table 10.1 Flashpoints	°F	°C
Polyester resin (liquid state)	90	32
Peroxide catalyst	176	80
Accelerator	86	31
Styrene	90	32
Epoxy resin (liquid state)	320	154
Epoxy hardener (varies – typical)	200	93
Acetone	1	–18
Polyurethane foam (liquid state)	190	88
Diesel fuel	150	65
Restrictions on transport below	131	55

is the glass content and lay up. Then the size, shape, position and orientation of the moulding. Fire is very complex, even more when the material is a composite and one burns, the other does not.

Flashpoint

The safety assessment of many materials is based on their flashpoint, the temperature above which the material gives off sufficient vapour to ignite readily in air if a flame is applied. Below the flashpoint the flame has to heat the material before it will ignite. Therefore the higher the flashpoint the safer.

The figures in Table 10.1 are for materials in the *liquid* state and for safety of more concern to moulders or for transport. Hard fibreglass behaves very differently and is not classified as hazardous.

Polyester resin

In the liquid state polyester is classified as hazardous because of the low flashpoint, 90°F, 32°C. In Britain, it comes under the Highly Flammable Liquids and Liquefied Petroleum Gases Regulations 1972. The inflammable component is styrene. A few polyesters use a different monomer but are little better.

Despite the formidable title of the regulations polyester is not as dangerous as petrol or bottled gas. Nevertheless common sense precautions are necessary. While mainly of concern to builders and moulders who will be required by law to take proper precautions, the hazards should not be disregarded by more casual repairers and owners.

There are restrictions on transport, carriage by air and post. Fibreglass repair kits are specifically mentioned. This can be inconvenient when needed urgently for repair and polyester is not available locally.

All self-extinguishing, low flammability, or fire retardant resins in the liquid state burn just as readily and are as hazardous as ordinary resins.

The catalyst has a safer flashpoint, but being a peroxide the high oxygen content will feed a fire. Consequently it is more dangerous than polyester.

Epoxy

Epoxy mouldings also burn and with much black smoke. In the liquid state it has higher flashpoint and is not rated as hazardous. Some hardeners have low flashpoints but may be banned for transport anyway as dangerous chemicals.

The fumes from burning amine hardeners are toxic.

Phenolic resin

Phenolics have a high resistance to burning and when they do ignite produce little smoke and no toxic fumes. Heat resistance is higher than polyesters. For engine spaces and hazardous areas it is surprising these superior properties over the generally specified, inefficient, self-extinguishing polyesters are so little appreciated.

Gel coat

The most inflammable part is the gel coat. If flames get out from inside through a hatch or window, the common case, they will spread along the gel coat outside. It can also be ignited from an external source and set fire to the rest of the boat.

There are endless rules about engine spaces. A seldom considered hazard are the gel coats on all internal mouldings, especially near the galley. Once a fire starts, these will spread burning below.

Self-extinguishing resins

Well meaning bureaucrats, itching to save us from our follies, often insist on the use of self-extinguishing resins. Of course they do sound a nice safety feature. But how effective are they? For boats they are not nearly so effective as people think and certainly not the reliable safety precaution supposed.

A self-extinguishing resin is basically an ordinary inflammable resin with an additive which stops it burning if the source of ignition is removed. But if something else is burning, as will be the case otherwise the fibreglass would not have caught fire at all, the resin will continue to blaze as fiercely as one that is not self-extinguishing; some kinds more fiercely.

There is no agreement about the terms commonly used; fire retardant, self-extinguishing, low flammability, reduced flammability and slow burning mean much the same.

All polyester resins burn with a lot of thick black smoke. Self-extinguishing grades produce even more smoke and it is astringent and toxic. Consequently by making escape and fire fighting more difficult they may increase the fire hazard.

Self-extinguishing resins are mainly specified for areas like engine and fuel tank spaces. But the fire will start from fuel or the engine, not the surrounding fibreglass. Only after the fiercely burning fuel has been extinguished will the self-extinguishing resin of the surrounding fibreglass go out on its own – provided it is not by then being kept going by half the rest of the boat on fire.

There are no completely non-inflammable polyester resins, although some, generally unsuitable for marine use, do have a higher rating. All polyesters and epoxies will burn given a plentiful supply of heat either self-generated or from another source.

It is not sufficient just to specify self-extinguishing resin. Manufacturers have many grades and claims vary depending on whether it is more important to reduce surface spread of flame, inflammability, or rate of burning; also whether for internal or external use. There are standards for building codes, and endless military ones. Unless it is specified which the resin is required to meet the term is meaningless. Even then they are based on simple laboratory tests. A moulding will behave differently. The resin cannot be considered in isolation.

The most effective are HET acid resins, where one of the basic constituents is changed during manufacture. But any polyester can be made self-extinguishing with additives. Common fire retardants mixed in later are halogens like chlorine and bromine compounds, and antimony oxide. Resin manufacturers get proper testing by a fire laboratory but if mixed in by the moulder it may be only a token amount. Unless stirred frequently during application the properties will be patchy.

In general self-extinguishing resins tend to have lower strength both wet and dry, limited colour choice, poor weather and water resistance and are unsuitable for external use. The self-extinguishing properties can diminish with age and the fire retardant constituents leach out in a wet place, eg bilges. Self-extinguishing resins should not be used underwater despite well meaning specifications.

Far better protection will be given by painting the vulnerable areas with intumescent paint or using intumescent gel coat on internal mouldings. In a fire these froth up to form a fire barrier and insulate the surface beneath. No self-extinguishing resin does that.

On sail training ships a surface layer of woven rovings is permissible in the engine space and galley areas as an alternative to self-extinguishing resins and acts as a fire barrier. However, the ordinary, fairly heavy woven rovings would still have a resin contact of about 50%. Close weave glass cloth would have less resin and be a better fire barrier.

Other materials

The dangers of petrol and bottled gas are well known, and there are strict laws, codes of practice and regulations. When they explode it matters little what the boat was made of. However, there are plenty of other less dramatically inflammable materials on board.

Most plastics foams commonly used for upholstery are a hazard, especially on older boats. Nowadays it should at least be self-extinguishing grade, easily tested by igniting a small piece. Burning foam is difficult to put out because its cellular nature contains enough air to support combustion. Polyurethane gives off a lot of smoke and toxic fumes. When burning fiercely these include phosgene, one of the first poisonous gases used in warfare before scientists developed fouler ones.

Whether a fire will start in upholstery depends largely on the covering. Cotton can be made non-inflammable and tends to smoulder rather than ignite. Plastics coverings, even if they do not actually catch fire, melt away from the source of ignition and expose the foam beneath. This is dangerous with that most common source, a dropped cigarette or match.

The Code of Practice for Sail Training Ships (1993) requires furnishings materials and mattresses to be Combustion Modified High Resilient (CMHR) type. Fabrics should satisfy the cigarette and butane flame tests of BS 5852 Part 1 1979 also BS7176 and 7177.

PVC and vinyl are inherently self-extinguishing but are far from non-inflammable. They will burn quite fiercely if there is a fire from another source. Moreover they do not self-extinguish immediately. A very serious hazard is the way they drip flaming globules and ignite anything beneath.

One modern cruiser of popular make had a fire following a modest gas explosion in the galley (meaning it did not blow the deck off) due to stupidly dangerous installation (on delivery from the builders too). Although the fire brigade were at the dockside promptly and so were nearby crews the entire vinyl deckhead lining had melted and burnt away. So had the expensive electronics opposite. But the fibreglass had not even started to burn.

Most fibreglass boats contain a lot of wood below, often the entire accommodation, and only the bare shell is fibreglass.

Even if the builder uses safe materials there is nothing to prevent the owner bringing inflammable bedding and pillows and other items on board. No matter how strict and comprehensive the regulations for construction and equipment, fire risk is far more in the hands of the crew than the builder.

Inflammable materials are not found only below. Barbecues are more hazardous than an engine. Many awnings, spray hoods and plastics winter covers burn readily, and drip burning globules to set alight the deck or cockpit beneath.

Fire ships sent into an anchored fleet were a much feared weapon in olden days. Close packed marinas are even more of a fire trap. (Yet insurers charge lower premiums!) In one case the plastics awning of a motor cruiser was set alight by a carelessly discarded cigarette from the shore. The fire completely destroyed that boat together with the cruiser in the adjoining berth, and severely damaged two more. Tightly parked boatyards ashore are as bad without the chance of casting off in a hurry. 'Watch thy neighbour as thyself' should be the watchword.

Radiant heat

Fibreglass boats can be very badly damaged by radiant heat, eg from a nearby burning boat or building, even a bonfire. There is probably cosmetic damage like blistered or crazed gel coat. But the really serious damage is extensive and unseen delamination. After any fire, inside or out, get a good survey and in particular suspect delamination. Repair will be a very big operation; what appears at first to be modest, easily repaired damage to the gel coat may turn out to be total loss. Be very cautious about buying a boat known to have been fire damaged.

Lightning

As well as the risk of igniting fibreglass, or other materials, there is the probability of delamination or structural damage due to vaporisation of moisture trapped in voids. After a lightning strike insist on a thorough hull survey. Because of their conductivity carbon fibre masts may explode if not fitted with a lightning conductor.

Conductivity

Unlike a metal boat the inside face will remain comparatively cool despite the outside being ablaze. Often it shows hardly a blister even when half the outside has been burnt away.

In a major sea disaster when the surface is ablaze with burning oil, the crew have a better chance of escaping in an inflammable fibreglass lifeboat than a non-inflammable metal one. It may emerge on fire, which can be put out with water, but in a metal boat they would be roasted.

Smoke

Polyester burns with a lot of black smoke. Epoxy creates even more and so does vinyl ester. Cynics say this aids rescue as a burning boat can be seen from afar. Of much more practical importance, the smoke will not only hamper fire fighting but be lethal if trapped in a cabin. More people die in buildings through being overcome by smoke, fumes and lack of oxygen than actual fire. A boat is much smaller than a building and the effects become lethal very quickly.

Ordinary polyester does not produce significant quantities of toxic fumes other than usual combustion products. But there are so many other materials on a boat, most of which will be burning fiercely well before the fibreglass especially those vinyl linings.

Construction

Hot exhaust pipes and chimneys must be lagged and have sufficient clearance so that no materials close to the pipe, especially structural, can exceed a surface temperature of more than 150°F, 65°C. Allowance should be made for lagging getting waterlogged, deteriorating or even crumbling away. The best safeguard is space. Water cooled exhausts get hot if the cooling water fails. No exhaust pipe should run close to a fuel tank.

There must be adequate clearance round a stove. All materials must be Class 1 spread of flame or suitably protected within 400 mm above a flame if horizontal and 125 mm if vertical. When heeled to 30° the distances are 200 mm for horizontal surfaces and 200 mm for vertical. Note this assumes a fixed stove. If gimballed the position of the flame will move. Nothing inflammable like curtains or dishcloths must be allowed to swing within 600 mm of any flame. (From DTI Safety of Small Commercial Sailing Vessels 1993.)

Finally, electrical wiring must not be embedded.

Fuel tanks

Fibreglass fuel tanks are permitted but local regulations may make it impossible to mould them. They should not be used for petrol, only diesel.

There have been worries that being an insulator, static electricity could cause sparks inside a fibreglass tank and lead to spontaneous explosion. This is impossible. Even if

there could be sparks, which is disputed, the free space in a tank is saturated with fuel vapour and the proportion of air too small for combustion. It is standard practice to bond all metal fittings.

The inside must be well coated with resin, preferably a better quality chemical resistant type. But higher resistance may be only when post-cured, impossible *in situ*. HET acid resins are more chemically resistant than ordinary ones. So are vinyl ester, their primary purpose. Fire retardant fillers offer lower resistance.

To reduce the risk of fibreglass tanks burning, fire retardant resins are often specified. Better protection would be multiple layers of high glass content woven rovings or cloth.

Tanks can be built in but should be done with caution and special care to avoid seepage via stringers or bulkheads. Being sealed, inspection or repair of the hull is impossible. Tanks should not be built into a sandwich hull. It is better to use fibreglass only for separately moulded tanks.

Dust

Like most basically inflammable materials the finely divided polyester dust from sanding can be explosive and should be swept up promptly.

Fire fighting

There are three principal scenarios:

1   A workshop fire involving liquid resin or other components. These are Class B fires. Use sand, carbon dioxide, dry powder or foam extinguishers. A major hazard will be thick, acrid smoke. Do not use water except to cool drums or tanks. When calling the fire service warn them what is involved. They should have been notified before starting moulding as a normal precaution.

2   An external fire. With no other materials involved water can be used. It would almost certainly be in a marina or on land with help available, probably a fire service, but in a general conflagration the boat might be of secondary interest.

3   An internal fire. If at sea, as must be assumed, no help will be near. The fibreglass itself presents no problems. Water can be used

and is generally plentiful but other materials will be involved, probably fuel, fat or electrical equipment on which water must not be used. Few fires are simple, especially on a boat where so many different substances and equipment are mixed together in a small space.

The boat's extinguishers must be capable of putting out a serious fuel or engine fire quickly. Until that is done the crew should not grab those buckets of water, except to damp down fibreglass and other materials.

All fire fighting is much easier in theory than in the frightening reality.

Fire extinguishers

The basic principles of fire extinguishing are

- Cool it below ignition temperature (the action of water).
- Cut off the supply of an essential constituent. Turn off the fuel.
- Smother the flames to cut off oxygen, either physically with a blanket, or by foam or carbon dioxide.
- Interrupt the flame front, by beating or blowing, or interposing non-inflammable elements, the action of dry powder and halogen compounds.

The rule is one extinguisher for the engine and one for the cabin, with a third if there is an aft cabin or the boat is over 45 ft, 15 m. The minimum size for dry powder or BCF is 3 lb, 1.5 kg. Some authorities require a fire blanket as well, and no boat however small should go to sea without one or more buckets fitted with lanyards.

In the early days there were horror stories about crews grabbing a fire extinguisher to put out a fire only to find the boat sinking as the extinguisher fluid dissolved the fibreglass! The choice, it was claimed, was burn or sink. It made a nice bar joke in the days when anything bad about fibreglass was good.

Certain vaporising liquid fire extinguisher fluids will attack polyester, although only slowly. They could never sink a good boat and only in large quantity damage a bad one. Even then it would need to be very bad. In any case those extinguishers have been banned for forty years, not for their effect on fibreglass but because they are too dangerous for humans. However, old ones may still be lying around and unscrupulous dealers have been known to dump stocks on other countries. Now even previously safe Halon extinguishers like BCF and BTM have been outlawed as environmentally unfriendly.

Foam extinguishers are good on fuel fires but too bulky for average boat use. Dry powder is effective, compact and inexpensive. Both make a mess. Carbon dioxide is clean but asphyxiating in a confined space. Halons are best for automatic engine space installations. Unfortunately, there seems no environmentally acceptable replacement now they are being phased out. For a small fire a fire blanket is effective, clean and reusable, and can also save someone whose clothes are alight.

Big extinguishers are expensive and to ensure they are always full are made for once only use. Once started they cannot be turned off. For a small galley flare up it is worth having a simple camping or car extinguisher, preferably on-off, so it can be stopped as soon as the fire is out. The only way to stop a big extinguisher from making the whole boat a mess is by throwing it overboard. More important, if at sea the big extinguisher is still available for a serious fire. Because of the expense and mess a crew may hesitate to use a main extinguisher for a small fire, and hesitation can be fatal. There need be no hesitation about grabbing a small, cheap one.

The most effective extinguisher of all, and by far the cheapest, is still a simple bucket and lanyard with a frightened person at the end of it. Water is unlimited and costs nothing.

Fire extinguisher types		
Safe on fibreglass	Phasing out	Banned
Water	BCF	BCM (Chlorobromethane)
Dry powder	BTM	CCl_3 (Carbon tetrachloride 'Pyrene')
Foam	Halon	Trichlorethylene
CO_2	Halogens	

Gas detectors

Most detectors are put in the bilges because LPG sinks so, in theory, that is where it will collect. But it may not get there. A fibreglass, close-fitting, or carpeted cabin sole means that a dangerous concentration can build up at floor level – a lot closer to a cooker flame or dropped match. Gas leaks will always be well above floor level not in the bilges. Regulations forbid gas pipes in the bilges.

References

Statutory Instrument No 917, The Highly Flammable Liquids and Liquefied Petroleum Gases Regulations, 1972, HMSO.

Fire and Related Properties of Industrial Chemicals, 1972. Fire Protection Association, London.

Health and Safety at Work No 22, Dust Explosion in Factories, HMSO.

Guide to the Safe Handling of Unsaturated Polyester Resins and Resin Systems. British Resin Manufacturers' Association and Scott Bader Ltd, Wellingborough, Northants.

Yachting Monthly, November 1989

Turning a bare moulding into a boat

A fibreglass boat must be first and foremost a boat. This tends to be forgotten with the emphasis on moulding and production.

The lines and technical matters like engine and rig are outside the scope of this book. This section covers the way a bare moulding straight out of the mould is, or should be, turned into a strong, seaworthy, trouble free boat, and something about how it should not be.

Wood and steel boats are forgiving. Fibreglass is not and is becoming less so as construction becomes thinner and more sophisticated. Many practices common on sturdy wood and steel are disastrous on fibreglass.

Better a good wooden boat than a badly fitted out fibreglass one.

CHAPTER

11

Glassing-in

By far the commonest way to make attachments, and most sympathetic to the nature of fibreglass, is by moulding, either a butt strap or the ubiquitous glass angle. This secondary bonding is known as glassing-in or matting-in. It is versatile and as well as joining fibreglass mouldings is used for attaching wood, and even metal with suitable precautions.

Moulded joins

'Wet' glass mat forms an intimate contact with whatever is being joined, particularly the rough side, and follows any shape exactly. In effect the surfaces act as a mould (Fig 11.1).

While the main moulding is fairly new a chemical bond will be obtained and it becomes part of the moulding not just an attachment. Even when cured the bond will be fairly good, if the surface is cleaned and roughened, and there will be the same intimate contact.

Most glassing-in is done during fitting out, not under moulding shop conditions, and by woodworkers or mechanics not trained

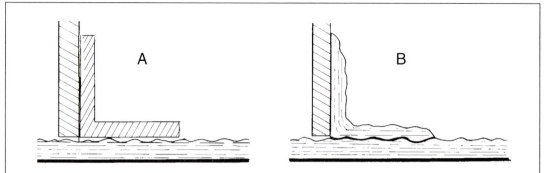

Figure 11.1   Intimate fit
A The natural inside of a fibreglass moulding is always uneven. No metal or preformed part can fit intimately.
B A glass angle automatically forms to the exact shape and contours of the moulding giving an absolutely intimate fit and therefore maximum bonding area.

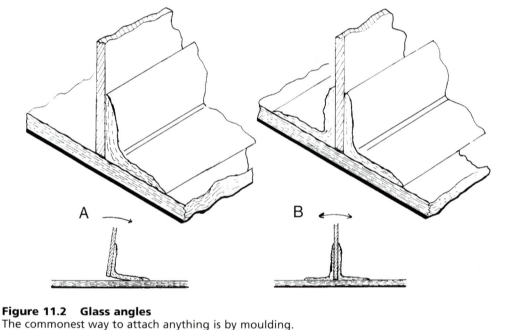

Figure 11.2   Glass angles
The commonest way to attach anything is by moulding.
A A single angle may peel.
B Where practicable angles should be double. Even if half the thickness they are stronger and unlikely to peel.

moulders. Sometimes they scorn moulding and when they have to do it themselves as part of their own fitting out work it may be done badly or given to an apprentice. This is the wrong attitude. Glassing-in is as important as primary moulding and, being generally fiddly, more difficult, and often done under awkward conditions, requires even more care; also a proper environment for moulding. This is what holds the boat together.

Glass angles

Good practice is to mould angles with mat because it conforms more easily to shape. Suppliers of stronger woven rovings, especially the more exotic kinds, extol their virtues. But they are harder to work into the angle and tend to bridge and are then not strong. Also, woven materials cannot get such an intimate bond to the irregular surface as mat. Multiple layers of soundly moulded mat are far better

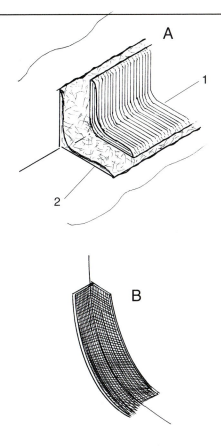

Figure 11.3   Attachment on a curve
Some authorities recommend using stronger woven rovings for angles, even unidirectional cloth or carbon fibre, orientated across the angle.
A Strong materials, 1, are more difficult to mould. Bond is poor so the first layer should be mat, 2
B Most angles are on a curve. Woven materials soon get distorted.

than fewer but badly moulded woven rovings however strong in theory. Also, most attachments are on a curve (Fig 11.3). A weave soon gets out of line.

A single angle tends to peel. Angles must be double wherever possible. Good design will ensure access to both sides for all structural attachments (Fig 11.2).

Gaps
Often there is a gap. Sound moulding requires a firm backing. So unless something is done there will be a weak line along the critical part, often showing as white, badly moulded glass. Production pressures seldom allow correct procedure (Fig 11.4).

Butt straps
Again, peeling must be prevented. However, as one side is often the gel coat, appearance rules out a double butt strap (Fig 11.5).

Changes of thickness
All changes of thickness must be gradual, whether the flange of an angle or a butt strap. Abrupt change causes a high stress hinge effect. An approximate rule of thumb is 1 in per 1 oz/ft^2 of glass mat, 30 mm per 300 g/m^2, for structural members. Non-structural attachments may be $^3/_4$ in, 20 mm. The width should not be less than 2 in, 50 mm, and the combined weight of glass both sides not less than the lighter member joined, with a minimum of 3 oz/ft^2, 900 g/m^2, or two layers of medium weight mat.

The equivalent strength is difficult to reckon when joining wood or metal but the main point is whether it is structural or not. In practice this rule is widely ignored and a two-layer angle used for everything. Often for the sake of speed just a single layer is used.

These figures are largely academic. It is impracticable to mould precisely, or circumstances may make them impossible. Nevertheless they should be considered the minimum. Being awkward resin content will be high. A common fault is skimping. Thorough wetting out is much more important than theoretical resin/glass ratio.

Gel coat/rough side
Bonding to a gel coat is bad practice. Stresses from glassed-on attachments are delaminating and the gel coat bond is the weakest part. Moreover the surface is very smooth and generally has traces of polish or release agent which prevent a good bond. It is better to attach to the gel coat by fastenings.

Not only is bonding more secure to the rough side but the appearance is similar. A rough angle looks out of place on smooth gel coat.

Surface preparation
The best secondary bond is while the basic moulding is still 'green', and it can be a chemical bond. No preparation is then needed provided the surface is uncontaminated. Some

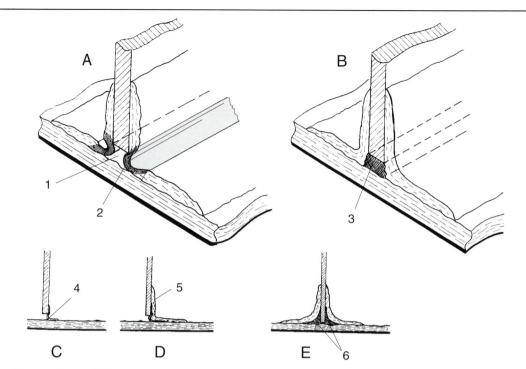

Figure 11.4   Filling a gap
Very often the angle must bridge a gap, 1. Fibreglass cannot be moulded soundly without a firm backing.
A If moulded directly over the gap there will be a line of bad moulding and weakness, 2, along the angle just where it is supposed to hold the pieces together strongly.
B The correct way is to fill the gap first with putty or foam, 3, or cover with adhesive tape to provide firm backing.
C Alternatively the gap can be moulded over with a single layer, 4, perhaps wetted out separately, and allowed to set. It will be badly moulded but firm enough to be a backing.
D When hard the full angle, 5, can be moulded over it.
E Regardless of whether there is a gap, when forming an angle with woven rovings the root angle must be filled out with a fillet, 6, for easier and sounder moulding.

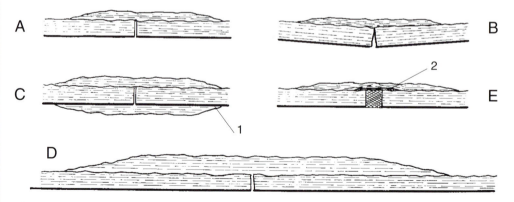

Figure 11.5   Butt strap
A, B A single butt strap is weak. The tendency is for a hinge effect along the line of the join.
C Where possible the butt strap should be double. But this will often be on the gel coat side, 1, and too unsightly.
D Therefore with a single butt strap it must be as thick or thicker than the parts to be joined and of generous width.
E As with angles a gap must be filled or covered first, 2.

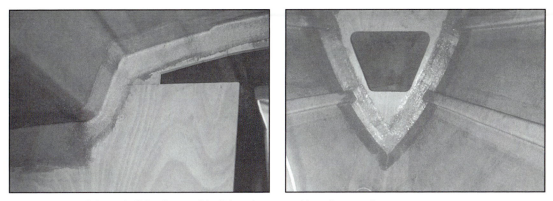

Photos 11.1 (a) and **(b)** Plywood bulkheads secured by glass angles.

authorities stipulate within 24–48 hours after moulding; after that it will be increasingly more difficult to get a chemical bond, although with a generous width it will usually be adequate. Even when aged, the styrene in liquid resin will attack the hard polyester to some extent.

Acetone will condition and clean the surface and frequently, due to restricted access, is all that is possible. The approved preparation is grinding. In theory this exposes fibres, although as they will have been sheared off flush intermeshing is either wishful thinking or very bad moulding. Because the natural inside surface is so uneven grinding has to go down to the lowest level of the hollows. This not only takes longer, and is therefore commonly skimped, but removes valuable material. If it has to be done by hand because access does not allow power tools it is certain to be skimped if attempted at all. A wire brush in an electric drill cleans hollows without taking off so much material, and also makes less mess.

Being uncured and still tacky the inside can get very dirty and contaminated during fitting out. Workers must walk around, there will be dust and sawdust, and resin drips to bind it together. It is also common to find odd screws trodden in.

Where it is known that important glassing-on must come, a tear-off strip or polythene can be used to expose the uncontaminated surface beneath.

By the time it is old and painted substantially clean is the best that can be expected. The most important part is to clean off oil and muck. Test a doubtful surface by laying up a sample with a slip of polythene under one edge. By inserting a screwdriver under the polythene the sample can be peeled off. If it shears untidily leaving jagged fibres the bond is good. A poor bond separates cleanly.

'Bond burn'

Anything bonded on inside can cause 'bond burn' or telegraphing, due to the bonding resin contracting as it cures and pulling the light moulding out of shape (Fig 11.6).

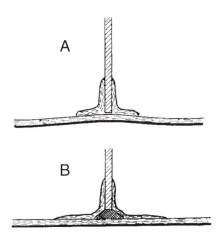

Figure 11.6   Bond burn
A Thick angles against a fairly light moulding will cause distortion due to the angles contracting as they cure. (Exaggerated but even slight distortion is conspicuous on a well polished gel coat.)
B Bond burn can be reduced by spreading the root and tapering the flanges over a wide distance.

Joins

We live in a solid world of metal, wood and stone. A major difficulty is our attitude of mind. Whether building or using we must think fibreglass, and realise we are dealing with a thin shell, not something solid, which needs sympathy not brute force. The nearest to something resembling a fibreglass boat is probably the shell of our morning boiled egg!

Access

A wooden or steel boat is built up piece by piece in contrast so there is always good access, fibreglass boatbuilding generally involves assembling comparatively large, pre-fabricated parts and access by anything but a trained rat may be impossible. That is no way to make sound joins.

A fundamental rule is: difficult work will be bad work. Ideally, there must be good access and reasonably comfortable working conditions. Joins must be designed to be joined, not left to the builder's ingenuity. Moreover they should be designed to be done under production conditions and pressures, where anything time consuming and fiddly will be bypassed or skimped.

Difficult jobs may have to be done by a slim apprentice because a more skilled man cannot get there or refuses to work in a dimly lit, fume laden hole. Out of sight does not mean only out of mind but uninspected, and very often uninspectable.

Joint design

The strength of the moulding is in the glass fibres. All joins between mouldings, whether by moulding or fastenings, should overlap with a wide area of contact. Butt joins give no continuity of strength (Figs 12.1, 12.2, 12.3).

Avoid sharp transitions

Changes of thickness must be made gradually, whether joining two parts of unequal thickness, or increasing or reducing a single moulding. A sharp step creates a weakening hinge effect (Figs 12.6 and 12.7).

The minimum rate of change of thickness for structural work is not less than 1 oz/ft^2 of glass per 1 in width, 300 g/m^2 per 30 mm, or more where space allows. If non-structural this can be reduced to $^3/_4$ inch, 20 mm. Other weights pro rata. It is not essential to hold the taper precisely. Accurate measurement under moulding conditions is practicable only in books.

Bends

When metal is bent it maintains a constant thickness. Fibreglass cannot be bent and has to be moulded to shape but in doing so thickness will vary. An inside radius will fill as succeeding layers take a shorter path and puddles of resin form. Woven materials tend to bridge or pull away. Conversely an outside radius will pull thin as mat tends to break up and resin drain away (Figs 12.8 and 12.9). (Remember: features on the mould are reversed.)

Thickness

The thickness cannot be held precisely. There is a manufacturer's tolerance on the thickness of glass, and resin content varies with the skill and habits of the worker. Overlaps will form bulges and the natural unevenness of the inside is usually $^1/_8$ in, 3 mm, between peaks and hollows.

Pieces intended to mate accurately should not involve an inside surface. Only gel coat side to gel coat, with dimensions controlled by moulds, will fit reliably (Fig 12.9).

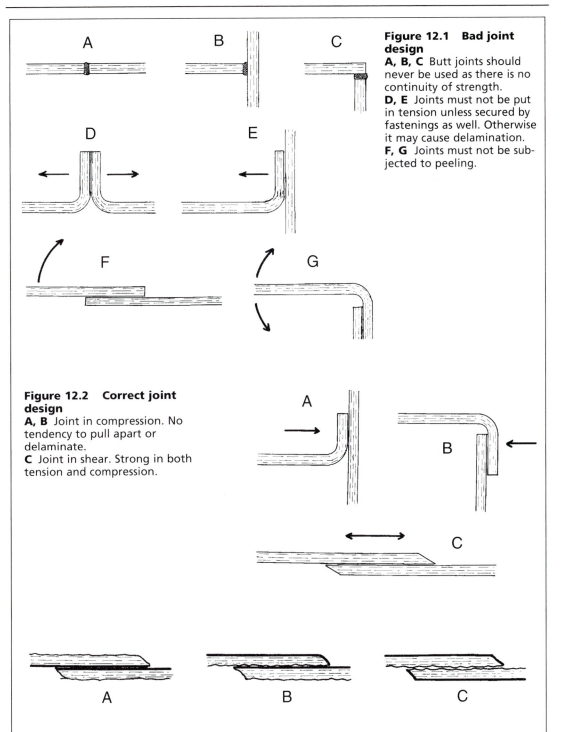

Figure 12.1 Bad joint design
A, B, C Butt joints should never be used as there is no continuity of strength.
D, E Joints must not be put in tension unless secured by fastenings as well. Otherwise it may cause delamination.
F, G Joints must not be subjected to peeling.

Figure 12.2 Correct joint design
A, B Joint in compression. No tendency to pull apart or delaminate.
C Joint in shear. Strong in both tension and compression.

Figure 12.3 Gel coat
The gel coat is weak. Therefore it is bad practice to bond to that side.
A Gel coat to gel coat. This gives the most accurate fit but is the weakest. To prevent the gel coat separating it should be supplemented by fastenings.
B One side gel coat. Also weak.
C Neither part gel coat. This is the strongest bond, but the fit cannot be accurate unless one is laid up wet.

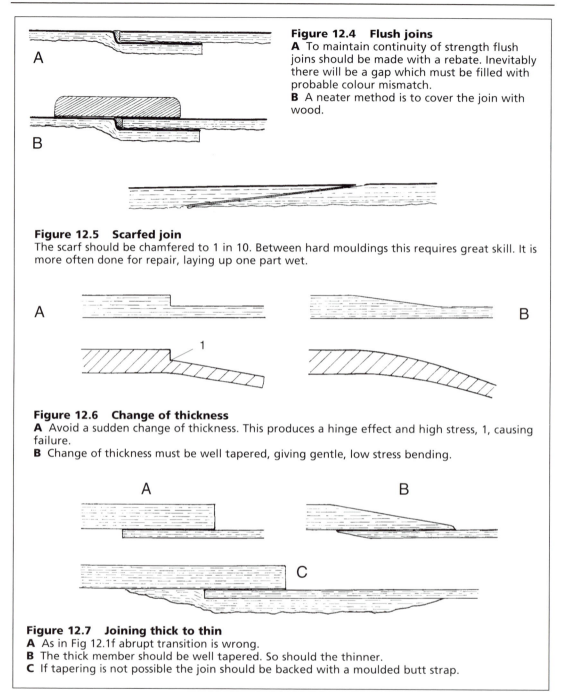

Figure 12.4   Flush joins
A To maintain continuity of strength flush joins should be made with a rebate. Inevitably there will be a gap which must be filled with probable colour mismatch.
B A neater method is to cover the join with wood.

Figure 12.5   Scarfed join
The scarf should be chamfered to 1 in 10. Between hard mouldings this requires great skill. It is more often done for repair, laying up one part wet.

Figure 12.6   Change of thickness
A Avoid a sudden change of thickness. This produces a hinge effect and high stress, 1, causing failure.
B Change of thickness must be well tapered, giving gentle, low stress bending.

Figure 12.7   Joining thick to thin
A As in Fig 12.1f abrupt transition is wrong.
B The thick member should be well tapered. So should the thinner.
C If tapering is not possible the join should be backed with a moulded butt strap.

Fastenings

A moulded join bonds over a wide area so it blends into the moulding. This is sympathetic to fibreglass. A fastening of any kind imposes a brutal local stress, but often no other way is possible and fastenings are used very frequently. This must be done with due regard to the nature of fibreglass.

Most other structural materials have ductility. If the stress around one fastening is too high the material will flow locally until stress is equalised among adjoining fastenings. Fibreglass cannot do this. Stress relief can occur only through local failure. The join strength depends on the bearing pressure on the fibreglass, not the strength of the fastenings.

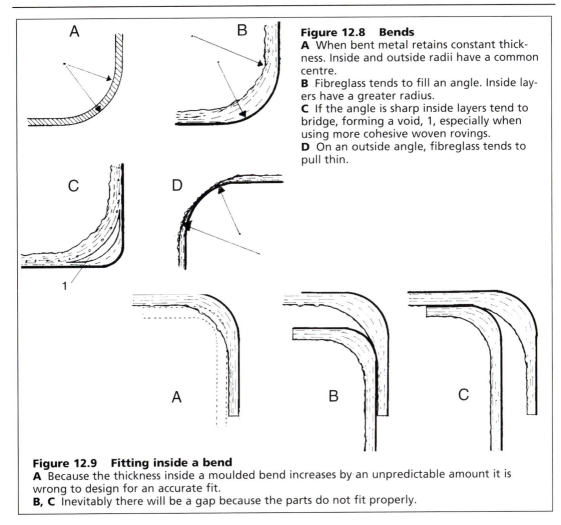

Figure 12.8   Bends
A When bent metal retains constant thickness. Inside and outside radii have a common centre.
B Fibreglass tends to fill an angle. Inside layers have a greater radius.
C If the angle is sharp inside layers tend to bridge, forming a void, 1, especially when using more cohesive woven rovings.
D On an outside angle, fibreglass tends to pull thin.

Figure 12.9   Fitting inside a bend
A Because the thickness inside a moulded bend increases by an unpredictable amount it is wrong to design for an accurate fit.
B, C Inevitably there will be a gap because the parts do not fit properly.

They should be a good fit and hole centres as in Fig 12.10.

Moulding soundly near an edge is more difficult so it is often thin and unprotected edges degrade where exposed to water and weather. For long term reliability the distance should be at least 1½ in, 35 mm, regardless of size.

A fastening can crush the brittle resin if tightened hard. The force must be well distributed. Preferably the fibreglass is sandwiched between wood or other resilient material (Fig 12.11). Otherwise there must be oversize washers, at least twice the hole diameter; better still 'penny' washers. For types of fastenings see Chapter 15.

Gap filling

The preferred method is rough side to rough side but because of the unevenness an intimate fit is impossible unless one member is laid up wet. Between hard mouldings the gap must be filled. Wet mat is often used but has poor flow. On long, thick gaps multiple layers can sag, or take so long the resin has started to set. The parts must be assembled and bolted together while the resin is still fluid so it needs to be slow setting. Polyester and epoxy putties flow better but also set quickly.

On a long, wide gap tightening the fastenings while the filling is soft will distort the mouldings. It is good practice to put spacers in way of fastenings. The gap is filled with putty later (Fig 12.12).

Glueing

Glue must be gap filling and not require pressure to avoid crushing or distorting the fibreglass with clamps. The size of mouldings

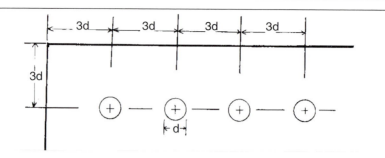

Figure 12.10 Spacing of fastenings
Holes must be at least 3d distance from the edge and 3d apart for bolts, where d is the diameter of the hole, not the bolt. This may be reduced to 2.5 for rivets. Spacing must be increased where d is less than twice the moulding thickness.

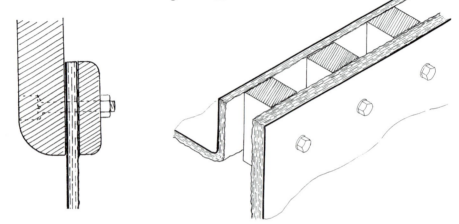

Figure 12.11 Bolting to wood
When bolting or riveting fibreglass to wood the preferred method is to sandwich the fibreglass between two pieces of wood to prevent local crushing.

Figure 12.12 Wide gap
Correct design will allow a substantial tolerance between large parts, eg hull and deck. To avoid distortion when bolting the gap should have spacers.

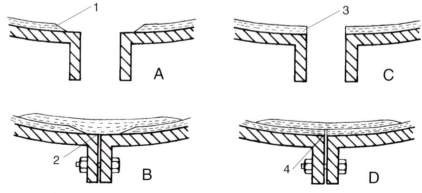

Figure 12.13 Split mould
To mould the unmouldable a split mould is used. The lay up is done conveniently while separated, the parts brought together while still in the mould and joined by a butt strap.
A The edges of the moulding are staggered, 1.
B When brought together this gives a flush join, 2, and smooth finish.
C Alternatively the edges are trimmed, 3.
D This leaves a gap, 4, which must be filled. If done badly, or it comes out, the trimmed edges of the moulding will be exposed and will decay.

usually means clamps are impractical anyway.

Glueing requires a precise fit and smooth surface. The uneven side must be ground flat and reduced to even thickness. Glueing to a gel coat is easier but bad practice (see page 65).

As epoxy or polyester putty does not contain glass fibre it lacks the structural strength of a glass angle or butt strap. A few do contain fibres but the proportion which can be loaded is low, much less than ordinary moulding, and the strength is illusory.

Woodwork is often glued together in prefabricated accommodation units. This is neat and strong but cannot be dismantled. Access for repair must be destructive. Screws used to be acceptable for high class wooden yachts and require no more labour. Boats would be cheaper to repair if that was still done today.

Split mould

How can the unmouldable be moulded?

With many things the shape is dictated by the production methods, eg a polythene bucket. But boats are designed on performance. Only after drawing the lines does a designer wonder how, or if, it could be moulded. Few designers have been moulders.

The easier to release, the sooner the next boat can be started and the less risk of damage, not only to the boat but also the valuable mould on which all further production depends. In the simplest case the moulding is designed to lift straight out, yet it still requires considerable force to break out because of the vacuum behind, especially with a large moulding.

A common approach is a split mould which can be dismantled. This allows shapes impossible to release from a simple mould, typically the fashionable forward sloping transom.

Commonly the hull mould is in two halves. Each half can be worked on from both sides, a particular advantage with a deep keel. Then the mould is bolted together and the halves, still inside, are joined with a massive butt strap (Fig 12.13).

While much of the butt strap will be accessible, a major problem is how to mould it deep down inside the keel, far out of reach or too narrow to use ordinary moulding tools. The usual approach is to 'push it in with a stick' (Fig 29.3), a bad way of moulding something

which literally holds the boat together. (See Chapter 29.) And sometimes does not.

Refined methods use side panels moulded separately and bonded on later, even complete sub-assemblies, or another material like wood.

Flush joins

The simplest case is a butt joint but to ensure strength it must be backed by a substantial butt strap. Planned flush joins between hard mouldings need to be properly designed, eg with a rebate and overlap. A flush join will require filling and fairing. A good colour and texture match will be difficult and probably not last. Flush joins are better hidden by woodwork (Fig 12.4).

A scarfed join between two hard mouldings requires precision and a high degree of skill. It would be too difficult for production (Fig 12.5). So it is only attempted for repair when fitting a new pre-moulded section. It is far easier if one part is laid up 'wet' as is more usual for repair. Laboratory tests have shown that even on an aged moulding and using polyester the join is as strong as the original if the chamfered edge has a long taper.

Forcing to fit

Forcing to fit will pre-stress the moulding and thereby weaken it. The sooner mouldings can be joined, ie. the 'greener' they are, the less harm done because they will cure in that shape. Most forcing to fit occurs because one or both mouldings have become distorted due to careless support during cure. Between two fibreglass mouldings there will be some mutual flexibility, but not against a massive keel. It is essential this is exactly the right shape too.

Pre-stressing is used in engineering to increase strength. That is different being designed deliberately to oppose known external stresses. Forcing mouldings to fit will not pre-stress in a beneficial direction.

Cleanliness

For a sound bond, even to a newly moulded hull, the surface must be clean. Cleanliness is relative. Fitting out does not require the clean room atmosphere of microchip assembly, and certainly never gets it. But the surface does

Keeping the inside clean

- Spread polythene over all vulnerable surfaces.
- Lay down cardboard anywhere walked on.
- Change to soft indoor shoes or overshoes.
- Wear soft overalls without hard buckles or buttons.
- Avoid carpentry work inside the hull.
- When the surface is sanded, vacuum clean dust at once.
- Delay oily jobs until all structural work has been done.
- Keep the workshop floor clean and dust free.
- Seal concrete floors.
- No drinking or eating inside the boat.
- Store resin, glass and solvents outside.
- Mop up spillages promptly.

need to be kept reasonably free from contamination.

The gel coat also needs protection to keep that beautiful shiny finish. Carelessness during the months of fitting out will scratch or stain it, especially the deck. All walked on surfaces must be covered. Some builders apply strippable coatings, but these can be loving when the time comes for removal.

Reference
Tests at Coleraine University 1980.

Stiffening

A fibreglass boat is essentially a thin shell made of expensive material. It is wasteful to build thickness so it requires stiffening. Moreover as a material it is only one-twentieth as stiff as steel, one-seventh as aluminium although of comparable strength. In this it is more like plywood, but being heavier, more expensive and easier to form to shape is always thinner (Table 1.2, page 4).

Do not confuse strength with stiffness or rigidity. A steel wire is strong but flexible; an eggshell rigid but weak. The main requirement on a boat is stiffness not high tensile or compressive strength, the properties generally quoted by suppliers. Generally when the boat is rigid enough it is strong enough.

Bending theory

When bending one side is in tension, the other in compression. The greatest stress occurs furthest from the neutral axis about which it bends (Fig 13.1).

Any stiffener works on the principle of the

girder. The stiffness it can exert, technically known as the moment of inertia or I, depends on the distance of the material from the axis of bending, not the total amount of material. A classic example is the I beam or RSJ, consisting of two flanges connected by a web. This puts the bulk of material where it works hardest and reduces weight and cost by eliminating material in the middle where it contributes little to strength (Fig 13.2).

With fibreglass stiffeners, one side of the 'girder' is the moulding itself, which is wide and thick compared with the flanges of the stiffener. Therefore the power of the stiffener depends on the amount of material on the further face and its distance (Figs 13.3 and 13.4).

This may be expressed approximately:

$$I = A\,d^2$$

where A is the cross sectional area of the face and d the distance from the moulding.

Hardspots

Stiffening members are the main source of hardspots (Chapter 17). Everything must blend into the hull, with nothing abrupt. In particular there should be no sharp bending under any circumstances, because the sharper the bending the higher the stress.

Strength through shape

The cheapest, most elegant and least wasteful way to get stiffness is to use shape. A flat panel is flexible. A curved panel has natural stiffness (Fig 13.5). This has been known for hundreds of years by architects, carriage builders and furniture makers. It is apparent in nature too: look at leaves, flowers, insects, shells.

With monocoque construction there are no

Stiffening methods

- Strength through shape, curvature, corrugations etc
- Decorative dents
- Use of natural or designed features
- Extra thickness
- Orientation of reinforcement
- Bulkheads (Chapter 14)
- Frames, ribs and stringers
- Angles and webs
- Beading and flanges
- Internal mouldings and accommodation
- Attachment to other members
- Space frame
- Sandwich (Chapter 19)
- S glass, Kevlar and carbon fibre

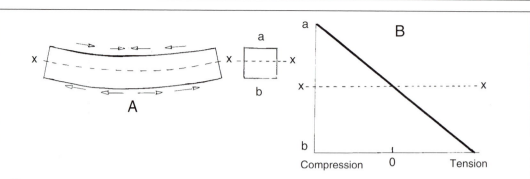

Figure 13.1
When anything bends, one side, a, is in compression, the other, b, in tension. The graph shows how stress reverses and is zero at the axis of bending x–x.

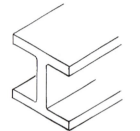

Figure 13.2   The common I beam or RSJ
Because stress when bending is greatest at the edges this is where material is concentrated. Solid right through would be heavy and wasteful. So in the middle it is reduced to a web, just sufficient to hold the edges together.

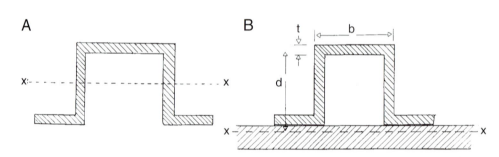

Figure 13.3
A simple channel section by itself bends approximately about its mid-section x–x. But when it is joined to the wider, thicker mass of the moulding the axis of bending of the combination will be close to or within the moulding. This makes the cross section area of the outer face, b x t, the more powerful, as it is proportional to d^2.

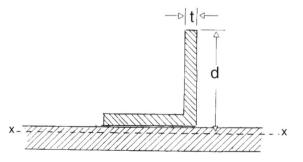

Figure 13.4
An angle has a small face area at greatest distance and therefore much less stiffening power.

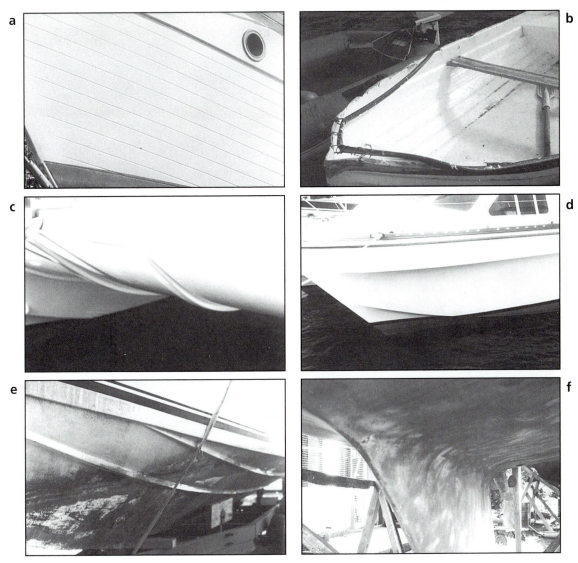

Photos 13.1 (a), (b), (c), (d), (e), (f)   Examples of strength through shape.

internal stiffeners and the hull relies on shape alone. This is easier with small boats.

Every part of a fibreglass boat should be curved not flat. Compound curvature in two directions is practicable because, unlike plywood or metal, we do not start with flat sheets which bend in only one direction.

Where the design does not allow natural curvature it can be contrived as with modern vehicle design. The raised panels on the flat side of a van are not decoration. They add stiffness, thereby it can be lighter and cheaper. Ridges, grooves, channels, swedging, dishing, bulges, depressions, knuckles, dimples,

pimples and other decorative dents can be integrally moulded at no extra cost. Such features need not be unsightly. The best way to disguise anything is make it look as if meant to be there. Simulated clinker is boaty as well as being good stiffening. In America 'mock planking' is popular. Other features are spray knuckles, cove lines, rubbing strakes, coamings, stub keels, bilge keels, spray rails on power boats, and many others (Fig 13.6).

Another familiar strength through shape is the ubiquitous corrugated roofing sheet. Corrugated hulls are unusual but a fishing boat design in South Africa was refined to this and

Naturally strong features	
Stem	Hull/deck join
Corners of the	Cabin top
transom	angles
Canoe stern	Cockpit angles
Chine	Coamings
Sheer strake	Mast step
Clinker lands	Keel
Mock planking	Keel stub
Rubbing band	Bilge keel
Cove line	

reduced the cost and weight of stringers. On decks it also gives better footing.

Natural features with a strong shape such as angles and channels can be thickened into structural members, or infilled with a core forming a box section (Figs 13.7, 13.8 and 13.9).

Extra thickness

A sheet of metal or plywood is of uniform thickness, dictated by the maximum stress any part of it has to bear. The rest is unnecessarily thick. That adds weight and is wasteful. The thickness of fibreglass can be graded so no part is thicker than it needs to be. Everything is put on, very little is wasted.

Over a wide area it is more economical to use stiffeners than extra thickness, although it is standard practice to increase thickness generally on the bottom and high stress areas.

Directivity

Metal is the same strength in all directions. With fibreglass, tensile strength and stiffness is orientated in the line of the fibres, like wood is along the grain. Compressive strength, in which the resin predominates, is not orientated.

The random distribution of fibres in glass mat gives uniform stiffness in the plane of the laminate. With woven materials it is strongly orientated in the line of warp and weft. (Fig 2.3) Designers can use this to emphasise stiffness in a certain direction; even more using unidirectional weaves with more fibres aligned in one direction. In the extreme case – single rovings – all fibres are aligned one way.

Bonding

Most stiffening entails bonding, usually after moulding. Unless soundly bonded stiffening cannot work (Chapter 11).

Bulkheads

The main stiffening on most boats is provided by bulkheads (Chapter 14).

Top hat stiffeners

The traditional and easiest form of stiffener for fibreglass is the top hat stiffener. Americans call it simply a hat stiffener, but Uncle Sam top hats were taller! Anyway top hat is a dignified description for what is generally more like a common bowler, billycock or boater.

Fibreglass is moulded over a core to form a channel section with flanges, the 'brim' bonding it to the moulding. The flanges, being against the moulding, contribute little stiffness because despite having as much mass as the face the distance is negligible. In theory it is not the most efficient use of material, but being simple is the most widely used (Fig 13.10).

The strength lies in the fibreglass, not the core which is just a former over which to mould the fibreglass. Some cores, such as wood, can contribute useful strength, but in general Rules require the strength of the core to be ignored. Sometimes it may have a secondary purpose like holding a screw or forming an incompressible insert.

Top hat stiffeners are very easy to make. They are moulded *in situ* and so fit and bond intimately and follow any curve. No steaming, shaping, offering up or fitting are necessary. Right first time. On curves the core should have no springiness or be in short sections (Fig 13.11).

They are extremely versatile and can form stringers, ribs, deck beams, panel stiffeners, keelsons, engine bearers, almost anywhere stiffeners are needed (even on wooden boats to strengthen or repair ribs). They can take many shapes and sizes from a thin narrow web, like a Covent Garden porter carrying baskets on his head, to a flat broad bulge like a fishmonger's straw boater (Fig 13.12).

Most forces on a hull or deck are inwards, putting the face of a stiffener, the part which carries most stress, in tension. It will be more powerful if thicker than the sides. For most purposes a few extra layers of mat would be sufficient. For greater stiffness, use unidirectional tape or single rovings with the fibres

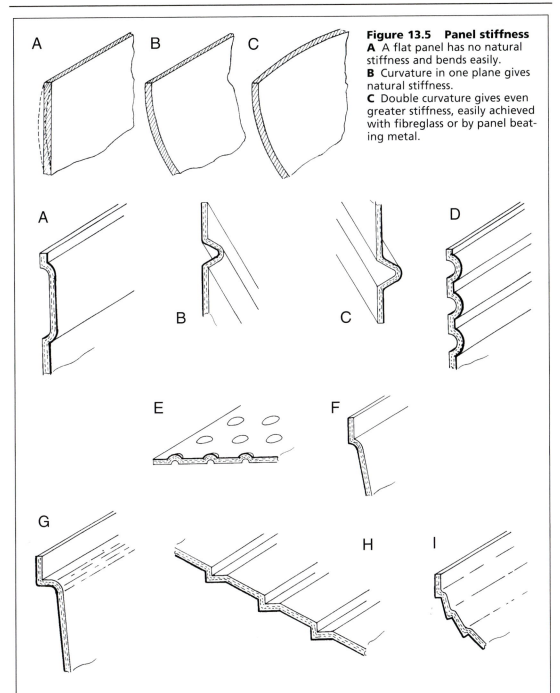

Figure 13.5 Panel stiffness
A A flat panel has no natural stiffness and bends easily.
B Curvature in one plane gives natural stiffness.
C Double curvature gives even greater stiffness, easily achieved with fibreglass or by panel beating metal.

Figure 13.6 Strength through shape
A Simple channel, eg a rubbing strake.
B Groove. Often seen as 'mock planking' on hulls.
C Ridge. Any raised feature like a toe rail or coaming.
D Corrugations. Very familiar in other fields, eg roofing. Sometimes seen on decks.
E Dimples and decorative dents, eg non-slip decks.
F Change of angle. Often forms a spray knuckle.
G Shelf. Typical of some hull/deck joins.
H Spray rails also stiffen the bottom.
I Mock clinker forms a naturally stiff hull.

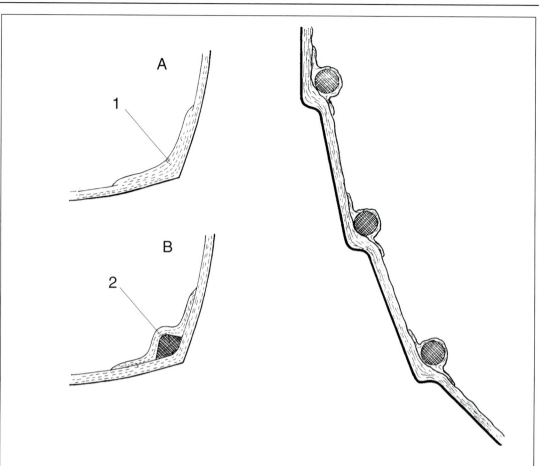

Figure 13.7 Emphasising strong features
The natural stiffness of an angle can be increased by extra moulding, 1, or infilling with a core, 2.

Figure 13.8
The good natural stiffness of mock clinker can be augmented by using a core at every land.

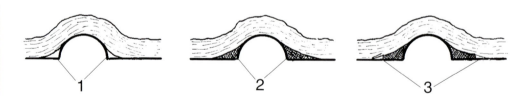

Figure 13.9
Simulated planking, popular in America, is formed by ridges in the mould. Cavities along the root, 1, are common and are a cause of blistering. These can be avoided by forming a fillet, 2, making it easier to mould. Note: the fillet must be well faired otherwise it merely transfers the blister forming cavity further outboard, 3. As is often seen.

running in the line of the stiffener. This is also where to put expensive carbon fibre so its high stiffness is used to greatest effect and economy (Fig 13.13).

Obviously the core cannot be removed afterwards so must be cheap enough to be expendable. Unless in the keel area where weight would be an advantage, it should be light. Almost anything can be used provided it neither harms nor is attacked by polyester, but must be firm enough to mould over (Fig 13.15). It must not swell, develop gas pressure or decompose into anything harmful if wet. Porous material should be sealed with resin first or wrapped in polythene. This can also protect anything attacked by polyester, eg polystyrene.

Wood is cheap, versatile, available everywhere often as scrap, and holds fastenings well. It can be in long lengths, short disjointed pieces or part sawn like a wriggling toy snake.

Strength must match appearance. Sometimes a massive looking frame has only a week, porous single layer of mat. The minimum thickness should be two layers. Two thin layers are stronger and less porous than one thick

Types of core

Suitable:	
Wood	Half sawn plastics pipe
Polyurethane or PVC foam	Premoulded fibreglass channels
Syntactic foam or putty	Extruded plastics sections
Somic paper rope	Rolled newspaper
Cardboard mailing tubes	Bent cardboard channels
Expanded metal	Wire netting
Slotted aluminium channel	Aluminium sections
Old rope	Bicycle tubes
Hose pipe	Polythene or PVC tube
Sand filled lay flat tubes	Lead

Unsuitable:	
Foam polystyrene	Plasticine
Soap	Anything damp
Some grades of phenolic based Tufnol	Preservative treated wood
Porous materials	Soft materials
	Cork

one, as well as being easier to mould. Woven rovings are more difficult to mould and likely to bridge. Ideally root angles would have fillets, but being extra work this is seldom done.

Do not assume the core can never get wet. Because of porous moulding, cut-outs, fastenings or damage it is quite possible it will. There are sure to be waterways. Voids and cavities are accepted as production tolerances. Hollow or porous cores can hold a bucketful of water, oozing for weeks after damage and delaying repairs (Fig 13.16).

It is common sense that fastenings should go into the sides of the stiffener to avoid weakening the more highly stressed face, but few bother about such details (Fig 13.17).

Where a stiffener ends at a bulkhead or partition it must be firmly connected, not simply butted (Fig 13.18). Often stiffeners must be positioned accurately to act as attachment points for accommodation or to clear other moulded or prefabricated units. If wrong they will be troublesome to reposition. Always cut away; wrenching off will damage the main moulding, probably causing delamination.

Inexperienced surveyors have been known to interpret the hollow sound of a core as delamination of the hull and require expensive, destructive and totally unnecessary repairs.

Integrally moulded stiffeners

Less weight is added and least material used when the top hat is formed within the lay up. Moulding is normal until the last few layers. Then the cores are laid down and moulding continued over them. This avoids the extra weight of the flanges. The core must be a very easy shape to mould over and lower edges faired with putty. The first layer over the core must be thin glass mat because it is important that it does not form voids. Good practice would apply several strips of mat to round off before any woven rovings (Fig 13.14).

With a soft core the hull will have a line of low impact strength.

Eggcrate

Stiffeners may run in two directions and join to form an eggcrate or waffle pattern, often used in the keel area or under decks. A weak feature is usually the intersection. Moulding

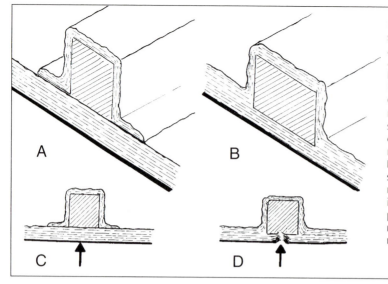

Figure 13.14   Integral stiffener
A Most stiffeners are added after the main moulding.
B They can also be moulded integrally.
C When added later there is no difference in impact strength because the soft core is protected by the full moulding thickness.
D If integrally moulded a soft core has less hull thickness between it and a point impact, and the hull can be punctured. Because there is no leak it is often not noticed.

Moulded frames

Stiffening can be pre-moulded giving a smooth, neat appearance, eg an eggcrate, engine bearers or waffle deck beams. The weakness is the bond. Unlike a stiffener laid up *in situ* soon after the main moulding, the bond is between hard mouldings. The fit cannot be intimate, as when laid up wet, and because hull thickness varies it cannot mate accurately (Fig 13.24).

It is feasible to bolt pre-moulded frames if the appearance is acceptable, and sometimes done for engine bearers. This is also done on some minehunters to resist explosions, a parameter seldom featuring in yacht design.

When damaged, moulded frames tend to break away in one piece whereas stiffeners moulded *in situ* remain bonded and fracture. This is not only easier to repair but also to detect there is damage at all (Fig 13.25).

Stiffening edges

It is bad practice to leave any edge unstiffened or unsupported, whether the trimmed edge of a moulding or a cut-out (Fig 13.26).

A flange may be vulnerable, eg a 'bathtub' hull/deck join. Where a rebate for a planned cut-out would interfere with release it can be formed by a detachable insert on the mould designed to come away with the moulding. Beading, as on old pre-polythene buckets, is easily made by moulding over cord. Unplanned or late cut-outs should be screwed to a wooden or moulded surround, or a fitting.

A plastics extrusion saves wear and hides the raw trimmed edge but gives no strength.

Accommodation

It is general practice to use the accommodation as part of the general stiffening, whether fibreglass or wood: on a small cruiser often the only stiffening. Using what has to be there anyway saves labour and expense.

Fibreglass accommodation is often thin, almost flimsy, and if a large one-piece moulding much of it will be inaccessible for glassing on. Plywood is thicker and stiffer, and being put in piece by piece, easier to glass on. An amateur fitting out a bare hull can build a stronger boat than a production conscious builder.

In theory fibreglass accommodation forms deep webs; in practice too deep. Damage and sometimes use puts too high a stress on the weak inboard side so it splits well before the hull it is supposed to be stiffening. Strength is unevenly distributed, being much reduced by openings for lockers, discontinuities, and meandering doglegs which form more weakening hard spots than stiffening.

The accommodation should be designed as stiffening, not on the assumption that whatever is there is bound to stiffen the hull.

Double shell moulding

It is common for the accommodation to be one large inside moulding – in America called

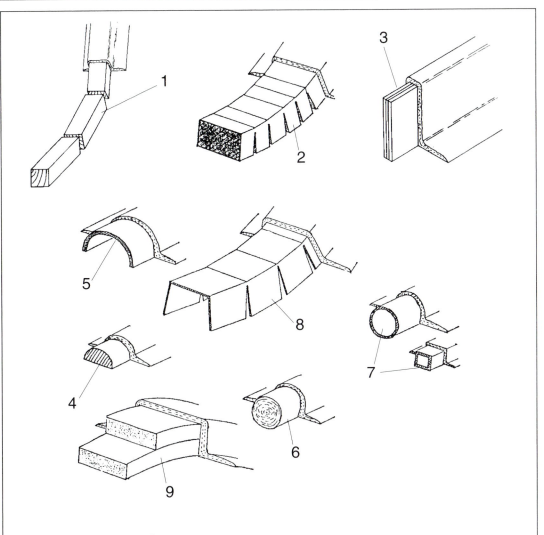

Figure 13.15 Types of core
Almost anything can be used as a core provided it is compatible with the resin. Eg wood, either disjointed pieces, 1, or part sawn, 2. Plywood, 3, is good for deep webs or to hold a fastening. Half round wood, 4, is easier to mould as also are cardboard tubes sawn in half, 5. Somic paper rope or rolled newspaper, 6, is cheap. Other choices are plastics or aluminium tube or sections, 7. High class early moulders used notched aluminium channel, 8. Cardboard does as well. Flexible PU foam, 9, is versatile, sometimes laminated or rigidised with resin.

a pan moulding, dropped in before the lid goes on. These can be sophisticated and incorporate all the stiffening (Chapter 18).

Space frame
A logical development used on some top level racing machines is an internal skeleton of tubes and wires linking the high stress points. The hull is just a shell to keep the water out. Unlike earlier racing yachts when outclassed a few years later, these make uncomfortable cruisers. Who wants to live with something like the Eiffel Tower through the middle?

Clearance
It is very common to find part of a stiffener, cut away for clearance leaving the core exposed (Fig 13.27). Probably the engine fitter had neither the material or inclination to make it good. This is very bad practice; not only must the core be sealed but the strength restored, if necessary fished. Moreover it

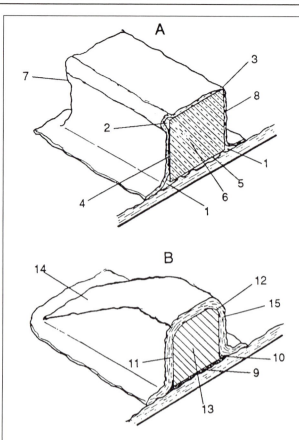

Figure 13.16   Waterways
A Water can get into a stiffener and travel far via many routes, mostly due to bad workmanship, eg Root voids, 1. Rucking on sharp angles, 2, or pulling thin, 3. Bad bonding to the core, 4. Gaps under the core where it can not lie snugly, 5. Porous core, 6. Difficult to mould square end, 7. Thin porous moulding, 8.
B Waterways can be minimised by good workmanship, eg Bedding the core to ensure a snug fit, 9, combined with fillets at the root angles, 10. Firm bonding to the core, 11. Well rounded angles for easy, uniform thickness moulding, 12. Non-porous core, 13. Tapered ends for easy moulding, 14 (but see also Fig 13.18). Adequate thickness, 15.

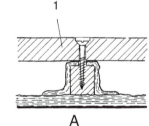

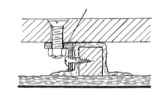

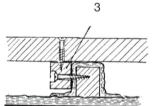

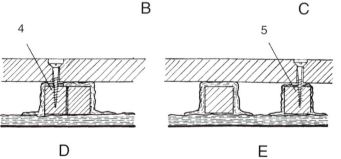

Figure 13.17   Fastening to a stiffener
A By far the commonest and easiest way to attach, say, woodwork, 1, to a stringer is to screw through the face into a wood insert or, worse, a self-tapping screw into the face. This is not good practice as it weakens the face.
B, C Good practice is to attach to a bracket, 2, or block of wood, 3, to the side.
D An easier way, when planned, widen the stringer, 4.
E Best of all, separate attachment points, 5. Being non-structural these may be lightly moulded.

Photos 13.2 (a) Moulded top hat stringers. Note how they continue to the bulkhead without any break.
(b) Egg crate in a keel area. Note the large plates under keel bolts. Also the way a pipe runs through the middle, not an edge.
(c) Massive top hat wooden cored engine bearers.

should be done at once. It would not have been cut away unless something was so close it would prevent access later.

From bending theory cutting a face is obviously more weakening than the centre. Clearance for pipes or wires should be drilled through the middle, not by cutting away an outer edge (Fig 13.28).

Where something unimportant fouls a structural member it is important to cut the unimportant one, never the face of the structural part. This is common sense of course. An old time boatbuilder would know it instinctively, but not those who build boats today. In one case the edge of a main web floor was notched to clear an unimportant batten. This was the direct cause of disastrous keel area damage later, and was done by one of the biggest and better builders too!

Limber holes

Dry bilges on a fibreglass boat are another myth. Builders who claim that only a dustpan and brush are needed to clean the bilges (without providing access to use one) have never been to sea. As any sailor knows the sea is a wet place. Bilges do collect water and engine oil makes them as foul as ever. A modern shallow bilge boat has no space to put it and in making life hell a little water goes a long way.

To get to the pump, water must pass a maze of frames and floors which therefore need limber holes. So do stringers, as water will collect outboard of them; also all parts of an eggcrate. Moulded accommodation can form unseen reservoirs and release water when the boat heels, raising fears it is sinking.

Limber holes should be planned, not drilled as afterthoughts (Figs 13.29, 13.30 and 13.31). When a lining or moulded cabin sole prevents access to any part of the bilges it is very important that generous sized holes or gaps are formed during construction. It will be impossible later. Limber holes need to be large to prevent clogging, especially where inaccessible. There may be less water but just as much dust, fluff, muck and matchsticks: probably more with the modern trend for maxiberth, high occupancy.

Holes through a top hat stiffener will expose the core. It may decompose into unpleasant or damaging products, or become soggy and block the holes. Even if not hollow there are likely to be waterways and many stiffeners are porous enough for dirty bilge water to emerge in clean lockers.

Limber holes should be moulded or have inserts to keep the cores watertight, even when formed later. So should scuppers through bulwarks or toe rail.

Rounding off

Unlike the general run of moulding, stiffening always means moulding some awkward shape. Difficult moulding is therefore likely to be bad moulding.

The easier the glass can drape the more likely it will be moulded soundly. If woven rovings have to be used, several layers of mat should be moulded first to round off, and fillets used in root angles. Only light woven rovings are suitable.

With integral stiffeners, good practice is to mould them separately and lay the heavy woven rovings if required in between.

Putties

On very awkward shapes the only way to form a core may be with resin putty. Syntactic foam, made with microballons, will reduce weight. Putty can also be used to round off, form fillets or fair features for sounder moulding.

Appendages

Fin keels, skegs and rudders can exert a large leverage. While a fin keel is usually adequately supported athwartships this is often forgotten with skegs. If bolted on, the hull inside needs strong floors. It is better to continue the skeg, or a metal or wooden core, up inside and bond to a stout web (Fig 17.14).

The common P bracket also needs good support inside. The vibration from a bent shaft or broken blade can tear it out, leaving a nasty hole.

Support while unstiffened

Until the stiffening is fitted the mouldings are flexible and easily distorted. It is very important they are not allowed to cure and harden in a distorted shape because that will become the natural shape regardless of what was moulded. Although initial hardening is quite rapid (a matter of days) it will not be fully cured for months. Therefore the moulding must be well supported in the shape it is to be until all the stiffening is in place. Ideally as much as possible should be fitted while still in the mould, but economic pressures seldom allow such luxury. Failing this it should be transferred immediately to a fitting jig.

The deck is a major structural part and with most production the 'lid' is put on at a late stage because it is easier to work on the hull while open. The boat should be kept in the jig until the deck is on.

Distortion will prevent other mouldings and major items fitting unless forced to fit, which will pre-stress and probably damage them. Moreover it may be the more important part, eg a distorted hull will be weakened if forced to fit the unchangeable but correct shape of a ballast keel.

A receiver will regard reject hulls as assets to be sold for the benefit of the rich. Do not think a reject hull carelessly dumped outside, unsupported, lying on dented bilges and weighted with rainwater is a bargain.

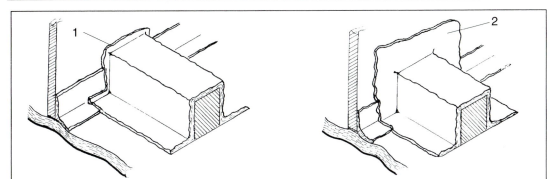

Figure 13.18
Where a stiffener terminates at a bulkhead or partition it must not simply butt, 1. The connection should be by as wide a flange, 2, as to the basic moulding.

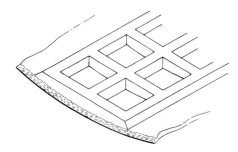

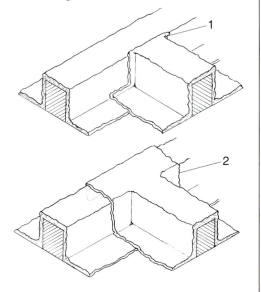

▲Figure 13.19
Stiffeners may run in two directions to form an egg crate pattern.

Figure 13.20 ▶
A weakness with many egg crates moulded in situ is the right angle connection, 1, which commonly breaks away. The connections must go right over the adjoining member, 2.

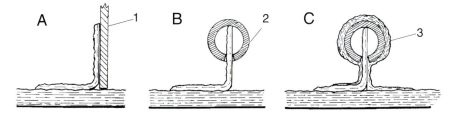

Figure 13.21   Bulbous angle
A An ordinary angle is formed by laying up against a temporary shuttering, 1.
B Over this is placed split plastics hose, 2.
C The stiffener is completed by moulding over, 3.

Figure 13.22   Z angle
A Z angle is made by laying up over a temporary core, removed later. In effect a top hat stiffener with one side not there. Useful where anything has to be bolted on.

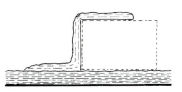

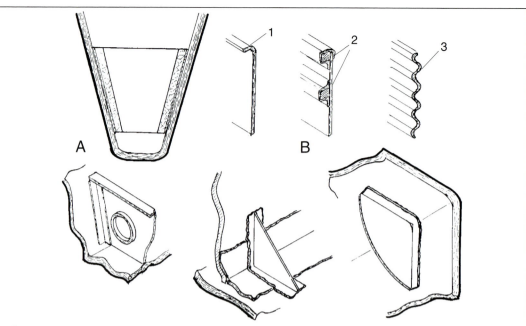

Figure 13.23   Webs
A Webs of fibreglass or plywood, or fibreglass covered plywood, are used to stiffen deep, narrow parts.
B The webs may themselves need stiffening by a top angle, 1, moulded stiffeners, 2, or corrugating, 3.
C Cut outs reduce weight and if flanged add stiffness.
D Small webs can also be used to stiffen a glass angle such as a bulkhead, or a moulded angle.

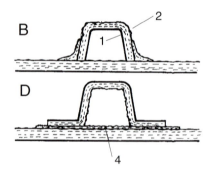

Figure 13.24   Attaching moulded frames
A If moulded with the gel coat outside, 1, it has a good appearance but attachment must be by moulded angle against the gel coat which is bad practice.
B Moulding inside out, 2, gives a better bond for the glass angles.
C An alternative is a thin moulded frame as a former, 3, over which can be moulded a thick, structural stiffener.
D If both are green, or using epoxy, a moulded frame can be bedded on wet mat, 4, but this requires a precise fit.

Figure 13.25
A stiffener moulded in situ will usually fracture, 1, while remaining firmly bonded. A separately moulded stiffener tends to separate, 2, and is often hard to detect.

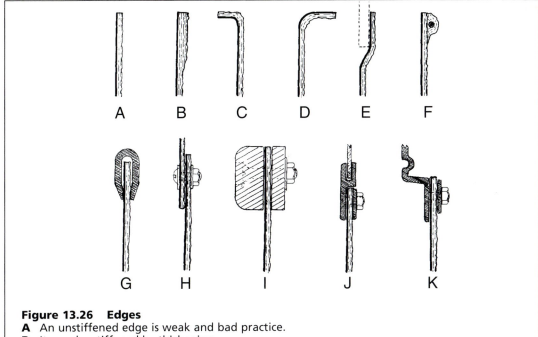

Figure 13.26 Edges
A An unstiffened edge is weak and bad practice.
B It may be stiffened by thickening.
C An outward flange can be vulnerable.
D An inwards flange is less vulnerable but may complicate the mould.
E A rebate stiffens as well as allowing a flush attachment to something else.
F Beading, by embedding a core or wire, has been used by tinkers for centuries.
G Extruded plastics protects an edge but does little to strengthen it.
H Where possible edges should be attached to other mouldings.
I Alternatively to woodwork. Note the fibreglass should be sandwiched between two pieces of wood.
J A common case is the cut out for a window which, for any seagoing boat, should have a metal frame.
K A metal hatch strengthens the cut out needed.

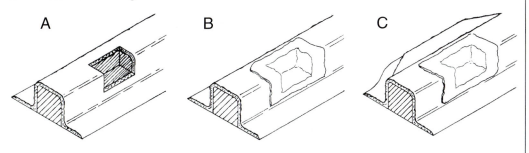

Figure 13.27 Cut outs
A Often a stiffener is cut away for clearance. It is very bad practice to leave it, as is commonly done.
B The cut out should at least be sealed by moulding.
C Where the cut away is deep strength should be restored by fishing.

The deck too needs good support while being fitted out separately. Being whippy and flat it has little natural strength.

No hull should leave the factory for fitting out elsewhere until it has main bulkheads, stringers and major stiffeners put in and the deck on even if only bolted temporarily. Also it should have had at least three weeks to cure under proper conditions. Until then the baby is not old enough to leave its mother.

An unfinished boat can collect a weight of rainwater which, if not noticed, can cause serious distortion. When the boat has to be stored outside or go on a long journey it should have drain holes in the bottom. It is not unusual to spend weeks in a rainy customs compound as inaccessible as if on the moon.

A boat cannot be supported properly by side struts when it is flexible. All support must be at bulkheads or strong points. Otherwise they just push the hull in and the dents will become permanent.

Carbon fibre

Carbon fibre is used for special applications where its superior stiffness – five or six times glass fibre – can be used to maximum effect and justify the high cost. It should be used only where stress is greatest, typically the face of a stiffener, and usually unidirectional.

Using carbon fibre as a direct replacement for glass is a waste of money. Usual practice is as a composite with conventional glass fibre, which is quite adequate to provide the bulk.

In the right place in the right way carbon fibre is very effective. But design can be complicated and in the wrong way disastrous, like the rudder failures on state of the art racing yachts in the 1979 Fastnet Race.

Carbon fibres have also been used to make high-tech composite wooden boats, more sophisticated than almost anything yet done in fibreglass.

When carbon fibre does fail it does so suddenly and catastrophically, unlike fibreglass and Kevlar which tend to hang on (Chapter 5). This is suggested as one reason for the dramatic breaking up of *Australia II*.

Kevlar

Like carbon fibre Kevlar's main advantage is greater stiffness. It is also cheaper than carbon fibre, less delicate, and more suitable for moulding large areas. Kevlar is half the weight of glass, but the greatest saving is because greater stiffness means high performance mouldings can be thinner and require less resin, the principal source of weight.

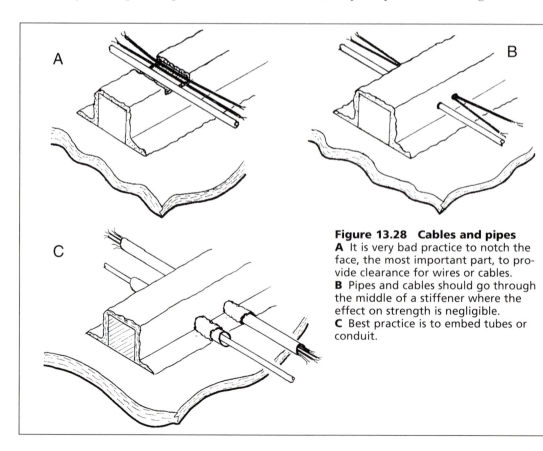

Figure 13.28   Cables and pipes
A It is very bad practice to notch the face, the most important part, to provide clearance for wires or cables.
B Pipes and cables should go through the middle of a stiffener where the effect on strength is negligible.
C Best practice is to embed tubes or conduit.

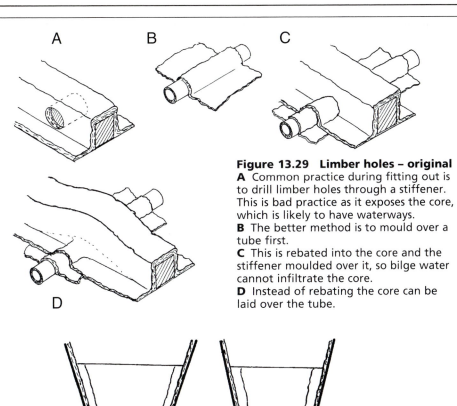

Figure 13.29 Limber holes – original
A Common practice during fitting out is to drill limber holes through a stiffener. This is bad practice as it exposes the core, which is likely to have waterways.
B The better method is to mould over a tube first.
C This is rebated into the core and the stiffener moulded over it, so bilge water cannot infiltrate the core.
D Instead of rebating the core can be laid over the tube.

Figure 13.30
Where limber holes are formed in webs it is important to seal the edges, 1. If the web has a core the better method is to embed a tube, 2.

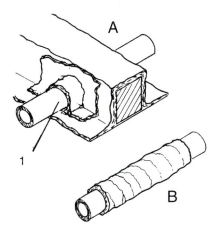

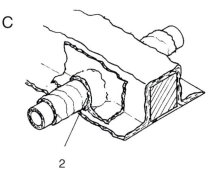

Figure 13.31 Limber holes – formed later
A Again these should not be unprotected. But as it is difficult to bond to a plastics tube, 1, especially underneath, there is likely to be seepage into the core.
B The recommended method is to bind the tube with fibreglass tape first (see Chapter 21).
C This provides a fibreglass to fibreglass seal when bonded in, 2, and less likely to be an opening for seepage.

Bulkheads

On most boats bulkheads and partial bulkheads are the principal structural members and maintain the shape. Often they support the mast and other heavy loads. However, bulkheads do obstruct the accommodation and often their position is decided as much by the layout below as structurally. They should be attached to the deck as well as the hull. A one-piece deckhead lining often prevents this.

Stresses

In theory the stresses on a bulkhead from the hull are in compression. Shroud plates and genoa blocks, however, pull powerfully upwards. This is common knowledge, yet overlooked is the upwards pull of turning blocks, commonly fitted to lead halyards aft to the cockpit, especially if added later.

Attachment

The usual way to attach a bulkhead to the hull is by double glass angles (Chapter 11). The box below shows the approved weights and widths for plywood bulkheads. Where, due to poor design, only single angles are practicable, these figures should be doubled.

Some authorities recommend that for higher strength, unidirectional cloth or tape should be used with the strands across the angle. Being more difficult to mould, and therefore more likely to be done badly, the advantages are largely theoretical.

The more newly moulded the hull when the bulkheads are fitted the better. Some authorities stipulate within seven days and, to preserve the shape, while still in the mould.

Bonding to the plywood is as important as to the fibreglass (Chapter 20). Failure is very common. To supplement bonding and prevent breaking away ingenious ways have been used to 'stitch' them. For security they can also be bolted. When there may be delay, angles can be moulded earlier as flanges and the bulkhead bolted on later. This also reduces twisting at the root (Fig 14.1 and 14.2).

A decorative veneer or melamine surface is often sanded off in way of the angles. Although this sounds logical it can affect the bond because an exposed phenolic glue line will poison polyester.

A complete inner shell prevents bulkheads being bonded to the hull so it must be in firm contact and itself bonded in way of the bulkheads (Chapter 18). But there is no way to tell if it really is and often breaks away in use or following damage (Fig 14.3).

Clearance

Tight fitting bulkheads, including partial bulkheads, create serious hard spots (Chapter 17), often noticeable as 'hungry horse' distortion of the polished topsides. There should always be a gap, relying on the width and taper of the glass angles to blend the incompressible bulkhead into the hull. To avoid a weak line just where strength is needed, the gap must be filled with resin putty or a trapezoidal section of plastics foam or wood (Figs 14.4, 14.5 and 14.6).

Plywood bulkheads

Bulkhead thickness		Glass weight		Angle width	
ins	mm	oz/ft²	g/m²	in	mm
Under ½	12.5	6	1800	5	135
½–¾	12.5–19	7.5	2250	6	150
¾–1	19–25	9	2700	7	175

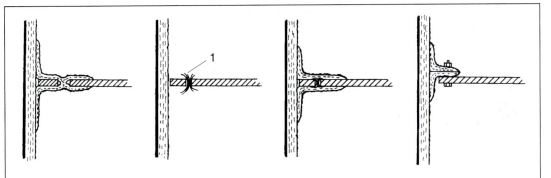

Figure 14.1
To make the bond to plywood bulkheads more secure large holes are drilled. The angles bond together and form dimples. Or they can be stitched by pushing rovings through holes, 1, which 'rivet' the angles together.

Figure 14.2 ▲
Bulkheads can be bolted to pre-moulded angles, a good way when fitted late.

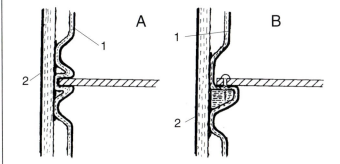

Figure 14.3   Inner shell
An inner moulding, 1, prevents the bulkheads being bonded to the hull, 2.
A Sometimes they are simply dropped into pre-moulded slots, and support the hull by pressure alone.
B Alternatively, and more securely, they can be bolted or screwed to flanges on the inner moulding.
  In both cases the inner moulding should be firmly bonded to the hull, 2.

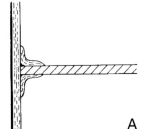

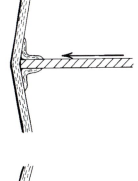

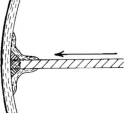

Figure 14.4   Avoid hardspots
A The bulkhead or partition must not be a tight fit against the hull or it will cause distortion and a hardspot.
B There must be a gap, which is then filled so it can be moulded over and avoid a line of weakness. This spreads the stress so the bulkhead blends into the hull.

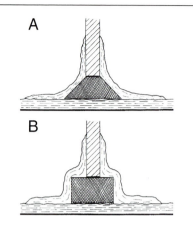

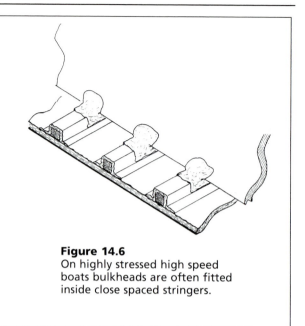

Figure 14.5
A Ideally the shape of the filler is trapezoidal.
B In practice for convenience it is more likely to be square. The effect is similar.

Figure 14.6
On highly stressed high speed boats bulkheads are often fitted inside close spaced stringers.

Buckling

As bulkheads are in compression they must be stiff enough to resist buckling. Plywood is cheap and being lighter than fibreglass can be twice as thick, and therefore for the same weight eight times stiffer, as well as less inclined to delaminate when edge loaded. It is the right material for the job.

To go-fast designers, always seeking to reduce weight, sandwich panels are attractive. But these are weaker and liable to delaminate under buckling, unless factory made or have interconnecting webs (Chapter 19).

An alternative, feasible with fibreglass, is to mould corrugated bulkheads, as commonly done with steel ships. The appearance would not be yacht quality unless covered.

Openings

A continuous bulkhead will be an intolerable inconvenience to anyone but a dedicated deepsea storm seeker. Bulkheads need openings, large enough for convenience while minimising the reduction in strength. Big or small boat, human beings come in roughly one size, and that can be swollen by bulky clothes needed to stay alive (Fig 14.7).

Jokes about bumped heads did not end with old sailing ships. Bald heads are particularly unfunny. Yet it is not essential to walk through upright. If you know you have to duck you

will. It is when you think you do not need to you may wish you had!

Material out of the middle reduces strength less than near an edge. It is a small inconvenience to step over a sill. The top is the problem. Where the bulkhead supports the mast the opening must have plenty of material above, at least 6 in, 150 mm, even on a small boat. If not possible it must be strongly reinforced.

To reduce stress concentrations all openings must be well rounded. This also looks more ship shape than square cornered domestic doorways (Fig 14.8).

Watertight bulkheads

Ships have watertight bulkheads. Why not yachts? So runs bureaucratic reasoning. But yachts are not built like ships. Anyone who thinks he can just fit a watertight door in his standard bulkhead needs to think again, very seriously.

A flooded fore cabin on a 35 ft, 11 m, boat would exert a force of around 10 tons on the bulkhead if static, and much more when surging at sea. No ordinary bulkhead could stand that. Even worse the glass angles would tear away, probably damaging the hull too.

The average yacht, especially a light cruiser/racer, is just not strong enough to convert however, even though misguided people

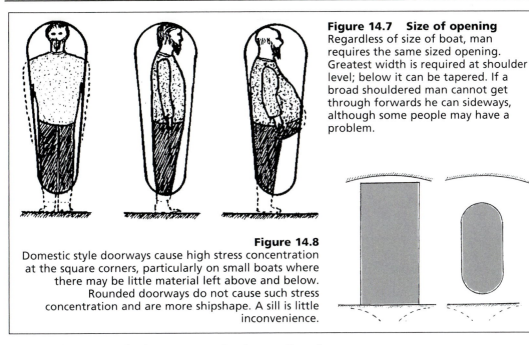

Figure 14.7   Size of opening
Regardless of size of boat, man requires the same sized opening. Greatest width is required at shoulder level; below it can be tapered. If a broad shouldered man cannot get through forwards he can sideways, although some people may have a problem.

Figure 14.8
Domestic style doorways cause high stress concentration at the square corners, particularly on small boats where there may be little material left above and below. Rounded doorways do not cause such stress concentration and are more shipshape. A sill is little inconvenience.

believe that watertight doors must make them safer.

Watertight bulkheads must be designed from the start as part of the whole boat including the strength of the hull and deck join. They cannot be adapted later.

Collision bulkhead

Safety authorities like to specify collision bulkheads, another misguided concern based on big ship thinking. I recall only one yacht with a crumpled stem dangerously near the waterline. It had a collision bulkhead too, but because the forward berths needed comfortable leg room was too far forward and high up to prevent the boat sinking.

Most boats, sail or power, have overhanging bows which absorb the shock of collision well above the waterline. A long bowsprit is better still! Boats are not cars on busy roads risking high speed head-on collisions. Boat bumps are nearly always bow against topsides. As the stem is strong and sharp and the topsides are not it is the other boat which sinks. It is remarkable what damage even a hard sailed dinghy can do!

The commonest accident is hitting something underwater. No collision bulkhead right forward will be any use. A double bottom makes more sense.

Repair

A white line along the angle following damage anywhere nearby shows it has been weakened. If still firmly bonded it can be moulded over.

Very often the angle has separated, usually from the plywood, due to damage, age, use or, more often, was never well bonded in the first place. Damp, muck, oil and access usually make rebonding impractical; bolting or screwing is safest (Fig 14.9). Wrenching off an angle may damage the hull, so cut or chisel away.

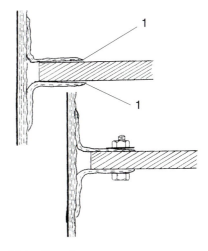

Figure 14.9   Repair
Angles frequently break away from woodwork, 1. The most practicable repair is usually to bolt or screw them together.

Attaching fittings

On a stoutly built wooden boat a cleat can be screwed almost anywhere, and steel will bend before it breaks. But with fibreglass, a wrongly fastened fitting can pull off a chunk of boat (Photo 15.1 and Fig 15.1).

What the designer or builder might have in mind, and what a crew may do in moments of stress, can be very different. There are occasions with the most competent sailor when things are not entirely under control. Bystanders, especially on the nearest boats which always happen to be the smartest and most expensive, are known to use other descriptions.

Large ropes get hitched round small cleats. Lines are made fast to whatever is nearest. Sheet winches are used just because they are winches.

Even normal use may exceed expectations. Everyone knows fenders just dangle over the side – until caught under the dock on a rising tide. I have found many small fender cleats which have pulled away a piece of boat.

Note: The rule must be that regardless of what load comes on the fitting, and what direction, it is the rope or fitting or fastenings which fail. Never, NEVER, the boat.

Reinforcement

Every fitting imposes a concentrated load, the worst thing for fibreglass. Therefore the load must be spread over a wide area to blend in. A heavily loaded fitting will require reinforcement of nearby structural members as well.

Tensile loads must be taken by the whole thickness of the moulding with never any tendency to cause delamination or peeling (Fig 15.2).

Thickening of the moulding and embed-

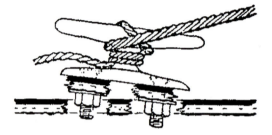

Figure 15.1 Do not copy common practice on wood or steel. A badly fastened cleat will pull off, taking a chunk of boat with it.

ding wood or metal inserts are usually practicable only during building and where the position is planned. Obviously they should be in the proper place and so must the fitting, particularly on a sandwich deck (Fig 15.3).

The approved method for fittings added later, and often during building too, is a wood pad or metal plate behind the moulding. Sometimes the join between mouldings, like hull to deck, is sufficient extra thickness (Figs 15.4 and 15.5).

Small fittings on comparatively thick mouldings can be backed with oversize washers, preferably penny washers, a term coined when a penny not only bought a bag of sweets but was big enough to see when dropped. Perhaps we should now call them 50p washers.

Methods of reinforcement	
Backing with wood	Backing with a metal plate
Large washers	
Use of accommodation	Penny washers
	Moulded features
Attachment to structural members	Tie bars

Fastenings

In most cases fittings will be through bolted. Large bolts can exert sufficient pressure to crush an unprotected gel coat or even the whole

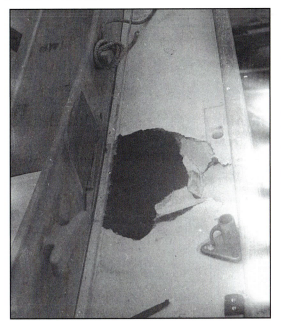

Photo 15.1 The hole is where a sheet winch used to be!

Photo 15.2 Countersinking: note how this by-passes the gel coat and exposes the moulding beneath. The chips around the hole show the effect of drilling from the reverse face. To avoid chipping the gel coat drill from the gel coat side.

moulding, and should not be overtightened, eg the bad practice of bolting shroud plates to the topsides without washers or load spreading because that would be unsightly. The distortion, revealed by highlights on the polished surface, tells its own story (Fig 15.6).

Fibreglass is too soft, fibrous, and generally thin to hold a screw thread unless lightly loaded. Repeated unscrewing will soon wear the thread. The preferred way is to screw into a wooden backing or insert, or tapped metal or Tufnol plate (Fig 15.7).

Self-tapping screws can be used for small fittings like instruments which carry no load and cannot have anything attached in a crisis. Thread cutting, not thread forming, types should be used. Sharp points protruding into lockers are an unwelcome hazard. Many a crew, nursing a cut hand after groping inside a locker, has cursed the thoughtless, slapdash builder. If a hand can grope where it can be scratched it can fit a nut on a blunt bolt!

The tightness of a bolt or screw can be adjusted. But there is no control with pop rivets. On thin mouldings the considerable pressure of setting can pull the rivet right through. They are often used on blind fastenings where it is impossible to fit a washer.

Small fittings can be bonded on. But being delaminating cannot be used with anything load bearing, especially on the gel coat (Figs 15.8 and 15.10).

Countersinking

Countersinking reduces strength and on thin mouldings the screw may pull through. The thickness of the moulding seldom allows countersinking deeply enough to fill for appearance as on wood. It bypasses the protection of the gel coat so in time the fibreglass decays if exposed to weather. If it has to be done the hole must be sealed with resin, a point generally overlooked (Fig 15.11).

Embedding fastenings

Nuts are often moulded over, an apparently simple way to hold when dismantling. It seldom works; fibreglass is too soft to prevent a common hexagon nut turning, especially if the thread is jammed with resin or distorted by

Types of fastenings	
Bolting	Tapped plates
Wood screws into wood	Self tapping screws
	Patent fastenings
Pop rivets	'Bigheads'
Toggles	
Bonding	

cropping. Also, being a fiddly job the moulding over it is generally poor. A square nut would hold better but only a tapped plate or 'bighead' is really reliable. It is far better to leave the nut exposed (Fig 15.12).

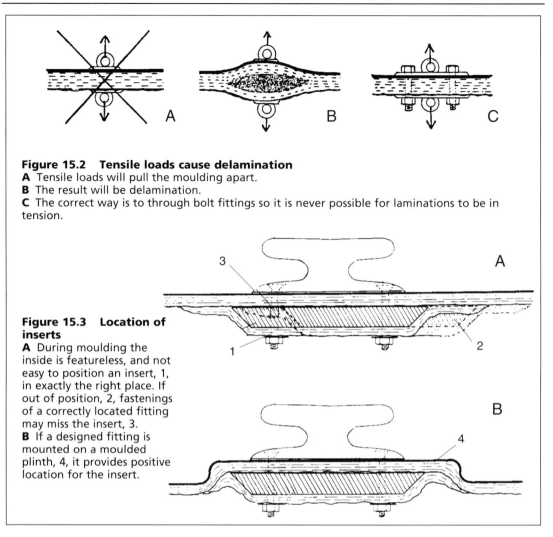

Figure 15.2 Tensile loads cause delamination
A Tensile loads will pull the moulding apart.
B The result will be delamination.
C The correct way is to through bolt fittings so it is never possible for laminations to be in tension.

Figure 15.3 Location of inserts
A During moulding the inside is featureless, and not easy to position an insert, 1, in exactly the right place. If out of position, 2, fastenings of a correctly located fitting may miss the insert, 3.
B If a designed fitting is mounted on a moulded plinth, 4, it provides positive location for the insert.

As a rough rule, if it needs a spanner to hold it, the nut will turn. Then the fibreglass must be hacked away. But if the intention was because the nut would be inaccessible it will be even more inaccessible for a chisel let alone a hammer! It is common to find irremovable parts have been fitted on top. Fate decrees those are the ones which turn!

Nuts should not be glassed over where anything may need repair, replacement or inspection, a probability far too often disregarded. The hull/deck join is very unlikely to be separated but the bolts securing it generally hold an aluminium toe rail or wooden rubbing band too, and these really are likely to be damaged. Keel bolts require regular inspection, if not tightening, and must never be glassed over or be inaccessible.

Embedding metal

Metal fittings do not bond securely and should not be secured by embedding where there is any possibility they could be pulled out. They should always be locked in. Stainless steel is not only impossible to bond but if there is any seepage, common with through-deck shroud plates, it can be destroyed or weakened by crevice corrosion. Replacement of anything embedded will be difficult and probably destructive just to gain access (Fig 15.13).

Bigheads

Bigheads are nuts or studs welded to wide perforated plates. They are designed to be embedded and distribute the local stress of a fastening.

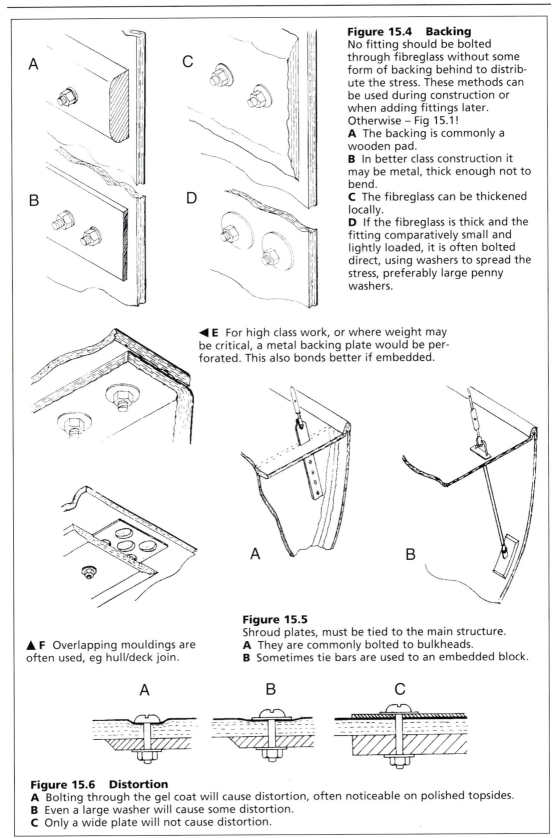

Figure 15.4   Backing
No fitting should be bolted through fibreglass without some form of backing behind to distribute the stress. These methods can be used during construction or when adding fittings later. Otherwise – Fig 15.1!
A The backing is commonly a wooden pad.
B In better class construction it may be metal, thick enough not to bend.
C The fibreglass can be thickened locally.
D If the fibreglass is thick and the fitting comparatively small and lightly loaded, it is often bolted direct, using washers to spread the stress, preferably large penny washers.

◄ **E** For high class work, or where weight may be critical, a metal backing plate would be perforated. This also bonds better if embedded.

▲ **F** Overlapping mouldings are often used, eg hull/deck join.

Figure 15.5
Shroud plates, must be tied to the main structure.
A They are commonly bolted to bulkheads.
B Sometimes tie bars are used to an embedded block.

Figure 15.6   Distortion
A Bolting through the gel coat will cause distortion, often noticeable on polished topsides.
B Even a large washer will cause some distortion.
C Only a wide plate will not cause distortion.

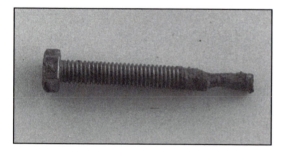

Photos 15.3 (a) 'Penny washers' as big as an old Britannia penny. For scale, the shrunken worthless token now called a penny today (and even that 50p will hardly buy one 'penny' washer!)
(b) 'Big heads': threaded fastenings for embedding.
(c) This stainless steel bolt protruded into the bilges where moulding had been 'pushed in with a stick' and was porous and anaerobic. The bolt formed an electrolytic cell with itself, as stainless steel can, between the part in the protected normally passive state and the active state where anaerobic.

On no account should important fastenings like keel bolts be inaccessible behind an inner moulding.

Surface protection
Metal fittings are hard and brutal. A gel coat is soft and easily crushed especially under the intense pressure from rough high spots (Figs 15.14 and 15.15).

Opinions differ about whether a ballast keel should be bolted tight or bedded on sealant. The massive keel will not move, so if bolted tight, as can be done with wood, all movement of either part must be absorbed by the fibreglass. That is not good. Moreover although the keel area of the hull will be thick, high spots on the casting must indent the fibreglass because the fibreglass is never going to make holes in the keel.

Bedding on sealant does allow slight movement to accommodate stress or thermal changes, a significant factor in cold winter climates.

Sealant
All fittings must be bedded on a marine quality flexible sealant as has long been proper practice. Otherwise leaks are inevitable – one of the myths is that fibreglass boats cannot leak!

Double shell
Major attachments such as keel, engine bearers or hull/deck join should not be made through a double shell or pan moulding. Good practice is end the double shell and bolt or bond to well thickened single skin.

Sandwich mouldings
Sandwich mouldings, very common for decks, have a soft core which is easily squashed. It is very important that fittings are through bolted only where there is an incompressible insert (Chapter 19).

Skegs
Some fittings will impose a severe bending stress. A typical example is a skeg which is not only subject to sideways pressure but generally supports the rudder as well. If not adequately stiffened it can distort the hull (Chapter 17).

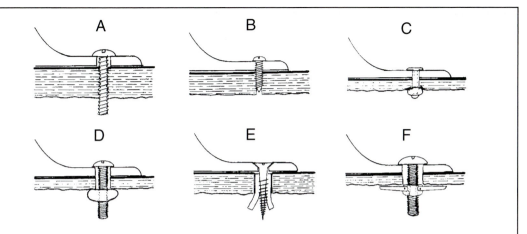

Figure 15.7 Blind fastenings
A If thick enough, at least twice screw diameter, the moulding can be tapped. The screw must be coarse thread.
B Self-tapping screws can be used into a thick moulding.
C Pop rivets should not be used on thin mouldings. The large pressure needed to set may pull them through. They should have washers behind to spread stress but this is not possible when used blind.
D There are numerous patent fastenings which squeeze a plastics insert into a bulge. Note the large clearance hole required in both moulding and fitting.
E Expanding wall plugs, as used in the building trade, are also best used in thick mouldings.
F There are patent toggle fastenings used in sheet metal work and building.

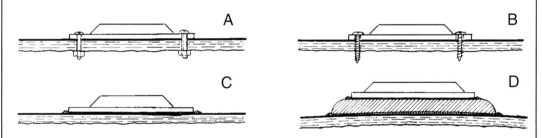

Figure 15.8 Mounting small fittings
A Where there is no load on a small fitting it is not necessary to reinforce the moulding.
B If not required to be removed it can be secured with self-tapping screws. The sharp point can be a hazard.
C Bonding is feasible but if it ever has to be removed the gel coat will be damaged.
D On a curved surface the fitting should be bonded or screwed to a wooden pad.

Deckhead lining

A moulded deckhead lining prevents access to the underside of the deck and there is usually a gap. The lining cannot be removed so adding fittings, even tightening or replacing existing fittings, is a big problem.

Owners often bolt through both deck and lining. It is essential to contrive an insert to prevent the lining being distorted and probably damaged (Fig 15.9).

A moulded lining may look smart, clean and modern, and be convenient for production. But as a practical, long term feature it is questionable. Much better are detachable panels. A fabric or foam-backed vinyl lining can be cut away neatly and replaced.

Electrolysis

Fibreglass is a good insulator so there are few problems with electrolysis, provided the normal rules are observed. An important exception is deep in a keel where it has been 'pushed

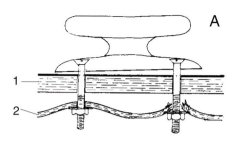

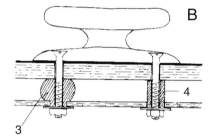

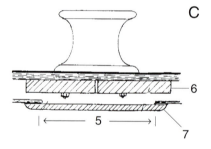

Figure 15.9   Deckhead lining
Frequently there is a gap between the deck, 1, and deckhead lining, 2.
A If bolted straight through the thin lining will be damaged. The fitting can never be tight and will leak.
B The correct way is to force in a hard filler, 3, and allow to set, or insert a metal tube or wooden plug, 4.
C With a large fitting like a winch the lining should be trepanned, 5, and backing fitted, 6, 7. A decorative wooden cover is fitted, 7, on the principle that the best way to disguise anything is to make it obvious.

in with a stick'. Here it is porous and exposed to bilge water. Being also anaerobic stainless steel rudder fastenings can switch from passive to active state and disintegrate rapidly.

Safety

Wherever safety is involved attachments must be firm, always through bolted *and be accessible for replacement, tightening and inspection.* Stanchion bases, commonly used for harness attachments, are often dangerously loose or broken because it is almost impossible to get at the fastenings beneath.

Marinas and anchoring

Another prevalent idea is that all yachts are kept in expensive marinas and crews just want to sail from one crowded marina to another even more crowded. Gone it seems are the days of freedom and lonely creeks. Whatever one's views about marinas this has had an important influence on yacht design. Massive centreline mooring cleats and sampson posts have been replaced by smaller, often inadequate side cleats for lighter mooring lines. Yet in storm conditions, when even marinas get rough and short lines snub, torn off cleats and fairleads are common.

Boats are not necessarily kept in marinas. In most parts of the world, places crews dream of cruising to, anchoring is still the custom. To many that is the attraction especially those who regard marinas as no better than very expensive slums. But the guidelines for anchor and cable size which most builders follow are minimum and less than serious cruising owners like. When a storm roars only the strongest ground tackle gives peace of mind. But where can you make fast with no cleat big and strong enough for a decent sized chain or rope? Or without one fastened securely enough?

Whether crews are getting weaker or lazier is a moot point but certainly it is commoner to fit a windlass, often retrospectively. This needs a strong kingplank, easy when new, a major problem later if the deck is sandwich. A strong centreline mooring cleat or sampson post also needs a kingplank.

If planning a dream cruise away from marinaland make sure that the boat is strong enough for the heavier ground tackle that is so essential.

Modern times

In earlier days everyone in a waterside boatyard would generally have come from a boat-

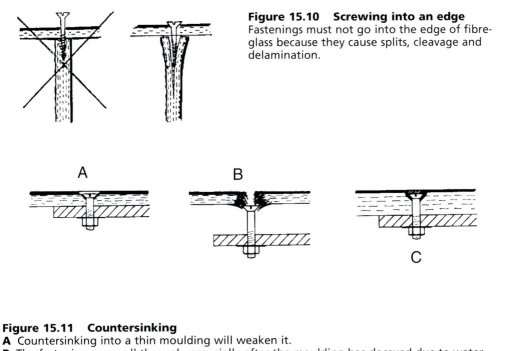

Figure 15.10   Screwing into an edge
Fastenings must not go into the edge of fibreglass because they cause splits, cleavage and delamination.

Figure 15.11   Countersinking
A Countersinking into a thin moulding will weaken it.
B The fastening may pull through, especially after the moulding has decayed due to water bypassing the gel coat.
C Countersinking should be done only where the moulding is thick enough and the fitting lightly loaded. Countersunk holes must be moulded or coated with gel coat or sealant to prevent water attacking exposed fibreglass.

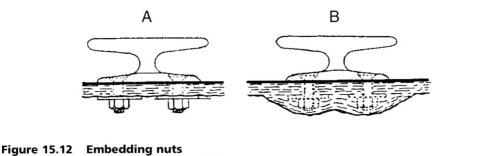

Figure 15.12   Embedding nuts
A Nuts should be left open and accessible.
B Embedding will seldom prevent nuts turning. Then the fibreglass must be hacked away. *If there is access.*

building or fisherman family, in and around boats all their lives. They had a feel for a boat and they knew what to do.

But in modern boatbuilding factories, often far from the water, most of the workers, and management too, do not have that background. To them boatbuilding is just another factory job. Most pick it up quickly, they are not stupid, but they do not have that feel for a boat and what is right and wrong. Small things done in ignorance, which a traditional boatbuilder would know instinctively not to do, can have a devastating effect.

What may be stupid boatbuilding may be sensible economics. Management are responsible for more than the workers.

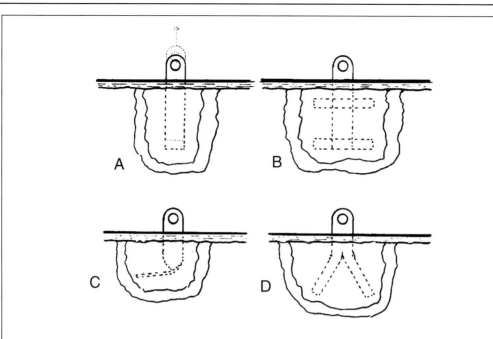

Figure 15.13   Embedding tangs
Where fittings are secured by embedding, eg shroud plates, it is important they are firmly locked in.
A A straight metal tang, relying solely on a metal to fibreglass bond, will probably pull out.
B The good class way is to weld lugs, but allow for welding weaking stainless steel.
C A cheap but effective way is twist and bend.
D Also cheap and easier to mould is a split tang.

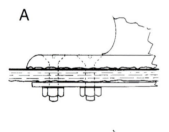

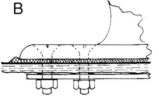

Figure 15.14   Protecting the gel coat
A Most metal fittings have a rough bottom. If bolted on directly high spots will bite into the gel coat.
B Small and medium fittings can be bedded on sealant.

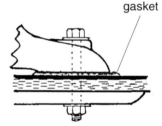

Figure 15.15   Gasket under a heavy fitting
Under heavy metal fittings the gel coat must have a neoprene gasket to prevent crushing especially if the metal is a rough casting. Alternatively a wood block.

Sealants

Nothing makes life on board more miserable than deck leaks. A few drips down the neck can end a well planned cruise quicker than anything. Hull leaks cause much less discomfort. They can be pumped out by the gallon.

A common myth is that fibreglass boats cannot leak. (This morning I was woken by a trickle on my face so can disprove that with feeling.) Certainly to those of us who started on elderly wooden boats the one-piece deck and cabin top is a boon. But decks can still leak if one of the many fittings or fastenings is not properly sealed. (This morning it was due to a cable gland ten feet away.)

In theory hulls too cannot leak. But to mould the impossible they are often in two or more pieces and the joins can cause very elusive leaks. So can the hull/deck join.

Wood can swell to seal a leak; fibreglass cannot. Moreover fibreglass boats are flexible so unlike robust wood or steel it can be the boat not the fitting which moves.

All fittings, fastenings, attachments, joints and openings must be sealed for life, including when new. More boats leak from building defects than age.

Joint design

Correct design is critical. Sealant is not something to bung in at the last moment to fill up

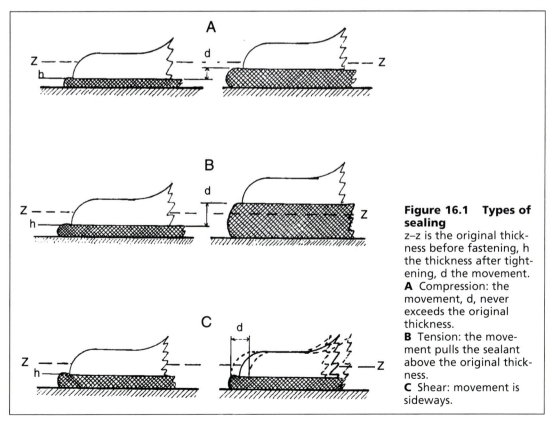

Figure 16.1   Types of sealing
z–z is the original thickness before fastening, h the thickness after tightening, d the movement.
A Compression: the movement, d, never exceeds the original thickness.
B Tension: the movement pulls the sealant above the original thickness.
C Shear: movement is sideways.

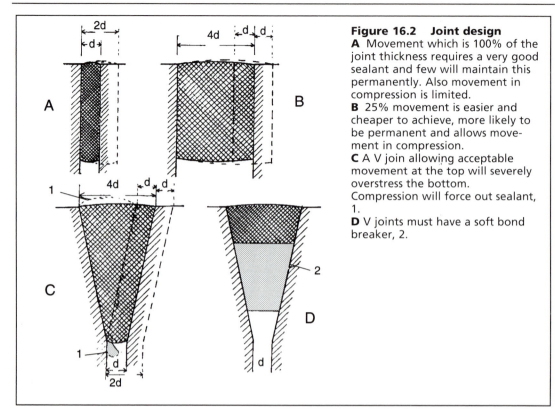

Figure 16.2   Joint design
A Movement which is 100% of the joint thickness requires a very good sealant and few will maintain this permanently. Also movement in compression is limited.
B 25% movement is easier and cheaper to achieve, more likely to be permanent and allows movement in compression.
C A V join allowing acceptable movement at the top will severely overstress the bottom.
Compression will force out sealant, 1.
D V joints must have a soft bond breaker, 2.

an awkward space between two ill fitting pieces. The joint must be designed from the start for effective sealing (Fig 16.1).

A joint not intended to move needs adequate fastenings in close fitting holes to make sure that it never does. Fastenings can and do work loose, as sealant settles or loses elasticity with age or use, so they must be accessible for retightening. No sealant will prevent a loose fitting leaking, and more leaks are due to inaccessible fastenings than anything else.

Intended movement requires not only an elastic sealant but a joint design that is wide

Recommended minimum depth to width		
	Depth	Width
Elastic	1	2
Elastoplastic	1	1–2
Plastoelastic	1–2	1
Plastic	1–3	1

Depth is the distance inwards, ie contact area.
Width is the distance apart.

enough. All movement is relative. Only the best sealant would accommodate 100% movement and then not for ever. 25% is not only within the range of more and cheaper sealants but more likely to remain good as it ages. For polysulphide rubber a joint width not less than three times the movement is recommended. Like other engineering components sealant should not be fully stressed and operate within a factor of safety (Fig 16.2).

Few sealants will bond reliably to stainless steel. Through deck shroud plate tangs usually leak. Neither will they bond to plastics like nylon, polythene or PVC. All sealing to these materials should be in compression.

Most fibreglass has a curvaceous surface, whereas fittings have a flat base. Places where it is known flat fittings will come should be designed with flat plinths, eg stanchion bases, cleats, winches etc. Otherwise sealant must fill a wide, uneven gap.

Recovery

The easiest to seal is a joint always in compression. This depends on:

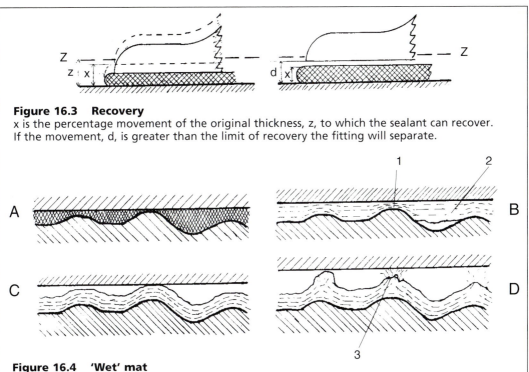

Figure 16.3   Recovery
x is the percentage movement of the original thickness, z, to which the sealant can recover.
If the movement, d, is greater than the limit of recovery the fitting will separate.

Figure 16.4   'Wet' mat
A A soft sealant will flow readily to fill hollows and thin out on peaks.
B Resin can flow but not glass fibre. On peaks the resin is washed out, leaving dry, incompressible glass, 1. In hollows resin is as likely to flow out of an edge as fill the centre, 2.
C If there is any delay and the resin starts to set it will not compress at all and the mat cannot seal.
D Movement will ruck the wet mat. Then the parts will bed on pulled up lumps or upstanding whiskers, 3.

- Original thickness.
- Thickness after tightening.
- The thickness, generally less, to which it will recover, ie memory (Fig 16.3).

A rubbery sealant will spring back almost to original thickness before being in tension, but a squidgy mastic is in tension, or more likely separation, almost at once. Most develop a set and recover only part way. Like us they get absent minded and their memory fades with age and fatigue.

To put a sealant in tension the bond must be strong enough to stretch it. So must the surface to which it is bonded. Although acceptable on wood or metal, tension is an unfair stress for fibreglass, particularly the gel coat, so design should ensure sealant is always in compression. Tangential stress is fair provided there is no peeling.

Requirements

No sealant meets all the requirements listed in the box below. Chose one with the more important properties for that particular situation. In general the more expensive the sealant the better and wider the properties. The cheaper it is the less likely it is to be suitable.

A sealant intended to be moulded over must not contain anything harmful to wet polyester or epoxy, nor exude oil or water. Wide chemical resistance is less important than being resistant to the same things as fibreglass.

Comparisons are difficult. Suppliers quote general properties, which vary considerably between makers. Even the type may not be stated. A builder buying in quantity from the manufacturer is in a better position to find out than an owner buying the odd tube from a chandler or hardware store.

Requirements for sealants

- Marine grade.
- Adequate elasticity and recovery.
- Resistant to weather and sunlight above water.
- Completely water resistant under water.
- Unaffected by high tropical sun temperatures.
- Not brittle in extreme winter cold.
- Life of the boat without renewal.
- Permanently flexible. Non-hardening with age.
- Bonds to fibreglass and paired material.
- Easily applied under ordinary working conditions.
- Separable without damage to gel coat.
- Harmless to fibreglass and material to be sealed.
- Will not bleed, stain or ooze.
- Not swollen or degraded by fuels, cleaners or solvents.
- Cleaned off without solvents harmful to fibreglass.
- Non-toxic, low odour and non-migrating if in contact with food or drinking water.
- Will not support mildew, fungi, algae or bacteria.
- Inedible or unpalatable to marine organisms, worms, insects, termites, birds.
- Not degraded by bird droppings or insect products.

Elasticity

The principal differences between sealants is their elasticity and recovery, ie ability to seal movement. Table 16.1 shows the classes of sealants but there is a wide overlap due to blending and the emphasis placed on the end use. Movement may be:

- Permanent and one way, while tightening the fastenings.
- Repetitive due to bending, sliding or shear of either the boat or fitting.

Cycles may be:
- Slow as with thermal movement or age.
- Moderate due to use.
- Very rapid under vibration.

Recovery may be:
- Negligible, eg soft putties, wet mat and hard setting sealants.
- Moderate but not to original thickness, eg most flexible sealants.
- Complete to original thickness, eg neoprene gaskets.
- Beyond original thickness. Only possible with the best elastomers.

Speed of recovery may be:
- Slow but sufficient to match thermal movement.
- Instantaneous to follow vibration.

Table 16.1   Types of sealant

Classification	Type	Movement %	Recovery %	Hardness Shore A	Years of life
Plastic	Oil based putty	0	0	Hard	5
Mastic	Mastics	10	0–10	0–5	5
	Bituminous	10	0–10	0–5	5
	Butyl	10	0–10	0–5	10
Plastoelastic	Acrylic	15	10–50	5–55	15
Elastoplastic (Elastomers)	Polysulpide, 1 part	25	50–100	15–55	20
	Polysulphide, 2 part	30	50–100	15–55	20
Elastic	Polyurethane	30	50–100	55–60	20
	Silicone low modulus	50	50–100	55–80	20
	Silicone high modulus (bath sealant)	30	50–100	55–80	20
	Neoprene gaskets	25	50–100	80	20+
Solid	'Wet mat'	0	0	Hard	Boat life
	Resin putties	0	0	Hard	Boat life

Movement is % of joint width.
Recovery is % of original dimensions.
Years of life refers to exposed edges in a marine situation.

Ideally recovery will be quick enough to follow any movement and elastic memory will return to the original position without developing permanent deformation.

Most properties alter with age; the best intentionally during early cure or hardening and are then stable. Others change slowly through exposure, time and loss of volatile constituents. Dark colours degrade more quickly than light.

Classes of sealants

Table 16.1 classes sealants in order of hardness. Most age to a harder, less elastic type. The best and most expensive age least and slowest.

Mastics include the common squishy sealants and caulking compounds. These are cheap, have good flow, squash down almost to nothing but no recovery. Good ones remain flexible.

Plastoelastic, Elastoplastic and Elastic are generally lumped together as elastomers, the expensive, high performance sealants which stretch as well as compress. These include silicones, polysulphide rubber (Thiokol, PRC etc), isobutylene, some neoprenes and urethane.

Gaskets of neoprene, rubber or foam have good elasticity and recovery but little flow and limited range of compressibility.

Putties are soft when applied but once hard, whether intentionally like resin putties or slowly through oxidation, have no elasticity and cannot accommodate any subsequent movement.

The common cheap sealants can be used under most conditions and in unskilled hands. But unless the high grade elastomers are applied properly and under the right conditions they will not be high grade though no less expensive.

Most two-part sealants are not only temperature dependent but sensitive to humidity. On a large job they may harden before the parts are properly positioned and fastenings tightened.

It is better to use a second rate sealant correctly than a super sealant applied under marginal conditions.

Wet mat

Wet mat, often used and recommended, is a leveller, not a sealant. It sets rock hard quickly, often too quickly, and thereafter allows no movement. Gap filling is not as good as claimed: on peaks the resin will be washed out leaving dry, incompressible glass, and in hollows is more likely to flow the easy way out of the edges than into gaps in the middle. A sliding fit will ruck up the glass (Fig 16.4).

If it sets prematurely the lumps will prevent proper bedding. Premature setting is most likely with parts that are large or difficult to position like a keel. Repositioning or moving will lift the glass and it must be smoothed out before trying again.

The resin must be slow setting regardless of theory. Not only must the mat stay wet while positioning but until the last bolt has been fully tightened. To hurry a tricky job because of the haunting knowledge that the bedding will soon set hard is courting disaster.

Resin putty flows well but has the same disadvantages of rapid setting as wet mat.

Temperature

Every sealant has a limited service temperature. Figures quoted vary widely even within types and to add confusion some are for continuous exposure and some intermittent. Only the more expensive sealants can withstand 158°F, 70°C, the design figure for tropical sunshine. Others will soften, bleed oil, ooze out, age rapidly or bake hard. Mastics and bituminous sealants may get sticky and messy at well below tropical temperatures, especially when black.

Equally important a sealant should not get hard and brittle in cold weather. Sailing in freezing temperatures is a peculiar pleasure, although the crews of work boats have little option. Yet even the most pleasure sailed boat lies out in the cold through the worst winter weather. Thermal movement will be greatest when the sealant is coldest and most brittle. Only a good sealant will not harden in the depth of a North American or Scandinavian winter, but these conditions are foreseeable. The occasional bad freeze up in Britain is not.

Silicones can be applied in a wide temperature range including unpleasantly cold. But chemically curing sealants must be used only within strictly limited temperatures. If too cold they will not react properly, if at all, or take too long. Under hot, humid conditions setting may be too rapid for proper positioning and tightening down. Even simple mastics become too thick to spread or force out when cold.

The better the sealant the more important it is applied under the recommended conditions and the more limited these are.

Preparation

To justify the high cost the best sealants demand careful preparation. Why waste money on an expensive sealant when a cheap one will do the job just as badly? On new work there should be little problem. But where a cheaper sealant has failed the solution is not simply to bung in something better. The joint must be cleaned out. It is useless putting good sealant into a dirty joint.

Some sealants will set underwater but the problem is the bond. They have to actually displace the water from the surface. That is much harder. Most sealants which claim to set underwater will not bond to a wet surface.

Waterways

Where the water comes out is generally obvious. But where and how it gets in is another matter and may be far away. But until that source is found and stopped the leak will continue. Stop it coming out in one place and it will just emerge somewhere else.

An old boatbuilder sent in a £100 bill for curing a leak. The owner complained that was ridiculous for just bunging in a blob of putty. So the boatbuilder revised his bill: £1 for curing leak, £99 for finding same. Even though that was a wooden yacht it emphasises that the source of a leak is often very difficult to trace.

With fibreglass boats it is even harder. The common moulded deckhead lining diverts it elsewhere and access is impossible. Finding which of the dozens of inaccessible fastenings is leaking needs a magician. Vinyl lining is as bad: the vinyl is waterproof but the foam is like a sponge.

An opening on the outside is still a leak even if nothing emerges inside. Trapped within the moulding water is a major cause of unseen decay (Chapter 6). Suspect seepage or stains where anything is embedded.

References

Sealants, Design Engineering Series, Morgan Grampian Ltd 1969.

Building Research Laboratory, various publications.

Sources of leaks

Deck fittings	Hull/deck join
Skin fittings	Hull joins
Plumbing	Joins between
Stern tube	mouldings
Rudder fittings	Joins to woodwork
	Porous moulding

Hardspots and stress concentrations

This subject is little understood and often ignored. A succession of owners, each adding his own improvements, can leave a boat dangerously weak. Boatyards can be as ignorant as owners, and builders by no means blameless. Remember: this book is as much about past ways as present.

The way fibreglass fails (Chapter 5) is crucial to understanding the effect of hardspots.

Stress concentration

Stress concentration means just that, places where the stresses on the boat are highest. Not the greatest forces but where, due to design or construction, usually of detail, stress is concentrated over a small area.

Everything must blend smoothly into the thin fibreglass shell. Traffic flow is an analogy: smooth flow is stress free, the essential feature of a motorway or freeway. In contrast a busy street intersection interferes with the smooth flow and creates stop-go stress (Fig 17.1).

Stress

Stress is not the same as load or force although the term is often used loosely. It is a function of the cross sectional area subject to that force.

Force v Stress

$$s = \frac{W}{A}$$

Where s is the stress, W is the force or load, A is the cross section area.
Stress is described as force per unit area, eg lb/in², kg/cm² etc.

On a hull that usually means thickness. The thinner it is the higher the stress.

It is not the load or force which causes a structure to fail but the stress which that force produces. The proverbial chain fails at the weakest link. A structure will fail at the point of highest stress (Fig 17.2).

A boat is a complicated structure subject to varying loads. Although large areas are of uniform strength the stresses will not be the same everywhere.

Hardspots

Less obvious, and sometimes very elusive, are the greatly increased local stress concentrations caused by hardspots.

So what is a hardspot?

All damage to a fibreglass boat occurs through bending in some form. The sharper the bending the greater the stress (Fig 17.3). A hardspot is anything which interferes with the smooth pattern of bending thereby making the fibreglass bend more sharply. This can drastically reduce the factor of safety or cause failure in a moulding which ostensibly is amply strong. Fibreglass fails progressively. Obviously the greatest excursions over the damage threshold, thereby the greatest weakening, are at points of highest stress. Cracks often reveal the stress pattern caused by a hardspot (Chapter 42).

Quite minor and seemingly harmless features, like sharp corners from a shelf or locker, can have a catastrophic influence. Often they are added later by unthinking owners or boatyards (Figs 17.4, 17.5, 17.6 and 17.7).

The designer's calculations can be seriously upset by hardspots. I once counted 68 on a

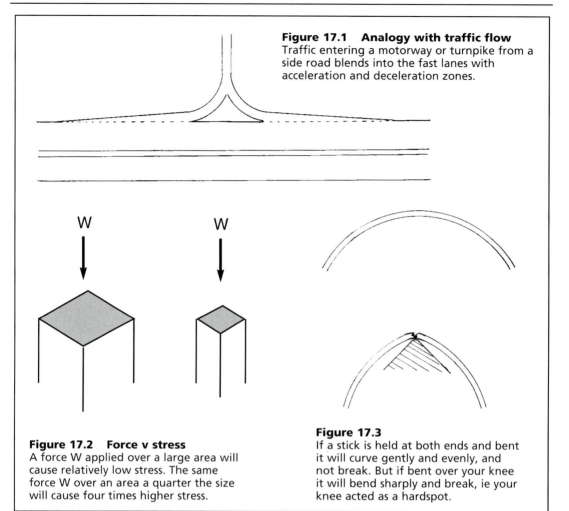

Figure 17.1   Analogy with traffic flow
Traffic entering a motorway or turnpike from a side road blends into the fast lanes with acceleration and deceleration zones.

Figure 17.2   Force v stress
A force W applied over a large area will cause relatively low stress. The same force W over an area a quarter the size will cause four times higher stress.

Figure 17.3
If a stick is held at both ends and bent it will curve gently and evenly, and not break. But if bent over your knee it will bend sharply and break, ie your knee acted as a hardspot.

monocoque hull, all added by the builders (now renowned for top quality!) and unforeseen by the horrified world famous designer. Details are generally left to the builder. Sometimes the designer supplies no more than the lines. Builders do have to turn the design into a practical, marketable boat, but their dominant considerations may be economics and production convenience. It is not unknown to tell the designer, whose reputation is equally at stake, not to interfere.

Hardspots are not peculiar to fibreglass. Wooden boats get away with them because of more massive construction, but not plywood. Steel ships have sunk because of splits induced by stress concentrations. Aircraft engineers are acutely aware. The Comet disasters, which ended Britain's lead in aircraft design, were due to stress concentration in a window frame.

Vulnerable areas

On a sailing boat the most vulnerable areas are the forward topsides and around a fin keel. On a fast power boat it is the bottom. Severe slamming on a power boat is expected, but the rule thickness for topsides of a sailing yacht is less than the bottom, even though this is the part which gets a hammering when close hauled. Moreover unlike the strongly curved bottom

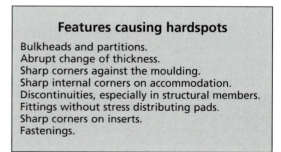

Features causing hardspots

Bulkheads and partitions.
Abrupt change of thickness.
Sharp corners against the moulding.
Sharp internal corners on accommodation.
Discontinuities, especially in structural members.
Fittings without stress distributing pads.
Sharp corners on inserts.
Fastenings.

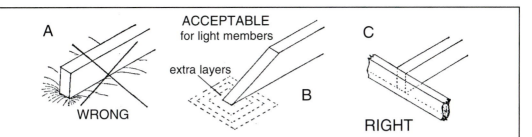

Figure 17.4   Terminating structural members
A WRONG. An abrupt termination causes a severe hardspot. The lines show the stress concentration at the end.
B For light members the member can be tapered. The moulding should be thickened at the end.
C CORRECT. One structural member terminates at another with a T joint.

◀ **Figure 17.5   Hardspots at partitions and lockers**
Partitions and semi-bulkheads must not end abruptly. Carry on to another structural member or the hull/deck join.
  Lockers and shelves with a sharp angle are particularly damaging. Always extend one part to join something else.

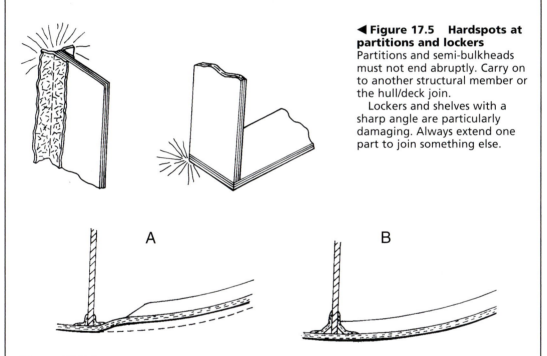

Figure 17.6 ▲
Hardspots can occur in shear also, notably where a stiffener ends short. Note how the moulding takes a sharp damaging S curve. Again continue to terminate at another structural member.

Figure 17.7
Sharp corners on cut outs are stress raisers and likely to split. All corners must be well rounded.

the shape is generally flattish with little inherent strength, especially on some go-fast designs, the ones which get the hardest sailing and lightest construction. Flexibility, panting and oil canning are common, the very conditions when hardspots are most devastating.

Effect of hardspots on damage

A great deal of damage from modest impact or grounding is made far worse and more expensive by hard spots, mostly foreseeable and due to thoughtless design, construction or additions. A hole is accepted without question. Nobody realises a better designed boat would have escaped with just a few scratches. Insurers could save themselves a great deal of money if they took more interest in yacht construction and less in their computers.

Damage does not happen only at the point of impact but also where the hull bends more sharply. If the impact was cushioned there may be hardly a mark. But nearby bulkheads or internal features can distort the pattern of bending so the hull bends sharply along that line. Even with obvious damage it is very common to find cracks at nearby bulkheads showing there is internal damage there too. It should be assumed in any case. This is frequently overlooked, or discounted, however. A hole cannot be disputed; distant cracks can and assumptions not accepted. (Fig 17.8).

Remember, cracks are not merely cosmetic, unimportant first stages of damage, but signs that internal damage already exceeds 50%. There may not even be cracks.

Keels

It is a peculiar thing that most modern builders do not seem aware that boats may go aground. But they do, frequently. The yachtsman who claims he has never run aground has probably never left his marina berth (and is the one most likely to run aground if he did!). Builders regard running aground as entirely due to the crew's carelessness and therefore no concern of theirs. Yet time and again I have seen yachts where, due to stupidly weak design, the fin keel has kicked back on impact, and the hull aft of the keel and often in front too has bent sharply (Fig 17.9).

Thoughtless hardspots in these areas have very often seriously aggravated the damage and needed far more expensive repairs. It is very important to avoid hardspots in all high stress areas of the bottom including potentially high stress areas when grounding accidentally. I have even had bad cases where yachts were severely damaged drying out intentionally and carefully. Too often the accommodation is designed with no thought about the effect of sharp corners and doglegs (Figs 17.10, 17.11, 17.12, 17.13 and 17.14).

On some classes the belly between twin keels is inadequately stiffened. Floors must extend right across to avoid any tendency for the bottom to flex when sailing or the keels to splay when aground. Vertical keels are supposed to be stronger than splayed ones. Not so. Both are subject to strong sideways forces

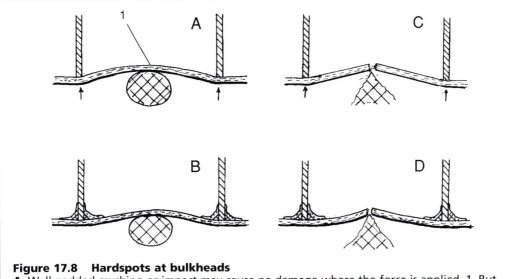

Figure 17.8 Hardspots at bulkheads
A Well padded crushing or impact may cause no damage where the force is applied, 1. But note the sharpness of bending at nearby bulkheads. That is where the damage will be. Never ignore cracks at bulkheads. They may be the only signs.
B Damage will be reduced if the bulkheads are blended to reduce the hard spot.
C With obvious damage there will be hidden damage too at nearby hardspots. Check for tell-tale cracks.
D Again this will be minimised by proper bulkhead design.

when dried out in any current or surge as well as while sailing.

Rudders and skegs can also bend the bottom unless well braced inside.

Cut outs

A cut out throws extra stress on adjacent material because what is left must still carry the load. To ease this transition corners must be well rounded. It is well known that sharp corners are stress raisers and often split.

When a moulding is forced to fit large areas are stressed. As cut outs concentrate that stress the worst distortion is around them. Commonly these are window or hatch openings. The cabin top is then forced back into shape by the metal frames, pre-stressing the moulding still more.

Heavily loaded parts should not be attached near cut outs. It is common to see shroud plates, cleats or winches fastened to cabin tops near or even over windows. This is obviously stupid.

The deck around a large, weakening foredeck locker needs to be very strongly reinforced. Mooring cleats or windlass should not be positioned close.

The edges of structural members should not be notched for passage of wires or pipes. A hole through the centre does not appreciably weaken. A cut out at the edge is in the area of highest stress. Moreover a notch will have square corners (Fig 13.28).

Hardspots and light weight

There are two ways to make something strong: the massive, rigid and unbending or the light and flexible. But nowadays weight is expensive. As well as the material cost it has to be moved, and needs a larger, more expensive engine or rig. Throughout its life the power boat will need more fuel, and may be uneconomic. Sail or power, weight steals performance in a market where speed is worshipped. So designers, builders and owners more and more go for light weight, sometimes to extremes. But the lighter the hull the more critical hardspots become, and the greater the skill and awareness needed to avoid them.

Avoiding hardspots will make a stronger moulding at lower cost and weight. Why add strength to resist a stress which need not be there? The stock remedy for local failure is to add more material, weight and cost. The

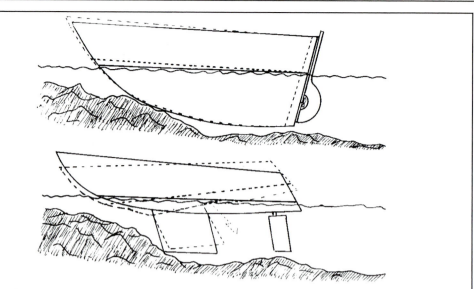

Figure 17.9
When a long keel boat hits a reef it will ride up and over with comparatively little structural damage. But when a fin keel yacht hits it will trip and stop suddenly. The keel kicks back, bending the hull, 1, unless stiffened against such a foreseeable event.

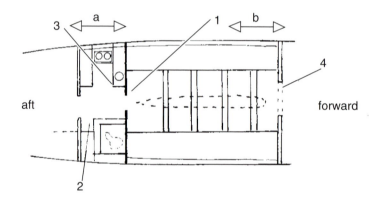

Figure 17.10
The area of a fin keel is usually stiffened adequately sideways with floors, but very often there is no stiffening forward or aft of the keel. If it kicks back the vulnerable area is (a) just aft, where it bends upwards and to a lesser extent, (b) ahead, where pulled down. Hardspots are then crucial. Common places are partial bulkheads, 1, foot well for navigation space, 2, glassed on galley units, 3, main bulkhead openings, 4.

elegant solution is to remove the high local stress which caused the failure.

Discontinuities

Hardspots can occur in shear as well as bending. A common case is when a stiffener ends short. In effect the intervening space is put into a sharp S bend. All stiffeners of any form should continue to another structural member, a bulkhead, stringer or to the hull/deck join.

Accommodation used as stiffening should run in a continuous line. But often the layout does not allow this. Every angle is a hardspot. There may even be gaps. On one boat the stern sagged as soon as the boat was ashore because of a discontinuity in the line of the bunks to provide space for the navigator's feet.

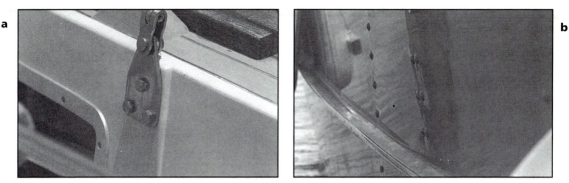

Photos 17.1 (a) It is obviously unwise to attach shroud plates where the cabin top is weakened by a window.
(b) Look closely at the distortion in the reflected highlights around the shroud plate bolts. This shows how such fastenings crush the topsides.

Intermittent hardspots

Hardspots can be intermittent, eg when part of the accommodation is not touching the hull yet can be in contact if the hull is forced inwards. Then it forms a knife edge or, worse, a point. Not being broadened by root angles this will be more acute than anything bonded on. In theory this could happen only under impact so builders discount the possibility. Yet many modern yachts have somewhat flexible topsides and 'pant' or 'oilcan'. Hulls can flex enough to contact these internal hardspots with considerable force during ordinary hard sailing.

It may be the internal part which moves. The accommodation is much lighter than the hull and less care taken to stiffen it. In one case the corner of a suspended water tank hammered a hole through the hull. In harbour it looked impossible.

Monocoque

Frameless or monocoque hulls are particularly sensitive to hardspots. With little stiffening other than shape they are deliberately designed to have some flexibility. Only essential and unavoidable attachments should be made to the hull, and even then with great care. Everything else should be suspended between bulkheads or an internal skeleton.

Signs of hardspots

Hardspots are often revealed by distortion in the smooth lines of the hull, especially the shiny topsides. Sight along the hull at an angle and watch how the reflection of something beyond changes shape as you move position. Distortion can also be felt by hand. But beware of red herrings. The distortion could have been picked up from the mould or pattern.

Suspect any pattern of cracks along or radiating from a feature behind (Chapter 42).

Rules for avoiding hardspots

- Everything must blend into the hull kindly.
- Do not fit bulkheads and partitions tightly.
- Structural members must end at another or taper into thickened fibreglass.
- Avoid sharp angles.
- Do not end structural members abruptly.
- Avoid discontinuities or sharp changes of direction.
- Make changes of thickness gradual.
- Taper edges of sandwich (cored) mouldings.
- Feather the edges of fillers.
- Radius internal corners of cut outs.
- Mouldings required to mate must fit accurately.
- Do not force mouldings to fit.
- Make woodwork, keels and major fittings to fit the boat, not vice versa.
- Pads behind fittings must have radiused corners.
- Keep everything not glassed on at least 2 in, 50 mm, from a lightly built hull.
- Minimise attachments to a monocoque hull. Attach to structural members only.
- The lighter and more high-tech the construction the more care essential to avoid hardspots.
- Wood and steel are forgiving; fibreglass is not.

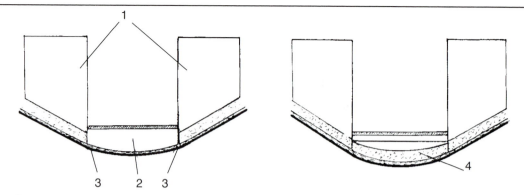

Figure 17.11
It is common to find partial bulkheads or partitions, 1, glassed into the bilges, 2, leaving a sharp angle which forms a bad hardspot, 3, in a very critical area. The correct method is to connect them with a floor, 4.

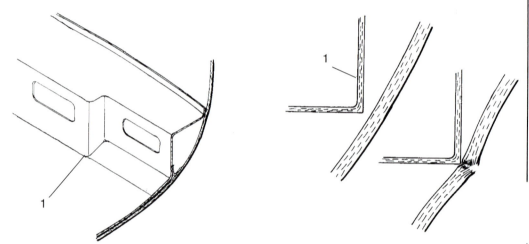

Figure 17.12 (Left)
Where accommodation forms stiffening it is important to avoid doglegs, 1, particularly small boats where the cabin sole is in contact with the hull.
Figure 17.13 (Right) Internal impact
The internal feature, 1, is normally not in contact with the hull. But under certain circumstances, eg damage or even hard sailing, the hull may be forced inwards and make contact with sufficient force to be punctured.

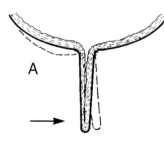
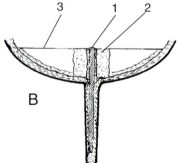

Figure 17.14   Skegs
A Commonly moulded as part of the hull. Sideways pressure will distort the hull which often has little stiffening.
B Better practice is fit a strong plywood or metal core, 1, and attach this by glass angles, 2, to a floor, 3. This not only strengthens the skeg but the hull too.

Double shell mouldings

It is common for the accommodation to be made as one or several large mouldings (in America called pan mouldings). This saves a great deal of fitting out. These inner mouldings are often very elaborate and incorporate major features: bunks, toilet compartment, cabin sole, otherwise made separately. Sometimes they include lockers, galley sink, companionway steps and masses of other details down to shaped recesses for bottles. This is fine if that is exactly what you want, but too bad if not because impossible to alter.

The price for the builder is a very complicated set of moulds which probably cost more than the comparatively simple shape of the hull and deck, and is feasible only when assured of a long production run. The builder must be sure it is absolutely right. Mistakes will be locked in. More sales are won, and lost, on accommodation than performance.

Accommodation goes out of fashion sooner than a hull which may go on for years with the occasional facelift of a new inside. One motor cruiser hull has been going for forty years and survived half a dozen bankruptcies!

An interior moulding can be outfitted separately as the deck usually is, then dropped into the hull and the lid put on. This reduces assembly time still further.

Fit

All the parts must fit perfectly. Making the moulds, especially where separate pieces go together like a jigsaw puzzle, requires higher mould making skill than the hull. It does not matter what shape the hull turns out. That is the shape of the boat. But the accommodation must fit that hull.

Stiffening

Often all the stiffening members like frames and stringers are formed in the elaborate inner moulding. However, because it is regarded as speed stealing weight or for the sake of economy, the accommodation moulding will generally be thin. To have serious structural value it needs thickening in important areas.

The inner moulding must be firmly bonded to the hull. The problem is how to get access to do it and, equally important, to know at any stage of the boat's life that it is still firmly bonded. Failure of the bond means the hull loses all stiffening. It cannot be added later.

Bonding – with access

With open lockers the mouldings can be glassed on securely. This is the most reliable way with the glass angles always visible for inspection (Fig 18.1). Because angles can, with care, bridge a gap, the inner moulding does not have to be a precise fit.

However, most inner mouldings still leave a large amount of inaccessible space. Openings are designed more to suit the accommodation than for access to make important structural attachments. Often only single angles are practicable. Sound moulding cannot be done blind by feel alone through an inadequate hole, as too often required, nor head down in a small space full of fumes far in excess of regulations.

Bonding – no access

The inner moulding may form a complete lining with no openings at all. The clean, smooth, modern looking interior is claimed as a sales point. The lockers are always dry. There are no openings for nasty bilge water (so they collect condensation and drips like a bucket!).

It is convenient for production. No time is spent moulding stiffeners or glassing on bulkheads and partitions. The inner moulding with its integrally moulded stiffeners is just dropped in and bonded on. But this vital bonding which literally holds the boat together

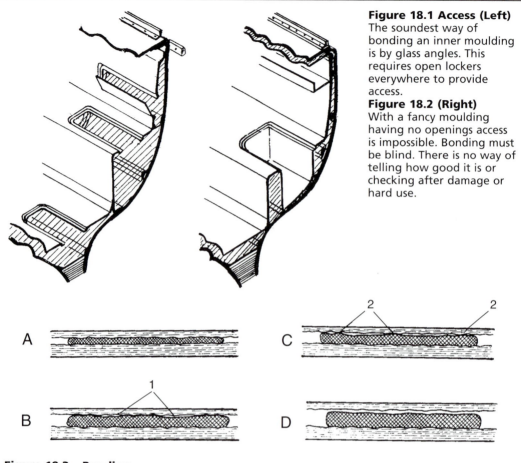

Figure 18.1 Access (Left) The soundest way of bonding an inner moulding is by glass angles. This requires open lockers everywhere to provide access.

Figure 18.2 (Right) With a fancy moulding having no openings access is impossible. Bonding must be blind. There is no way of telling how good it is or checking after damage or hard use.

Figure 18.3   Bonding
A The bonding agent is assumed to squash out evenly and be in contact everywhere. Yet contact alone does not ensure bonding. It could have broken away, even never bonded at all.
B When the gap is too wide the adhesive will not squash out properly. The bond will be spotty with gaps between, 1. This weaker bond is impossible to check.
C Even worse it may be in contact at high spots only, 2. Likely if timing was wrong and it was already hardening.
D In the extreme case, much commoner than realised, the gap is too wide for the adhesive to make contact at all.

has to be done completely blind. It cannot be seen or checked, so nobody knows how good it is, then or later (Fig 18.2).

More often than realised it was never properly bonding in the first place. Later it can fail through damage, hard use or natural ageing. Testing equipment will not reveal if the bond is weak or spotty, nor whether it is in contact but not actually bonding (Fig 18.3).

The mouldings must be made accurately to be in intimate contact at all important points to be bonded, with special care to avoid distortion after moulding. It is not practicable to

bond over the whole area of the hull. Mouldings could not be made sufficiently exact. Usually they will be in contact only at edges and along designed lines, like bulkheads or integrally moulded stiffeners (Fig 18.4).

Some builders splodge bond overall with dollops of adhesive putty put on to a pattern or at random. This is quick and can be applied with a gun.

Bonding will be rough side to rough side. Therefore the adhesive must be gap filling with good flow to allow for the uneven surfaces. Although nominally in contact there may be

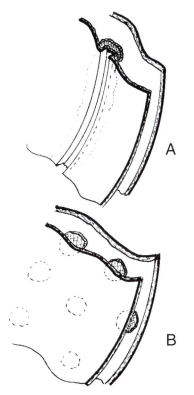

Figure 18.4   Bonding methods
A Channels, 1, purposely formed in the inner moulding are bonded to the hull along their whole length.
B Splodges of adhesive, 2, are applied by gun in a pattern or at random and the inner moulding bedded on them.

Figure 18.5
The space between the mouldings may be filled with plastics foam to make the boat unsinkable. But the foam is essentially too light to be structural so the hull can still be damaged. Proper repair from inside is difficult and because there is no leak damage may be unsuspected.

quite a gap due to moulding tolerances plus the largely unpredictable contraction and change of shape during cure of both mouldings. There is no precision about fibreglass moulding.

The time interval is critical and should always be the same. The more newly moulded and hence more flexible the inner part the better.

Generally an epoxy or polyester putty is used. Improved adhesives like polyurethane, silicone and methacryalate could also be used but all must be very slow setting – an hour at least, preferably a day. Depending on the size it will take time to apply. The large, unwieldy inner moulding must be carefully and exactly positioned, perhaps several times, reforming the adhesive after each attempt. Finally the moulding will need to be weighted or a vacuum bag applied. It is essential that everything is in place and weighted down before the adhesive starts to harden. Premature setting is the cause of numerous failures.

Thick putty is much weaker than a glass angle. Bedding on wet glass mat might seem a stronger method, but as the fibres lie in the plane of contact there is still no cross linkage as with a glass angle and it is purely bonding. The resin must be much slower setting than normal moulding. There will be a large area to lay up, probably several thicknesses. If disturbed by repositioning or moving it will be lifted into whiskers and lumps which must be worked smooth again (Fig 16.4).

Reliable contact requires pressure, not easy to apply evenly if the inner moulding is thin and flexible and much of the area vertical. Nowadays a volume builder would probably use a vacuum bag but in the past they just hoped for the best. The pressure required is no more than necessary to maintain intimate contact over the bonding areas. However, until the inner lining is firmly bonded and provides essential stiffening the hull itself will be floppy and can distort under pressure or weights.

Bonding two large mouldings of highly irregular shape, uneven surface, variable thickness and large tolerance is a lot harder in practice than in theory. I have found numerous cases where it was not as good as blissfully assumed to be. A double shell boat, bonded blind, must be considered suspect if it has been damaged or is elderly. But do not take it for granted that a new one is perfect either.

Bulkheads

Ideally inner mouldings should span between bulkheads already firmly glassed on to the hull.

But that requires more precise positioning than is practicable. Therefore most builders bond the whole inner moulding to the hull then bolt or bond the bulkhead to moulded flanges. Some slot it into grooves relying on the bulkhead supporting the hull by pressure alone. The inner shell should be in contact and bonded along the line of the bulkhead (Fig 14.3).

Attachments

Major attachments such as keel, engine bearers or hull/deck join should not be made through a double shell. Good practice is to end the double shell and bolt or bond to well thickened single skin. On no account should important fastenings be inaccessible behind an inner moulding.

Non-structural moulding

Larger hulls may have conventional top hat stringers or frames and the lining fits over them. This requires precise positioning of the stiffeners, which is not easy in a featureless moulding. If wrong, cutting away and repositioning are tedious and waste much time.

Damage

With anything more than minor damage to the hull the inner moulding must be cut away for proper access and inspection. This needs careful planning and skill to ensure cuts are made where least conspicuous, generally along angles or features, or where hidden by woodwork or upholstery.

The inner moulding is usually damaged too. Repair may mean remoulding complex parts in a conspicuous position, often more difficult than straightforward repairs to the hull. All this makes modest damage inordinately more expensive than with a single moulding.

The bond commonly breaks away. Inspection of the extent of damage will require the inner moulding to be cut away to nearby bulkheads and stiffening features, a lot further than the obvious damage. Not unnaturally the owner may be displeased if no damage is found.

A very serious safety aspect, which never seems to be considered despite authorities' concern with so much else, is how to cope with damage at sea (Chapter 39). With a single skin moulding there is a chance of being able

to locate a serious leak and do something. But how can you reach or even locate a leak behind a complete inner moulding?

In theory it will be contained, unable to pass the edges. That was thought up by someone safe ashore. It assumes:

- that edges or bonding areas were perfectly continuous in the first place which is not likely
- that the bond has not been broken by the damage, which is likely
- that the inner moulding is still intact, whereas it is probably split
- nobody has made holes for wires or pipes.

It is far more likely the crew will find a sinking leak pouring out of splits or flooding through an inaccessible edge, from an invisible hole in an unknown position.

Many experienced sailors declare fibreglass boats with continuous inner mouldings are not safe. But nobody will take any notice until enough people have been drowned.

Unsinkable boats

Here the space between inner and outer skins is deliberately made much greater and filled with plastics foam. This also bonds the mouldings together but they are too far apart to give effective mutual support and impact strength is low (Fig 18.5).

For good buoyancy the foam must be light. That means friable with poor compressive strength. Some disintegrate with use, age or damage. If waterlogged they can go soggy and decompose, and once wet a foam filled space will never dry out. Do not think there are no waterways or never will be.

The distribution of the foam is critical. The best method is foam injection through multiple filling holes. With poured foam *in situ* it is difficult to fill all the space with certainty. The shape is critical: in a deep narrow cavity the foam often collects on the sides and does not reach the bottom. Generally it solidifies and jams before rising to the top or filling corners. A closed cavity where some pressure builds up has a higher proportion of closed cells than open, free rise. The pressure built up is sufficient to lift a man and may distort or damage a light moulding.

Sandwich mouldings

This chapter concerns sandwich or cored mouldings made in a female mould. For 'mouldless' sandwich, which really means a male mould, see Chapter 31.

In theory a sandwich moulding, consisting of two fibreglass skins separated by a lightweight core, the classic engineering principle of the girder, is the ideal way to increase stiffness without adding weight. It makes feasible the moulding of larger vessels up to small ship size. But the high cost compared with steel limits this mainly to naval vessels like minehunters where the major attraction is a nonmagnetic hull. A few gin palaces have been built in this way, the attraction being ostentatious speed through lighter weight.

Most sandwich construction is more modest. It is increasingly being used for hulls as the techniques become better understood. Sandwich decks have long been common, the major attraction not weight saving but stiffness over a wide span without head bumping deck beams. Also the flattish shape is easier to mould than a hull.

As a sandwich, fibreglass can be stiffer than almost anything else in the same strength, weight and price range. This intrinsic stiffness means a hull can be a true monocoque. Combined with Kevlar and other hi-tech reinforcements very sophisticated light weight racing machines have been built.

However there are disadvantages. Moulding is not nearly so easy as often thought. Much more expertise is required than ordinary fibreglass moulding. Most early sandwich mouldings were badly made, often disastrous, especially hulls. There has been more structural trouble from bad sandwich moulding than anything else.

Theory

The theory of a structural sandwich is similar to a stiffener in Chapter 11 with the face extended to indefinite width (Fig 19.1).

Basic principle

The core binds the two faces together so the sandwich behaves as a single structure. Despite claims to the contrary, generally by builders trying to avoid expensive repair, a delaminating or separated sandwich is definitely not a structural sandwich, and is not

Sandwich mouldings

Advantages	Disadvantages
Greater stiffness	Higher cost
Less weight	Difficulty of moulding
Insulation	Tendency to delaminate
Sound deadening	Limitations of shape
Resistance to heat and cold	Difficulty of making attachments
Buoyancy	Vulnerability to damage
	Low impact strength
	Deterioration from water inside
	Permeability through thin skins
	Difficulty of testing
	Serious effects of failure
	Difficulty of repair

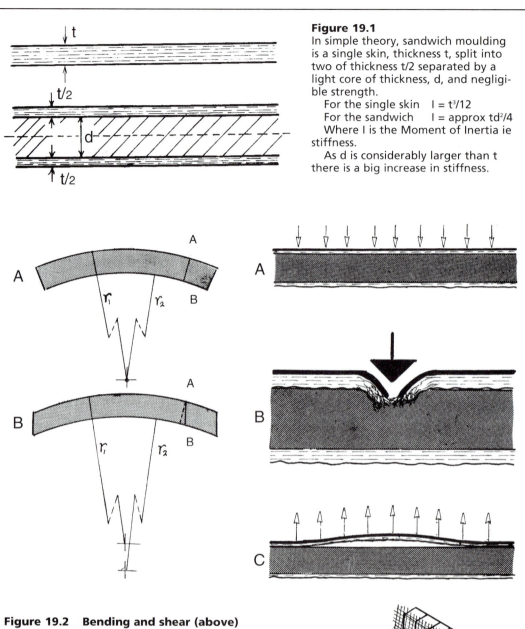

Figure 19.1
In simple theory, sandwich moulding is a single skin, thickness t, split into two of thickness t/2 separated by a light core of thickness, d, and negligible strength.

For the single skin $I = t^3/12$
For the sandwich $I = approx\ td^2/4$
Where I is the Moment of Inertia ie stiffness.

As d is considerably larger than t there is a big increase in stiffness.

Figure 19.2   Bending and shear (above)
A Ideally both sides bend on radii about a common centre and maintain their relative positions.
B A flexible core allows shear. The radii do not have a common centre and faces slide relative to each other.

Figure 19.3 (above right)
A Taken overall a sandwich moulding behaves according to theory as a homogeneous structure.
B Under point impact it is a skin of half thickness backed by a weak core and vulnerable to impact damage.
C Note it is also vulnerable to forces tending to pull it apart, notably cavitation. A major consideration also with mine sweepers which must resist nearby explosions.

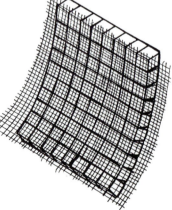

Figure 19.4
To allow a solid, rigid core to follow curves it is made in disjointed small blocks attached to a scrim cloth.

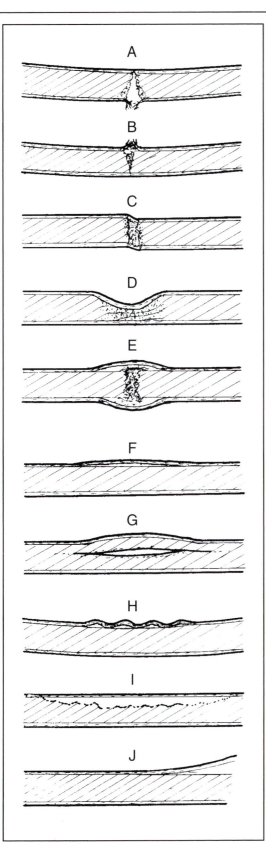

Figure 19.5   Modes of failure
A Failure of tension face in bending.
B Failure of compression face in bending.
C Failure in shear.
D Failure of core under compression or impact.
E Buckling under edge loading.
F Delamination and bond failure (commonest).
G Cleavage or splitting of the core.
H Wrinkling of compression face in bending.
I Disintegration of the core from age or damage.
J Peeling from an edge.

strong as well as having other very serious deficiencies. The bond is as important as the core, and by far the commonest source of failure.

A flexible core is not a structural sandwich either. Some peculiar decks have been moulded with furniture foam, said to be like dancing on springy turf. Yet one of the most successful materials, semi-rigid PVC foam, does have some flexibility, better described as resilience. In theory this is not a true sandwich, but thanks to careful compromise it retains adequate stiffness (Fig 19.2).

Behaviour of the core

The core is weak in comparison with the faces. Therefore it is usual to assume all stress is taken by those faces and the core can be discounted. This is true to a limited extent only. In theory the lighter the better. In practice a very light core will be too weak to hold the faces together. It must have adequate shear strength to transfer stress between the faces and also enough compressive strength to withstand the loads imposed. These can be quite large and local, eg the crew jumping on to the deck (No heavy man lands with such a thump as a child!). It must not be friable, or come apart and the bond to either face must never separate.

Most stresses are caused by bending, usually inwards, and it is the inner face in tension which fails. But a sandwich can also fail in other ways, most often by bond failure or wrong design (Fig 19.5).

Taken over a wide area loads are distributed and a sandwich moulding behaves as a structural entity according to theory. But over a small area it is only a thin fibreglass skin backed by a soft core. Consequently it is vulnerable to sharp impact because the core is unable to transfer the high local stress to the

Core requirements

Light weight	Low cost
Adequate compressive strength	Compatibility with polyester
Adequate shear strength	Easy forming to shape
Adequate integrity	Life of boat durability
Good water resistance	Low water absorption
Smooth surface for bonding	Low resin soakage
Closed cell	No harmful decomposition
Resistance to fuel	Low flammability
Resistant to bacteria	Ease of repair
Not attacked by insects	Resistant to styrene
Resilience	Not plasticised by solvents

moulding as a whole. As the outer face is about half the thickness of an equivalent single skin it will have much lower impact strength anyway. A sandwich moulding is often damaged when a single skin would have suffered no more than scratches (Fig 19.3).

Most quoted figures are based on static loads, and are misleading. On a boat, especially a hull, stresses are dynamic and although compressive predominate they may at times be tensile which pull the sandwich apart. This must be avoided.

The core, and the all important bond, needs good shock resistance and energy absorption. Many cores are too rigid and have no resilience.

Properties

Some plastics foams are as light as 1 lb/cu ft, SG 0.015. But these are too weak. In practice the minimum density needs to be about 6 lb/cu ft, SG 0.1, although a few can go as low as 4.5 lb/cu ft, SG 0.075. Around this density most will have adequate compressive and shear strength. Ideally the strength will be perpendicular to the surface.

Compressive strength should be over 100 lb/in^2, 700 kN/m^2. In way of fastenings it must be higher, about 1000 lb/in^2, 7000 kN/m^2. *Note:* Dynamic forces at sea, including the weight of the crew, will greatly increase stress.

A friable material will have poor shear strength. It frequently fails through cleavage or disintegration within the core itself. Friable foams also have poor energy absorption and

are easily damaged. Being internal this cannot be seen.

The core and its bond must be absolutely water resistant. Despite theory water will probably get into the core at some time. Decomposition products, whether caused by water or naturally, must not be harmful to polyester. They will be in contact for a long, long time. Neither must the core build up gas or vapour pressure, wet or dry, hot or cold, or offer dinner to any microbe. Durability must be life of the boat, come what may, and the life of the boat must not be limited by the durability of the core. Replacement would be very expensive and by then uneconomic.

During moulding the core will be in contact with wet polyester, or wet epoxy or adhesives. It must neither inhibit the resin or adhesive nor be attacked by it. Some PVC foams are slightly softened by styrene. This is claimed to improve the bond and when the resin sets the PVC hardens. But when hot some PVC foams release solvents, which subsequently plasticise and soften the polyester, or gas which causes internal pressure, blistering or delamination. Heat resistance and distortion should be above any possible working temperature.

Sandwich mouldings improve thermal insulation. Sound insulation too: a claimed virtue over the alleged sounding box of single skin although it has never disturbed me.

Curvature

Few parts of a boat are flat. Yet a thick, rigid core has to follow the curves exactly (Fig 19.4). Even if forced to shape and stuck down it will be under stress and tend to separate. Some cores are sufficiently thermoplastic to be formed by heat, but the commonest method is to divide the core into small pieces glued to scrim (Fig 19.4). This will follow even moderate compound curves. The glue must be compatible with polyester. Unsuitable adhesive has caused failures.

Voids

Cells of the core will be nuclei for blisters. They should be small and the surface preferably skinned not sawn. Large open cells will swallow resin like a thirsty chief stoker on a run ashore.

Types of core material

Orientation (Fig 19.6)	Material
Unidirectional (strength perpendicular to plane)	End grain balsa Honeycomb
Isotopic (strength in all directions)	Rigid polyurethane foam Rigid or semi-rigid PVC foam Phenolic foam Syntactic foam
Lamina (strength in the plane)	Plywood

The weight of resin filling open cells or soaking into the core makes nonsense of claims for light weight. It is also lost from the fibreglass which ends up dry.

Core materials

Quoted figures may be derived from different methods and conditions of testing, and short time scales. Most manufacturers' data is biased and disadvantages are glossed over unless referring to a rival.

Unidirectional

This is the ideal with strength orientated across the plane of the moulding.

End grain balsa

Balsa is the commonest core material (Fig 19.7). As model aircraft builders know balsa is the lightest wood but very soft. It is cheap, plentiful, quick growing and environmentally friendly. Balsa is used in blocks or sheets which, unlike planks, are sawn across the grain.

Being a natural product the properties vary widely. Density ranges from about 2–15 lb/cu ft, SG 0.03–0.3, and is graded according to weight. The lightest are very weak. Strength increases with weight and should not be less than about 6 lb/cu ft, SG 0.1.

Shock resistance is moderate, although once cells are crushed there is no recovery. With little tendency to shear across the grain it retains integrity well.

Heat resistance is well above any resin. It is unaffected by cold although the bond may be, and is a good insulator, although anyone who claims condensation is eliminated has not spent a winter on board!

Suppliers claim balsa is very durable wet or dry. This contradicts the Forest Products Research Laboratory classification as non-durable. Kiln drying kills rot spores, but does not prevent reinfestation during transport and

Table 19.1   Compressive strengths

Material	Density lb/cu ft	SG	Compressive strength lb/in²	kN/m²
Rigid foam polyurethane	2	0.03	22	150
	4	0.06	90	620
	6	0.10	150	1,000
Rigid foam PVC	2	0.03	31	220
	3	0.05	95	660
	4	0.06	151	1,040
Semi-rigid PVC at 72°F, 22°C	3	0.05	80	600
	4	0.06	115	800
	5	0.08	175	1,200
at 140°F, 60°C	3	0.05	59	445
	4	0.06	85	593
	5	0.08	130	890
End grain balsa*	6.5	0.10	945	6,520
	9.5	0.15	1,870	12,900
BaltekMat (plus resin)	45	0.70	?	?
Plywood	45	0.75	10,000	70,000

* Figures for balsa vary quite widely

Values are typical and taken from various sources.
There are differences between some authorities' minimum figures and those quoted by suppliers.

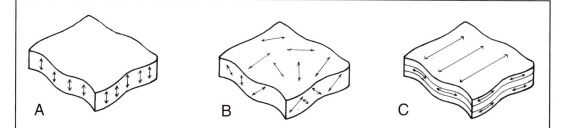

Figure 19.6   Core orientation
A Isotopic. Ideally, as principal loads are compressive, strength is orientated across the plane of the moulding, eg end grain balsa and honeycomb.
B Orthotopic. Strength the same in all directions, eg plastics foam. Much strength is wasted.
C Lamina. Main strength in the plane of the moulding. Even more wasteful. Typically plywood but as it is cheap, readily available and has good compressive strength across the laminate it is the commonest material for inserts.

Figure 19.7   End grain balsa ▶
The commonest core, usually in the form of small blocks bonded to a scrim backing so it can conform to shape.

◀ Figure 19.8   Honeycomb
Seldom used on boats because of the limited bonding area. Nida-core, however, is fused to a glass fibre backing so it can be bonded by conventional moulding techniques.

Figure 19.9   Foams
Also common are plastics foams.

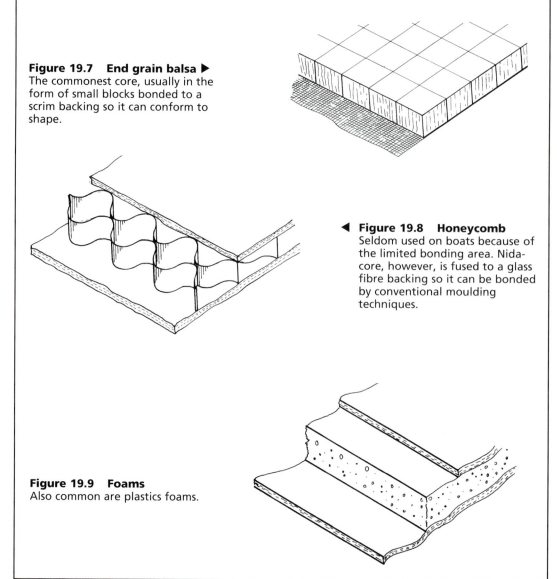

storage, nor through damage. Experience shows balsa cores do disintegrate when exposed to water and weather. Balsa is only durable if kept dry but the chance of it staying dry is where theory and practice diverge.

In theory moisture cannot migrate from one cell to another so leaks are confined to a small area around the point of entry. This assumes, with an optimism seldom well founded, there are no waterways. Wood swells when wet, but suppliers, so confident a balsa core will never get wet, do not mention that. The *Kon-Tiki* nearly sank because the balsa became waterlogged.

Honeycomb

As the name suggests this consists of interlinked cells formed by thin glass cloth, paper, plastics or aluminium. It is the lightest being mostly air, but expensive (Fig 19.8).

The area of contact is small. While not difficult to bond to the first surface it is impossible to lay up the second face directly on to the open honeycomb. Consequently it can be used only between two hard, accurate mouldings, and is more suitable for the sophisticated techniques and money of the aircraft industry. However, it has been used for flat bulkheads and accommodation on racing craft. A major disadvantage for a hull is the large amount of water retained within the cells following damage or seepage.

The bonding problem has been overcome by Nida-core. This is an extruded polypropylene honeycomb, fused to a non-woven polyester fabric backed by polythene as a resin and water barrier. The fabric makes it feasible to bond by normal lay up methods. This is an interesting new material.

Isotopic

Plastics foams have equal strength in all directions (Fig 19.9). This is unnecessary so theoretically they are more wasteful, but they are convenient and some are cheap.

Closed cells do not interconnect. Open cells do, like a sponge. Obviously the less chance there is for water to migrate the better. No foam is completely closed although a good one should be 90%.

Polyurethane foam

Rigid polyurethane tends to be friable, especially in lighter weights, and may disintegrate or shear internally. Impact strength and energy absorption are poor. It can break down with age, and some are attacked by bacteria or fungi. Being a thermoset polyurethane does not melt as thermoplastics do, so heat resistance is good, although prolonged heating will hasten degradation. Its principal advantage is cheapness.

Polyurethane is supplied in sheets. The best are formed to finished thickness with a solid face. Cheaper grades are sawn from thick blocks and have an open cell surface.

Phenolic foam

The cheapest with properties similar to polyurethane. It needs sealing with epoxy.

Polystyrene

The very cheap white foam polystyrene is the lightest but too weak for structural use. Polyester dissolves it instantly but not epoxy.

Rigid PVC

Sometimes called cross-linked PVC. This, the first plastics foam, was developed in Germany during World War II. It is stronger and durable. Being a thermoplastic it can, to a limited extent, be softened and bent to shape.

Klegecell is used with Kevlar for top class racing machines, but for such boats strength and lightness are more important than prosaic requirements like impact strength.

Semi-rigid PVC

Also known by trade names, Airex and Divinycell. This is a more expensive, better quality foam made from pure PVC. Although not the strongest it has the best compromise of properties. Being tough and slightly flexible it has resilience, giving good impact strength and energy absorption. Consequently it can be used in lighter densities and theoretically less compressive strength.

The surface should be primed with a thin coat of orthophthalic polyester. There are problems with isophthalic, vinyl ester and others but not epoxy.

Sheets can be softened and bent by heating

to about 200°F, 90°C, in a simple oven and retain that shape on cooling. This softening is a disadvantage on a deck where high sun temperatures can cause permanent indentation. Otherwise durability is good. It is little affected by water and is closed cell.

Being formed by high pressure gas, not a chemical foaming agent like others, it can be made only in thick buns and then sawn into sheets. Faces are always rough.

Syntactic foam

A putty made with lightweight filler, used where curvature is sharp or to taper from sandwich to single skin. Weight is fairly heavy, over 20 lb/cu ft, SG 0.3 even with the lightest fillers.

Light weight fillers	
Microballons (Plastics bubbles)	Q cells
	Pumice
Ballotini (Glass bubbles)	Pozzolana
Diatomaceous earth (Fuller's Earth)	Cork granules
	Wood flour
Vermiculite	
Ground coconut	

Lamina

Plywood

The layers of plywood run in the plane of the core. In theory this is wrong but being virtually incompressible, compared with a light core, it is the usual choice for solid inserts. Also, being strong, for large flattish high stress areas like king planks or transoms of outboard or stern drive boats. Bonding needs care (Chapter 20).

Bonding

Reliable, certain, life-of-the-boat bonding is the critical part of sandwich moulding. That has always been the greatest weakness and source of most failures. The techniques have improved, but a great many boats were built before sounder practice replaced blind faith.

Most separated mouldings were badly bonded right from the start, often never bonded at all. A bad bond can only get worse.

Sandwich mouldings are made by laying up the outer skin in the mould, allowing it to set hard, bonding the core and laying up the inner skin over the core. The inner, laid up wet, will bond naturally but bonding the core to the outer, and now hard fibreglass is essentially a glueing operation, not moulding. This is where so many go wrong.

Glueing requires the two parts to be in intimate contact (Fig 19.10). Yet the naturally uneven surface and high spots mean an intimate fit is impossible. So gap filling is necessary.

Generally polyester in some form is used. The outer face will be newly moulded, green and uncured. Adhesion to that is good, like another layer of moulding. But to the core it is a physical bond. Although beastly sticky, polyester is not a good adhesive.

A common method is to lay up one or more layers of wet mat and bed the core on to this. However, wet mat does not flow well. It must be an unusually wet, high resin content lay up because an unpredictable amount will be absorbed causing dry patches. Environmental resins cannot be used because of their waxy surface.

A better method is to bed on resin putty or highly thixotropic paste. This fills gaps better and there are no patches of dry glass. Epoxy putty will bond better than polyester but can be affected by styrene in the uncured polyester. Urethane acrylate is claimed to be tougher and more flexible. Other adhesives should be used with caution and never resorcinol or phenolic.

Timing is critical. The core must be properly positioned and pressure applied before the bonding agent begins to set. On a large area this will take a matter of hours. Normal polyester or epoxy starts to harden in minutes. So the resin must be unusually slow setting, and the area no larger than can be positioned *with certainty* in the time available. Movement while setting will be disastrous. Some theoretically excellent and approved adhesives like methacryalate set too quickly.

On no account should the core be laid on to the outer structural skin until that has set hard and cannot be disturbed. With a tight production schedule the temptation is to lay the core straight on to the wet outer skin. But this risks disturbing the structural moulding. As this should be moulded with properly

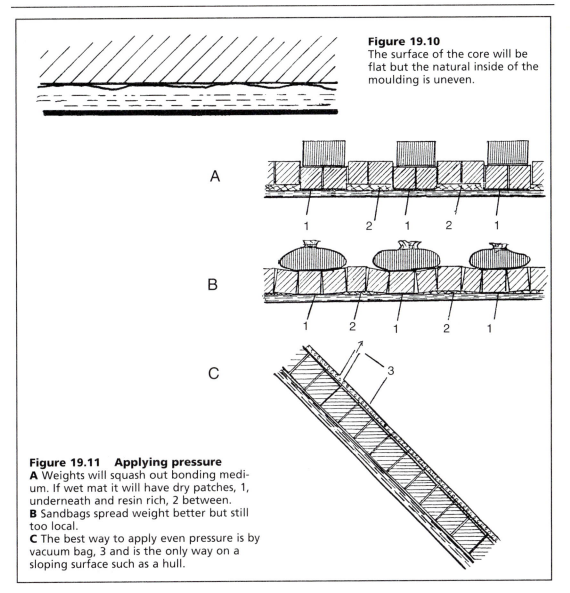

Figure 19.10
The surface of the core will be flat but the natural inside of the moulding is uneven.

A

B

C

Figure 19.11   Applying pressure
A Weights will squash out bonding medium. If wet mat it will have dry patches, 1, underneath and resin rich, 2 between.
B Sandbags spread weight better but still too local.
C The best way to apply even pressure is by vacuum bag, 3 and is the only way on a sloping surface such as a hull.

timed resin, it will set too soon for carefully laying down the core as well. Certainly on a high performance boat it would avoid the unwanted weight of a bonding layer but there are better methods.

Solvents or styrene may be absorbed selectively and weaken the resin. Balsa is highly absorbent. Others have large open cells into which resin can drain as if down a plughole. Sealing with epoxy will prevent sensitive materials being attacked by polyester, but polyester will not bond well to epoxy. Solve one problem, create two more!

After bonding and before applying the inner skin the core must be tested for unbond-ed areas by tapping. Hollow sounding patches must be cut out and rebonded, particularly important with a hull. Testing has been one of the greatest weaknesses and could have avoided most troubles. But making good disrupts production; often it is nicer not to know.

Pressure

For a sound bond the core must be in contact. This requires pressure, not clamping or a powerful press but just enough to overcome springiness and maintain intimate contact (Fig 19.11). Even flat panels and decks need this. Sand or shot bags distribute weight better than solid weights. But any weights press

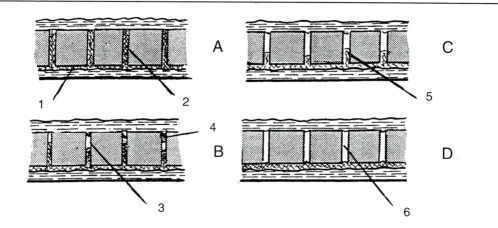

Figure 19.12   Filling gaps
A In theory the bonding medium, 1, will fill perfectly every gap between every joint of the core, 2, all thousands of them. This is likely only when vacuum bagged.
B In practice there will generally be some voids, 3, even when vacuum bagged. Resin flowing from the inner face, 4, will seldom fill completely either.
C When not vacuum bagged the bonding seldom fills any gaps completely, 5.
D Until recently builders saw no need to fill gaps. So on most existing boats they are completely unfilled, 6.

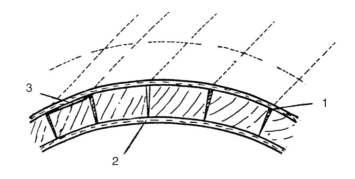

Figure 19.13
Gap filling is more difficult on curves and therefore even less likely, because the gaps open more widely one side, 1 or close tightly on the other, 2. A wide core may bridge, 3.

heavily over a limited area causing dry squashed out patches and resin rich between.

The preferred method now is a vacuum bag which exerts a uniform pressure. Being atmospheric no extra weight is involved so the same fibreglass moulds can be used. A vacuum bag is essential on a hull because of the curvature and vertical surfaces, and the much greater importance of being sound. As the whole moulding, perhaps quite a large hull, must be done at once not in sections and then it takes time to rig the membrane and apply vacuum the adhesive has to be very slow setting or heat assisted.

Filling gaps

No core is in one piece, even a flat panel. On curved surfaces with segmented cores there will be thousands of inch square pieces. Every gap between every single piece is supposed to be filled perfectly. In theory they are filled automatically as the core is bedded. But it is much too optimistic to expect the filling really will be perfect. A conscientious moulder would try, but inspecting and filling later is tedious and therefore likely to be skimped.

Only recently have better moulders, using vacuum bags, made serious efforts to fill the gaps properly or had a reasonable chance of

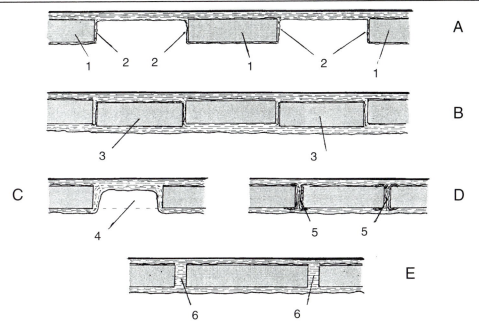

Figure 19.14   Interconnection
A Webs are easily formed by laying down the core in alternate strips, 1, and laying up a thin layer, zig-zag, 2.
B Next the intermediate cores are laid down, 3, and the inner layer moulded over all.
C With a plywood core like a transom large holes are often drilled, 4, so in places the inner skin can contact the outer.
D Rovings, 5, can be pushed through smaller holes to 'rivet' the skins together.
E On large hulls shear stress requires an uneconomically heavy core. Gaps can be left between sections, 6, and fibreglass worked in to form a geodesic structure.

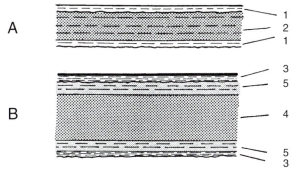

Figure 19.15   Volumisation
A Glass fibre reinforced cores, which can be moulded like mat, can be used to mould stiffer, minimal weight mouldings, eg racing dinghies. The faces, 1, are reduced to the absolute minimum and the main strength lies in the structural core, 2, giving a thicker moulding for the same weight.
B A weakness with normal sandwich moulding is the sharp change of stress between the faces, 3, and the core, 4. By using a layer of reinforced core, 5, there is more even transition and less stress on the bond.

doing so. On earlier boats they did not try, or even see the need (Fig 19.12).

Any gap is a potential waterway. If not filled, or not filled properly, the fishnet pattern will run the length of the boat, as moisture meter tests after damage have shown. The bond to the side of the gaps will be indifferent anyway and can break away as the unseen resin contracts on cure or due to use and age.

The weight of filling will be substantial and

offset the advantage of a light weight core. Certainly for high performance not filling saves weight. The saving in cost does not go unnoticed in other quarters.

Remember: this book is not just concerned with how boats should be made today (and sometimes are) by skilled moulders, based on years of experience, but also how boats were made in years past. How *your* boat was made.

Interconnection

Various methods have been tried to interlink the two faces and overcome complete dependence on this unreliable and indifferent adhesive bond (Fig 19.14).

Volumisation

A recent approach is a bulky, light weight reinforcement like Spheretex, a glass mat mixed with microballons or similar light filler. As a core this can be moulded like ordinary mat so there is no break in production. Weight is comparatively high, about half solid fibreglass, so it is a way of increasing thickness and hence stiffness without adding weight rather than reducing it (Fig 19.15).

Delamination

This is the commonest defect, especially on earlier boats when sandwich moulding was considered easy. In the 1960s most sandwich decks had some delamination, seldom less than 10%, many over 50%, and I have found 100%!

Delamination can occur through damage, use, age, ingress of water, but most is still original, due to a bad or patchy bond. Unless damaged, apparent development is usually because nobody noticed before. A delaminated patch of deck looks much the same as a sound one.

It nearly always occurs between the outer skin and the core, the bond to the hard moulding, seldom on the side laid up wet. Consequently mouldless construction, where both sides are laid up wet, rarely delaminates. On a deck most loads are downwards. Separation is pressed together and may appear strong. A limited area will be supported by sounder moulding around. But on a hull any delamination is very serious and dangerous.

Decks often delaminate due to bad support

Signs of delamination

Creaking	Movement under foot
Flexibility	Vibration
Hollow sounding	Cracks
Bulges	Large blisters
Depressions	Distortion
Weeping	Patches of condensation

---

while being fitted out separately with workers scrambling over it. Worse damage can be done when difficult to release from the mould. Common practice is to use the long leverage from one end. This bends the deck which, unlike the more robust hull, has little strength from shape. A deck with delamination often has telltale signs of sticky release.

Testing for delamination

Delamination is seldom obvious, although an experienced person may notice the faint signs. Patches sound hollow when rubbed or tapped gently. Hard tapping or a hammer will push separated parts together so they sound solid. A moulded or painted non-slip deck is a good sounding board but if covered, eg with Treadmaster or teak, delamination is impossible to detect.

Often the deck has delaminated but the shape holds it in contact so it sounds solid. So does a weak or spotty bond. Even sophisticated equipment is unlikely to detect that.

Beware of red herrings. Hollow sounding patches may be bonded on bulkheads or stiffeners, core edges and joins, recessed cable dusts or around inserts.

Water in the core

As well as weakness a very serious feature of delamination is the water trap formed by delaminated spaces. Even without damage water will permeate naturally (Chapter 26) especially as the outer skin will be thin.

Opinions differ about the effect, generally tempered by the money involved. Material suppliers and boatbuilders, if reluctantly forced to admit that the theoretically impossible might just be possible, will, of course, claim it does no harm. Experience shows otherwise, however. Water in the core is definitely harmful in the long term and often short term too.

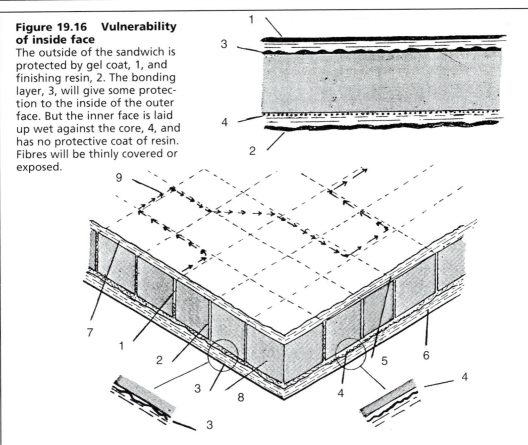

Figure 19.16   Vulnerability of inside face

The outside of the sandwich is protected by gel coat, 1, and finishing resin, 2. The bonding layer, 3, will give some protection to the inside of the outer face. But the inner face is laid up wet against the core, 4, and has no protective coat of resin. Fibres will be thinly covered or exposed.

Figure 19.17 (Above)   Waterways

Only in theory are there no waterways within a core. In practice there are numerous possibilities even before more are opened by damage, age or use.

Eg partly filled, 1, or unfilled gaps, 2, in the core. Gaps where the flat core beds on the uneven fibreglass, 3. All very common. Also common is delamination of the outer face, 4, and less commonly of the inner, 5. A thin outer moulding, 6, may be porous, although more commonly it is the inner face, 7, especially when moulding with a single layer of heavy woven rovings. The core itself may be porous, 8. The arrows, 9, show what a devious, three dimensional path water may take.

Figure 19.18 (Below)   Repair of delamination

A To repair a patch of delamination, 1, drill holes, 2, about ½ in, 12 mm, apart.
B With a small syringe inject resin into one hole until it oozes out of all others, 3 and no more bubbles appear.
C Apply weights or use temporary self-tapping screws with polythene, 4, to prevent sticking.

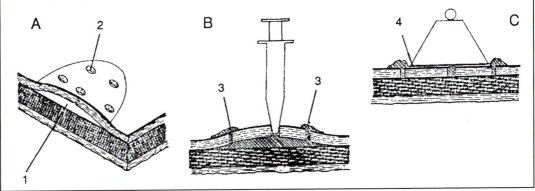

Water may reduce the strength of the core, cause deterioration or even complete disintegration. Some foams become friable or shrink. Gases may be generated. Wood can rot or swell. The bond can be hydrolysed. Even if the core is unaffected the vapour pressure due to the heat of the sun, or expansion from freezing, will force further delamination.

A damp core or fibreglass surface will be difficult to rebond. Repair will be unreliable or impossible. Pockets might be drained but the dampness will remain, or be fed from unlocated reservoirs. Dampness is usually unsuspected and difficult to detect. With skins of average thickness the core will be beyond the accurate range of most moisture meters and indicate dry when actually sodden.

The time scale must be years not months: total water resistance for the life of the boat. Moreover not just water resistance: trapped water will attack the fibreglass (Chapter 6), and become aggressive 'blister juice', leading to insidious, unseen decay from within or the dreaded 'osmosis' (Chapter 26). The adhesive will add to the brew, like a boy mixing all the contents of his Christmas chemistry set.

Normally fibreglass is protected by a thick gel coat on the outside and finishing resin on the other. But the inner surfaces of a sandwich are in the middle and do not have this protection (Fig 19.16). The inner skin was laid up directly on the core, like a moulding without the protection of a gel coat. Worse, resin may have been lost into the core, sucked away from fibres. The outer skin was before the thick finishing resin stage so also lacks protection. If the bonding layer was wet mat resin can be squashed or soaked out of that too.

These poorly protected and exposed fibres are perfect for wicking. To reduce soakage cores should be sealed, although this is unlikely to fill the innumerable holes or include the sides of jointed pieces.

One new yacht had a moderately delaminated deck. Rain water entering through the unsealed mast cut out ran to, and became trapped in, the hull/deck joint. Within two years the deck parted from the hull due to internal decay. The lawyers did well.

Waterways

Everyone assumes water will never get into the core, but anyone who knows about boats should ask why not? It gets everywhere else! Once inside, especially from damage, water can travel far by internal waterways (Fig 19.17).

Even when new nearly every sandwich moulding will have some internal waterways and after hard use and natural ageing there will be many more. Older boats were made with crisscrossing waterways like the creeks of a marsh. Unlike the microscopic capillary paths in fibreglass these are wide channels, and they form a substantial reservoir.

Water in the core, unseen and generally unsuspected, adds weight and will affect performance. Not only for a racing machine: fast

---

Waterways

Assumption	Fact
• There is no possible way water can get into the core.	• Water gets in by many ways, eg damage, fastenings, cut outs, permeability
• Even if it does, water cannot get beyond the entry point.	• Waterways, gaps, poor bond, decomposition of core mean it can and will.
• There are no gaps in the core.	• There are. Perhaps few on modern boats. Between every piece on older ones.
• The bond is perfect everywhere.	• Seldom so on modern boats. Patchy or poor on older ones.
• The moulding is made as perfectly as by their skilled laboratory technicians under controlled laboratory conditions.	• Boats are made under factory conditions and production pressures by factory labour.
• The core retains its integrity under all conditions.	• It can be damaged, decay, decompose, disintegrate.
• Nothing is altered by age or use.	• Most cores degrade, some disintegrate, bonds fail.
• Damage is not builders' concern.	• Easier to blame the owner than their own poor standard of moulding.

motor boats may become too heavy to plane; a soggy fishing boat uses more fuel to bring home a smaller catch.

Hull

Delamination in a deck, even if extensive, will seldom affect the safety of the boat. However, with the hull lives are at stake and a delaminating hull should be condemned.

For any boat, it must be possible to mould the hull under the circumstances, cost and available expertise. A builder specialising in one-off top class racing machines, where cost is no object provided the boat wins, may succeed. A production builder moulding down to an economic price on a tight schedule with less skilled labour is a different proposition. Anything difficult or time consuming will be avoided or skimped, and it is then that things really can go wrong.

The fluctuating stresses on a hull require a core with good fatigue resistance as well as resilience. Because of this risk of water penetration many wise builders use sandwich for the topsides only, a policy approved by some authorities. Moreover these are usually flatter and more easily moulded and so more likely to be soundly moulded.

Be very cautious when buying a boat with a sandwich or cored hull. Enquire if it was made using a vacuum bag. The newer the boat the more likely the builder got the technique right, but most earlier ones were built 'by guess and by God'.

Repair of delamination

Provided the core is dry, modest delamination can be rebonded by injecting epoxy. Assume the void extends beyond the area detected. The bond will always be spotty round the edge (Fig 19.18).

Damage is sure to mean water has got in, and probably muck too. Simple rebonding is impossible and it must be repaired by cutting away and remoulding, a major repair demanding proper conditions.

Delamination should never be accepted on a new boat. It is a serious building defect. While a small amount on deck might be repaired at the builder's expense, nothing less than zero tolerance is good enough on a hull.

Ignore the builder's assurances that it does not matter. They know it is going to be expensive, and if one boat has delamination the rest probably have or will have too. Make a bee-line for your lawyer.

Attachments

The core must always be replaced locally with an incompressible insert. Otherwise it will be crushed as the fastenings are tightened. The two sides will just be squashed closer and closer yet the fitting will still not be tight. Leaks into the core are certain. Attachments must not be delaminating either. It is easy to pull a sandwich apart (Figs 19.19 and 19.20).

When planned the insert is put in during moulding. However, unless designed with a moulded plinth the inside of a moulding is featureless. It is common to find a crushed core because the insert was not in the right place. The sandwich should be reduced to single skin and well reinforced in way of major attachments, like keel and engine bearers, and also for skin fittings (thru hulls).

The inner skin must be continuous behind bulkheads. Ideally the core would have an insert although common practice is to rely on a wide root to distribute the stress.

It is equally essential to avoid crushing the core when adding a fitting later, as will be needed many times during the boat's life. The biggest problem will generally be access. A lot else may need to be cut away (Figs 19.21 and 19.22).

Inserts	
Plywood pads	Metal tubes
Denser foam	Premoulded fibre-
Syntactic foam filler	glass tubes
Proprietary fittings	Wood plug
	Resin putty

Do not underestimate the compression exerted by a fastening. A $^3/_{16}$ in, 5 mm, stainless steel bolt, a modest size, can exert a pressure of 500 lb. Four would be about a ton, and those are small bolts.

Every fastening is a potential leak into the core, and the commonest source. Fittings must be well bedded, and fastenings coated with

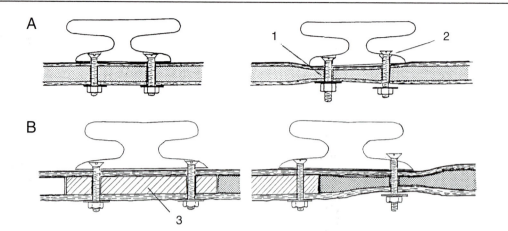

Figure 19.19   Attachments to a sandwich
A WRONG. Fittings must not be bolted straight through a sandwich core unless it has an incompressible insert. Otherwise the core will be crushed, 1 and the bolts impossible to tighten, 2.
B CORRECT. The core is replaced locally with an incompressible insert, 3.
Obviously when inserts are put in during moulding they must be in the right place. The fitting too.

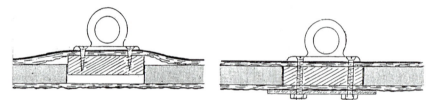

Figure 19.20   Attachments – delaminating
Fittings must not be screwed into an insert. All attachments must be through bolted so the load is taken by the whole sandwich, preferably with a backing plate or pad.

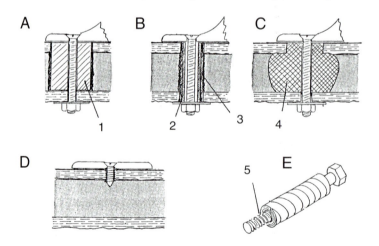

Figure 19.21   Adding inserts later
It is equally important to prevent crushing the core when adding fittings later.
A Drill a larger hole and bond in a wooden plug, 1. The plug can be full depth or just as far as the opposite face.
B A metal tube, 2, needs a smaller hole but must be well sealed in, 3.
C Scoop out the core and fill with resin putty, 4.
D Small fittings carrying no load can be attached by self-tapping screws.
E Tubes are easily made by moulding fibreglass over a waxed bolt, 5. Being fibreglass it will bond more securely than a metal tube.

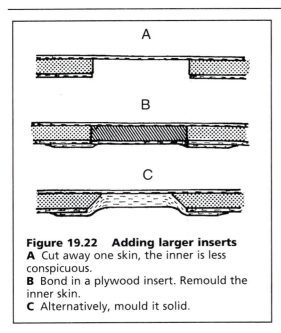

Figure 19.22   Adding larger inserts
A Cut away one skin, the inner is less conspicuous.
B Bond in a plywood insert. Remould the inner skin.
C Alternatively, mould it solid.

sealant before inserting and holes not drilled oversize.

Single skin or sandwich?

It is often hard to tell. The core pattern may be visible through the inner skin or it shows as an opaque shadow from inside. A single skin will be slightly translucent. The surest clue is to feel for the change of thickness at the edge. Tapping is ambiguous even for an expert.

Decks

A moulded non-slip tread poses no problems. Neither does non-slip paint. Stick-on treads bond readily provided the surface is smooth and keyed, but pulling off if need be will cause delamination. Ideally the deck will be designed for this tread. Applied later a moulded tread must be ground smooth which destroys most of the gel coat.

Laid teak is the highest class deck covering but should be solid. Veneer tends to delaminate and being bonded on is difficult to chisel off without damaging the deck. Traditional solid teak must be bolted or screwed on and that requires inserts spaced at regular intervals. It must not be bolted straight through and needs to be well bedded on mastic. On the whole, laid teak is better applied over a single skin deck, which it will stiffen, thereby making sandwich unnecessary anyway.

Edges

A sandwich moulding must not end abruptly but taper into single skin at a ratio not less than 2:1, preferably 3:1 (Fig 19.23). Some cores are available as fillets. Awkward places can be filled with syntactic foam or resin putty (Fig 19.24). Underwater the edge must be feathered otherwise voids will cause a line of blisters.

Sandwich to single skin forms a high stress area unless properly blended. Moulding over a hull/deck join does this naturally, but the production oriented method of bolting together does not. A shelf or flange will add some strength but not the common 'tin lid' join or 'bathtub' flange.

Cut outs

The edges of cut outs must be sealed. This is frequently a cause of water seeping into a core: a simple, cheap detail during building but very expensive to repair later (Figs 19.25 and 19.26).

Sawing will tend to delaminate. Use a fine tooth saw, never a wood saw. Large openings are better cut with a router.

Joins

To join two sandwich mouldings, whether designed or for repair, butt the core and overlap the fibreglass (Fig 19.27).

Permeability

In seeking higher performance the trend is to make the faces as thin as practicable and forget permeability. Some are not even watertight. With single skin, permeating water can evaporate from the inside face. But in a sandwich it will be trapped. Sound, low permeability moulding is therefore important.

The opposite is common. To speed production moulders like to use as few layers as possible, wetting out one thick layer, or even two at a time, rather than thinner layers individually. Speed and good moulding do *not* go together.

Particularly bad is the common practice of using a single layer of heavy woven rovings. At any time 24 oz, 750 g/m², woven rovings is difficult to wet out well, and tends to have dry strands and multiple voids in the interstices.

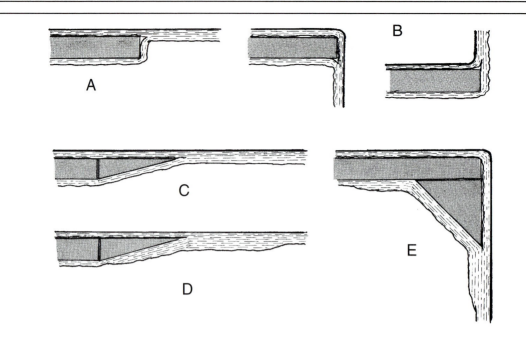

Figure 19.23   Sandwich to single skin
A WRONG. An abrupt step causes high local stress and a hinge effect. Very common because it is easier.
B WRONG. It is less obvious that an angle like this also forms an abrupt step.
C CORRECT. The sandwich is tapered to single skin.
D Better still is to reinforce the transition.
E An angle needs a fillet to make a proper transition.

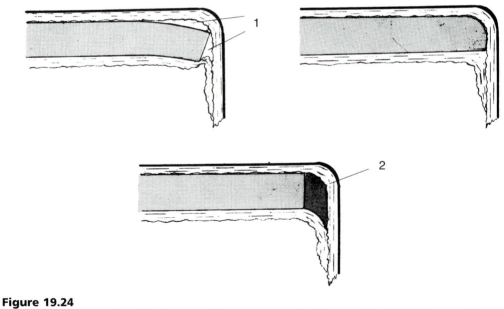

Figure 19.24
Because of the rounding off when moulding a square edged core will not fit into an angle. Consequently there will be voids, 1. The core must be shaped to fit the angle. Even so a precise fit is unlikely. The better method is to end the core short and pack the space with syntactic foam, 2, extended to form a fillet.

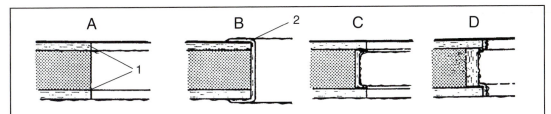

Figure 19.25   Cut outs – unplanned
A WRONG. Both core and moulding edge are unsealed. Also cutting has probably initiated delamination, 1.
B The edge is moulded over. This may be unsightly and the raised lip, 2, makes it difficult to bed a fitting snugly.
C A neater way is to scoop out some core before moulding.
D Scooping out more core and filling with putty provides an insert for fastenings.

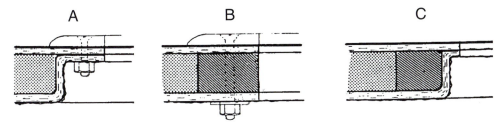

Figure 19.26   Cut outs – planned
A The core is omitted and the moulding reduced to single skin. The abrupt step is acceptable here provided the cut out is comparatively small and supported by the fitting.
B Insert put in during moulding and cut out later. But the moulding edge is exposed and sawing may cause delamination.
C A shaped insert put in during moulding and moulded over.

Figure 19.27   Joining sandwich mouldings
The correct way is to lap the mouldings and butt the core. When planned the conspicuous face can be rebated or arranged as a tongue and groove.

Only layers of mat between ensure it is not actually porous. Two thin layers are better than a single thick one. The inner face too must not be porous. To ensure this the inside face should always be finished with mat.

Damage

Only in a laboratory will damage be confined to the immediate area of impact. On a boat damage will always be associated with bending which will break the bond and cause core failure over a wider area. The edges will be shattered and the core exposed.

Inevitably water will get in and travel the waterways created by the damage even if not original. On most old boats there is nothing to stop water filling the whole core. The first indication of minor damage could be a list or that terrible calamity, not winning.

If the outer face is damaged, it is claimed as a virtue that the inner face will prevent the boat sinking. But not if the inner face is porous. The probable effect will be water oozing like sweat all over the inside with no indication where it comes from.

A 40 ft, 13 m, catamaran I surveyed had a single layer of heavy woven rovings on the inside. In theory this was adequate for strength, but, was, as usual, porous with pinholes everywhere. Helped by waterways throughout the core, water from a leak in the transom bubbled up through the galley floor amidships having passed under three bulkheads, a bunk and a tank.

Temperature

Nowadays, regardless of where a boat was built, it may end up anywhere in the world. Most yachts among which I am anchored in this tropical paradise were bought second-hand in Northern countries. Some plastics foams soften and indent at semi-tropical deck temperatures. This does not mean the equator; the Mediterranean and Florida are quite hot enough.

In cold weather many plastics become brittle or lose their resiliency. The bond too can be weakened. When trapped water freezes it will spread delamination or break down cell walls.

Water cushions a hull against temperature extremes. Cold is limited by freezing, and it is never like a hot bath. But a hull stored ashore can roast in hot sunshine, especially if stored upside down, and in winter will be exposed to the iciest winds. The colder the winters the more likely the boat will be ashore.

Styrene is often trapped in open cells. Some foams retain the gas from blowing. When heated by the sun the vapour pressure can initiate delamination. So can water trapped by permeability or damage.

Thermal expansion of the core should match the fibreglass. If considered at all, reliance is placed on the value being small and accommodated by resilience. But if not resilient the difference between extremes of heat and cold is sufficient to break the bond or shear the core.

The insulation of the core will distort thermal expansion. The sunny outer face will get hot. The other will be shaded. On a wide deck like a catamaran the difference in expansion can be too much for the core to absorb without shearing, delaminating or distorting. Being daily not seasonal fatigue is a factor. Shape and features will cause large local stress.

Rudders

Fibreglass rudders and similar shapes are made in two halves. Often they rely entirely on a polyurethane foam filling to hold them together. This is bad practice. The forces are large and the common internal armature tends to split the rudder. Edges should always be moulded over as well. External straps are not so neat but a lot stronger.

Most rudders leak because it is impossible to seal the metal shaft. In theory foam filling keeps the water out but seldom completely and disintegrates with age. Flooding should be assumed and inside faces well coated with finishing resin to reduce unseen decay within. When a rudder does flood it creates anaerobic conditions and stainless steel can corrode invisibly, another reason why external straps are safer.

Buoyancy

It is commonly claimed that a sandwich hull makes the boat unsinkable. This is a dangerous illusion. Unless so thick that the faces are not effectively in structural contact, no sandwich hull will contain enough buoyancy material to support a keel boat or motor boat with engine.

References

Conference on Fishing Vessel Construction Materials. Montreal 1968.

Karl Brandl, *Cellular Plastics of pure PVC as a sandwich core for large FRP boat hulls*.

Speciality foams, Airex Ltd.

Technical manuals from Divinycell Ltd, Baltek Corporation, Polimex Corporation, Spheretex American Inc, Nido-core.

Det Norske Veritas Rules for vessels under 15 m.

Wood and fibreglass

It is common to regard fibreglass as the new wonder material superior to wood for every purpose. That is quite wrong. Wood and fibreglass are complementary. For many applications on a fibreglass boat wood is the correct choice.

Accommodation

There are two schools of thought: mould the lot, everything fibreglass; or hull and deck only in fibreglass and accommodation in wood. Neither view is right or wrong. Each depends on what the builders can do best and make a profit. Most cases fall somewhere in between anyway.

Boatbuilders moulding their own hulls will have good moulding facilities, but woodwork requires a parallel line and large investment in totally different machinery, buildings and more skilled staff. Moreover they are probably a factory not a boatyard. So it makes sense to mould everything possible. However, that does require investment in intricate moulds, the skill to design and make them, a substantial production run, and accurate assembly. Modifications are difficult and bad features are locked in.

All wood accommodation appeals to a traditional boatbuilder who already has woodworking facilities, especially one who buys in hulls and does limited moulding. It is also the obvious choice for short runs, special designs and amateurs.

Some big production builders find it cheaper to set up furniture factory style production lines to make prefabricated units in wood. Design changes are easier and mistakes can be corrected.

A common compromise is to form the major part of the accommodation as one large moulding or 'pan' to which are attached simpler or decorative parts of wood.

More boats are sold on their accommodation than performance. Market research indicates many yacht buyers do not like the 'plastics' look of moulded accommodation. They are happy to have a fibreglass boat provided they cannot see it! The current trend is away from all moulded accommodation, or the fibreglass is hidden by woodwork. Builders boast of exotic woods, generally the thinnest of veneers on the commonest plywood. Often it looks more perfect than any wood and is in fact printed melamine.

Wood as protection

Fibreglass is a thin shell and has poor abrasion resistance. Wood is cheap, more resistant to wear and can have much greater thickness to absorb it. Moreover it is separate and renewable, whereas an integral part of a large moulding cannot be replaced. Therefore it is good practice, as well as common sense, to protect fibreglass with wood in areas subject to wear (Chapter 35).

For production adding wood takes time and material, eg it is cheaper to mould a coaming as an integral part of the deck. It is claimed fibreglass can be touched up, yet it is difficult to do so inconspicuously and get a lasting colour match. It is far easier to touch up wood and it can be done as routine maintenance.

Maintenance? Ay, that is the rub. The antithesis of the 'no maintenance' aura. Builders are terrified the thought will discourage sales. Yet it has sales appeal itself. Varnished wood looks nice, traditional, boaty. In practice the amount is small. Most owners accept the modest maintenance for the sake of appearance and take real pride in it.

Durability

Woods vary greatly in durability. The box gives ratings by the Forest Products Research Laboratory. Some descriptions such as teak or mahogany cover a range of similar species with different durabilities. The list includes types not generally considered for boat-building. Yet it is common to see attractive wood, normally used for indoor furniture, forming accommodation. Note the perishable position of balsa, despite the suppliers' claims, which emphasises the importance of keeping water out of balsa cored decks and hulls.

Marine plywood is classed as durable but WBP, often stained to look like something better, means the glue not the wood. In theory the durability of inner layers is secondary but edges are where plywood is vulnerable.

Wood preservative

Do not use preservative on any wood in contact with 'wet' polyester however desirable it may seem. Polyester resin itself is claimed to be mildly preservative. Most preservatives contain phenol or copper salts, both of which poison 'wet' polyester and prevent it setting properly. Obviously the part most affected will be the vital bonding layer.

The contents are seldom marked on the tin. They are probably a trade secret. Even if the principal constituents are quoted or guessed (a green preservative contains copper salts, creosote and brown ones phenol), unmentioned minor ones may be harmful. They will be meaningless to most people anyway.

As dry wood cannot rot, many preservatives do not release their active components until in contact with moisture. If harmful to fibreglass the effect can be long delayed.

Ventilation

Traditional good wooden boatbuilding practice, based on generations of experience, is ignored by modern production builders even if anyone still remembers or cares. Everyone used to know that unventilated spaces and pockets of stale air were breeding grounds for rot. Now fibreglass boats are full of them. This may not be serious if entirely within fibreglass. But very often these spaces contain wood as well, generally structural. It is common to find toadstools and rot behind the pretty veneer where nobody is supposed to see. Moreover many fibreglass boatbuilders use wood no better than firewood to a wooden boatbuilder.

References

Forest Products Research Laboratory Technical note 38, *The Movement of Timbers*, May 1969.

Forest Products Research Laboratory Technical note 40, *The Natural Durability, Classification of Timber*, October 1969. Reference 19.3.

Forest Products Research Laboratory. Various publications.

Practical Boat Owner, 'Plywood', June 1993.

Durability

Very durable	Durable	Moderately durable	Non-durable	Perishable
Afrormosia	Agba	Douglas fir	Deal	Ash
Greenheart	Cedar	Gurjun*	Elm	Balsa
Iroko	Mahogany	Keruing*	Ramin	Beech
Makore	(American)	Larch	Redwood	Birch
Opepe	Meranti*	Mahogany (African)	Scots pine	Poplar
Purpleheart	Oak*	Pitch pine	Spruce	Sycamore
Teak	Utile	Sappele		Willow
Western red cedar		Yang*		

*These can vary according to the exact species

Fibreglass and other materials

Metals are very different from fibreglass. They do not go well together but have to be used. Bonding to most plastics other than polyester is unreliable or impossible.

Bolting

The preferred method of joining metal to fibreglass is by bolting or similar fastenings (Chapter 15).

Bonding

Adhesion of polyester to metal is poor. You may have used it on that heap of rust with four wheels you call a car (as I have for over forty years!). But anything will bond to steel if rusty and rough. For new steel there are proprietary primers and some can be used on aluminium. In general, for bonding to metal use epoxy.

Copper, bronze and anything containing copper or tin inhibit polyester and prevent it curing properly. Seal first with epoxy before embedding or bringing into contact with 'wet' resin.

Use special adhesives for bonding to rubber and flexible materials.

Wrapping

The preferred method of attaching pipes, whether plastics or metal, is by proper screwed fittings. If simply moulded in they usually leak. If moulding in is unavoidable, mould tape over them first, pulled tight. As this sets it will contract and grip as well as bond. Then when moulding in the fibreglass bonds firmly to the tape (Fig 13.31).

Embedding

If fully embeded metal inserts or plates will be held securely whether bonding or not, but tangs must be designed so they cannot be pulled out. Even if mechanically secure the bond is unlikely to prevent leaks (Fig 15.13). It is bad practice to embed a fitting which might ever need replacement.

Stainless steel

Nothing bonds reliably to polished stainless steel.

It should not be embedded underwater or anywhere that leaks are possible. Stainless steel has a passive and an active state. The normal and assumed condition is passive but when air is excluded it can switch to the active state with different electro-potential, forming a destructive electolytic cell with itself. Examples are through deck shroud plates and rudder fittings. Corrosion will be invisible and, such is the confidence in stainless steel, generally considered impossible.

Plastics

Most other common plastics are waxy, eg nylon, polythene, PVC, and impossible to bond reliably. With some grades of PVC pipes the plasticiser is attacked by styrene and a bond of sorts is possible. There are special polyesters for this.

Melamine should be well sanded to break up the polished surface. Being non-absorbent the bond is indifferent.

Ballast

Close fitting blocks are often set by pouring resin round them. It must be low viscosity to flow to the bottom of deep narrow spaces and allow bubbles to rise.

Loose fillings like shot or punchings have low bulk density and high resin demand. To limit exotherm they must be pre-mixed with resin and poured a little at a time. If resin is poured over loose ballast it will set before it reaches the bottom. Thixotropic resin will never get there. Some boats actually rattle and when damaged the ballast trickles out.

Ballast is sometimes set in cement. This is not crude building labourer's work. Drying will be very slow, if at all, before fully encased. Therefore the water must be gauged accurately and be the absolute minimum. A rich cement/sand ratio is needed, about 1:2, not a builder's 1:7 or more, to make a waterproof mortar. The aggregate must be fine sand only, dry or with measured water content. The technique is closer to casting garden gnomes than laying a concrete floor.

Cement contains lime which, if it gets damp or contains too much water, will attack the fibreglass. Therefore the inside of a keel must be very well moulded and sealed. Keels are vulnerable and damage at some time must be assumed. If not a waterproof mortar the water will soak far, as in a damp house, and liberate aggressive alkali. Also it can freeze and burst the fibreglass. In any case over the years moisture will penetrate through normal permeability. Unlike the inside of the hull, the moisture cannot evaporate and will be absorbed by the concrete or, worse, be trapped in voids. This is a long term problem, worse when boats are kept afloat continually, especially in warm waters where permeability is faster.

Modulus

The modulus of fibreglass is much less than steel and most metals (Table 1.2). Therefore stressed metal fittings attached to fibreglass must blend in so that the stress is evenly distributed, eg by enlarging the area of contact or making the fibreglass much thicker than the metal.

Rust

When steel rusts it expands. The increase in volume can be five times or more, enough to burst embedding, although experience suggests it is probably self-limiting.

Thermal expansion

Metals and fibreglass have different co-efficients. Movement will be similar to mechanical stress. It is generally considered significant only on decks or topsides in hot sunshine. But metals also contract in cold weather.

Long or irresistible massive fittings should be bedded on flexible sealant to allow adequate range of movement without stressing the fibreglass.

Sheathing

In the enthusiastic early days fibreglass was hailed as the salvation for a rotten wooden boat: 'Cover it with fibreglass and scoop out the old boat.' Like many rosy-eyed ideas it was economically impractical. Since materials became cheaper, a lot of old boats have been covered with glass mat and most look like horrible floating doormats. The economics are still questionable. The proper application is on a boat in good condition, otherwise you may end up with rot *and* osmosis.

There are good and bad ways. Forty years ago I pioneered the good. Sadly the bad methods of those early days are not only still being repeated but recommended by suppliers and specified by authorities.

Sheathing is not the same as moulding. The materials may seem similar but the principles, purpose and method are quite different. Refer also to Chapter 20 (Bonding to wood).

Principles
The boat is the important thing. Sheathing is just a covering, so it must give with the boat yet still be strong enough to retain its integrity, bond and watertightness. If stronger it will pull the boat apart. If of similar strength there will be conflict, the likely outcome being failure of the bond and the sheathing peeling off

---

Ideal requirements for sheathing

Good adhesion
Watertight
No porosity
Smooth surface
Attractive finish
Simple application

---

intact. So the sheathing must be weaker than the boat. Conversely if the boat needs fibreglass to hold it together it is not worth the expense!

Strength should be related to the size and construction of the boat. Carvel or clinker could hardly be worse to sheathe. Movement is concentrated along the plank edges and imposes lines of high local stress. Plywood and double diagonal are suitable but they do not have leaking seams, the common reason for sheathing, all else having failed!

Glass fibre
Correct choice is the key to success. For strength without rigidity it must be thin. Only strong cloth fits the bill. But not just any cloth. Most of the confusing range are for pressure moulding to aerospace standards and the weave is too close to wet out by hand. For strength it must be close weave, yet not too close to wet out easily. As a rough guide it should look close yet be possible to see the time on a clock through it. A suitable weight is 7 oz/yd^2, 250 g/m^2.

The common, loose, very open weave scrim cloth is quite useless, although still very commonly used in ignorance because it is cheap and often the only cloth available. Suppliers even recommend it which shows how little many of them know about sheathing boats. Scrim has little strength and requires a

---

Pros and cons of sheathing

Advantages	Disadvantages
Cures leaks	Risk of peeling off
Waterproofs	Possible porosity
Low maintenance	Permeability
finish	Difficulty of application
Protection	Cost
against worms	Vulnerability
Non-slip finish	
Extra strength	

Wood preservative

It may seem a good precaution to douse the surface with preservative. But most contain either phenol or copper which poison polyester and prevent proper cure. On old wood it is difficult to tell if it has been used but should be the first thing suspected after inexplicable failure. In case of doubt use epoxy. Polyester itself is claimed to be a mild preservative.

Decks

Cabin tops and decks are sheathed more often than hulls, either as replacement for old canvas or from new. Modern plywood decks have a good, seam free surface. For a proper job fittings must be removed. The position can be marked by matchsticks in the screw holes which will pierce the cloth. Edges should be secured under beading rather than relying on bonding alone.

Certain weaves, notably mock leno, have a knobbly finish which gives a non-slip surface similar to a moulded pattern provided it is not flooded with resin. A prominent pattern is difficult to lay neatly in straight lines, and conspicuous if not. The natural uneven surface of mat is often used. This is wrong: if adequately finished with resin it will be too smooth, and if resin starved the fibres will be needle sharp (very nasty for barefoot sailors), wear badly and may not even be waterproof. Scrim cloth is disastrous. The only way the shallow weave can be prominent is by using too little resin, and then it will be like a sieve.

The best non-slip surface is sand or cork granules mixed into or sprinkled over the final coat of resin. Or use non-slip deck paint.

Translucent sheathing

When glass fibres are moulded they become almost invisible. They are not dissolved, as is sometimes thought. The resin makes good optical contact and as anybody knows, glass is transparent. A moulding is too uneven to be clear. Yet like ground glass, anything in contact is seen clearly. So a thin layer of translucent fibreglass reveals the wood like varnish. It has sometimes replaced varnish on deckhouses which persistently leak at the joints.

The bond must be perfect and the glass fibres thoroughly wetted. Special translucent resins based on methyl methacrylate instead of styrene have a near perfect refractive index with glass and give even clearer effect.

Unfortunately the varnishlike effect fades as the surface gets dull, dirty and scratched. Also, with natural ageing the resin/glass bond breaks down and fibres become visible.

A variation is laying up wood pattern printed paper behind a clear gel coat, before backing with ordinary moulding. This looks very convincing. But when the unreinforced gel coat cracks the paper fades, giving the show away. It is as effective and much stronger behind gauze or a layer of cloth.

Preparation

As with painting preparation is all important. Old paint must be removed down to bare wood. Sheathing is expensive. To rely on the bond of old paint is stupid. Ingrained paint will be difficult to remove; substantially clean, say 80%, is adequate.

Tar is particularly difficult. When burnt off it melts and soaks in further. Try soaking with paraffin (kerosene) or other solvents. In practice what will not come out will not come off either. Because of possible phenol epoxy is safer, but may be too expensive for the sort of old boat painted with tar for generations.

Dryness

The wood must be dry. Yet if it is too dry it will crack, and seams open wide. When it takes up the seams and cracks will close and force off the sheathing. The optimum state is 'dry' as in the table on page 146, ie atmospheric equilibrium at 60% RH. As a rough rule of thumb, by the time the boat has been ashore for a few months with the paint removed it should be dry enough. Unlike fibreglass, the commoner probe type moisture meters can be used.

Rot

Sheathing will not cure rot although by keeping wood below the critical moisture content it can halt or delay it. But the wood may still get wet from the other side and rot spores are persistent.

It is often alleged that wood will rot if it cannot 'breathe' and sheathing prevents this. Yet many a sound old boat has layers of paint

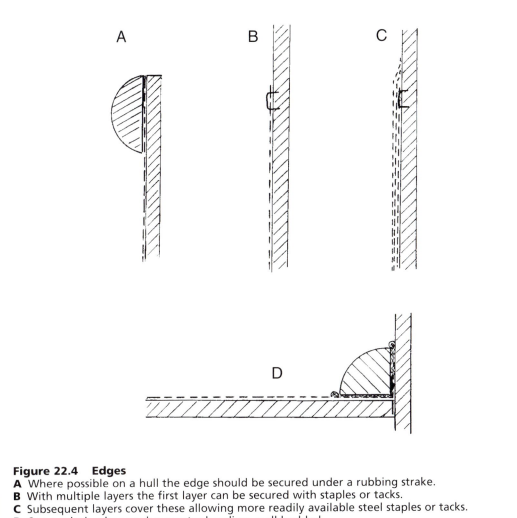

Figure 22.4   Edges
A Where possible on a hull the edge should be secured under a rubbing strake.
B With multiple layers the first layer can be secured with staples or tacks.
C Subsequent layers cover these allowing more readily available steel staples or tacks.
D Secure deck edges under quarter beading, well bedded.

on the bottom and in the bilges thick enough to suffocate anything. (It should be good protection against blistering on fibreglass too but it is unfashionable to suggest it!)

Edges

If sheathing is going to come off it will generally start at an edge. Therefore where possible edges should be secured (Fig 22.4). On a small boat, sheathed overall, the gunwale rubbing strake can be used. Deck edges should have beading as with a canvas deck. Where the edge cannot be under anything it should be fastened with screws, tacks or staples. Only the first layer needs to be secured.

Protection

Being thin sheathing is easily damaged, cut, crushed, and even torn off. Like all fibreglass, abrasion resistance is poor. Vulnerable areas therefore need protection with wood or metal, or built up locally with thick mat.

Damage

Sheathing can be patched easily. But what happens to the boat meantime? An exposed seam could be a serious leak. In tropical waters, teredo worms will exploit any breach in the defences as quickly as a commander in battle.

When the boat itself is damaged a wide area of sheathing must be removed to repair the wood beneath. Generally the sheathing is stronger than the bond and determined pulling will rip off what damage has not done already.

Practical difficulties

Convenient working conditions make a great difference to the quality of the sheathing. Unless small enough to turn over the bottom will have to be done overhead. If that means the worker lying on his back in mud with resin dripping into his face and hair the work is sure to be done badly. Do not underestimate the difficulties, discomfort and sheer unpleasantness of working underneath a boat.

It should be high enough to sit underneath. Use long handled rollers. Keeping one's hands at waist level is much less tiring. Wear protective clothing, especially head covering, and goggles are essential.

When weighted with wet resin the cloth will sag. Work with smallish, easily handled pieces. They may need to be held temporarily with ice-picks, staples or wedged with polythene covered battens. Long lengths can be pre-impregnated and wound on rollers, but generally it is easier to work with small, easily managed areas.

Gauze sheathing

A form of sheathing once advocated used surfacing gauze, the weakest form of glass fibre, to hold a thick layer of resin without providing strength. The idea was that if it came off it would flake away in small pieces instead of whole sheets as cloth sheathing would, possibly endangering the boat or damaging the screw. It had the blessing of the Admiralty. Now it has passed into limbo.

Caulking

At one time it was assumed that caulking was not necessary because sheathing made the hull watertight, especially for a leaky old boat that nothing else could keep afloat. That confidence sometimes extended to new boats too. The folly was amply demonstrated when a brand new boat had not gone more than a few miles out to sea before the badly applied sheathing came off and it sank.

The boat is the important thing. With or without the sheathing the boat must still stay afloat. Even if not indefinitely. That is plain common sense.

References

Instructions for Sheathing, Hugo du Plessis. Issued by Newtown Industries and Fibreclad Ltd.

Fibreglass Sheathing, Hugo du Plessis. Privately published, obtainable from the author.

Access

Access

One of least satisfactory features of modern boatbuilding is lack of access. After many years as a somewhat stout, stiff, surveyor, as well as yacht owner, I am convinced there must be great opportunities in the boat business for dwarfs and fairies or workers exceptionally small and slim. My fear, surveying a yacht up a lonely creek, was of getting stuck like Winnie-the-Pooh!

General practice is to fit out the hull and deck before joining together. At that stage access is easy, but very different after the lid goes on. Production convenience dominates building; maintenance and repair of the boat afterwards is of no concern to the builder. What does it matter if a repair costs a hundred times more than it need provided a few pounds or dollars can be saved in building? That is what insurance is for. The amazing thing is that insurance companies put up with it.

Engine

Engines interfere with the accommodation. Therefore they are boxed in tightly so builders can boast of ingeniously squeezing in berths for more people than any sane person would want to sail with. Yet no part of a boat, whether sail or power, needs attention more frequently or so importantly. The number of toilets is not nearly so important as access to the engine.

Routine maintenance, oil and water checks, oil changes etc must be convenient, otherwise they will not be done, yet done they must be. The absolute minimum requirement is to open a hatch and not have to reach over a hot dirty engine to get at an invisible dipstick. It sounds ridiculous but not uncommon. The stern tube must also be accessible by creatures larger than a rat.

Cleaning a fuel or water filter must not only be easy but very easy. Sooner or later it will have to be done at sea by somebody not feeling at all well and with patience minimal.

For seasonal servicing and minor repairs it is acceptable that some accommodation has to be dismantled. Good design will allow that. No work on the engine should require a devotee of extreme forms of yoga and the determination of a speleologist. Most do. Unfortunately, owners are apt to be stout or elderly, often both. So are the more experienced mechanics. Few people in this world can have been cursed so often and so vehemently as those who install boat engines.

During the life of the boat the engine will have to be taken out for major overhaul, repair or replacement, often with only on-board facilities. It is much easier and cheaper with a straight lift through the cockpit or wheelhouse. It is far harder, much longer and disgustingly dirty if it has to be levered up, slid somehow into the cabin, then up and out through a main hatch which may not be big enough, scarring fibreglass and woodwork as it goes and leaving a trail of black oil. And back again of course. What should be a simple half hour job becomes a day long struggle, plus a far bigger bill for crane hire. I speak with feeling from recent experience!

The choice of engine may be limited by simple matters like which side is the oil dipstick. Would it really be difficult for engine makers to have alternative positions for dipsticks and oil changes? Or to standardise?

Underwater fittings

More boats sink through defective plumbing than tempest. All through hull fittings are holes in the bottom. Seacocks must not only be easy to reach but easy to inspect, dismantle and replace. These too are installed when access is easy. Afterwards accommodation is often glassed on so close there is no room to use the large spanner needed or even unscrew the fitting. Pipe runs, now generally plastics with limited life, must also be accessible for regular inspection and replacement, especially the clips at both ends.

Services

All other pipes should be accessible too. Tanks, also built-in early, will need renewal without wrecking the accommodation. Wiring must never be embedded. Gas pipes should be exposed; hidden joints are very dangerous.

Decks

We nostalgically look at the exposed deck beams on friends' wooden boats but are persuaded the smoother, less cluttered inside of fibreglass is ugly and must be hidden.

A one-piece fibreglass deckhead lining looks clean and smooth but, being fitted at the same time as the deck, it too is there for keeps. Yet behind lie dozens of completely inaccessible fastenings, any one of which can break, work loose or leak. Also it is difficult to add extra fittings or update.

Detachable panels are far more practical and allow access to wiring too. A vinyl or fabric lining stuck to the underside of the deck moulding can be slit or cut away and replaced inconspicuously.

Repair

At any time a boat may be damaged, as likely when new as old. The only satisfactory repair is from inside (Chapters 40 and 41), which allows proper inspection and reinforcement of weakened areas beyond obvious external damage. If the attractive inner lining prevents access it has to be cut away. Replacement without leaving conspicuous scars requires much care and skill. Glued woodwork is even worse.

This makes repair far more expensive. If it is an insurance job the repairer can be ruthlessly destructive, although the owner who loves his boat may have very different views. So may the insurers.

At sea it must be possible to reach a bad leak (Chapters 18 and 39). A liferaft is a very poor and expensive substitute for a sock stuffed in the hole.

Additions

Many builders ignore the possibility, let alone necessity, that additions will be needed: the boat is perfect in every way; the owner should buy the latest model if he wants something better. Yet no owner is ever completely satisfied even with a new boat, and still less with what previous owners have done. Always he wants to improve his boat or add some new gadget, and every chandlery and boat show is full of temptations. Then the problems start. How to fit the new toy without pulling the boat apart? How to gain access to the inaccessible? Simple jobs become fraught with difficulties and end up being bodged.

Electronics, just science fiction when the boat was built, require wires and more wires. Large linings make running these difficult. Some far sighted builders run conduit to strategic points, yet generally underestimate the escalating demands.

The gel coat – that shiny fibreglass look

Beauty is skin deep, they say. What more of our body is seen? Similarly the gel coat is the only part seen of a fibreglass boat. To most people the gel coat is 'fibreglass'. But it is also the part exposed to weather and water, and bears the brunt of wear and damage.

CHAPTER

24

Gel coat

Fibreglass consists of glass fibres embedded in resin. This fibrous finish is not attractive. So it is hidden by a thick layer of unreinforced coloured resin, the gel coat, which also takes up the smooth, shiny finish of the mould in very exact detail. Being polyester the gel coat melds into the main moulding, and actually becomes part of the moulding in a way no paint or coating of dissimilar material could ever do.

Gel coats are somewhat different from moulding resins and formulated for good appearance, colour, water and weather resistance, freedom from crazing and cracking, abrasion resistance and other properties. The primary properties meet recognised standards but secondary ones depend on the emphasis placed on them by the manufacturers.

To cure properly gel coats depend on the mass of resin behind curing at the same time. Used alone they will not cure properly, so should not be used as surface coatings although this is often specified wrongly.

Purpose of gel coat
Just as important as the shiny, eye catching, coloured finish, is the protection given to the delicate structural fibres. Yet even more convenient for production because the boat comes out of the mould with a superb coloured finish needing no further work.

Application
The finish of a fibreglass boat is put on first. This may sound like putting the stern in the bows. Yet obviously it must be so because in

the usual female mould the gel coat is the first stage of moulding, applied to the mould face before the structural lay up.

The preferred method is by spray and to apply evenly the mould should be of contrasting colour. Timing is critical. The gel coat must set before moulding starts, otherwise it will be lifted or softened causing cosmetic defects. But delay will allow the surface to become contaminated and cause poor bonding. Evaporation of volatile constituents will cause undercure. Some gel coats contain wax and must be overcoated within a few hours.

Thickness
The thickness must be about 0.020 in, 0.5 mm, with a minimum of 0.012 in, 0.3 mm, and maximum 0.024 in, 0.6 mm. This is much thicker than a coat of paint, and would horrify a professional painter. But it is not decoration; it is part of the moulding.

If too thin the gel coat will not cure properly and be attacked by the next resin. The colour will be shadowy and it will be porous. Check thickness with a wet gauge (Fig 24.1).

Types of gel coat
The terms orthophthalic, isophthalic, vinyl ester and others refer to the acid from which polyester resins are made. No need to go further. Leave chemistry to the chemists!

Orthophthalic resins
In earlier days there were only orthophthalic resins, and they are still the cheapest. Most boats built before about 1980 have orthophthalic gel coats.

Isophthalic resins
Recommended gel coats for marine use are now isophthalic because they are somewhat less permeable than orthophthalic. But the

changeover was gradual. A few good moulders are still sceptical.

Being more expensive to make some suppliers add a modest quantity of isophthalic resin to an orthophthalic and call that isophthalic. To be effective it must be 100% isophthalic, but only a chemist can tell the difference.

Vinylester
Vinylester has even lower permeability and is yet more expensive. It has greater flexibility and hence is the preferred choice for thin hi-tech hulls. It is now recommended as a barrier coat behind an isophthalic gel coat.

Other resins
Gel coats have been developed with still less permeability but, like wonder drugs, often have undesirable side effects for marine use. The main ones are neopentyl glycol-isophthalic, and bisphenol polyester. All are expensive, some are not yet approved whereas good old polyester is universally accepted.

Builders often make exaggerated claims for their own secret formulae despite not having been proved for long enough by practical use in all waters. But with worry about 'osmosis' super gel coats are good for sales. It is wise to distrust secrecy. It may be just a poorly tried bright idea. The owner will not be told his boat is a guinea pig. A resin manufacturer has far better facilities for research and testing than any moulder and a reputation to uphold.

The merits of epoxy tend to be overrated. Although commonly used to repair or replace a gel coat, it should not be used during moulding. Epoxy will bond to polyester, but only if cured because it is affected by free styrene. Polyester will not bond to epoxy gel coat.

Epoxy gel coats should be used only with all-epoxy mouldings. But suppliers do not make special gel coats or supply resins ready coloured. The finish and weather resistance are generally not as good as polyester.

Colour
All colours change with exposure to sunlight and weather so they are difficult to match even with a batch of original gel coat. Moreover a good match may fade differently and become conspicuous later.

Types of gel coat

Orthophthalic
Isophthalic
Vinyl ester
Neopentyl-glycol
Bisphenol polyester
Copperclad
Epoxy

Photos 24.1 (a) Streaky gel coat due to differential weathering. The gel coat was badly mixed and settled out when brushed. Being coloured it was probably hand mixed.
(b) Worms? Not yet. Selective non-absorption of waterline stains. Various possibilities: mixing (in this case marginally better), overspray or cosmetic repairs after moulding.

Whites and pastel shades are the most durable and should last ten to twenty years but do tend to yellow, generally unnoticeable unless compared with a new 'Persil White' boat or repaired with a supposedly matching colour. There are several hundred thousand shades of white. Lower permeability is claimed for light colours possibly because white being the strongest and most opaque pigment less is needed.

Dark blue, green and black weather badly and can get blotchy after a few years. Brilliant red and orange cadmium colours are good but banned in some countries as cadmium is no longer 'green'. Few good yellows do not contain cadmium and may soon become hard to obtain. Non-cadmium reds and oranges are little better than blue and green. The worst are glitter colours behind a clear gel coat. This soon dulls and so does the sparkle of the dyed aluminium flakes beneath.

Bright colours, like brilliant dirty dawn orange, and also black and dark colours can be almost translucent, not nearly as opaque as anaemic baby blue and pastel shades based on white pigment.

The densest colours are obtained by grinding pigment into the gel coat with a ball mill, normally by the manufacturer as a standard colour. For non-standard colours the moulder must stir colour paste into uncoloured stock, but this cannot be done as thoroughly. Consequently more paste has to be used, and the carrier, a plasticiser or non-marine polyester, has an adverse effect. Being impossible to repeat hand mixing precisely, all gel coat needed must be coloured in one batch. Even small differences are conspicuous.

As colours take no part in the reaction they are passengers, a possible source of WSMs and sometimes contaminants. They can affect the setting time by as much as 100%. There seems no particular rule.

Double gel coats

Some claim double gel coats are better. To avoid the combination being too thick, each must be thin so may not cure properly, or may be attacked by the following resin. Timing is critical: they often separate if the interval is too long, or the interface contaminated by condensation.

Clear gel coat

Uncoloured gel coats are often used underwater to eliminate a possible cause of blistering but being more difficult to control thickness, may itself be a contributory cause. Surveyors bless it as the moulding quality can be seen.

Copperclad

An early claim was that weed and barnacles would not grow on smooth shiny fibreglass. Nobody told the barnacles, however. A fibreglass bottom is as desirable a residence as anywhere else. Evidence suggests they may prefer it.

Yet a self-antifouling bottom has long been a dream. Copper foil can be glued on but is still an external cladding. Copperclad developed by Scott Bader Ltd, but now supplied only by Ferro in America, is a gel coat containing 70% finely powdered copper. The only treatment needed is abrading the surface before launching to expose copper. Afterwards it is claimed bottom painting will never be needed. However, it is a necessary part of the guarantee to clean off slime every 3–4 months which could mean frequent haul out or employing a diver. Some users find annual abrading is needed.

It can be applied either in mould or later but only by an approved contractor. Reactivation after 3–5 years must also be done by a contractor as well as any repairs. Ordinary anti-fouling is certainly much simpler and probably cheaper. It seems more suitable for boats kept in well serviced home waters than those more distant where it really would be valuable.

Some boats have had problems with electrolysis.

Permeability

Polyester is not the sieve it is reputed to be. *All* plastics including epoxy are slightly permeable because their long chain molecular structure allows the much smaller water molecules to slip between. No paint is impermeable either although some are better than others.

Relative permeabilities are roughly:

Two pack polyurethane	1
Epoxy	2–4
Polyester	6

But that is not the full story. Permeability also depends on thickness. Polyurethane paint is always very thin. Epoxy can be built up to a thicker coating but still generally thinner than a polyester gel coat. Thickness evens the score. So does price.

Polyester gel coat will be applied under controlled moulding shop conditions, maybe not ideal but close. Epoxy and polyurethane will be used under field conditions which vary widely, especially epoxy with its claim to be applicable in cold, damp weather. Figures for the superiority of epoxy are generally cooked and apply only when heat cured. At room temperature it is only 75–80% at best.

Consequently a good polyester gel coat is probably about as impermeable as other coatings despite their theoretical superiority. Blistering, widely attributed to the permeability of polyester gel coats, is basically due to imperfections in the moulding behind (Chapter 26). Certainly gel coats can be improved. But a better gel coat to protect a bad moulding is not the right solution.

What goes in with difficulty will come out with difficulty. Therefore water which does penetrate a lower permeability gel coat is trapped to a greater extent. So blistering is more likely although it may take longer.

Most research has been directed to lower permeability gel coats. Yet some experts suggest this is the wrong approach. Why not deliberately make gel coats permeable so that what gets in can get out? Moreover, being in effect free flooding, the concentration would not develop into aggressive 'blister juice'.

However, it does require sound moulding, probably beyond the present ability of most moulders under production conditions and, even more, present inclinations. It raises the interesting, albeit heretical, idea that boasting of a wonderful new impermeable gel coat does not indicate technical excellence but an admission the builder cannot mould a sound boat!

Increasing water resistance

A common precaution is painting with epoxy. The ideal time is when new as the hull is absolutely dry. Later it traps water which, although not evident, may already be aggressive 'blister juice', thereby making things worse.

Epoxy is not magic. To be effective it must be of comparable thickness to a gel coat and more expensive than most owners feel necessary. A thin coat gives no worthwhile protection, although often offered as a profitable sales gimmick. Epoxy underwater must be solventless. Most epoxy paints contain solvents which get trapped and are themselves a source of blistering. I have seen epoxy paint blister worse in six months than bad polyester in six years!

An epoxy interlayer has been used between the gel coat and lay up, a typical poorly tested bright idea that does not work. The gel coat is isolated so the essential melding with the main moulding is lost and it does not cure properly. Epoxy may bond to the gel coat, but the moulding polyester does not bond to the hard shiny epoxy. Consequently the gel coat plus epoxy separates. The same happens when epoxy is used for the whole gel coat.

Vinyl ester makes a better interlayer because it is compatible with polyester and bonds chemically.

Permeability can be reduced by incorporating silica flakes (Fig 24.2). These align in the plane of the coating so water has to traverse a longer zig-zag path. Loading with water repellant filler makes resins brittle. Microballon filler behind the gel coat has been seen but came away in chunks.

Increasing thickness is logical. But if total gel coat thickness is much above 0.024 in, 0.6 mm, it becomes liable to crack. The correct approach is to reinforce with surfacing gauze.

All coatings yet developed or likely to be are permeable. It is a matter of degree. A supposedly better coating may have disadvantages, eg poor colour or low resilience. Some may require specialist application, heat curing or exceptionally good conditions, otherwise they are worse than theoretically less efficient coatings.

There is still little to beat a good polyester gel coat. Many have now lasted twenty-five years without painting. Compare that with most paints under marine conditions and the average guarantee of only five years for epoxy gel coat replacement.

Cracks

Gel coats crack mainly because the underlying resin or moulding has cracked due to over-strain and are therefore a valuable guide to hidden damage (Chapters 5 and 42). They are not a minor cosmetic problem but a warning that internal damage has already reached a significant level.

Nowadays some authorities stipulate gel coats must have higher elongation than the underlying resin to prevent cracking. This eliminates those vital warning signs so invaluable to an experienced surveyor. However, it is likely the substrate will still win and cracks appear but not until nearer catastrophic failure.

Cracks invariably extend the full depth of the gel coat, never mere surface cracks as often supposed. Consequently they bypass the gel coat and open the moulding to water and weather. If, as is probable, this is cracked too, capillary paths will go deep.

Gel coats usually crack in tension, less often in compression. New cracks will be flush, almost invisible. As they weather the edges tend to curl and dirt makes them visible. This indicates their age.

Gel coat defects

Most gel coat defects occur while moulding but are not apparent until after release from the mould. By then the moulding is painfully expensive to scrap just because of cosmetic blemishes. A good moulder will take trouble to make them good. It is time consuming but with skill they can be invisible, although often reappear later, after the guarantee has expired due to weathering and age.

Cavities

Cavities occur on almost every boat. Good moulders know this and look for them. Others leave them for the owner to find. They should be few, although I found 365 on one deck (at that point I gave up counting).

Gel coat defects	
Cavities	Fisheyes
Wrinkles	Streaks
Crazing	Blotchiness
Delamination	Fading
Pinholes	Speckles

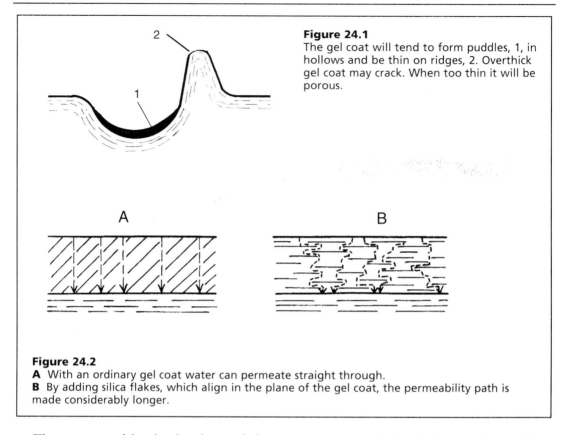

Figure 24.1
The gel coat will tend to form puddles, 1, in hollows and be thin on ridges, 2. Overthick gel coat may crack. When too thin it will be porous.

Figure 24.2
A With an ordinary gel coat water can permeate straight through.
B By adding silica flakes, which align in the plane of the gel coat, the permeability path is made considerably longer.

They are caused by the first layer of glass not being in intimate contact with the gel coat, usually because it was not worked fully into features; less commonly on flattish surfaces due to rucking. The first layer must be thin glass mat, 1 oz/ft², 300 g/m², which can be worked easily into difficult places. It should not be thick mat, as sometimes used for speed, still less two layers at once, and never the cohesive, more difficult to mould woven rovings. When sprayed, cavities can be due to premature setting, bad gun adjustment, trying to cover too large an area or hold ups.

The first couple of layers are by far the most important of the whole boat and must be very carefully moulded regardless of how long it takes. There is skill to moulding but too often emphasis on production speed does not allow it. Cavities reflect the management policy.

It may be years before the eggshell thin crust of the gel coat breaks and the cavity appears. It has not developed as often thought but was there all the time. (One has just appeared on my own boat, now twenty years old.) Cavities are easily detected by tapping or running a rounded tool along angles and features (Chapter 43). They should be broken open and filled, especially underwater. If one is found look nearby for more; they usually come in groups (Fig 24.3).

Wrinkles
These look like a centipede or dried apple. They are caused by the next resin, whether lay up or a second gel coat, being applied too soon and softening the first before it has properly set. Also if the gel coat is too thin. The treatment is to fill with gel coat or coloured filler, and polish to match.

Crazing
A widespread pattern of cracks like crazy paving is now uncommon. Unlike other defects this can appear later. It may be one of the terminal factors. Local crazing is common due to heat around exhaust pipes or from pouring hot fat into fibreglass sinks and also exposure to fire.

In early days crazing was a common problem. Soon more flexible gel coats were developed

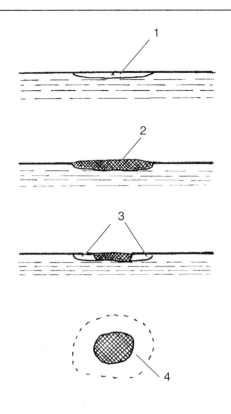

Figure 24.3 Gel coat cavities
Small cavities behind the gel coat, 1, are extremely common. Most boats have them. When found they should be opened and filled, 2. Note: they must be opened completely. Very often only the middle is filled, 3, leaving a halo, 4.

but brought other problems including a serious epidemic of blistering. Since then general crazing has become very uncommon, although there is evidence that it will be a feature of age and weathering. Some gel coats are too good, emphasis on weather and water resistance has reduced their resilience so they have a tendency to crack.

Delamination

Properly applied a gel coat forms a chemical bond with the moulding beneath. Any separation of the gel coat shows the bond was poor, probably due to contaminated interface eg condensation, or delay so the waxy surface of some gel coats prevented good adhesion, or wrong moulding technique.

Pinholes

Here the gel coat is full of champagne sized bubbles and pinholes are the tips. Permeability will be high as water takes short cuts through the bubbles.

A common reason for this is using cold gel coat brought in from outside storage. Other causes are over vigorous stirring coupled with short setting time, a badly adjusted spray gun, or spraying in high humidity. Patches indicate a locally thin gel coat, places the moulding stuck, or an unobtrusive repair.

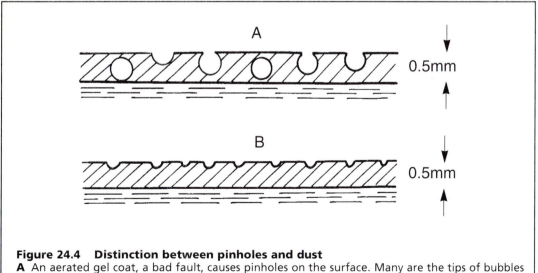

Figure 24.4 Distinction between pinholes and dust
A An aerated gel coat, a bad fault, causes pinholes on the surface. Many are the tips of bubbles beneath.
B Dust on the mould leaves a similar appearance and can be mistaken for aerated gel coat. The difference is easy to see as dust pits are blind and shallow.

Photo 24.2 Badly etched gel coat due to using strong paint remover not approved for fibreglass.

Dust on the mould causes a deceptively similar effect, but on close inspection the holes are blind (Fig 24.4).

Fisheyes

Spots of thin gel coat surrounded by weak colour are caused by the gel coat not wetting the mould surface; usually due to wrong release agent or condensation on the mould.

Streaky colour

Brushing can induce colour separation. Colours can settle in the can so always stir before use. Colour pastes must be very well mixed otherwise the gel coat will be patchy or fade differentially later.

Along the waterline oil can be absorbed and form brown stains. Selective absorption or leaching forms patterns which sometimes resemble worms, and fuel interesting speculation.

Speckles

Speckles of different colour are common when a two-coloured gel coat is used for a boot top or styling flash due to overspray or drips settling on the adjoining part. Nothing can be done because they are as much part of the gel coat as the rest. It may also be overspray from adjacent moulds or even paint.

Is a gel coat necessary?

As gel coats cause so much trouble why have one at all? Both protection and appearance could be obtained by other means. With mouldless construction gel coat is impossible anyway. In most manufacture finishing in some form is normal practice. A few moulders in early days did dispense with gel coats, using familiar industrial finishing techniques.

The advantages of a gel coat lie mainly with the builder; the disadvantages with later owners. The boat comes out of the mould with a perfect finish requiring no costly paint system. The builder just gives a final polish before it goes out of the gate. For production this is a tremendous saving.

Gel coats are fashionable and now considered a basic part of 'fibreglass', the essential basis of the 'no maintenance' myth. Although now accepted that fibreglass does need painting after some years and modern paints last almost as long as gel coat, it would be suicidal for a builder to say the boat was painted and, by implication, would need repainting. Even at long intervals. Actually some new boats are painted, especially non-standard colours or to hide defective gel coats, but the owner does not know.

A really soundly moulded hull does not need a gel coat to keep the water out. But with the present state of the art and under normal production pressures no boatbuilder can mould sound enough hulls and few want to try.

At present there is nothing so suited to production techniques. Like them or not, gel coats will be around for a long time yet.

References
J A Raymond, Scott Bader 8th International RP Conference (1973).
Glass Reinforced Plastics, edited by Brian Parkyn.

25

Weathering

Early claims that fibreglass would last for ever and never need maintenance were audaciously optimistic. Those who believed them were naive to fly in the face of common sense. Yet the myth lingers.

Nevertheless polyester gel coats on the whole do give a good long lasting finish, much better than most paints and plastics including epoxy. However, emphasis on improved physical properties may be at the expense of weathering.

Effect of weather

When new a gel coat will be very smooth, glossy and easily polished. It is solid, sheds water and shrugs off stains. As it ages the weather will etch and erode the surface where exposed. The gloss fades, it becomes difficult to clean and feels rough. A tonneau cover leaves a shadow. So will a former name. The boat looks dingy like the ruins of a Greek temple once a glory of polished marble.

Soluble constituents of the gel coat are leached out by rain. The surface becomes absorbent. Along the waterline it soaks up oil, especially light harbour oil.

In good condition red penetrant stain, a favourite tool with experienced surveyors, can be wiped off without leaving a trace. When weathered it soaks in like water into sand. Testing can be embarrassing; the boat looks as if the surveyor has murdered someone.

Obviously leaching starts on the surface. Yet in time the whole gel coat becomes like a sponge. Gel coats showing other defects like pinholes or blotchiness weather more quickly than good ones. As most boats have the same gel coat above and below the waterline, prematurely weathered topsides are a warning that the bottom is probably poor too.

Colour

All colours fade (Chapter 24). Bright colours lose their brilliance, largely from reduced surface gloss. Constituents are leached selectively with white being the least affected.

Abrasive polishing will bring up fresh colour from underneath but thins the gel coat and can be done only occasionally.

Hot climates

All weathering is faster and more severe in hot climates. When wet it is wetter, when dry the sunlight more intense. Generally both, not only seasonally but often several times a day. Yet crews are drawn to sunny waters like flies to a honey pot without considering the effect on their boats when they get there.

White and light colours are cooler, as is well known, and reduce degradation by sunlight. Particularly severe conditions are where rainwater lies on deck. Fresh water heated by the sun to hot bath temperature is an aggressive combination.

Boats are commonly laid up ashore during the hottest or wettest months. Stored upside down, conditions for the bottom will be similar to accelerated weathering tests in a laboratory.

Cold weather

Once the surface becomes etched and porous the gel coat will absorb and hold water. When this freezes it spreads physical breakdown, like frost damage in concrete. Gel coat cavities are extended further like highway potholes, especially the very common pinholes in the peaks of diamond pattern moulded tread.

In extreme cold fibreglass contracts. Some high quality gel coats do not have sufficient resilience and crack. So does putty and fairing.

Boats built for the intensely cold but very dry Scandinavian and North American winters often weather badly in milder, wetter climates.

Time scale

A good gel coat should last unpainted at least ten years even in an aggressive climate. Many have gone twenty or more. A modern gel coat which deteriorates because of weather in less than ten years was sub-standard.

Red herrings

Beware, it might not be the gel coat at fault. Old polish gets dull and dirty. Weathered paint can seem like a faulty gel coat. Many owners are unaware the boat has been painted perhaps from new. It may be a clue that a second-hand boat has been repaired.

Crazing

Some old decks and cabin tops show a fine pattern of crazing all over. The boats which I have seen had all been exposed to North American winters so it may have been aggravated by contraction in extreme cold. It could be one of the long term effects, perhaps terminal for gel coats, if not protected by paint.

Protection

The topsides get the attention but the deck and cabin top are the parts most exposed to the weather.

Gel coats last longer and better if protected. Of that there is absolutely no doubt. While 'no maintenance' has sold millions of boats it has probably ruined even more!

The best protection, like Sir Joseph Porter KCB in *HMS Pinafore*, is never go to sea. Many a sailor on a dirty night, and even more seasick passengers, might agree. Yet the ravages of weather are as bad in a marina as at sea.

The first protection which should be applied from the start is polish (Chapter 36). This will keep the gel coat in good condition for many years, perhaps indefinitely. Many owners polish their boat to keep it smart all summer, when it is less needed. Come winter when protection really is needed the poor thing sits naked and forlorn.

A good winter cover keeps rain and snow off the deck where it does most harm. It must be padded at points of contact to prevent wear and well tied down. A cover flapping all winter will make deep scratches. Undercover storage is best of all, although there is an old saying that the more expensive the storage the more the roof leaks! Plus the dust of ages and fallout from roosting pigeons and sparrows.

26

Nasty little lumps

Nothing turns bold sailors with fibreglass boats so pale with fright as that dreaded word 'osmosis', popularly known as 'boat pox': nasty little lumps on a boat's bottom which were not there before. Blisters may be a terminal factor, but more economic than physical.

Blistering is one of the undesirable features we have discovered since those optimistic pioneering days when we boldly proclaimed fibreglass boats would last for ever, perfect in every way. However, it is not confined to boats. Swimming pools and showers are as bad (what is a pool but a boat inside out?), and I had a case of 'churchpox': blisters on a fibreglass spire!

Note: I deliberately say blistering not osmosis. Blistering is a large family of similar effects. The main thing in common is causing owners sleepless nights. They take many forms and there are hundreds of causes. Osmosis is never a cause. It is sometimes an effect.

Much research has been done in recent years to discover the basic causes. The principal conclusion is that the subject is very complicated, and the more discovered the more complicated it gets. There is no one simple cause. Always it is a combination. To generalise is to be wrong. Even researchers cannot agree and weight different factors according to whether they are chemists, physicists, or practical fibreglass specialists, often biased by commercial interest and a rodeo of hobby horses.

Even osmosis is far from simple. It can occur for different reasons and take different forms during the course of development.

This research has, or should have, led to better boats. But that is no help to the owners of the great majority built earlier, now mostly middle aged and ripe for blistering. They want to know why *their* boat is blistering. The

effect is obvious. The important thing is the cause.

Blisters are nothing new. My first case was in 1958: a deck. Osmosis? Not at all. The cause was bad moulding, like most blistering still. A Kestrel dinghy had been stored upside down; water in the forepeak soaked through the porous moulding until stopped by the gel coat. Nearly forty years later I have found a similar case in an almost new boat. Is this to be the pattern? Errors repeated generation after generation? A cynic might ask why fibreglass boats should be different from any other activity of mankind!

Gel coat replacement is now accepted treatment: far too accepted and often unnecessary. Simpler options are not considered. It is not even as permanent as the original gel coat.

The most undesirable aspect is the acceptance that expensive treatment has to be repeated at, to me, unacceptably short intervals. Or that it is necessary at all. That was never the dream of the founding fathers of fibreglass boats, however misjudged our idealism. It makes nonsense of the low maintenance image which played such a major role in getting fibreglass boats accepted at all and still does. It is part of the regrettable resurgence of the view of yachting as a rich man's sport. Or nowadays a 'Yuppie' sport.

Moreover it compares very badly with all but the worst wooden boats.

History

Many early boats have shown little tendency to blister. Why? (Admittedly, plenty developed so many other defects they did not last long enough to blister!) It was before the days of marinas, an influence seldom appreciated. The custom was to lay up ashore every winter

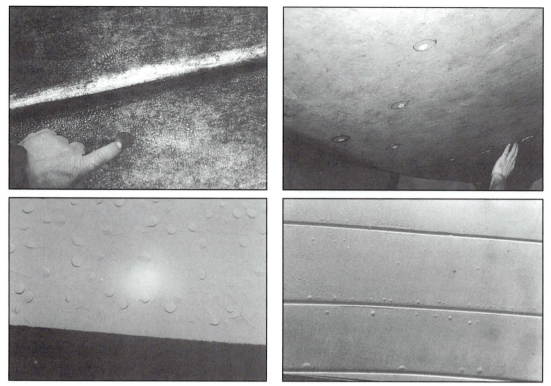

Photos 26.1 (a) Extensive overall blistering after five years afloat in fresh water. Too late to save the gel coat.
  Interpretation: poor moulding behind with masses of voids.
(b) Random blisters on a Sadler after nine years. The well known expert surveyor insisted the gel coat must be replaced.
  Interpretation: quite unnecessary to remove the gel coat. The fault is clearly voids in the moulding. Opening and filling blisters as they appear every few years will keep this gel coat going for many years.
(c) Crescent shaped cracked blisters.
  Interpretation: old blisters, at least five years, possibly ten. Once broken they cannot develop further, osmosis is impossible, but the moulding beneath is exposed and the gel coat will be gradually undermined.
(d) Lines of blisters parallel to a feature, viz, 'mock planking' grooves.
  Interpretation: the groove was rounded off with filler for easier moulding but not feathered (Fig 13.9).

so the boats regularly dried out. Nowadays many boats lie afloat in sheltered berths all year and consequently do not dry out regularly.

In early days materials were subtly different and in many ways better. Most improvements have been directed to easier production, quicker wetting out, faster moulding and mould turn round, not to better water resistance and fewer water soluble molecules. Only recently has it been realised there were such things. It would have been heresy to suggest fibreglass was not completely water resistant for ever.

Although large, the boat industry is not the

biggest user. In the USA it ranks third and a large part of that is small boats. For most other uses, easy, fast, economic moulding is a main requirement. Unlike boats added value tends to be small. But if there is economic advantage, production orientated boat moulders will also be strongly attracted. Most are minor subsidiaries of large conglomerates, with head office accountants on their backs.

That these easily moulded, more economic materials may have undesirable long term effects is ignored, even if anyone realises. In most cases nobody does until years later. To most builders the main consideration has not been whether the boat will blister but would it do so before the guarantee expired?

This search for cheaper production is a major reason why fibreglass boats, especially those of middle age, are prone to blister. Yet the savings are small compared with the fully equipped cost of the boat.

The disease

In the popular view there is one disease – 'osmosis'. Most clinics, surveyors and other experts seem to think so too. As with our bodies many ailments can cause a rash, blister or lump on our skins, from midge bites to chickenpox to cancer. It is similar with boats. There are many causes and many forms of blisters, all needing different treatment. Adding to owners' worries are red herrings, not blisters at all.

Blisters are not an option like rot in wood, that may or may not destroy originally sound material. Fibreglass boats blister because they are built to blister. Sooner or later they will, and keep on blistering because the moulding has fundamental defects. As that includes nearly every boat built so far, it is endemic under past and present standards of moulding, and the future looks little better.

The relevant point is how soon it occurs. That depends on the state of art at the time but above all on quality of moulding. This is the obvious factor far too often forgotten. Some good boats have gone twenty, even thirty years without blistering. Badly moulded ones – no more than as many weeks.

Conditions during moulding have a crucial influence. There is now greater awareness and control. Yet most boats afloat today were not moulded under ideal conditions: nowadays they would be regarded as downright unsuitable yet they were acceptable at the time.

The improved modern gel coats are mostly directed to keeping the boat blister free until the guarantee has expired. Basically this means a more waterproof gel coat so the hulls can be moulded with greater production speed and lower quality. Improved gel coats may delay but never solve the problem. Only improved moulding quality will ever make boats blister free. Marginal moulding quality, not 'osmosis', really is the disease.

Diagnosis

The first and most important thing is to discover the root cause. Without accurate diagnosis any treatment is guesswork. It may work – for a time. But it is not a professional repair, merely treating the symptoms, not the ailment.

Some surveyors know little about fibreglass. Their impressive qualifications often mean they know more about steel supertankers than fibreglass boats. Like the Red Queen in *Alice in Wonderland*, their stock remedy is 'Off with his head'. Or in this case 'Off with the gel coat'. They have heard it is the thing to do but their knowledge is too limited to realise there may be alternatives, or not the right thing at all. To them there is only one defect – 'osmosis' – and therefore only one remedy.

Proper diagnosis requires an expert on fibreglass moulding, a specialist in plastics not steel or wood. Moreover he needs to be something of a historian because he must know how boats used to be moulded, as well as the latest research into the causes. An ordinary surveyor is like a GP. Medical practice is to refer a patient to a consultant.

To most people a surveyor, just because he calls himself a surveyor, is regarded as an expert on everything to do with boats. Few owners question his verdict, but surveyors are very far from infallible. (Only an honest and humble surveyor knows how fallible!) They are generally expert in only one material and a few of the many parts of a modern boat.

Yet as well as technical knowledge and experience the most important and frequently overlooked ability is simply taking the trouble to examine blisters carefully. Distrust any surveyor who does not examine blisters with a microscope or powerful magnifier. Too many jump to conclusions.

Why does fibreglass blister?

Would that we really knew. A lot has been written in recent years about what is now known following further research, but very little about what we still do *not* know. Fibreglass is by no means the simple material we used to think. There are unlimited variables. Every boat is different, even within the same class, and some a lot more different than others. A great many things can go wrong during mould-ing, generally minor but some catastrophic, without anyone having the faintest idea. And in most cases nobody bothers to find out – until the boat starts blistering ten years later!

It is generally assumed that because blisters appear on the gel coat it must be the gel coat at fault. This is true only when blisters appear early, eg two years. In nearly all other cases the cause is in the moulding beneath or the inter-face. The gel coat blisters only because it is in the way. Often it is the best part of the boat.

What are these hidden time bombs?

In general they are water soluble molecules, WSMs. But that covers a great many things, to some extent everything the boat is made of. Another myth bites the dust. The idea of a fibreglass boat dissolving in water may sound alarming – a good bar horror story. (What about steel boats rusting away?) However, sol-uble does not mean instantly like a lump of sugar. It takes years.

Polyester resin is not a single compound. As well as being a blend of resins, to make it usable it has solvents, monomer, hardeners, thixotropic agents, plasticiser and other things. Left over from manufacture is a small excess of unreacted components, usually gly-cols. Because moulding is a crude process there are small pockets of resin which have not set or cured properly, or even cured too well. Water from condensation and the atmosphere can be in there from the start. There may be dust too and that may be anything. Whatever falls into the mould becomes part of the boat.

Although technically insoluble polyester can be hydrolysed, ie broken down into sim-pler substances which are soluble. When poly-ester resin polymerises it forms vast crosslinked chain molecules hundreds, even thousands of groups long. It is unrealistic to assume every crosslink is perfect. There will be many which did not find a partner. If, later, a water molecule can grab a free linkage it will break that chain into smaller units. The mass of large molecules will still be enmeshed in the glass fibres and retain considerable strength but some of the molecules which split off will be small and soluble.

Other constituents may be unaffected yet absorb moisture, notably finely divided silica thixotropes. These wet pockets then attack the surrounding resin.

Components which do not actually take part in the reaction will be left embedded like raisins in a plum duff. Nobody seems to have wondered until recently what effect they might have. Harmless passengers or fifth column?

It is too simple to say what should happen. 100% perfection does not happen even in a laboratory. It is very different under practical production conditions and economic pres-sures. The polymerisation, the 'making' of the fibreglass, is done in the mould with virtually no control. Workers may know what to do but not why. None are trained chemists, scientists or even laboratory assistants, and in earlier days, working on the boats giving trouble now, they were often untrained labourers doing what was regarded as unskilled messy work. There is absolutely no comparison with the close, carefully monitored control of a chemical factory or indeed a modern factory production line making cheap washing machines.

The wonder is that the complicated chem-ical reaction of polyester polymerisation turns out as well as it does!

Glass fibres contribute too. No glass is pure silicon dioxide. Although inert enough in the form of a bottle, very fine fibres are more easi-ly eroded releasing soluble salts. Glass mat has a binder to hold it together for handling. Emulsion binder based on PVA, much used earlier as it wetted out more readily and was fully approved, is now known to be hygroscop-ic and a major source of WSMs. It is no longer approved in Europe although sometimes still used in America. Cloth too has a size to lubri-cate for weaving.

Glass is difficult to bond on to so fibres are given a special coating which is usually silane based. This is the least water resistant compo-nent and one reason fibres soon become visi-ble as white strands.

Glass fibres and resins used in boatbuilding are general purpose materials. This fibre treat-ment is a typical case where development to improve strength or speed of moulding for other industries was discovered later to have undesirable side effects for marine use.

Very few moulders understand the finer points of their materials. They are not organic chemists and rely on their suppliers who are not boatbuilders and may not understand either. Anyway, choice of materials is usually based more on ease of moulding and price.

So much for the materials, even assuming perfect moulding. But practical production moulding is never perfect, and quality of moulding is critical.

The single key factor is water and all fibreglass mouldings are permeable no matter how waterproof the claims. When water permeates through the gel coat into the moulding, it slowly dissolves the WSMs. Plain sea or fresh water is relatively harmless, which may seem a contradiction. But in dissolving WSMs it becomes acid. The concentration increases if trapped and becomes aggressive and self-accelerating. It is this 'blister juice', not water itself, which does the damage.

Permeability

All plastics are slightly permeable. The water molecule is very small and mobile. It can slip between the huge chain molecules of polyester like a small, thin child in a crowd. On a larger scale, fibreglass is a composite of resin and glass fibres; a jungle not a brick wall. So there will be capillary movement along fibres.

Hydrostatic pressure, another claim, is unlikely as blisters are not related to depth and often worst in the splash zone above.

The surprise is not that it is slightly permeable but waterproof at all, and a few fibreglass boats have not even been that.

Permeation is inevitable, a law of nature, but not enough to sink the boat even when badly moulded. Normally it would never be noticed as moisture goes right through and out the other side, like it does with wood. The important thing is what happens on the way.

Bilge water

It is sometimes claimed that blisters are caused by bilge water attacking the gel coat from behind. In practice, with a sound moulding the amount will be insignificant compared with permeation from outside. It could happen only with thin, very bad moulding and obviously be limited to that area. It is a warning sign, although if the moulding really is that bad it is probably badly blistered all over anyway.

Bonding

A perfectly bonding gel cannot blister. Obviously the easier it is to separate the gel coat the easier it is to force it into a blister. In theory the gel coat melds into the main moulding and forms an integral part not just a coating. In practice this bond is often far from perfect. The first lay up should follow as soon as the gel coat is hard enough. If left too long, notably the common habit of leaving overnight, the gel coat surface can become contaminated especially by invisible condensation.

If the underside of a broken blister is smooth the bond was poor. Well bonded gel coat cannot be chipped off. Some contain wax to prevent air inhibition and give a better cure. Unless timing is exactly right, difficult with a boat sized moulding, the waxy surface prevents a perfect bond. Environmental resins can also prevent good adhesion.

The bond between the first and second layers is equally important. There should be no pause until built up to about $1/8$ in, 3 mm.

Water absorption

Wood is a honeycomb of cells which, in a boat, can fill fairly harmlessly with its own weight of water. In contrast fibreglass has no cells to store water. So when the resin swells the only way is up. The gel coat is first raised into solid pimples before being forced into blisters, often dry. It usually means a poor quality gel coat, accompanied by other signs like poor finish. Osmosis is not involved.

Normally water absorbed by the resin will be small. 3% is a wet moulding, mostly confined to the surface layers and evenly spread. Only in a bubble sized void can it become concentrated. Even so most blisters, and hence voids, contain only a trace, a smear, barely enough to smell. Large, deep ones still contain no more than a few drops, perhaps half a teaspoonful.

Water may be trapped during moulding. If careless there can be condensation on the glass fibre, mould, gel coat or in resin drums.

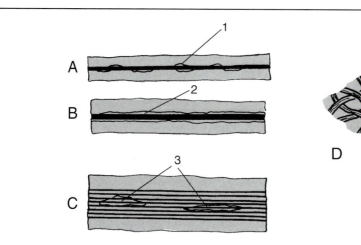

Figure 26.1   Microvoids
A Fibres do not wet completely. There will be microvoids along every fibre, 1.
B With age, use, water absorption, hydrolysis of coupling agent, damage etc, these will spread, 2.
C Fibres are bunched into strands which also do not wet out completely and will have small dry patches in the middle, 3.
D Woven materials crimp at crossover points. This doubles thickness and tightens strands, making it even harder to wet out completely. Every crimp will have microvoids.

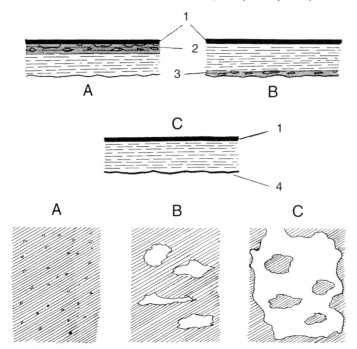

Figure 26.2   Coloured moulding
A If the first layers, 2, behind the gel coat, 1, are coloured the worker is unable to see what he is doing. Consequently this most critical part will be full of voids.
B If denser colour is needed a deeper layer, 3, is as effective and voids will be less harmful.
C Better still, paint the inside, 4.

Figure 26.3   Patchy bond
A A normal moulding will have numerous voids of insignificant area. As nuclei for blisters they lack the power to raise more than the gel coat.
B Poor moulding will have larger voids of significant area but being bonded all around are difficult to detect. New or eroded these have the power to form interlaminar blisters.
C An area of dry moulding is often bonding in patches. This too is difficult to detect if not at the surface. Structurally the surfaces are joined but weak. The first indication would probably be extensive hydrolysis.

Spraying draws in atmospheric moisture unless humidity is kept below 40%. Water does not mix with resin so it coalesces to form voids already water filled. Also, by affecting the cure of surrounding resin, they make it less resistant.

Voids

Every fibreglass moulding has voids; millions of them from coin size to microvoids along fibres (Fig 26.1). The commonest visible ones are champagne bubble size due to trapped air, inevitable with hand lay up, even worse when sprayed. They may also be caused by styrene vapour due to exotherm or hot conditions. Where strands of cloth or woven rovings cross there will be small dry patches due to double thickness and tightness. Poor moulding can have large dry patches with little resin at all.

Some fibres and strands will always be incompletely wetted. The worker has to wet out a thousand miles of fibre a minute, a pretty formidable task. Water can wick along these microvoids, eroding as it goes and enlarging the capillary paths, helped by the hygroscopic silane coupling agent. Consequently the voids spread as the bond breaks down with age, use and water absorption.

Unfortunately at present it is not possible to mould void-free hulls, although claims are made for the SCRIMP vacuum process. The quality of moulding, especially care taken with the critical layers close to the gel coat, decides whether a boat will be a blistering problem. Not the gel coat, however super. Good moulding will have as few voids and as small as can be achieved in practice: about 2–3%. Bad moulding can have 10% or more and larger voids.

Spray moulding traps air and has a high void content. It will pick up atmospheric moisture too. Consequently spray moulded boats are more inclined to blister. Naturally spray moulders deny this. Special resins and airless spray do now reduce voids, but that benefit is for the future. How boats were moulded in the past is why they blister today.

Mouldings made throughout with coloured resins, as was common in early days, always have a high void content because the worker cannot see what he is doing (Fig 26.2).

Most early mouldings also have a high void content. The glass was harder to wet out and the resins more difficult to use. Nobody appreciated voids might be harmful. To put it bluntly nobody really knew what they were doing anyway.

Safe depth

Moulders often switch to cheaper materials at what they consider a safe depth, generally after the first two or three layers. Some authorities say 0.1 in, 3 mm.

There is no 'safe' depth. Given time water can permeate right through. Hydrolysis can occur at any depth. The moulding may be too strong to blister. Nevertheless the bad effects will be there. Holes have been eaten right through the thickness of a keel (see photo p. 43).

The white fibre pattern, plainly visible on older boats, is often due to hydrolysis of the glass/resin coupling agent, and shows how deep water can permeate.

Blister free moulding

We now realise fibreglass moulding involves complex chemistry and physics. Very careful attention to detail and choice of materials is

---

Voids	
Voids are commonly of these forms:	
Microvoids	Along fibres forming capillary paths
Disc cracks	In resin plasticised by water
Strands	Along strands not properly wetted
Crossovers	Where woven strands cross over
Interstices	Between the weave of a cloth
Bubbles	Champagne bubble size trapped air
Cavities	Common gel coat cavities
Delamination	Within the moulding (may be large)
Dry moulding	Unwetted, or partly wetted glass

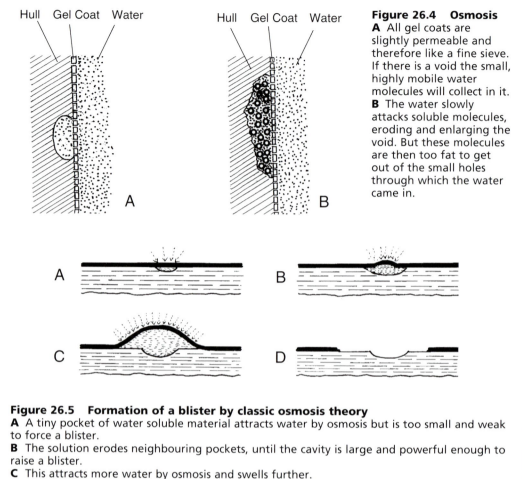

Figure 26.4 Osmosis
A All gel coats are slightly permeable and therefore like a fine sieve. If there is a void the small, highly mobile water molecules will collect in it.
B The water slowly attacks soluble molecules, eroding and enlarging the void. But these molecules are then too fat to get out of the small holes through which the water came in.

Figure 26.5 Formation of a blister by classic osmosis theory
A A tiny pocket of water soluble material attracts water by osmosis but is too small and weak to force a blister.
B The solution erodes neighbouring pockets, until the cavity is large and powerful enough to raise a blister.
C This attracts more water by osmosis and swells further.
D Eventually the blister bursts, destroying the gel coat.
   Note the conditions: a pocket containing soluble material, water permeating into that pocket, a gel coat bond weak enough to be lifted.

essential if the boat is to remain blister free (Chapter 29). Yet knowing is not the same as doing in the face of economics and production convenience. That is the real root of the problem.

The reason some boats blister early and others do not under similar circumstances depends more on the care taken to eliminate voids in the first layers than fancy gel coats or anything else. Not until that is appreciated will the blistering problem be overcome.

Nuclei

A blister requires a nucleus. No nucleus, no blister. Voids provide the nuclei. The smaller the voids the slower blisters develop because until they are eroded to a certain size they do not have the power to raise a blister. The deeper they lie the more power needed. So microvoids can be discounted except as contributory factors.

By far the commonest are the tiny air bubbles. Like champagne bubbles on the side of a glass, they tend to collect on a surface, in particular the gel coat interface, the ideal place to raise a blister.

Dry moulding, typical of poor quality, forms large but generally deeper voids (Fig 26.3). Often, like a marsh, good spots are surrounded by voids. Sometimes half the boat is like that.

Delamination and bulges are caused by deep seated nuclei and cannot occur until

Figure 26.6 Wicking
A Normally water has to permeate into a void slowly through the thickness of the moulding above.
B If the void is connected to the gel coat or surface by a fibre water can wick along it by capillary movement. In so doing it will erode the resin/glass coupling agent and the surrounding resin, forming a tunnel and waterway. The void will fill and blistering occur sooner.

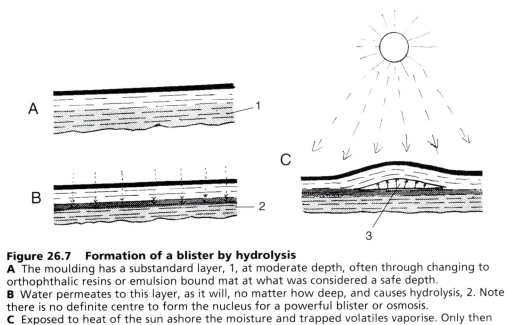

Figure 26.7 Formation of a blister by hydrolysis
A The moulding has a substandard layer, 1, at moderate depth, often through changing to orthophthalic resins or emulsion bound mat at what was considered a safe depth.
B Water permeates to this layer, as it will, no matter how deep, and causes hydrolysis, 2. Note there is no definite centre to form the nucleus for a powerful blister or osmosis.
C Exposed to heat of the sun ashore the moisture and trapped volatiles vaporise. Only then is the pressure sufficient to cleave the moulding and raise a bulge, 3.

hydrolysis over a prolonged time has eroded voids powerful enough to cleave the laminate.

Osmosis

Blisters may be raised by osmotic pressure but osmosis is not the root cause. There has to be permeability and WSMs, and the solution must be trapped in a pocket where critical strength and pressure can develop (Fig 26.5).

Opinions differ about the role osmosis plays in water absorption. Some say absorption would occur anyway, like a sponge. Others say it is drawn into pockets of WSMs by osmosis. Probably both occur. Which predominates may depend on moulding quality, osmosis being more likely with poor moulding.

Osmosis is not peculiar to fibreglass boats, but a well known physical phenomenon, very widespread in nature, a foundation of life. Essential functions of our bodies depend on it. In simple terms it is transfer of a fluid through a semi-permeable membrane which allows small molecules to pass but blocks larger ones, like a molecular size sieve. (Actually much more complicated but this explanation will suffice.) The slight permeability of a gel coat behaves as a membrane, and allows water to pass but traps fatter WSMs. (Fig 26.4).

Water goes from the weaker to the stronger solution to equalise the concentration on both sides. If the stronger solution is trapped, as it is in a void, the flow will build up pressure. This is what raises a blister and the panic stricken wails of 'osmosis'.

All blisters require power, a certain minimum pressure depending on the depth. Therefore the pocket has to be large enough and the concentration of sufficient strength. If the voids are too small there will be no blisters until the aggressive blister juice has dug a big enough hole. Similarly, until enough WSMs have been dug out to make a strong concentration there will not be enough osmotic pressure (Fig 26.5).

A blister can form only by shearing along the interface. A well bonded gel coat or interlayer would not shear and would contain the pressure. Osmosis cannot continue to build pressure indefinitely. When the pressure exerted by the moulding balances the osmotic pressure osmosis must stop.

Absence of blisters does not mean all is well. There could be substantial hydrolysis without a blister showing because no nuclei was large enough. At considerable moulding depth pressure will not be enough to cleave the moulding apart so nobody will realise how bad it really is inside.

Chemical attack, osmosis and permeability get faster as temperature rises, roughly doubling every 18°F, 10°C. Hence blistering is worse in warm seas and icy waters are safe.

Pressure from other causes

Osmosis is not the only pressure. As WSMs are dissolved the volume will increase and exert pressure. In hot climates deep bulges often do not appear until the boat has been a week ashore, and are due to the sun's heat vaporising trapped moisture. In osmosis theory these should have appeared when afloat.

Blistering in fresh water

Blistering is much commoner in fresh water, yet waters vary, even different parts of the same river. Fresh water does not mean pure. (Fortunately. Distilled water is aggressive: one reason laboratory tests are misleading.) Rivers, lakes and canals always have natural dissolved minerals, and as for what man may add . . . Even in rural areas away from industrial and urban pollution there is run off from modern farming. As in sea water, the higher the mineral

content the less likely to blister. Polyester is more resistant to acids than alkalis which may also be why blistering is worse in some waters than others.

Many enclosed seas are partly fresh, eg the Baltic and Black Sea, and the estuaries of rivers. Lots of yachting centres are on rivers which are fresh seasonally, or a low salinity layer overrides tidal seawater. Rivers can be fresh even where tidal. The Seine is tidal above Rouen, a hundred miles from the sea, but salt only for the first ten miles. Some coastal marinas enclosed by lock gates are notorious for blistering. Few realise they are largely fresh water from streams and drains.

All vessels float inches deeper in fresh water. Unless the painted waterline is raised they will blister along the lower topsides.

Where ice is little danger boats are kept afloat all year round. As antifouling is not needed they lack the paint protection that seagoing boats have. Haul out facilities are often non-existent. Consequently nobody realises how badly the bottom is blistered.

Rainwater is still as pure as one can find in nature. Places where it forms puddles on deck are prone to develop blisters. They have also been found behind badly sealed woodwork. Absorbent pads on supports ashore will be almost continually damp.

Wet ground is as bad as being afloat and has higher concentrations of aggressive chemicals. Boats left ashore, either way up, should be raised off the ground.

Blistering in sea water

It is easy to see how osmosis starts in fresh water, but what about sea water? Initially the solution will be stronger outside, built up since the world began, so osmosis ought to suck water out not in. Yet blisters certainly do develop in sea water although more slowly.

The osmosis theory is that due to poor moulding, or even inevitably, there are pockets of unreacted polyester, trapped solvent or impurities in the moulding. In particular the silane treatment on glass fibres. By forming nuclei with a salts concentration already higher than sea water, they suck in water by osmosis.

In another theory permeability will happen

anyway. When solution strength in nuclei inside substantially exceeds the sea water outside osmosis can start and pressure builds up.

Probably both occur simultaneously which shows how complicated this problem is.

Pollution

Fortunately waters really foul from pollution are few. Who wants to sail for pleasure in stinking sewage or black sludge anyway? However, accidents can happen. The clean up can be worse than the pollution when authorities panic and use lethal detergents. The only place for a fibreglass boat is far away or out of the water.

Glass fibre

Emulsion bound glass mat, fully approved and extensively used before about 1980 because it was faster to wet out, is responsible for much blistering. The PVA (polyvinyl acetate) emulsion is hydrolysed into acetic acid which speeds attack on other WSMs. Being used right through blistering can occur at any depth. Approved practice now in Europe is powder bound mat throughout.

Woven rovings and cloth do not have a binder but being harder to wet out usually have a higher void content and dry strands, especially thick woven rovings used to build bulk. Chop or spray moulded fibres do not have a binder either but have other problems like high air entrapment and, especially in earlier days, undercure due to misadjustment.

There will always be millions of microvoids along fibres, too small to raise blisters but forming capillary paths and, like the seams of a coal mine, are where many of the WSMs come from. Chromic chloride silane, commonly used for improved resin/glass bond and faster wetting out, is not water resistant, thus opening up more capillary paths along fibres. Being also hydrolysed into acid compounds it is immediately aggressive and attacks surrounding WSMs.

Some moulders are careless about condensation on the glass. This prevents a good bond and causes pockets of undercured resin. As moisture is trapped around the fibres from the start hydrolysis need not wait for water to permeate from outside.

Kevlar

Kevlar is claimed to be blister free. There seems no reason why, other than different coupling agent, especially as it is harder to mould. Other factors may be the reason. Being used mainly on sophisticated expensive racing machines it must be more carefully and skilfully moulded, and often used with vinyl ester. Like early fibreglass claims it has probably not been around long enough.

Gel coat

Attention has been concentrated on the gel coat because that is where the blisters appear and people assume the troubles lie. Better gel coats are good for sales. But at best they only delay blistering. They cannot prevent it. Only better moulding will do that.

Isophthalic gel coats are now generally specified. But simply specifying isophthalic is not sufficient. Some makers just add a modest quantity of the isophthalic component to a general purpose resin. To be effective it should be 100% isophthalic but only a chemist would know.

Improved gel coats have been developed based on other resins. All are considerably more expensive, although negligible compared with the total cost of the boat. Among these are neopentyl glycol-isophthalic (NPG), biphenol polyester and vinyl ester. There can be disadvantages, like increased brittleness.

Results as good as these expensive gel coats are claimed for ordinary 100% isophthalic resins if thickness is increased by surfacing gauze behind the gel coat, thereby lengthening the permeability path. The first layers of mat must always be isophthalic too.

A few good quality moulders claim a sound orthophthalic gel coat backed by gauze and followed by carefully moulded laminate is better than isophthalic.

The higher the heat distortion temperature the less susceptible to hydrolysis. Technically the resin is more cross linked. However, they are more brittle and achieve full properties only if post-cured. A reasonable compromise is a medium HDT resin.

Gel coats do sometimes blister because they are defective. Nearly always this will be within the first two years and is a job for a lawyer. The only satisfactory solution is replacement of the whole boat. Any repair is just bodging a new boat and should not be accepted. The boat is and always will be second class. Early blistering could also indicate a bad, perhaps dangerously weak moulding.

Avoiding blisters

Forget early claims for immortality. We pioneers have been hoist by our own petard so often it is painful to sit down! If boats are built to blister is it inevitable? Can the owner prevent or delay it?

Blisters are caused basically by water absorption. Racing dinghies are wrapped in cotton wool and in some areas small motor cruisers are stored in pigeon holes. But all larger boats are berthed afloat and will therefore absorb water. Therein lies the problem.

Allowing the hull to dry out regularly is strongly recommended. If stored ashore every winter the level of water absorption will fall and must build up again. So an aggressive level takes years longer. Even winter storage ashore every few years will help, or a few months when out of use. The worst thing is leaving the boat afloat indefinitely, especially in warm or fresh waters. Many owners lay up afloat in their expensive marina berths for which they have paid a full year's rent. The saving will not offset the expense of early gel coat replacement.

Boats in use year round are more difficult, although commercial craft have a shorter working life and can be written off sooner than yachts. However, even blue water cruisers and liveaboards have to leave their boats occasionally when family, business or health call them home. They should take every opportunity to leave the boat ashore.

Applying an epoxy coating will help but must be thick. Not the thin, token coat offered as an expensive extra by some builders. Even epoxy only delays permeation. Vinyl ester can be applied as an interlayer during moulding but not as a separate coating later.

The best way to avoid blisters is to be able to specify how the boat is to be moulded and what type of gel coat, interlayers and materials used throughout. And then pick a moulder who can be trusted to take special care to mould the first layers soundly. If you can find one: most production builders, would not be interested, or would charge a deliberately discouraging price.

Few owners will deliberately choose waters where blistering is less likely (ideally cold waters like the Arctic and Antarctic). Fresh water is always bad, and those dreamy tropical islands worst of all.

Types of blisters

All blisters are a combination of the characteristics described in the box below and, with examination of the moulding beneath, give clues to the cause (Figs 26.8, 26.9 and 26.10).

It is possible to give a few generalities:
- Blisters within about two years, all over, close spaced and virulent, ie developing quickly, indicate a seriously defective gel coat.
- Widely spaced, slowly developing blisters after ten years are to be expected. Break and fill them every few years but retain the gel coat as long as possible.
- The longer before blisters appear, the slower they will develop and the less need for early treatment.
- An unblistered boat will often develop blisters when transferred to different waters, eg warm or fresh.
- A wet blister may have dried by the time it is examined. Blisters may collapse when they dry. They will be back.
- Common gel coat cavities, more often revealed by depressions than blisters, are static and generally dry.
- Most slowly developing blisters are caused by voids, so filling the void will be the end of it. Yet they may seem to keep reappearing like the Hydra because there are always other voids to spawn more.
- Small blisters may not show until patches of antifouling are removed. Sometimes it is easier to feel than see them.
- Bulges have to mean delamination within the moulding. This is the most serious kind. In way of a structural member they are a warning of bad design, weakness or failure. Often they are not apparent on haul out but appear days or weeks later when heated

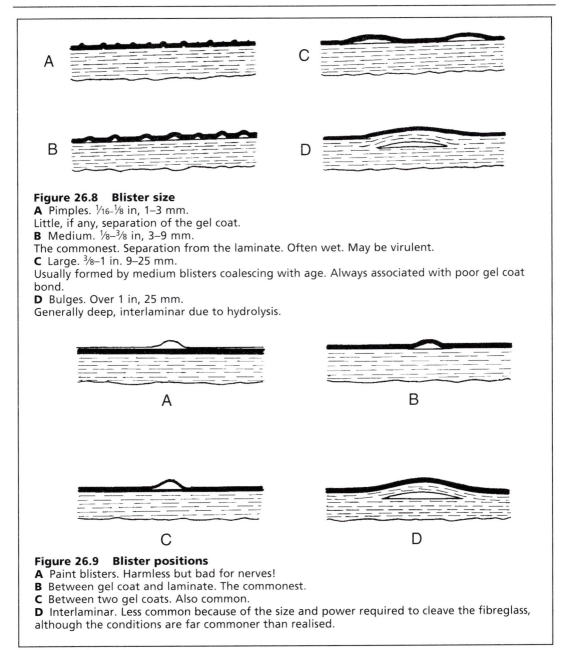

Figure 26.8   Blister size
A Pimples. $\frac{1}{16}$–$\frac{1}{8}$ in, 1–3 mm.
Little, if any, separation of the gel coat.
B Medium. $\frac{1}{8}$–$\frac{3}{8}$ in, 3–9 mm.
The commonest. Separation from the laminate. Often wet. May be virulent.
C Large. $\frac{3}{8}$–1 in. 9–25 mm.
Usually formed by medium blisters coalescing with age. Always associated with poor gel coat bond.
D Bulges. Over 1 in, 25 mm.
Generally deep, interlaminar due to hydrolysis.

Figure 26.9   Blister positions
A Paint blisters. Harmless but bad for nerves!
B Between gel coat and laminate. The commonest.
C Between two gel coats. Also common.
D Interlaminar. Less common because of the size and power required to cleave the fibreglass, although the conditions are far commoner than realised.

by the sun. Open and fill or inject epoxy but assume there are many more which lack the power to force delamination. In bad cases it may mean remoulding.

- Patches may be an area of substandard moulding or just the more visible signs of widespread blistering. They are common along the unpainted waterline where easily seen. Patches may be a warning of overall blistering to come.
- A fabric pattern of blisters reveals badly moulded woven rovings or cloth beneath, or too close to the surface.
- Along a feature inside that could hold or trap water, or where bilge water lies, blisters show water has soaked through and is attacking the gel coat from behind. This is usually warning of a bad or porous moulding. In high stress areas or near repairs they can indicate hidden damage.
- Broken blisters have distinctive crescent or circular shaped cracks before becoming a

crater. Being free flooding the moisture will no longer be aggressive.

• Elongated blisters reveal wicking due to exposed or badly wetted fibres or laying up the first layer before the gel coat was hard. Wicking is a path for moisture to penetrate deep into the moulding (Fig 26.6).

A vinegary, acidic smell is typical of the old emulsion binder and also some silane fibre treatments. Styrene can be trapped in pockets by hot moulding conditions, excessive exotherm or thinning stale resin. Some authorities claim voids are filled with styrene vapour not air. The rather nasty amine smell

suggests a booster which would not be used unless conditions were cold. As that implies undercure watch for a host of other problems. It could also be epoxy which is liable to blister too if unsuitable or badly cured. Diesel or fishy smell suggests the moulding is so porous it has seeped through.

A low pH figure (acid) means the blisters have been developing a long time or the moulding is substandard and easily dissolved. **Note:** there are so many different WSMs, some not even identified yet, this indicator is not conclusive. Their acidity will vary and some are alkaline. The proportion can alter with time and rate of solubility.

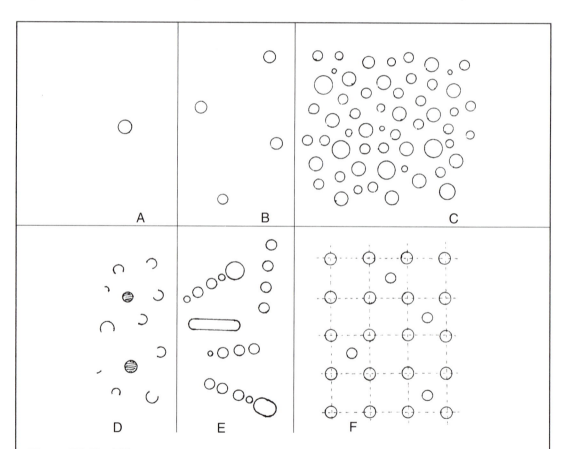

Figure 26.10   Blister patterns
A Isolated blisters. Nothing to worry about.
B Random and well spaced. Fill as they appear. May be forerunners of more widespread blister-ing. If appearing through antifouling look for more underneath.
C Widespread, close spaced assorted sizes. Too late to save the gel coat.
D Crescent shaped cracks and craters. Old blisters. If random fill as B but probably more like C.
E Lines, often with a 'head' or elongated. Wicking due to fibres near the surface.
F Regular fabric pattern. Blisters occur at crossovers of heavy woven rovings close beneath. (Dotted lines show the pattern of the weave.) Blisters also occur at interstices.

Types of blisters

Blisters can be: Wet Dry Solid Broken Not blisters at all	*Development:* Static Developing slowly Virulent
Position: In paint Gel coat/laminate interface Between double gel coats Between laminates In a gel coat replacement In a repair	*Time:* First season Three years Ten years Longer
Distribution: Random patches All over Localised in way of features, outside or in	*Spacing:* Isolated Wide apart Close spaced
Size: Pimples 1/16–1/8 in, 1–3 mm Medium 1/8–3/8 in, 3–9 mm Large 3/8–1 in, 9–25 mm Bulges over 1 in, over 25 mm	*Pattern:* Random Fabric pattern Lines
pH value: 4–5 Prolonged development 5–6 Moderate development 6–7 Early stages 7 Neutral. Fresh water 7.8 Sea water 8–9 Alkaline. Amine booster or epoxy	*Shape:* Round Elongated Crescent
Smell: Vinegary, acidic Aromatic, pear drops Styrene, the 'polyester' smell Amine Paint Musty Miscellaneous	*Colour:* Clear Honey Red tint Brown Rusty Coloured

Sea water is mildly alkaline, 7.8. (Neutral is 7.0). What passes for fresh water may be quite a way either side.

The fluid from new blisters is clear, thin and mobile. In older ones, it is thick, sticky and honey coloured, particularly in bulges from widespread, long standing, deep hydrolysis.

A red tint shows pockets of excess catalyst. (The clear catalyst favoured in Europe gives no indication.) Brown stains come from wood flour filler, favoured on Taiwanese built boats, or absorption of accelerator into filler. Rust, a sign of trouble, must come from embedded steel or stainless steel and indicates deep capillary or seepage paths. (Do not confuse with rust stains from etched-in filings. Chapter 36.)

Colour is probably embedded paint but could be leaching from coloured moulding. If a spillage inside has seeped right through the moulding is bad but there is the nasty possibility it is something corrosive which has eaten through.

Probably more boats have blisters in the paint than the fibreglass. Lumps and pits too can set alarm bells ringing but are more likely due to a worn mould, lumpy paint, weed residues, old barnacles, repairs, even mud splashes.

Causes

There are hundreds of causes of blistering. Table 26.1 lists some of the three hundred I know, and I certainly do not claim to know

Table 26.1   Causes of blistering   *(Continued)*

Cause	*Effect*
Low temperature, heating failure during moulding	Undercure, condensation
Contamination	Resin does not set or cure properly
Porous moulding	Bad moulding allows water through and attacks the gel coat from behind
Production schedule too fast	Insufficient time for gel coat to set
Unfeathered filler rounding off features	Lines of blisters along unmouldable sharp edge
Foreign bodies	Anything falling into the mould becomes part of the boat

Materials
Defective materials are uncommon. Trouble is more likely through wrong choice or careless use.

Water soluble molecules (WSMs)	The principal culprits and constituents of aggressive 'blister juice'
Emulsion bound mat	Although fully approved earlier now known to be a major source of WSMs
Orthophthalic resins	Generally considered less water resistant than isophthalic but universal earlier
Change from isophthalic to orthophthalic	The 'safe' depth may not be beyond the permeation level
Undercure	Massive increase in WSMs. Very common
Wrong treatment on glass	Bad resin/glass bond, microvoids, wicking
Chromic chloride silane coupling agent	Readily hydrolysed, glass/resin bond failure, capillaries
Bad mixing	Undercure, bad setting
Catalyst forgotten	Failure to set, undercure
Over vigorous stirring	Excessive air entrapment, voids
Contamination	Undercure or failure to set
Bad housekeeping	Contamination
Cold resin	Slow setting and undercure
Moisture	Undercure, voids
Condensation on glass	Poor bond, voids, undercure
Job lots	Almost anything
Improvements	Undesirable side effects
Coloured laminating resin	High void content, dry moulding

Mould
A few causes can be traced back to the mould, especially worrying things that look like blisters.

Wrong release agent	Bloom, contaminated gel coat, fisheyes
Dusty mould	The impression of pinholes
Hygroscopic dust	Water absorbent nuclei
Contaminated dust, sawdust, fibreglass dust	Undercured gel coat, nuclei
Cold mould	Undercured gel coat
Worn mould	Pits and lumps

Use
Will not actually cause blisters but can hasten natural development.

Cleaning	Abrasive polishes reduce the gel coat thickness
Sanding	Reduces the gel coat thickness
Abrasion	Wear or damage reduces the gel coat thickness
Sand scour	Abrasion reduces the gel coat thickness
Time afloat	Boats afloat continuously absorb more water than if regularly laid up ashore
Wet ground	Contact with wet ground is worse than being afloat
Wet support pads	If continuously wet it is similar to being afloat
Freezing	Enlarges water filled cavities
Hard use	High stress and fatigue cause resin/glass bond failure, capillary paths and voids
Age	Resin/glass bond breaks down naturally with age
Cavitation	Lifts the gel coat

Table 26.1 Causes of blistering *(Continued)*

Cause	Effect

Outside causes
While seldom causing blisters, outside causes can attack the gel coat and increase the chances, or create effects which resemble blisters.

Exhaust drips	Local heat blisters
Heat	A nearby fire will cause extensive blistering
Salt crystals	By magnifying the sun's rays can cause heat blisters on susceptible gel coats
Chemical attack	Solvents, cleaners, polishes, paint remover etc can blister the gel coat
Pollution	Water or air. A modern hazard
Fall-out	Particles or rain from power stations, industry or nearby central heating flues
Anodes	Corrosive products reported near anodes (disputed)
Infection	Chemical, not biological, eg blister juice from contaminated slings or close marina neighbours
Science fiction	Heat blistering from high power equipment is possible near a defence establishment or research laboratory

Paint
Blisters are often in the paint not the gel coat.

Paint remover	Some paint removers will attack polyester
Polyurethane	Used underwater can blister too
Epoxy	Some trap solvent
Epoxy for above water steel	Underwater can blister worse than any polyester
Primers for fibreglass	Bond chemically. May be too aggressive for marginal gel coats
High humidity	Retards solvent evaporation which then becomes trapped
Osmosis treatment	May blister worse than the gel coat it was supposed to cure. Common with early treatments, boatyards, working under unsuitable conditions, moonlighters, etc

Water quality
Where the boat is used has important influence on blistering.

Fresh water	Blistering is far commoner in fresh water than sea
Warm water	Chemical reactions causing blistering are faster
Water composition	High mineral content delays osmosis, as in sea water
Alkalinity	Polyester is less resistant to alkalis than acids
Salinity	Seawater varies widely, locally as well as worldwide
Oxygenated water	Blistering is more likely in oxygenated surface waters

Repair
Non-marine materials or repair under unsuitable conditions can cause blisters.

Absorbent filler	Blisters, pinholes, porosity
Repair not done under proper conditions	Undercure, lower quality than original moulding
Sanding and burnishing	Reduces gel coat thickness
Abrasion	Most damage includes abrasion which reduces thickness

Red herrings
'Cowards die many times before their deaths/The valiant never taste of death but once' (Julius Caesar). A lot of things can look like blisters and start an owner worrying. It is cheaper to look carefully yourself before calling in an expert. Less embarrassing too!

Barnacles, tube worms, etc	When painted over the lumps look ominous
Weed residue	Can retain moisture for weeks. Small spots resemble weeps
Repairs	Raised repairs look like bulges from deep blisters
Fungus	Can grow on weed residue, slime or mud when ashore
Lichen	Spots resembling pinholes
Mudsplash	Too simple? At first sight it can look very worrying

Commonest causes of blistering

Water absorption	Paint blisters
Marginal or bad moulding	Gel coat replacement
Poor bonding	Contamination
Undercure	Emulsion bound mat
Dry moulding	Worn mould
Voids	Fresh waters
Too thick first laminate	Tropical waters
	Hard use
Woven material near surface	Age
Wicking	

Note: most of these are general headings and cover a variety of actual causes.

indefinitely, on some yachts thirty years already. The amount of work is modest although tedious. Nevertheless it is greatly cheaper and easier than gel coat replacement and within an owner's modest capability, an important point as ageing boats move down the social and economic scale. Tackling part of the hull only each year makes the job less formidable.

Interlaminar blisters

Blisters below the gel coat, appearing as larger bulges, are more serious. They indicate long standing hydrolysis and can form only by delamination. In theory they can be at any depth but beyond $\frac{1}{4}$ in, 6 mm, would need to be unusually large and powerful to lift such a strength of moulding. A typical depth would be the first layer of woven rovings because a cloth interface is easier to cleave than mat.

Common practice with cost conscious moulders is to use better quality isophthalic resin for the gel coat and the first one or two layers of the moulding. Then, at what they consider a safe depth beyond water permeation, they change to cheaper orthophthalic. Hydrolysis often starts at this transition.

The 'safe' level may be sufficient, with a boat kept in Northern waters, stored ashore every winter, to last until the guarantee expires. But it underestimates the depth that water will permeate when kept afloat year round, especially in fresh or warm waters. There is no safe depth to which water will not permeate. How long that takes and the damage hydrolysis does depends, like much else,

on moulding quality.

It is significant that deep blisters often do not appear until the boat is ashore, exposed to sunshine and ambient heat which vaporises the trapped moisture. Without heat they would probably not appear. This shows the cause is water absorption leading to hydrolysis (Fig 26.7). In osmosis theory blisters can form only underwater. In cool climates, without heat to raise blisters a great many hulls must have unsuspected hydrolysis deep in the moulding beyond the shallow range of moisture meters.

In any case moisture will be in discrete pockets, often following wicking paths, yet overall, which is what a meter measures, the average value will be low. In my experience the pockets are almost indetectable, and it is difficult to predict where bulges will rise. Small ones never will until they have eaten away more of the boat.

The obvious fear is bulges spreading until laminates peel off like an onion. Although the number will increase individual bulges seem self-limiting. Greatest pressure and amount of water are found in new ones where the fluid is mobile with low acidity. As concentration and acidity increase the fluid becomes thick, so although more aggressive it is unable to spread by capillary movement along fibres.

Treatment of deep blisters

In theory the only way is to grind, peel or blast off defective layers down to sound material. Assuming any can be found, which will not be until much of the boat has gone! Then remould.

That is the sort of recommendation from a surveyor who has never done any practical moulding and never likely to. Remoulding in a boat's normal upright position is far more difficult than original moulding in a female mould. One might compare it to pouring water into an upside down bucket. Turning over a fully fitted boat is impractical and dangerous even if heavy lifting tackle is available.

The chances of remoulding being done well are slim, especially on a flattish bottomed motor boat or twin keeled yacht where it has to be done overhead. This is really difficult

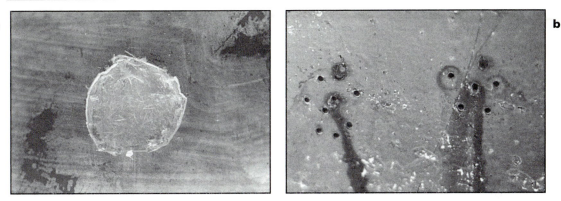

Photos 26.3 (a) Interlaminar hydrolysis blister, about $1/8$ in (3 mm depth) and 1 in (25 mm) across, cut out with a chisel. Note: if this had been ground out, as is common practice, an area twice the size of the photograph would have been destroyed.
(b) Alternative, non-destructive repair of deep interlaminar blisters. First a central hole is drilled to drain the cavity (note the stain from the tiny trickle). Later holes are drilled round the edge of the blister. Finally thin epoxy is injected into the holes.

moulding and requires special techniques. Remember the rule: 'Difficult moulding will be bad moulding'. Furthermore it will not be done under proper moulding conditions by experienced moulders, but by workers who are basically painters and at best in an ordinary shed. Others will attempt it in the open. This is structural moulding, as important as the original boat. It must be done with the same skill and under the same controlled conditions, and also with similar materials, although the lay up is probably unknown.

The depth of defects will vary, so the hull will be ground away unevenly, and probably no one will know how much has been taken off or where. The owner will be having kittens anyway. Besides, where do you stop? Water will have permeated further. Deeper layers will be damp and partly hydrolysed too.

Whenever anything is taken off the thickness should be checked all over before and after with a non-destructive electronic tester (Chapter 43). Once gone nobody will know what used to be there.

It is more practical to leave the original and mould over that after drying out as much as possible. It will still have a lot of strength, especially when dried. The repair will be much cheaper and easier, an important point with an old boat as the owner is likely to be impecunious. Also, both the original and added thickness will be known with reasonable certainty.

This method is safer in tropic islands where deep blistering is common. Boat yards are generally crude, trained specialists unknown, workers rough and ready and all work done in the open – conditions very far from the bare minimum essential for sound moulding. One needs to be desperate, or foolish, to embark on such a 'cure'.

It is far better to try to contain the problem until returning home or to a well serviced area where such a major operation can be done under proper conditions by a skilled firm who really know what they are doing.

Alternative treatments

These methods are well within the capability of the average handyman owner, which remoulding and gel coat replacement are not.

If the total area is relatively small, as is usual initially, individual bulges can be cut out. To restore strength they must be moulded, not filled with putty. A grinder, as commonly used, is clumsy and destroys too much boat. A chisel, router or countersink drill is kinder. It is important to cut back to sound material all round. This is hard to see. Although separated it may be in contact, leaving a delaminated halo to blister again.

A simpler, less destructive alternative is to bond the bulges by injecting epoxy. Although delaminated the layers will still have structural strength. Drill shallow holes to drain the bulges. They are easier to see by sighting along the hull or feeling by hand and better on a shiny wet surface than dry. Mark indelibly because they will collapse.

Leave to dry out as long as conditions, climate and time allow but because the moisture is deep it will take a long time. Remove antifouling if possible but avoid sanding as this will shave thin the gel coat over blisters. Use paint remover before drilling holes otherwise it may penetrate (Fig 27.1).

Drill ⅛ in, 3–4 mm, holes no deeper than the blister, all round and across, about ½ in, 12 mm, apart. (Friends will think you intend to scuttle the boat in despair!) Plot the extent by tapping.

Bulges must still be cleaned and traces of moisture and salts washed out. Inject methylated spirits, denatured alcohol or acetone into the holes with an unused oil can. Unlike steam cleaning, also suggested, solvents carry moisture away.

By this time the bulges will have collapsed, hence the importance of marking. Using a crude syringe, not a hypodermic, inject a very thin epoxy, or standard grade cautiously warmed (Chapter 20), until it bubbles out of other holes. Light pressure is needed, so the syringe should fit the hole. Keep holes topped up. Some suppliers recommend a thick, paste consistency, but only thin resin will follow capillary paths and flow between collapsed faces. Paste will bond but leave a halo into which it has not penetrated, meaning voids which will blister again. Uncollapsed bulges may need flattening temporarily with a self-tapping screw.

Epoxy can be thinned with acetone but loses tackiness if more than 10%. Polyester, thinned with styrene, can also be used but epoxy is a better adhesive and less affected by traces of moisture or slime.

With the same conditions of use blisters are likely to appear again but can be treated in the same way. Even on a short haul out, draining blisters and plugging is beneficial as it will take a few years for blister juice to regain strength.

Theory v practice

Surveyors, authorities, clinics, boatyards and owners too, based in major yachting areas with every service available, have a very different outlook from those far away from such facilities. Plus a predominantly wealthier clientele. Theory and practice become further apart with distance from both facilities and money. A theoretically makeshift method done sensibly is better than a correct treatment done unskilfully under unsuitable conditions.

Waterline

The bottom needs good water resistance but is protected to some extent by antifouling and anyway nobody can see it. The topsides are in full view and the boat is judged by the smart shiny appearance. These are conflicting requirements. Where do you draw the line? The waterline? But that is a nice straight line only on paper. Moreover the theoretical waterline will alter according to load, and whether in fresh or sea water, and there is no certainty that either the designer or builder got their sums right.

Consequently the lower part of the topsides, the splash zone, will be persistently wet and even more blister prone than the bottom because it has no protective antifouling. Surface water is more highly oxygenated too. The splash zone is exposed to sunlight and caked salt which is not only aggressive but magnifies the sun's rays. No part of the boat endures tougher conditions.

A wide boot-top will give some protection to this vulnerable zone. It needs to be at least 4 in, 100 mm, above the loaded waterline and must be painted even though that means maintenance. A bi-colour gel coat sounds nice, avoiding a fiddly bit of maintenance, but blisters before anywhere else.

Colour

Pigments are a suspected contributory cause. Therefore some moulders use clear gel coats underwater. But the transition complicates and delays moulding. The topsides must be coloured so the splash zone is still vulnerable.

The culprit is the carrier more than the pigment. White is the strongest pigment so less is needed and it is the least prone to blister. Also, being the most popular, it is economic for manufacturers to supply gel coat with pigment ground in using no carrier. The problems arise when moulders stir in colour paste. This cannot be done as thoroughly as a manufacturer with a ball mill so more pigment and carrier are needed. Colour is one reason why boot-tops blister sooner.

Thixotropic resins

The usual thixotropic agent is finely divided silica. One school of thought claims that in forcing this through the strands some gets filtered out leaving microscopic patches without resin close to the surface. Silica can absorb moisture and thereby plasticise adjoining resin although unaffected itself.

Therefore in the critical first layer, thixotropic agent should be reduced to the minimum. But this is a vicious circle. Good first layer moulding requires a lot of resin to be applied to the mould and the glass bedded on to this. To get it to stay it has to be thixotropic. The alternative is to work fast but that is the antithesis of the careful moulding so essential for this critical part. In most cases the moulder buys thixotropic resin and has no control anyway.

Spraying the first layer is claimed to eliminate fibre filtering. Against this is the higher void content and inclusion of atmospheric moisture.

Cure

Undercured resins are not only more susceptible to attack by water but have greater permeability. The amount of catalyst is important. Too little and although the resin sets there is less crosslinking and a more open structure. Too much and the resin sets too quickly to link properly, and traces of unused catalyst remain.

Water soluble molecules

We now know WSMs in their many different forms are the main root cause. How can these be minimised? With the exception of extraneous things which fall into the mould, all come from the materials. Some material manufacturers are taking greater care to reduce them but most materials used in boatbuilding are general purpose, largely for non-marine applications where WSMs are of no concern. Vinylester and epoxy both have fewer WSMs and free linkages but are harder to use and considerably more expensive. The problem is to persuade moulders to pay the small amount extra for better materials.

The major source of WSMs is the moulder. Only the utmost care and attention to detail while moulding will reduce them. Amongst these details are:

- Repeated checks of spray equipment, catalyst ratio, spray pattern, air pressure, oil leakage, atmospheric humidity and setting time, plus frequent cleaning but avoiding residue of cleaners. Less incorrect mixing occurs with internal mixing airless spray than external where it can also vary with distance.
- Gel coats in particular are sensitive to spraying faults. Build thickness with few passes. Multiple thin coats are more porous. Check thickness with a gauge. Thin coats will be undercured.
- Setting time is critical. If prolonged, monomer loss causes undercure. If too fast glass binder and coupling agent do not have time to dissolve, resulting in dry strands. This is particularly likely with environmentally more acceptable low monomer resins (California 1162).
- Polyester that has not crosslinked fully is a common source of WSMs. Therefore special care is needed to avoid undercure from any cause. This not only requires proper temperature control but also avoiding contamination and innumerable other factors causing local undercure at any scale from molecular to whole boat.
- Catalyst has a carrier. This is usually dimethyl or dibutyl phthalate which takes no part in the reaction and is a plasticiser. Use the strongest catalyst and therefore least carrier, and always fresh. It loses strength with age.
- All materials can absorb atmospheric moisture. Keep containers sealed, including part used drums of resin. Cover rolls of glass at night to keep them clean, and warm before use to drive off condensation. Also sandwich cores: most fillers, including silica, absorb moisture. Do not open sealed packages before use.
- Drums of resin should be stirred daily with a mechanical stirrer to prevent settlement,

and always before use, particularly important with gel coats.

- Concrete floors need to be sealed. Vacuum clean them; do not sweep as it raises dust, usually hygroscopic, which settles in the mould and on half finished mouldings. Roofs and ceilings too must be kept dust free. Incoming air should be filtered and personnel doors have air locks and absorbent doormats.

- The bond between the gel coat and first lay up is critical, and also between two gel coats or to a vinyl ester back up. Timing must be right and as short as possible to prevent contamination or condensation. It is common sense that a well bonded gel coat will be harder to raise into a blister.

- Hard rolling and thorough consolidation not only ensure better wetting out and a minimum of the tiny air bubbles, but also a final mixing of constituents.

- Use clean gloves when handling glass fibre and core materials. Just as finger marks cause rust on steel, so they contaminate these materials. In particular, barrier cream is intended to be insoluble in resins but wash off after use. That means traces transferred by handling are water soluble.

- In hot conditions avoid perspiration dripping on to the work. A worker with a streaming cold should not mould hulls. Perhaps hair nets too should be worn as in catering.

Many of these may seem unimportant even trivial details. Yet it is only by very careful attention to such details that WSMs can be minimised, and blistering tackled at its source. Such conditions are a far cry from the sticky fibre covered floors of old. Yet not as stringent as standard practice in catering or even most engineering factories.

Yes it costs money. So many builders will still follow the cheaper course of bemusing buyers with extravagant claims for waterproof gel coats so they can continue to load the mouldings behind with ever more WSMs.

Records

All blistering starts in the mould. What went wrong with that boat on that day years ago?

What was not up to standard? Indeed what was the standard?

History is a guide to techniques and materials in vogue at that time, but can anyone remember what the moulders were like? Did they have a proper temperature controlled moulding workshop or just a curtained off end of the factory? Were they trained, experienced staff or builders' labourers? Quality conscious management with long experience of boats or caravan builders interested only in greatest profit?

Despite the popular assumption, fibreglass boats are not alike, even from the same mould. Apparently insignificant things can cause trouble years later. Few moulders kept good daily records. Even those still in business may be unwilling to dig back years. What was the weather? The season? Were the doors opened to let another boat out? Were there power cuts? What crises national, international, material shortages, strikes, recessions? Were the builders or moulders in financial trouble?

Fibreglass hulls are made by hand. Who were the workers? Did anyone have a cold? Hangover? Monday morning blues? A grudge? Personal problems? Was the foreman away sick?

It is difficult enough to find the specification, how the boat should have been built. So many builders have gone. Boatbuilding is a notoriously risky business. Classification societies ought to have records of what they approved, in particular the types of material. Yet these too can be so vague one wonders if the surveyor knew.

Heresy?

The more waterproof the coating the worse the blistering will eventually be even though delayed. The reason is obvious. All coatings are permeable to some degree, no matter what claims are made. But what goes in with difficulty can come out only with greater difficulty. Therefore WSMs are trapped more efficiently.

Now instead of the impossible task of trying to make gel coats waterproof suppose they were made more porous thereby allowing these fat WSMs to get out easily. The concentration of blister juice would not reach aggressive levels, osmosis could not build up pressure, hence no blisters. However, it does require a higher standard of moulding than most production dominated moulders try to attain although vacuum bag methods have promise.

Don't panic

Some owners panic at the first faint suspicion of dreaded 'boat pox'. Look at the boat calmly and consider these questions.

1 Are they gel coat blisters at all? Could they be paint blisters, lumps from the mould, old barnacles, or simply marks, weed or mud?

2 What is the boat's age? In middle age, say ten years, blisters can be expected. They will develop slowly, so there is plenty of time to consider what to do. Cheap, owner maintenance may contain them indefinitely.

3 If the boat is new blisters are likely to be virulent and develop quickly. This is a moulding defect. See your lawyer, and pray the builders are still in business.

4 What is the spacing and coverage? All over or just in patches? Wide apart or close? Scrape off antifouling in places to see developing blisters not yet showing through.

5 How big are they? Burst open a few. Are they wet? (Probably a mere trace.) What is the smell? Test for acidity. Ignore the Sherlock Holmes taunts and look for tiny voids or dry fibres with a magnifier or pocket microscope.

6 How deep are they? Smallish blisters in the gel coat or interlaminar bulges?

7 Where are they? Blisters often appear in the vulnerable splash zone before the bottom, protected by antifouling or epoxy. These are advance warning. Drying out and perhaps epoxy coating may at this stage forestall trouble.

8 Are blisters cracked or open? These are old and show blisters have been developing for years.

9 Has the boat been afloat continuously? When was its last chance to dry out?

10 Where has the boat been used, or kept afloat? Sea or fresh water? Warm, temperate or icy?

Before consulting anyone with a vested interest in major repair, the owner should assess for himself whether or not he has a serious problem.

Isolated random blisters are little to worry about. They can be treated cheaply but will be an ongoing maintenance problem. Pimples are the early stages and likely to develop further, but if caught in time might be delayed. Only close spaced, all over, well developed blisters mean it is too late for cheap remedy and complete gel coat replacement will be required sooner or later. Deep, interlaminar blisters indicate hydrolysis and perhaps major remoulding needed.

Do not be rushed into treatment which may not be necessary. Get a second opinion. There is no need for haste and time to plan several years ahead. The boat will not sink.

Blistering is a complex subject impossible to cover comprehensively in this book. The author's companion book *Fibreglass Boats – Blistering and Osmosis* to be published shortly goes into the subject in greater detail.

Finally, when on the EEC committee attempting to produce standards for fibreglass boats I referred to blistering 'popularly known as boat pox'. The excellent translators, I was told, translated this in medical terms!

References

There has been more written about blistering than any other aspect of fibreglass boats. Also more nonsense. Among the more useful are:

Blisters, Professional Boatbuilder Magazine's Guide to Understanding, Preventing and Repairing Them, 1994. (Strongly recommended. The best I have yet seen.)

Practical Sailor, June 1989.

Repairs to Blisters in Glassfibre Hulls, British Plastics Federation, November 1979.

The Osmosis Project, International Paints.

Osmosis, Cause and Effect, YBDSA 1978.

Practical Boat Owner, March–June 1983.

Replacing a gel coat

The principal advice is: don't. The gel coat is as much an integral part of a fibreglass boat as our skins are of our bodies.

Replacing a gel coat is a major operation to be avoided if possible, a last resort and not, as so often regarded, the first and only treatment. When unavoidable be very careful it is done under proper conditions, the equivalent to an operating theatre, and by competent workers. There are plenty of untrained cowboys, boatyards too, working in the open, whose confidence far outstrips their ability and knowledge.

Is it necessary?

A lot of gel coats are removed quite unnecessarily. It should never be considered until simpler treatments have been tried and failed (Chapter 26). The boat will never have anything as much part of it as the original gel coat. Keep it as long as possible. Most blistering is caused by defects in the moulding behind. The gel coat is just where they show and often the soundest part. Only if blistering when new is the gel coat likely to be faulty – a matter for a lawyer not a repairer.

No gel coat should be removed unless the blisters are too tedious to fill separately. Before that stage many gel coats have been kept going for twenty or thirty years by filling the blisters as they appeared. The older the boat the slower blisters appear and the easier to control by inexpensive regular maintenance. Recurring blisters do not mean the treatment has failed. They are a fresh crop in different places. In one early class, Nicholson 32, original gel coats on boats with wise owners have outlasted repeated replacement on others.

There is no need to replace the gel coat, as soon as the first blisters appear, on the grounds

that the gel coat is now useless. As too many clinics, surveyors, paint suppliers and others with vested interest in the expensive repair maintain.

Get independent advice before you let anyone touch the boat, and if wise, a second opinion. Never go by the advice of a specialist clinic or boatyard. They want work and are often very ignorant.

No gel coat removal should start until inspection of several small areas has revealed what is underneath. Otherwise there may be nasty surprises, inevitably meaning big extra expense and delay. Removing the gel coat is not the panacea for all ills. More likely opening a Pandora's box. Be certain the drastic and expensive treatment really is going to cure the problem. That means you must know *why* the gel coat is blistering. There is no single disease 'osmosis'. Blisters are the outward symptoms of a wide variety of causes, usually a combination. Good diagnosis is the essential preliminary.

This is also the time to decide if the boat is worth it. Would it be better to scrap before wasting money on a fundamentally unsound hull? Carry on a few years more despite the blisters? Bodge it up cheaply and sell as 'treated for osmosis' (without saying how little!)? But once that gel coat comes off there is no turning back. You are irrevocably committed to open ended expense just to make the boat saleable or even afloat again.

Early mouldings

Few now remember what moulding was like in early days. Yet without this knowledge one cannot understand what is happening to old boats today. Void content was always high, inevitable with the less easily moulded materials and unskilled workers, but does not mean the boat was unsound. It is probably thicker and still stronger than many modern boats.

Approved materials have since proved to have deficiencies that encourage blistering. By present best standards the fibreglass may not be good. But if it has lasted twenty or thirty years it would have to be in a bad state right through, obvious in other ways, if not likely to last a good few more.

Removing gel coat

This is a messy business. The boatyard may not allow it. Owners of adjoining boats may complain; at home neighbours or the council may object. Do not underestimate the time and cost of protection and clearing up.

In theory gel coat thickness will be indicated by change of colour. But when abraded all fibreglass turns a light grey similar to white gel coat and the dust on the surface. It is not easy to see when to stop. Exposed fibres may be the first warning. Judging thickness is particularly difficult if the gel coat is clear like the moulding underneath, and even worse if through coloured as was common early practice.

Methods of taking off gel coat are banned for removing antifouling because of toxicity. Antifouling must be taken off first but toxic traces may remain.

No chemical stripper will remove gel coat and leave the boat behind.

Grinding

This is the simplest method, suitable for an amateur or small boatyard, but brutal destruction not delicate finishing. It requires a high speed industrial grinder and coarse, resin bonded discs. More efficient diamond discs are now available. An ordinary electric drill is too slow and paper discs tear quickly. A powerful sander is heavy and difficult to handle. It is easy to gouge deep into the fibreglass.

Frictional heat softens the resin and discs clog unless used with plenty of water. The muddy run off may be difficult to control.

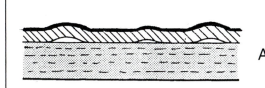

Figure 27.1   Effect of sanding
A It is common to remove antifouling by sanding.
B The effect is to shave the gel coat thin over some blisters, 1, leaving them vulnerable yet undetected. Others are opened, 2, but some to a barely noticeable pinhole, 3. Note how the crater extends further than the opening.

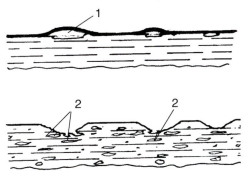

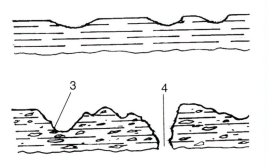

Figure 27.2
Grit blasting will open voids, 1, preferentially so material is removed to a greater depth than the general level of the gel coat. If, as generally the case on older boats, there are voids right through, 2, an inexperienced, over enthusiastic operator may chase void after void down to a considerable depth, 3. Even right through, 4.

Grinding creates clouds of itchy dust, unpleasant for those nearby as well as the worker. A good mask, goggles and protective clothing are essential. Polyester dust inhibits fresh resin. Grinding should not be done near a moulding workshop air intake.

Grit blasting

This is a job for a contractor with special equipment and a big air compressor, well beyond an ordinary paint or garage compressor.

The choice of grit is absolutely critical. Most contractors are accustomed to working on steel, using a hard, sharp, cutting grit in a near supersonic jet. This will blast holes right through fibreglass! It must be something gentler, using a soft, blunt compound, although still resembling a hurricane force sandstorm. Some compound will remain deeply embedded. If hygroscopic or contaminating it will be nuclei for further blisters.

The quantity of grit can be tons – quite an expense even if cheap. Then it all has to be cleaned up along with the remains of the boat, by which time it will have blown all over the yard, every other boat and half the surrounding area. Finally everything has to be disposed of according to regulations. Slurry makes mud instead. Ordinary sand and anything containing free silica is prohibited in Britain and some other states.

Factory regulations are strict. Grit blasting is dangerous not only for the boat but for the operator, anyone on nearby boats and even casual passers-by. A danger area must be marked out and other people excluded to protect them from flying particles, breathing dust or harming their eyes. The operator must have a spacesuit and breathing apparatus.

This is definitely not for amateurs or casual, untrained, ill equipped labour. Although quick and efficient, it is expensive. A large part of the cost will be transport of materials and equipment, rigging protective screens, preparation and cleaning up. The topsides and all parts which could be damaged must be masked, and windows, especially acrylic, covered to prevent them becoming frosted. Every opening must be sealed to keep out dust. Nearby boats must be protected too.

Grit blasting keys the surface and preferentially opens and enlarges cavities (Fig 27.2). An enthusiasic operator who, like a dentist, considers any cavity bad, may go chasing voids deeper and deeper until, quite literally, he comes out the other side. Judging depth is as difficult as when grinding but material disappears much faster. Before anyone realises the operator may have blasted half the boat away. One clue is skin fittings (thru hulls) standing proud like a golf ball on a tee.

Make sure, *before starting*, that the operator has experience of fibreglass and never allow one accustomed to working only on steel anywhere near the boat. Give very clear instructions that the gel coat, and *only* the gel coat, is to be removed and on no account is the operator to go further without express permission from the owner. To make sure, get independent non-destructive thickness tests before and after. And insist the contractor has good liability insurance!

On a routine survey I really did discover a boat that had been blasted to the Canadian winds. The alarming thing was, nobody knew half the boat was no longer there. A well qualified surveyor had actually declared it was quite impossible, even though the operator had blasted holes right through! Which suggests it was not the only yacht to have suffered that fate and serious damage is commoner than anyone realises.

Heating

This should not be confused with burning off paint. The gel coat is heated no more than enough to soften so it can be scraped or peeled off. The best tool is a hot air gun. As little equipment is needed this method is suitable for an amateur but it does need care and there is potential for damage (Chapter 9).

Mechanical Stripper

This is the latest development. Strippers shave off a precisely controlled thickness, leaving the fibreglass beneath untouched. This assumes the gel coat is of constant thickness which is seldom the case. On convex curves they are bound to bite deeper. The smooth surface is claimed to need less filling but this is no real advantage as voids, the major source of blistering, are not opened.

Hand held machines are more versatile, as well as much cheaper, than the elaborate model with a computer controlled arm. There would be so many places that arm could not reach. Experience shows claims for controlled removal thickness are exaggerated. Many boats have been badly damaged by going too far and shaving off layers of structural fibreglass, too. A lot more skill is needed than is generally thought.

Ordinary portable planers have been used but there is no control over thickness and the abrasive nature of fibreglass blunts blades. But they are simpler and readily available.

Waste disposal

The constituents of finely divided fibreglass are readily leached and can contaminate water courses. They may also include toxic antifouling. On site dumping is seldom approved nowadays (Chapter 4).

Washing down

Repeated washing down is essential to get out aggressive blister juice which will have wicked into the moulding, as well as salt, slime and antifouling. Being hygroscopic some of these will delay drying if left. In theory it will wash out WSMs but as these will still be locked in it is unlikely mere washing will get them out.

Washing should be by high pressure hose, not by hand, and repeated daily for several weeks. More mess! By getting rid of hygroscopic particles it will speed rather than delay drying. Fresh water is preferred but unlimited sea water is better than skimping on fresh. Some authorities advocate steam cleaning.

Inspection

At this stage inspect carefully to see if the hull is worse than feared. There is still the option of doing nothing. Additional work means big extra expense and the owner may well consider an oldish boat not worth it. The decision must be the owner's alone, never the clinic, boatyard or surveyor however much they consider it necessary. Nothing beyond what has been agreed must be done without the owner's consent. If wise he will get independent opinion.

Remoulding

In theory soggy hydrolysed areas should be ground away and remoulded, but discover how deep first. On an old boat they may be right through. Beware of glib assurances about remoulding. It sounds easy; in practice it is not. The boat cannot be turned upside down so much has to be done under difficult and unpleasant overhead conditions by workers who are not trained moulders and not under moulding shop conditions. Their remoulding is likely to be even worse than the original. Gel coat clinics are basically painters, not moulders.

Yet it is vital that any fibreglass ground away *must* be replaced. It is structural. If not replaced, the boat is obviously weakened. Moreover those first layers would be the only part moulded with better quality isophthalic resins, and the ones most carefully moulded (Chapter 29).

Some specialist repairers grind down to the first layer of woven rovings (if they can find one). This is the layer most likely to bridge, have voids in the interstices and dry spots at crossovers. Nuclei for further blistering. Moreover they claim that epoxy alone will restore strength. That is utterly wrong as anyone who knows the first thing about fibreglass should realise.

Hydrolysed layers still retain much of their strength. Once dried out it is more practical to remould on top rather than grind away, as well as kinder to the boat.

If the first layers have large voids it will almost certainly be the same right through, so there is no point in grinding them away. They are probably still as strong as they have ever been.

Deep voids

Many repairers attack deep class 3 interlaminar blisters clumsily with a grinder which destroys a wide patch of sound structural fibreglass. The more elegant, less destructive method it to cut them out with a chisel, or use a countersink drill, rotary file or router like a dentist attacking a tooth. Delamination extends beyond the obvious blister. Cut back as far as the gel coat is undermined. To maintain strength repair with fibreglass not putty.

Conditions

Because of the mess, removal of the gel coat is best done in the open away from other boats and buildings. Drying is mainly a matter of time and most of it can also be done in the open with a cover to keep rain off.

Only the final drying and replacement are critical. This must be done indoors, preferably in controlled conditions similar to moulding. It should not be attempted in the open even under a cover.

If proper conditions are not available, less harm will be done by leaving the job until it can be done properly than attempting such an important operation under unsuitable conditions. The boat is not going to sink. Plan ahead for the boat to be somewhere with the right facilities. Do not believe anyone who claims they can do the job just as well in the open. They can't.

A hot climate does not mean dry weather. Most hot countries have a higher rainfall than the wettest part of Europe, a high humidity and often heavy showers even during a nominal dry season.

Insist on proper conditions or not at all.

Drying

This is very important. Going to considerable expense to keep water out is pointless if trapped inside. The boat will blister again because it is caused by water in the moulding, not the gel coat.

Having taken years to permeate deep into tiny capillary paths water will be in no hurry to get out. The best way is to leave the boat ashore for as long as possible, months not weeks, and let it dry naturally. A winter outside exposed to the winds but protected from rain will dry more thoroughly than indoors or by forced drying.

The amount of moisture absorbed will depend on the quality of moulding, age and materials but principally on the time continuously afloat. A boat stored ashore every winter will never attain the moisture content of a boat afloat year round.

For those who cannot wait, forced drying with heaters or dehumidifiers is commonly used. Also vacuum drying if you want to get complicated. Forced drying is less effective than claimed. Moisture will have permeated deeply. Tests have shown that it can go right through.

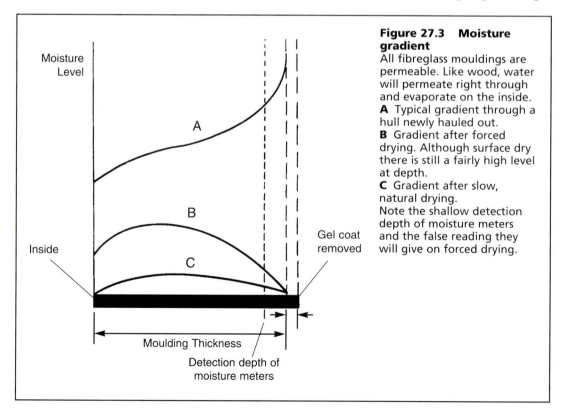

Figure 27.3   Moisture gradient
All fibreglass mouldings are permeable. Like wood, water will permeate right through and evaporate on the inside.
A Typical gradient through a hull newly hauled out.
B Gradient after forced drying. Although surface dry there is still a fairly high level at depth.
C Gradient after slow, natural drying.
Note the shallow detection depth of moisture meters and the false reading they will give on forced drying.

Drying evenly is a false assumption. Forced drying will dry the surface layers but it is obvious there will be a moisture gradient (Fig 27.3). As moisture meters have a shallow detection depth, they will give a false indication. A moisture gradient is denied in some circles, mostly by makers of moisture meters and dehumidifiers, but has been confirmed by analysis.

The common forced drying is by heaters within a polythene tent. Avoid gas or fuel heaters, including catalytic or flameless types. As well as being dangerous, combustion produces a lot of water vapour. In a tent that is like trying to dry a boat in a Turkish bath. Oil fumes can contaminate the surface. Electric heaters or pig lamps are fume-free and dry, but moisture must still be extracted or it will be reabsorbed. So will moisture from the ground unless sealed off. To avoid damage the hull surface should nowhere be too hot to touch. As well as softening the resin leading to structural distortion there is risk of severe delamination.

Claims made for dehumidifiers (gallons of water extracted every day) would be impressive if not absurd. It may come from the air but very definitely not out of the fibreglass. Even straight out of the water a fibreglass boat can not have more than a few bucketfuls absorbed (Chapter 6). Some quantities quoted would be equivalent to filling the boat to the gunwales!

All forced drying is expensive. Therefore it will not be maintained any longer than necessary and in most cases not long enough. Air and wind are the best way to dry a boat.

There are hundreds of causes of blistering but water is the key to most of them. So drying is the crucial part. If rushed failure is probable. Some suppliers say three weeks is sufficient, but even if forced that is too short. Allow at least three months for a boat regularly laid up ashore; six if afloat continuously for the previous two years. If you cannot spare this time, wait until you can. A few years will make little difference.

How dry?

Theoretical chemists say a boat should have 0% moisture content, but this is impracticable. Surveyors like to see below 5% reading on a Sovereign moisture meter, which represents about 0.5% in fibreglass (Chapter 43), less

than some other meters can read.

In practice it just has to be as low as can be got under the circumstances. This may still be too high theoretically. But with the gel coat off and storage costs escalating the job has to start if the boat is not to sit there for ever. A boat afloat a long time in tropical waters and made with older materials might take years.

Although the fibreglass can be dried to a very low moisture content without harm, woodwork cannot. Forced drying to a theoretically low level may cause considerable damage inside, and to keels, rudders and external woodwork.

Testing for dryness

The approved method nowadays is to use a moisture meter. But unless used with caution and awareness of the limits of that meter, plus a good knowledge of the structure of fibreglass, the results will be misleading. Amateurs buy them, and a lot of professionals too, with no idea what the readings really indicate; even more, what they do not.

Because of the very variable nature of fibreglass, moisture meters cannot be calibrated. Therefore use relative readings. Mark test points and take measurements until the readings are steady regardless of absolute value, showing the moisture is as low as it is likely to get.

If the bottom persistently reads high suspect something else. Meters do not detect only moisture. Antifouling may contain a lot of metal, or itself retain moisture or traces of weed. Certain fillers give false readings. So do trapped solvent and hydrocarbons. Some hulls can absorb a film of oil, as can antifouling which, like an invisible film of condensation, will send a meter haywire. The topsides should give a baseline. If this reads high too there is a whopping red herring. Many owners have been lured into expensive work on the basis of false moisture meter readings.

A crude test is to tape glass or polythene on the surface and leave it for several days. Condensation shows there is moisture still but even apparently dry is not dry enough. Leave for another month or two.

Filling and recoating

These are covered comprehensively by the suppliers' literature and one should always read the instructions. However, people who write instructions are not usually those who do the work.

Many failures have been caused by absorbent fillers. Nowadays they are usually epoxy based. On high-tech boats, where the thought of extra ounces or grams makes the owner scream, light weight fillers can be used. The hull must be sanded repeatedly for a fair surface. Adding a little talc makes it easier.

Mechanical strippers and heating do not open voids. As these are the main nuclei for blisters the surface must be sanded afterwards to expose them for filling (so much for claims about the benefits of a smooth surface).

Replacement

Epoxy is now the recommended gel coat replacement but must be solventless. Many early failures were due to trapped solvent. The thickness should be comparable to the gel coat. Only solventless epoxy can be applied thickly enough. Epoxy is expensive and there is temptation to skimp. As permeability is inversely proportional to thickness the improvement over polyester will not be obtained without equal thickness. So regardless of cost the epoxy must be thick. Skimping this final stage will jeopardise the whole expensive project.

Polyurethane used to be specified. It is one of the least permeable coatings, better than epoxy, and does not need heat curing for optimum properties. But it is a thin paint and cannot be built up to adequate thickness. Also, in multiple coats it has been found to blister as badly as the gel coat it replaces.

Blistering is seldom confined to the bottom but includes the splash zone of the topsides, especially on cruising yachts venturing into tropical waters, inevitably floating deeper. Consequently the topsides will need painting or at least an unusually broad boottop. Being unprotected by antifouling blisters commonly appear first on the lower topsides: a clue to what may be still hidden below.

Epoxy is less resistant to sunlight so parts above water need painting anyway.

Do not underestimate the difficulties, time and expense. Repeated filling, sanding and building up are tedious. Running out of patience is as common a cause of failure as running out of money.

Rehydration

After gel coat replacement, the moisture level may increase substantially in a year or two, suggesting the expensive process has been no use. This is not necessarily so. More likely it indicates incomplete drying in the first place, especially if force dried. Moisture from a deeper level may have migrated to the surface, or even, with a poor moulding, been reabsorbed and permeated through from inside.

Before recoating, the moisture level may also rise after apparent drying. As well as deep moisture migrating the surface will reabsorb moisture from the atmosphere. Any surface will trend to the ambient humidity level, so a hull cannot be dried properly where humidity is high or there is condensation. This does not imply a steamy jungle. Mist, and fog too, are 100% humidity. The roughened surface left by gel coat removal will consist of exposed fibres and shattered resin. Ideal conditions for wicking, especially as a blistered hull is likely to be sub-standard anyway.

A liveaboard cruising yacht may be occupied while ashore and, in a hot, humid country, often has air conditioning. But by maintaining the hull at a cooler temperature this will encourage condensation.

Many clinics shamelessly seek work regardless of whether the gel coat really needs to be removed. One manager saw some lumps on the bottom of a yacht and, putting on his gloomiest face, advised the owner he must have the gel coat taken off immediately or the boat would sink. The owner did not have the heart to tell him it was a steel boat!

References

Gougeon Brothers, WEST system.
Gougeon Brothers, *Epoxyworks No 4 1994*.
International Paints, Gelshield and Interguard.
Blakes paints manual. Hempel's paint manual.
Moisture meters, Trials on GRP test panels, Southampton Institute of Higher Education, Oct 1992.
How good are moisture meters? Hugo du Plessis, *Practical Boat Owner*, 1990.
Blisters, Professional Boatbuilder Magazine's Guide to Understanding, Preventing and Repairing Them, 1994.
Practical Boat Owner, March 1995.

In the beginning – moulding

Everything stems from the way the boat was moulded and the expertise and care taken by the workers in the mould. Of particular relevance to owners of older boats, the great majority now, is how boats used to be moulded. *Your* boat, not those shiny new, state of the art boats at the shows. Only that will explain what is happening today.

Conditions for moulding

Authorities lay down stringent conditions for moulding fibreglass. The best moulders have always tried to observe them, although the requirements were not then as stringent as now. But most in the past have been wide of the mark; some were primitive even by the standards of those days. Unsatisfactory conditions during moulding are responsible for many troubles affecting older yachts today.

Life was so much simpler when a wooden boat could be built in a leaky old open shed on a misty waterside.

Temperature

Polyester and epoxy resins are formulated to be used within a strictly limited range of temperature and conditions. They set and cure by chemical action which is temperature dependent. For serious moulding, authorities stipulate a temperature of not less than 65°F, 18°C, ± 5°F, 3°C, *maintained day and night*, regardless of weather. For repairs and amateur work outside a professional moulding shop ordinary polyester resin can be used successfully down to 55°F, 12°C. Epoxies are more tolerant but proper cure is still temperature dependent.

Speed of reaction doubles with every 18°F, 10°C, rise, but slows by a similar amount when temperature falls. Worse, when well outside the range for which they are formulated, the complex reactions may be incomplete or not work at all. They are also sensitive to damp.

Cold conditions

The setting time of polyester can be speeded in cold conditions by increasing the amount of catalyst to about 7%, or adding an amine booster. But although persuaded to set it will not cure properly or develop full strength and water resistance. Below 40°F, 5°C, it may not set at all. Polyester must set within about an hour, otherwise there will be evaporation from the surface and absorption of atmospheric moisture.

Epoxies have a wider temperature range but as the resin/hardener ratio cannot be altered the only control over setting time is by using special hardeners. Some allow working at freezing temperatures.

Although usable, resins become thick and difficult to work. The recommended solution is warming the resin, but the surface must be warmed too.

Subsequent normal temperatures, even months later, will improve the cure but mouldings made under cold conditions will never become fully cured.

Low temperature working must be an expedient for emergencies, *never original moulding*, and should be replaced later under better conditions (see Hints p. 264).

Hot conditions

In hot conditions polyester will set too quickly, often catching the worker unawares. Decrease catalyst to maintain adequate working time, but not less than 1%. If not pre-accelerated, reducing accelerator is preferable. High temperature is equivalent to post-curing so except for some surface tackiness due to styrene evaporation strength and water resistance will be good.

With epoxy use a less reactive hardener, or work faster with smaller quantities. In emergencies put the resin in a refrigerator.

Shelf life of polyester will be short. It may become too thick to use easily. If it pours it will set, but will be difficult to use and bad moulding is probable.

Too hot is better than too cold.

Humidity

For professional moulding humidity must not exceed 80% to prevent condensation on the mould and glass fibre. When spray moulding the humidity must be below 40% to prevent moisture being drawn into the resin stream.

For professional moulding these levels must be monitored and maintained under all weather conditions, which requires a purpose built workshop and expensive air conditioning. This is a far cry from a polythene screen across one end of a shed, typical conditions when many older boats were moulded. In Florida and other areas where heating is not necessary, humidity control is commonly ignored despite being generally high, and quality therefore suffers.

For repairs and amateur work using hand lay up humidity is not so important as temperature provided the resin sets within the proper time and conditions of high humidity are avoided. This does not just mean a steamy jungle: mist and fog are 100% humidity.

Condensation

Much trouble has been caused by condensation during moulding. Like mist collects on a window, moisture will condense on glass fibre. Therefore, whether for production or repair, glass fibre should be warmed before use. Otherwise trapped moisture will form nuclei for blisters. Also the glass coupling agent is destroyed from the start.

Condensation on the mould will cause blemishes and undercure of the gel coat. During moulding it can lead to poor interlayer bonding and hydrolysis. Surfaces must be dry when secondary bonding.

Acclimatisation

Materials must be brought into the moulding area at least 48 hours before use, particularly resin which fire regulations require to be stored outside. In winter a drum of resin will take several days to warm up. Moulds too should not be used until acclimatised. Porous gel coats were once a feature of Scandinavian boats moulded in winter.

Ventilation

Draughts on to the mould must be avoided. Authorities do not now allow open windows and doors, although they were very common in the past. Draughts, whether natural or from ventilation, evaporate styrene, chill the resin and cause reduced cure.

Fitting out
Ideally all major structural attachments like bulkheads and stringers should be done under moulding shop conditions, but they seldom are. Yet structural attachments are as important as the main moulding; they hold the boat together.

Cure
The most critical part of cure is the first three weeks. The mouldings should remain under moulding shop conditions for that time. But with rapid mould turnover and space there at a premium it is common to shunt bare shells into fitting out bays as soon as possible. Here the company accountant can rule and expensive controlled conditions are not maintained. A cold night or weekend with heating turned off is enough to halt the cure. Although it will resume, the damage may have been done.

In earlier years conditions during cure were often primitive. Sometimes newly moulded hulls were stored outside in winter weather to await their turn for fitting out or transport. Day and night heating was exceptional even in moulding workshops.

Amateur building
Amateurs will seldom have access to the conditions of a proper moulding workshop, and generally are more economy conscious than even the meanest company accountant. The fibreglass work fitting out a bare hull is often done under poor conditions, perhaps in the open and during winter. After some changes of ownership nobody may know if a boat of a popular class was fitted out by the company or from a bare shell. It is sold as a boat of that class, supposedly on a par with factory built boats.

In early days we rigged polythene tents inside leaky sheds and, some of us anyway, managed to do pretty good moulding. Polythene is an effective and economical way to retain heat and exclude draughts.

Warning: A polythene tent can be a fire risk. Any combustion heater can cause asphyxiation. Hydrocarbon vapours affect bonding and the large amount of water vapour, a product of combustion, will cause massive condensation. Use only electric heaters.

Dust
On the mould dust will cause blemishes and pinholes. Concrete floors should be sealed. Some kinds of dust will affect the setting and cure of polyester, notably from sawing or sanding plywood as the glue line contains phenol.

Cleanliness
The idea of a moulding workshop being clean may be greeted with hollow laughter. Nevertheless the cleaner the conditions the better the moulding.

This also applies to the inside of the boat during the important fitting out stages.

Repair
Moulding repairs should also be done under acceptable conditions; the bigger the repair the more important they are (Chapters 39–41).

Crises
Despite the best will in the world power cuts, strikes, breakdowns, material shortages and weather can thwart the best intentions. Unless seriously abnormal, troubles will not be apparent until years later, by which time it is very difficult to trace the root cause of puzzling problems.

That is where knowledge of fibreglass history and boat vintages is invaluable. Some crises, like impending bankruptcy, would affect one firm, others boatbuilding worldwide.

Moulding

The general principles of moulding are assumed to be familiar, just as a book on wooden boats does not describe basic carpentry. However, many finer points are still often neglected, especially by moulders more interested in production speed.

Moulding is not the crude, slapdash bucket-and-brush job for unskilled labourers that was widely assumed in the earlier boom years of the 1960s and 1970s. Most boats of that era are second class. Or worse.

Recent research into the causes of blistering has shown what everyone should have known since the beginning: only scrupulous care and attention to detail will produce good quality mouldings.

Rounding off

All parts need to be well rounded and easy to mould. This does not always suit yacht designers (who have seldom been practical moulders), and the unfortunate builder often has to mould the shape he has been given as best he can.

It is not easy to work glass mat or chop into sharp angles, grooves, ridges and other difficult detail, nearly impossible with woven rovings. It is sound practice to mould these first with narrow strips to infill and round off before laying up the general area. Otherwise there will probably be cavities and voids.

On sharp ridges or edges mat tends to pull thin. An experienced moulder lays on extra strips to compensate (Fig 29.1). Woven rovings will ruck especially heavy weight.

Bridging

Glass mat breaks up readily but woven rovings is too cohesive and tends to bridge. Also it gets pulled out again when working nearby.

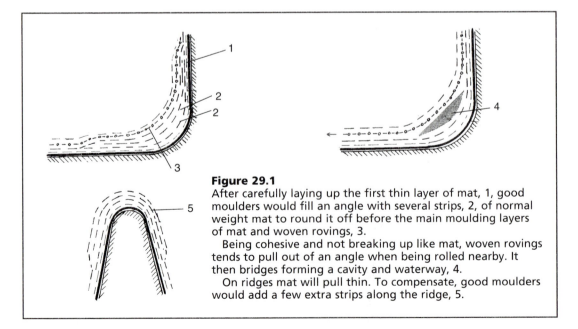

Figure 29.1
After carefully laying up the first thin layer of mat, 1, good moulders would fill an angle with several strips, 2, of normal weight mat to round it off before the main moulding layers of mat and woven rovings, 3.

Being cohesive and not breaking up like mat, woven rovings tends to pull out of an angle when being rolled nearby. It then bridges forming a cavity and waterway, 4.

On ridges mat will pull thin. To compensate, good moulders would add a few extra strips along the ridge, 5.

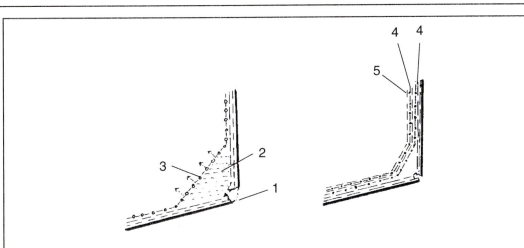

Figure 29.2
Actual example. Because of weak moulding the chine suffered minor damage, 1. This allowed water to fill an extensive cavity, 2, running the length of the boat where woven rovings had bridged. This was a single layer of heavy weight, 3, and, being over a gap, was porous. Result: insignificant damage sank the boat.
This would not have happened, even with woven rovings bridging in places, if properly moulded using two thinner layers of rovings, 4, with an inter layer and sealing layer of mat, 5.

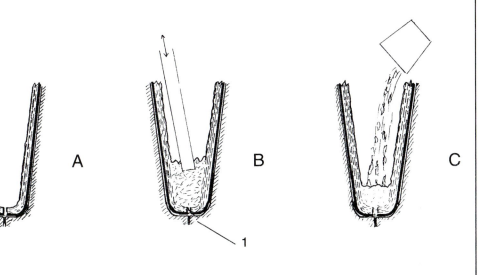

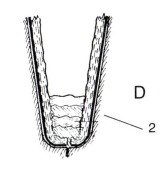

Figure 29.3   Moulding the unmouldable
A Problem: a deep keel, too narrow and deep to get a hand or tool inside, has been moulded in two halves and the half moulds brought together. Now it must be joined at the bottom by an important butt strap.
B The usual way is to 'push it in with a stick'. Inevitably the moulding will be bad and porous. Note the gap still at the bottom, 1.
C Another method is to pour in a dollop of resin mixed with fibres. The amount of glass which can be mixed in is small and the moulding therefore weak.
D Both these methods mean a large mass of resin and high exotherm as it sets. To reduce exotherm the moulding must be done a little at a time, 2.

Unless very careful the result is a line of cavities or voids in a conspicuous place. Underwater this can cause a serious leak. When bridging, woven rovings will be like a sieve because it is impossible to mould soundly without a backing. Moulded on the few and thickest principle it may be a single layer. So if a vulnerable chine or spray rail is slightly damaged, and water gets into the long void where the woven rovings have bridged the boat may sink (Fig 29.2).

Thickness

For cheapest production moulders want fast build up of bulk, so some use the thickest materials wetted out and rolled several layers at a time. That is not good moulding and always has a high void content, dry strands and often wide dry areas. Good, trouble free mouldings are made with thinner layers laid up individually. Even if rolled as multiple layers they must be wetted out singly, preferably with resin worked through from underneath.

Thick woven rovings build bulk faster but are difficult to mould into detail and should be used only on flattish, featureless areas. It usually has more voids and nuclei for blisters, and is commonly porous due to pinholes in the interstices. Rovings should always be interlayered with mat. It is becoming common to stitch them together but some are now too thick to wet out readily.

There must always be mat or gauze on the inner face to make a solid, non-porous surface. A layer of mat followed by a single thick woven rovings, as is not unusual with a light moulding or sandwich, is bad moulding however quick and economic to mould.

Two thin layers of woven rovings will be better moulded and less likely to be porous than one thick one. Similarly, with two layers of mat or chop, thin or pulled apart patches are less likely to coincide.

With the coloured gel coat one side and opaque finishing resin the other, a bad moulding looks much the same as a good one. Unless seriously defective it is hard and sounds solid enough. The difference seldom becomes apparent until troubles develop years later, comfortably after the warranty has expired.

Economics may be important, but so is quality. Compared with the overall cost of the boat, and the equipment now considered so essential, the money difference between good and bad moulding is small.

Moulding the unmouldable

Design and fashion dictate shape, not ease of moulding or release. Undercuts, parallel sides, forward slope transoms, twin keels, often require two, three or more piece moulds. So do out of reach places like deep keels. Sometimes impossible parts are moulded separately and grafted on later.

'Pushing in with a stick'

One of the rules of moulding is that 'difficult moulding will be bad moulding'. Too often designers leave the moulder to work out how to mould the unmouldable. A very common place is out of reach, deep in a narrow keel. Even moulded in two halves the vital butt strap holding the hull together still has to be moulded somehow, and moulded well because it holds the hull together (Fig 29.3).

The usual way is to 'push it in with a stick', relying on a generous mass to compensate for the very bad moulding, or pour in a bucketful of 'gunk' ie, mixed fibres and resin. Such moulding is spongy, with a myriad of voids and waterways. Being where water will collect in the bilges, decay is inevitable, not only in the pushed-in fibreglass but also the inner face and trimmed edges of the hull. Leaks along these edges due to attack from inside are common on older boats. I have known decay eat right through the thickest part of the keel.

The exotherm with a mass of resin will be high. Thermal stresses will crack the resin and the heat can damage the moulding, including unseen delamination. To reduce exotherm the resin should be low reactivity or deliberately inhibited, and the bulk built up a little at a time, allowing it to cool in between.

Colour

In early days everyone assumed a moulding must be coloured right through, like the new polythene buckets. It was some years before moulders realised a coloured gel coat alone was sufficient, and even longer to discover that coloured resins meant bad moulding. In fairness nobody really knew what good moulding was. Anything was good if fibreglass.

With uncoloured, clear resin the worker can see what he is doing. Air bubbles and dry patches are obvious. But coloured resins are opaque so he cannot see them. Consequently there is a massive void content. The foreman cannot see either, nor a surveyor or repairer later.

The need for through colour is a misconception. Remember your grease spot experiments at school? As long as the light outside is brighter than inside, as it normally will be, the colour will seem solid. From inside the reverse happens. Light shows through and the colour appears patchy giving the impression the hull is thin in places, causing many an owner to panic. Wise builders paint inside or make sure it cannot be seen. Actually any patchiness is in the gel coat and has no relation to the thickness of the translucent moulding. It is like looking through a painted window.

A coloured layer behind is sometimes needed with semi-translucent colours but should never be in the first layers. These are the most critical and must always be very carefully moulded. It is equally effective in the last layer.

Custom moulding

As builders buy in engines, masts and hundreds of other items, some buy hulls from a custom moulder. The practice has much to commend it. Specialist moulders can put all their capital, equipment and expertise into moulding, whereas a boatbuilder must have equipment and staff for many trades. Unlike wooden boatbuilding, fibreglass moulding with its expensive special buildings and separate staff does not fit well with anything else.

The moulding must be selected on quality, not price. A bad moulding can never be a good boat no matter how prestigious the builder.

The moulder

Those who go to sea trust their life first and foremost to a sound and seaworthy hull (as true today as in Noah's time). It does not matter how much safety equipment is carried, whether compulsory or voluntarily, nor the amount spent on electronics. The safety of the crew depends absolutely on the moulder just as with a wooden boat it depends on the skill and integrity of the builder.

Management need not be trained chemists but must know how to use resins and, even more, how *not* to, and recognise when things are going wrong.

What of the workers? Moulding used to be regarded by many companies as crude, unskilled dirty work. Inexperienced labourers were put on to moulding hulls, the most important part of any boat. No wonder so many old boats have troubles now; even supposedly high quality boats by famous names.

Fortunately sound moulding is no longer considered a labourer's job. In Britain and Europe it is recognised that workers do need to be trained, although not through years of apprenticeship, and there are training courses. Most moulders still train their own, but nowadays good companies do not put them straight on to moulding hulls. Workers start on unimportant hatches or internal mouldings. Only their most experienced workers are trusted to mould hulls. It was not always so. In the USA and perhaps other countries, it has been reported that some faulty mouldings have been due to language problems with immigrant workers, probably inevitable with such a manual process.

The most important and seldom appreciated qualification is character – something no training can give. The person needs to be conscientious and honest. Mature, steady workers, men or women, usually make better moulders than youngsters. Some of the best moulders I have known have been women as they are very conscientious. This attribute, however, can make them less popular with employers as they tend to work slower.

Blister-free moulding

It is unlikely with the present state of the art, that any fibreglass boat will be completely free of blisters throughout its life, which should be fifty years at least. But a lot can be done during moulding to reduce and delay the problem. As has been emphasised, careful moulding, not fancy gel coats, is the reason why some builders' boats are trouble free for many years.

Until that simple fact is realised owners will keep on having to pay huge maintenance bills to replace gel coats every few years.

It is not wooden or steel boats that are now expensive to maintain but fibreglass. Yet it need not be so. That early dream of low maintenance is as true as ever – but *only* if fibreglass boats are moulded properly.

Resin manufacturers Scott Bader Ltd have done research on preventing blisters, in contrast to paint manufacturers' emphasis on repair and setting up expensive clinics. To them the more boats that blister the better.

Scott Bader advocate the following:

1 100% isophthalic gel coats, not an ordinary resin improved by adding a proportion of isophthalic.

2 A layer of surfacing gauze or tissue behind the gel coat to build a thick resin rich layer.

3 The first layer to be a thin mat, 1 oz/ft², 300 g/m², very carefully and thoroughly worked in and consolidated. This is the most important part of the whole moulding.

4 The resin should be applied first and the glass laid on top, so it is forced up through the glass, displacing air as it goes. The common, speedier practice of applying resin on top of dry mat traps air underneath, and bubbles are left clinging to the interface. These are the commonest nuclei for blisters. (An American expert claims the first method filters silica grains from thixotropic agents and these form hygroscopic nuclei. In my experience the recommended technique is better as air bubbles form much larger, more powerful voids, evident behind most blisters.)

5 Two more layers of mat are applied in the same careful way, again using 100% isophthalic resin. As the angles become filled and rounded the mat may be thicker.

6 An alternative is to use vinyl ester or neopentyl glycol-isophthalic resin for these first layers. Vinyl ester is the more expensive. A layer of moulding or gauze is more effective than the thin barrier coat often recommended.

7 All mat must be powder bound, never emulsion bound.

8 All glass should be pre-dried before use to ensure there is no condensation.

9 Not until after three layers of mat should woven rovings be used. Even then the first layer must be light or medium weight, not thick bulk building.

10 If isophthalic resins cannot be used throughout the change to cheaper orthophthalic must be done at depth, and not before at least three layers of mat.

11 All glass must be applied one layer at a time, carefully rolled and consolidated.

12 The issue of resin should be catalysed at source to make sure that it is not overlooked, and controlled but not rationed. If the job needs more for proper wetting out it should be issued. Dry moulding must be avoided.

13 The critical first few layers of mat should be hand laid. This is disputed by those who claim chop eliminates the bad effects of binders, especially in America where emulsion binders are still sometimes used for faster wetting out.

14 Spray moulding or chop is faster but the quality is lower. Unlike a team laying up rolls of factory made glass, chop is completely dependent on the skill of the one person operating the gun. As air and atmospheric moisture get picked up in the stream there are more voids.

Middle age

So much for how fibreglass boats should be moulded today. How were they moulded yesterday? The early years when the pioneers were feeling their way. The boom years when shady builders jumped on the bandwagon and many neither knew nor cared as long as they could sell their rubbish. The oil crisis and inflation when prices went through the roof helped by the imposition of VAT in Britain. The mad competition to build faster, lighter boats, more stuffed with toys.

All along price has never been a criterion of quality. Good moulders have not necessarily been the most expensive. Some builders of cheap boats, like Hurley, were among the best. Sadly they, with several others, were sunk by an unannounced 'improvement' in a gel coat which caused an epidemic of blistering. The manufacturers, Artrite Resins, sank too. Luckily such epidemics have been few and most troubles have been the moulder's fault.

The best moulders have always been conscientious about conditions and have built or adapted proper buildings. However, concern about maintaining heating day and night has often been related to the cost of fuel. During and after the worldwide fuel crisis in 1974, many moulders were forced to economise. Those years are a bad vintage.

Outside the best moulders there was little concern about maintaining proper conditions. Temperatures fluctuated widely. Nature decided humidity and nobody bothered about condensation. Materials were brought straight in from cold, damp storage outside; drums of resin left open; doors and windows opened wide; draughts and dust blowing on to the mould; dirt, debris and insects trodden in. Everything that nowadays would be bad practice!

A properly built and insulated workshop was uncommon. Often it was a curtained off portion of the main building, with extra heating during working hours. Dust blew through from woodworking, the floor a foot thick with dirty, trodden in resin and glass.

Avoid a boat moulded during the winter. Not when it was completed, the date on a certificate, but when moulded. More recent ones have the date embossed on the stern. Otherwise guess three months earlier.

The remarkable thing is how some moulders managed to mould good boats under theoretically poor conditions. Even more remarkable the number all along who have consistently turned out bad boats under good conditions, and still do. Good conditions alone do not make good boats. Although many moulders did their best, conditions generally were unsatisfactory compared with the required standards today. Many more just did not care.

Those are the sort of boats still afloat today, the great fleet of middle aged boats. The ones with the problems, so many of which stem from the way they were moulded. Some good, a lot bad, but mostly indifferent. According to modern theory they ought not to be afloat at all. Strangely, most of them are! Even stranger that many will still be afloat when the sophisticated flimsy ones being built now are not.

Preaching how fibreglass boats should be moulded is as useful to the owner of a middle aged boat as telling someone in a geriatric home how he should have spent his life. The relevant thing is not how a fibreglass boat *should* be moulded but how it *was* moulded. Unfortunately that is very hard to tell, although if you really want to know there are laboratories able to analyse samples, destructively of course and at a cost.

Like wine, one needs to know the vintage.

Moulding faults

What can go wrong, one might ask, with such a simple process? Sloshing resin on to layers of glass fibre. Any fool can do that – it's unskilled, messy work unlike the craftsmanship of the wooden boat builder.

That is how people used to think and is the root cause of much trouble on older boats. Moulding is *not* a job for the lowest grade workers. Moulding is semi-skilled work on a par with a professional painter. There are many tricks to sound moulding only learned by experience. A great many things can go wrong.

Unusually in this age, and not generally appreciated, fibreglass boats are made by hand. In a mould, it is true, but the actual moulding is a manual process even when mechanised.

Design

Good moulding starts on the drawing board but few designers have been moulders. They are more interested in the go-fastest shape. The moulder will do his best, but 'difficult moulding will be bad moulding'.

Initial inspection

Every moulding should be examined very, very carefully before any work is done to turn it into a boat. Scrapping a bare moulding will be painful and expensive, yet far more expensive after a lot of money, equipment and weeks of work have been poured in. So will the cost of putting right fundamental errors. Most builders lack the courage, and finance.

Careful inspection is particularly important when the moulding is subcontracted, and faults are not the builders'. All they can claim from the moulder is the value of the bare hull but the aggrieved owner will demand the full value of the boat, perhaps three or four times more. Only lawyers benefit from this.

Gel coat flaws

Almost every boat is likely to have a few subcutaneous cavities (Chapter 24). Good builders search out and fill them. They know by experience where to look, generally along angles and ridges. Bad builders wait for the owner to complain.

Materials

The basic materials are made by big chemical or glass companies under close control. Defective materials are rare nowadays but in the past an epidemic would affect many boats and other companies. Far commoner is incorrect use by the moulder, or disregard of conditions.

Resins and reinforcements have become more sophisticated and specialised. But unless used correctly for the right purpose their superior properties will not be attained. They may not even be as good as cheaper general purpose materials. Some have undesirable side effects. Where a critical design requires a certain material substitutions can be disastrous.

Nowadays small quantities are obtained from secondary suppliers, often of unknown make without data sheets. A moulder short of his usual supply may turn to a local wholesaler or retailer, or another moulder perhaps not marine – anything to keep going.

Even though fully approved a material can turn out years later to have critical deficiencies unknown at the time. Much blistering today is due to emulsion bound mats which twenty years ago were considered superior to powder bound.

The science of fibreglass moulding has developed so quickly we lack the experience built up over generations with other materials. There has been steady improvement, but much has been put into use without long term trial. Big boats moulded under production conditions and afloat for years do not behave like small laboratory samples tested artificially for unrealistically short times.

Moulding defects

The box below lists common defects, many covered elsewhere. Most are multiple, one leading to another. Except close to the gel coat they will be difficult or impossible to detect, especially when small or spotty, eg massive delamination over an area of 1 ft, 300 mm, should be detectable, but not 1 in, 25 mm. A patch bonding in spots, typical dry moulding, will be weak and porous yet seem quite solid (Fig 26.3).

Cure is a matter of degree. No practical mouldings ever attain theoretical 100% cure but most are good enough. Undercure leads to weakness, lack of stiffness, high water absorption, blistering and is a major initiator of other defects. The general reason is cold or damp.

Even for good moulders wetting out every single fibre in the time available is impossible. Nevertheless the moulding should look substantially translucent with few dry, white strands visible. Due to natural ageing and hydrolysis of the coupling agent they become more visible later but there should never be large white areas at any time, nor the more common small patches and spots. Dry moulding is most serious near the surface as absorbed water can then wick deep into the hull. It is commonest when, for speed, the first layers are moulded carelessly and with thick mat, even two at once.

Common contamination

These inhibit (delay setting) or poison polyester:

Phenol and compounds	Certain wood preservatives
Resorcinol	Some pesticides
Plywood dust	Copper, copper compounds
Water	Pyridine
Dust from sanding fibreglass	Some disinfectants

These affect bonding:

Condensation	Release agent
Oil	Grease
Diesel	Trodden in dirt
Dust	Wood preservatives
Phenolic and resorcinol glues	
Anything which inhibits polyester	

Sandwich mouldings

Sandwich or cored mouldings are more likely to give trouble than single skin (Chapter 19).

Distortion

Forcing to fit was common in earlier years when bare hulls and decks were treated casually and allowed to distort during cure.

Contamination

For a sound interlaminar bond the surfaces must be free of contamination. This is no problem when one layer follows immediately, but in practice delays and intervals are inevitable.

During the night or weekend the surface can become contaminated with dust or condensation which prevents a good interlaminar bond when work is resumed. Most boats are laid up one complete layer at a time. On the big fibreglass minehunters one smallish section was moulded to full thickness before moving on to the next to avoid long intervals between layers.

Elusive troubles have been caused by certain kinds of dust, notably phenolic glues from plywood. Ventilation systems may suck in fumes from neighbouring industrial plants, perhaps only occasionally. Even in a pollution free rural area drift from pesticides has played havoc. In most cases the effects will be marginal and not apparent until years later when memory of the original cause has been long lost.

Moulding faults

Inadequate cure	Thick glass in first layer
Dry moulding	Cloth in first layer
Excess resin	Poor interlaminar bond
Bridging angles	Delamination
'Pushing in with a stick'	Contamination
Coloured moulding resin	Condensation
High void content	Telegraphing

a

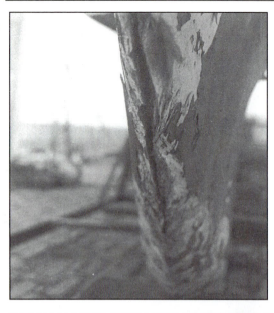

b

c

Photos 30.1 (a) Split keel, showing how weak the butt strap holding the halves of the boat together can be. Obviously it was difficult to mould so was probably 'pushed in with a stick'. **(b)** The two part mould for this boat (Elizabethan 29). Easy enough to mould while separated but imagine what it was like in that deep keel slot when trying to mould the vital butt strap which holds the two sides together. (In 1960 this special, insulated moulding workshop was good by early standards. Its predecessor was just a polythene tent in a leaky, uninsulated, ex-wartime shed.) **(c)** Deck for a 38 ft Nelson patrol boat still in the mould. Unusually this mould is split athwartships. (Note the improved conditions now essential even for small moulders.)

During fitting out workers often walk about on the still tacky surface with dirty shoes which, as they get stickier, get even dirtier. They cover it with shavings, sanding dust, spilt tea and worse. Dust, bugs and leaves blow in through open doors and windows. Everything which falls into the mould becomes part of the boat. Important structural members are still expected to bond.

Clinical cleanliness is impractical. Nevertheless the inside must be kept as clean as possible and all surfaces protected with polythene. Newspaper or cardboard will stick.

Speed of moulding

In the early boom years workers were often on a speed related bonus. Naturally they did not want to lose their bonus so defects, obviously numerous with such a system, were not put right or bodged. This was not confined to the lower end of the market. Some of the better builders bought in hulls at the cheapest price to fit out as luxury yachts.

A lot of boats were made that way in the 1960s. Quality was as it came. The idea that fibreglass could be bad was inconceivable. It was enough that it was fibreglass: the new wonder material, perfect in every way.

Nowadays that attitude has gone. Production pressures and the demand for rapid moulding speed are even greater, but moulders now turn to spray moulding and other semi-mechanised processes. Yet in general speed and good quality still do not go together. The best moulders still use hand lay up.

To build bulk quickly some moulders lay up

several layers at a time. They must still be wetted out separately even when rolled down together. Others use the heaviest woven rovings and extra thick mats. Thorough wetting out is difficult and quality generally poor. If the large amount of resin needed is stinted there will be innumerable pinholes in the interstices. The hard rolling is commonly stinted too. Being easier to wet out properly and mould to shape two thinner layers do not really take much longer.

Centreline join

Boats often split along the join, usually in the keel area where it is difficult to mould a butt strap. It is unlikely along the whole length but can cause a baffling leak especially when it opens only while sailing.

State of the art

The standard of moulding and materials have steadily improved. Yet most improvements have been for economic reasons and benefit the moulder not the owner. In any case only the best are ever built to state of the art. Most fall short in varying degrees.

The great majority of fibreglass boats afloat today were built between ten and thirty years ago. Soon it will be forty. For those owners state of the art today is irrelevant. What was it when their boat was moulded? How did the builders rate then?

In the glamour of new developments, revised rules and standards, the way boats used to be moulded gets very little attention. The best were never better than marginal. Most would now be rated second rate. Yet without knowing that, one cannot understand what is happening to them today, and why, and how it could be put right. Even if it is worth putting right.

Few remember earlier days. That generation are now retired or dead. Most were very soon out of it anyway. Who in the industry today can recall the primitive conditions under which most boats were moulded? The hard to mould materials. Mistakes and misjudgements. Regular recessions every ten years which always hit boatbuilding first and hardest. International and national crises. And not least the economic and social attitudes in which it all happened.

Mouldless construction

Since the earliest days of fibreglass people have tried to build boats without a mould. Indeed especially in those early days, for traditions of conventional boatbuilding were strong and the idea of producing yachts by the hundred was unthinkable. A gentleman's yacht was just not built that way.

Yet there is still a need for boats not mass produced from a mould for amateur backyard construction or special one-off commercial boats, top flight hi-tech racing machines and very large boats for which the numbers would not justify a conventional mould.

Mouldless construction is a misnomer. Some sort of former is essential to give the shape. Before the resin sets it is as shapeless as a wet blanket and must have support. What it generally implies is a cheap expendable mould or former.

This description is brief. There are many methods and materials used, which are better described in other literature.

Advantages	Disadvantages
Cheap, expendable mould	Rough finish
Suitable for one-off	Work needed to fair
Suitable for hi-tech yachts	Problem of turning the boat over
Suitable for large vessels	Difficulty of fitting frames
Suitable for superstructures	Mouldings require painting
Suitable for amateurs	Poor impact strength
Versatility	Little scope for detail
Relative freedom from blistering	
Less risk of sandwich delamination	

Mould

Usually this is a simple male mould, upside down even for quite large sizes, comprising frames plus stem and stern, on which wood battens are fastened to form a skeleton hull. Over this is laid the sandwich core using any of the materials described in Chapter 19.

Another method is to strip plank using conventional boatbuilding techniques, eg with pultruded rods similar to fishing rod blanks, pre-moulded or sawn narrow fibreglass planks, end grain balsa in long strips or ordinary timber. Whatever is used it must have a solid surface to mould over.

Bruce Roberts claims it is as easy to make a simple female mould using cheap hardboard, any extra work being more than compensated by eliminating the tedious fairing which is unavoidable with a male mould. However, this assumes a hard chine design as for plywood or steel, whereas the male mould can be round bilge.

Moulding

The fibreglass outer skin is laid up by conventional moulding except there is no gel coat. When the mould is to become the core, no release agent is used. Instead it must bond, and bond well.

Inner skin

Next the mould is turned over, a major problem with a large boat or wide multihull, and must be planned before starting. It requires suitable tackle or crane hire, a job for professionals, plus space. Do not underestimate the difficulties. A boat is a big ungainly thing and can be dangerous.

When turned over the framework is

Photos 31.1 (a) 'Mouldless construction'. Skeleton male mould made of battens.
(b) 'Sewing' sheets of plastics foam on to the battens (both Bruce Roberts-Goodson Designs).

removed, and the inner face laid up, plus bulkheads, and stiffeners.

Fairing

In a female mould the polished mould face imparts a smooth finish to the gel coat so the moulding needs no further work. But there certainly is with a male mould. Hard, tedious work, sanding with long battens, to get a good finish. The boat is 'inside out'. Instead of smooth gel coat on the outside, uneven finish inside, the uneven surface is now outside. In effect it is like the mould in Fig 1.2.

To avoid bulges, reinforcement should be butted relying on staggered multiple layers for continuity. Marrying is even better.

Yacht finish will take weeks or until patience is exhausted. It is easier to put on filler than take off. Unless ruthless the thickness and weight of filler will end up quite substantial. On racing machines this must be the bare minimum. Syntactic foam will reduce weight. Sanding cannot start until the hull is hard and largely cured.

Despite the similarity of purpose gel coat resins are unsuitable for the finish. Use waxy top coat or finishing resin as for a normal inside and then paint.

Superstructures

Cabin tops, decks and superstructures can be made in a similar way, and often done for commercial and military craft, where appearance is secondary, giving versatility on a standard hull.

Delamination

Because both faces are laid up wet on the core the bond is generally good. Delamination between the outer face and core, the common curse with a female mould, seldom occurs.

The Kelsall 'one-piece' hull

David Kelsall, one of the most experienced and successful builders, has developed true mouldless construction. In this the hull is laid up flat on a moulding table. After setting it is bent to shape along pre-planned lines where the inner skin has been omitted. Then the inner skin is completed and frames added. Bow and stern have cut-aways and are bent separately.

A somewhat similar, bent sheet construction is used by South American Indians at El Dorado to make conchas with bark from the copaiba tree. It is easier to make another than portage round rapids.

Prefabrication

Instead of moulding *in situ*, boats have been made by laying up sandwich panels on a table and using these like plywood. Joins are by butt straps and moulded rebates. Gentle curvature can be induced while green. Being moulded on a smooth surface the finish is good and can be gel coat. Standard designs for plywood or steel can be adapted. A refinement is to mould smaller, difficult sections like bow and stern in female moulds.

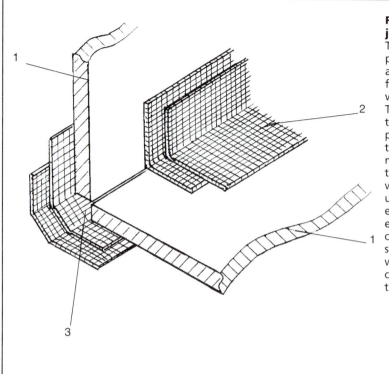

Figure 31.1   Taped joints
Two pieces, 1, commonly plywood but could be anything else including fibreglass, can be joined with strong glass tape, 2. Two layers should be used to reduce the risk of pinholes coinciding. As the outer layers must be moulded over a gap, 3, the first should be pre-wetted. This would usually be the side exposed to water and even if the edges are chamfered to fit there will still be a small gap. It would be good practice to cover it first with sticky tape.

The newspaper boat

An interesting 1940s dinghy was made of newspaper, soaked in epoxy and rolled into tubes in a home-made machine like a large cigarette roller. Nowadays one could use polyester. I would be interested to learn its fate.

Taped joints

Fibreglass tapes can be used to join pieces of rigid foam, plywood or metal, a method I developed in the early 1950s, originally for a

Photo 31.2 Using fibreglass tape to join pre-cut pieces of plywood. The popular Mirror dinghy (Bell Woodworking Ltd).

balloon gondola but it did become a boat in mid-ocean. Stitching them together first, a very old idea, was resurrected for the amateur built Mirror dinghies, and is now widely used (Fig 31.1).

The tape not only holds the boat together but must keep the water out. Open weave scrim tape is too weak and is like a sieve unless flooded with more resin than inexperienced amateurs like to apply.

The tape should be a strong fairly close weave, similar to the cloth recommended for sheathing (Chapter 22). Epoxy is the better adhesive but cheaper polyester is more often used and adequate provided surfaces are properly prepared and primed. Some tapes are not suitable for epoxy whereas most readily available ones can be used with polyester.

References

Trade catalogues, Airex, Di-Vinyl, Baltek and others.
Boat Building by Bruce Roberts, 1994.
Various technical articles and correspondence with David Kelsall 1964–94.

Thickness

The reinforcement is assumed to be glass fibre and the boats ordinary production cruisers. Different parameters apply to Kevlar and carbon fibre.

Thickness is easy to alter. Add more if higher strength is needed. Reduce if somebody thinks it too heavy, or expensive. It can also go either way by mistake without anyone realising. Few moulders have bothered to check. Some, like Tylers, colour rag layers.

Specification

In popular theory the glass fibre alone gives strength. So specifications quote glass weight, type and distribution, which is easy to apply. The resin/glass ratio may be specified but being the major component and harder to control is the principal variable. Consequently a fibreglass boat is as thick as it turns out to be.

However, thickness is the only parameter easy to check. So it is useful to know the approximate relationship between specified weight of glass and the thickness it ought to be.

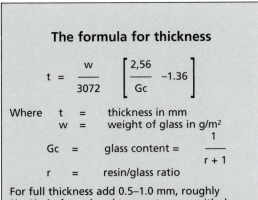

The formula for thickness

$$t = \frac{w}{3072}\left[\frac{2{,}56}{Gc} - 1.36\right]$$

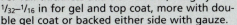

Where   t   =   thickness in mm
  w   =   weight of glass in g/m²
  Gc   =   glass content = $\dfrac{1}{r+1}$
  r   =   resin/glass ratio

For full thickness add 0.5–1.0 mm, roughly ¹/₃₂–¹/₁₆ in for gel and top coat, more with double gel coat or backed either side with gauze.

This assumes the specification is known. With a new boat some builders are stupidly cagey. Or afraid of being caught out. Secrecy is unjustified; owners have a right to know what they are buying. It is much harder to discover the specification for an older boat. Even when the builder is still in business and cooperative it may not refer to that boat but an earlier or later model. Neither are classification societies who approved the design or actually supervised construction more forthcoming.

The most relevant guide is how it compares with boats of the same class, or similar size, type and vintage.

Design

By increasing the glass content, using woven materials instead of general purpose glass mat, or stronger kinds of glass fibre, the tensile strength can be increased. Therefore it is claimed thickness can be reduced in proportion to the increase in tensile strength, thus reducing weight and placating the god of speed.

This is wrong thinking. The important factor is not tensile strength, but stiffness. They go together but not in proportion (Chapter 13). Shape, curvature and features have greater influence.

Glass fibre

Glass mat and woven rovings have different resin ratios and thickness by weight of glass. But being usually in combination the differences tend to average out.

The manufacturing tolerance for glass reinforcement is ±10%. In theory this affects thickness. In practice nobody is likely to know or bother to adjust the resin.

Resin/glass ratio

Regardless of the nominal weight, weave and type of glass in a layer it is the resin/glass ratio which determines thickness.

Glass content

Normal glass content for mat will be 25–30% and woven rovings 38–47% (see Table 32.1). These are less than the target figures but more likely in practice. Individual workers develop their own pattern. Moulders concerned with speed will have high resin ratios because slushy moulding is easier and faster. High performance moulders taking more time and effort to consolidate can reduce the resin and hence weight. In general polyester is cheaper than labour.

The thinnest mouldings are wet-on-wet so a subsequent layer squashes down into the previous one. But much moulding is wet-on-dry where the previous layer has already set. That layer will be thicker and is another reason why practical mouldings tend to have a higher resin ratio.

Only with bad material control and workers drawing resin ad lib, would glass content be below 20%, and affect the moulders' solvency more than strength. Tight resin control is necessary for economic survival but may be worse for the boat, eg if a worker runs out and is afraid to ask for more he will make do with what he has and leave resin starved, dry patches. Conversely if he has a little left over the natural inclination is to put it into the boat rather than waste it. Too much is better than too little. Actual resin ratio will depend on how evenly he distributes the resin and how hard he rolls and consolidates the glass fibre.

A company that wants to stay in business will maintain a close check on resin used and keep fairly close overall to the target resin/glass ratio. But it will still vary between individuals and different parts of the boat.

It is nonsense to specify precise figures. Fibreglass moulding is not a precision process.

Thickness

With different glass types and unknown lay up thickness may seem an unreliable method of checking quality. Critics will say a weak moulding with too little glass and too much resin will be the same thickness as a high strength, high glass one. True. Yet extremes will be obvious in other ways. With experience and examination of the moulding, the type of boat and quality, age and perhaps knowledge of the class it is possible to get a good idea compared with similar boats.

The average thickness is usually taken to be 0.7 mm per layer of 300 g/m^2, or roughly $1/32$ in per 1 oz/ft^2 (mat is usually supplied as 300, 450 or 600 g/m^2 equivalent to 1, $1^1/_2$, 2 oz/ft^2), based on a glass content, Gc, of 30% or resin/glass ratio 2.3. This is typical for most ordinary production cruisers built since about 1970 with the usual combination of woven rovings interlayered with mat. Early boats, when all mat was usual and harder to wet out, would be higher, 0.8–0.9 mm. Only with poor materials control would it be over 1 mm. A carefully moulded, very thoroughly consolidated boat might get as low as 0.5 mm, Gc 40%, R/G 1.5, but would be an obviously top flight racing machine (see Table 32.2).

The inside surface is undulating. Does the

Table 32.1   Glass content/thickness

R/G	4.0	3.0	2.75	2.5	2.33	2.25	2.0	1.75	1.5	1.25	1.0
Gc%	20	25	27	29	30	31	33	36	40	44	50
t mm	1.1	0.86	0.79	0.72	0.70	0.68	0.62	0.56	0.49	0.43	0.36
t in	0.043	0.033	0.031	0.028	0.027	0.026	0.024	0.022	0.019	0.017	0.014

<-------------------------Mat----------------------> <-------------Rovings------------>

<-------------------Composite------------------>

R/G	Resin/glass ratio
Gc	Glass content
t	Thickness in mm or inches of unit layer of glass, ie 1 oz/ft^2, 300 g/m^2

0.7 mm, the thickness underlined, is the generally accepted figure for a composite moulding formula mean the peaks or the hollows – a difference of 1 mm or more? Nobody has ever said but obviously spot checks by drilling are hit or miss.

Note: in Tables 32.1 and 32.2 glass ratio applies regardless of whether mat or woven rovings. Cloth, however, varies according to the weave: high with close weave, very low with open weave scrim cloth. Woven materials, rovings and cloth, tend to maintain thickness regardless of resin. But mat varies more according to thoroughness of consolidation and amount of resin. With hard work and minimum resin, mat can be rolled quite thin. Dry, resin starved mat will be thick but obvious if visible.

Tables 32.3 and 32.5 give rule weights of glass for different sizes of boats (based on the 1982 EEC draft directive, an amalgam of European standards). Tables 32.4 and 32.6 convert them into approximate thickness. Being based on 0.7 mm per 300 g/m², they must be used with discretion.

Tolerance

Pundits will claim measurement is futile. How can you quote a thickness when the resin ratio can vary from 1.5 to 3 and nobody knows anyway? In practice an ordinary production cruiser based on glass mat and woven rovings will not vary much from the average overall 2.3. Stepping up the ratio to 2.5 or down to 2.0 makes a difference in thickness of less than 12%. Compare this with the manufacturing tolerance on glass of 10%, plus a vague, variable and probably larger moulding tolerance and an imprecise undulating surface.

The tables are a guide, nothing more. If within about 10% there is little to worry about. 25% less would warrant explanation. Anything thicker is on the right side even due to excess of resin. However, in recent years the trend is to thinner, lighter, cheaper hulls based

on computer optimised design rather than established rules.

If you want accuracy you have to know the exact resin/glass ratio and lay up, only possible by laboratory analysis of cut outs which is expensive and destructive. Even then only for that place. Many cut outs are necessary to get an accurate average figure. Conclusive evidence for the court but, if you still want a boat, thickness tests are a rough guide, cheap, quick and easy.

Yes it is crude. But so is fibreglass moulding.

Thickness will not be reliable on a high tech boat with exotic reinforcements and deliberately low resin ratio. But that sort of owner will worry himself sick about thickness, not thinness. Thinner could squeeze another microknot.

A few boats, generally a whole class, may have a very high resin content due to slack materials control. The 29 ft, 9 m Shipmans were consistently half a ton heavier than the prototype (which, I discovered on survey, explained why it won every race!). However, they survived accidents which would have wrecked a normal boat. Two things distinguish an overweight boat: the waterline will be above the designed and the builders bankrupt!

Variation of thickness

Rules and good design specify the thickness based on glass weight for different parts of the boat. The dominant thickness is the bottom merging into greater thickness along the centreline and keel area. Topsides are generally about 80%, although for simplicity of moulding on small boats they are often the same. High stress areas need extra thickness, eg shroud plates on sailing yachts and the transom on outboard or stern drive motor boats. Decks and superstructures should be topside thickness but most are now sandwich (Figs 32.1 and 32.2).

Table 32.2 Weight of glass per mm

R/G	3.0	2.33	1.85	1.5	1.22	1.0
Gc%	25	30	35	40	45	50
g/m²	400	480	525	625	675	725
oz/ft²	1.3	1.6	1.75	2.0	2.25	2.4
	<-------------Mat------------->			<-----------Rovings----------->		
	<---------Composite-------->					

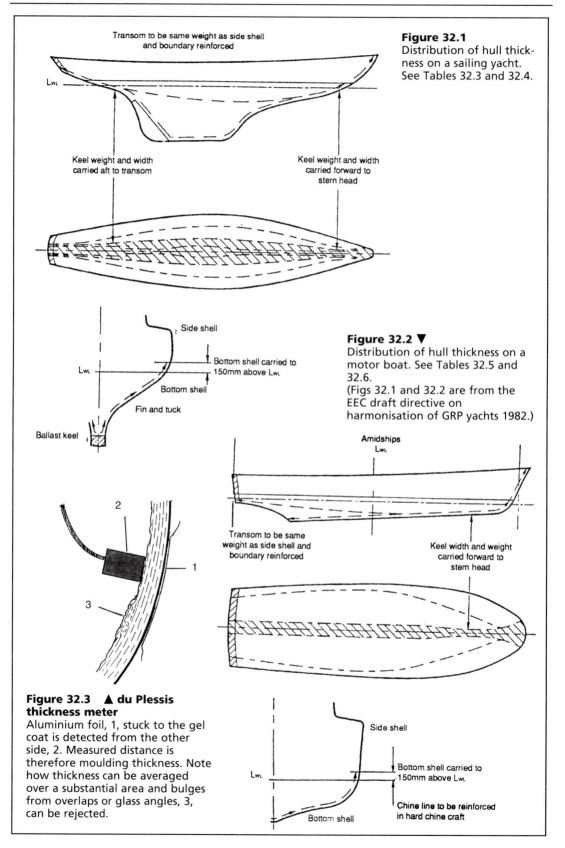

Figure 32.1
Distribution of hull thickness on a sailing yacht. See Tables 32.3 and 32.4.

Transom to be same weight as side shell and boundary reinforced

Keel weight and width carried aft to transom

Keel weight and width carried forward to stern head

Side shell

Bottom shell carried to 150mm above L$_{WL}$

Bottom shell

Fin and tuck

Ballast keel

Figure 32.2 ▼
Distribution of hull thickness on a motor boat. See Tables 32.5 and 32.6.
(Figs 32.1 and 32.2 are from the EEC draft directive on harmonisation of GRP yachts 1982.)

Amidships
L$_{WL}$

Transom to be same weight as side shell and boundary reinforced

Keel width and weight carried forward to stem head

Figure 32.3 ▲ du Plessis thickness meter
Aluminium foil, 1, stuck to the gel coat is detected from the other side, 2. Measured distance is therefore moulding thickness. Note how thickness can be averaged over a substantial area and bulges from overlaps or glass angles, 3, can be rejected.

Side shell

Bottom shell carried to 150mm above L$_{WL}$

Chine line to be reinforced in hard chine craft

Bottom shell

The requirements for motor cruisers are dominated by speed. (Sailing yachts are not considered fast!) The first category in Tables 32.4 and 32.6 covers most displacement and semi-displacement hulls.

Measuring thickness

Edges tend to be thinner and do not indicate thickness elsewhere. Cut-outs are less misleading and should always be kept. Most surveyors drill a hole, but this is a crude method, much too hit or miss and destructive. Measurement must be averaged over an area (Chapter 43), to discard confusing overlaps, flanges and places where the glass has pulled thin or puddles formed. From inside, these areas can be located. But that means drilling towards the gel coat and chipping it. Access inside is usually so restricted anyway, most test drilling has to be from outside with no idea what is inside.

With glass mat and woven rovings the material is of fairly constant thickness and the principal variable is the amount and distribution of resin. With spray-up or chop the glass/resin ratio is set by the machine. But where it goes is entirely in the hands of the operator. Thickness can vary widely. I found one boat with the port side twice as thick as the starboard. Everyone swore it was absolutely impossible. The right weight of glass had gone into the boat. Nevertheless one side was half the thickness it should have been.

Nowadays non-destructive methods are well developed in other industries and should be standard practice on boats. Ultrasonic testers are expensive and require considerable experience and knowledge, not only of fibreglass but sound transmission too, if results are to be interpreted correctly. Thirty years ago I devised a simple electronic thickness meter based on an inexpensive industrial proximity meter (Fig 32.3).

A very important advantage with non-destructive testing is being able to measure over a sufficient area to average the peaks and hollows, and reject overlaps and bulges. Doing this with a drill on ordinary survey would need a lot of holes and owners tend to object to their boats being turned into sieves.

How thick should it be?

How thick does anyone want it to be?

'Not a micron thicker than the rule minimum' screams the racing fanatic. An ocean cruiser, with reef bashing in mind, wants 'tougher than steel'. 'As cheap as we can get away with', says a production builder for whom the criterion is the number of toilets, and seaworthiness ends at Force Four. 'Our reputation is at stake', claims the builder of quality yachts.

Each in his own way is right.

Various standards and rules have been produced and more are coming, notably the EU directive which, whether one likes it or not, should at least harmonise European standards. Before the first Lloyd's Rules were published, about 1963, there were no guidelines. It was an unexplored wilderness. Time has shown they have been a fair guide to a sound, strong boat. Many builders say too strong; a few not strong enough. It is always possible to build a faster boat. That does not mean a better boat. Also a cheaper boat, which many people do think is better.

Lloyd's Rules are regarded as conservative, based on a seaworthy vessel able to weather a storm at sea. Not a fast, fun to sail weekend boat for coastal cruising in fine summer weather. Which is all most people want. Many claim they are unrealistic. Modern boats are just not built like that. Whether they should be is a moot point.

Although the majority of classes built in Britain for many years have been Lloyd's approved (meaning the design is approved but not individual boats), very few, generally only big ones, fully comply with Lloyd's Rule Book. Nowadays builders submit their design or computer print out and if it agrees with the Society's calculations the design is approved regardless of what the book may say. The same applies to other societies and authorities.

What of the owner who just wants to know if his boat, or one he wants to buy, is thick enough. An approved design should be but is no guarantee that a particular boat is. The design may have been modified. It may have been built before approval. Some overseas builders have claimed approval they did not have.

Boats are not always moulded to specification. Mistakes can creep in. The impossible can happen and after many years as a surveyor I know well how it can, even on top-class yachts.

Beware of a boat which seems flexible when sailing. Even more if flexible when not sailing. Compare it with another of the same class and vintage. Often it is a design feature; some light, cheap boats are notoriously flimsy.

Panel size

Glass weights are based on specified panel sizes, ie the area between stiffeners, and should be increased or reduced according to spacing, shape of panel and width of glass angles. Other factors are materials of different stiffness, moduli of the stiffeners and curvature. Panel size is where rules and practice differ most, and is commonly larger than it should be.

There are practical problems. Grading glass weight according to numerous individual panel sizes would require complicated positioning with unacceptable scope for error. It is simpler for moulders to select an appropriate bottom or topsides weight throughout and plan panel size accordingly. Simpler still to forget about it, and arrange panels to suit the accommodation.

An amateur builder, altering the standard lay out, should be careful not to alter the spacing of the stiffeners, including accommodation glassed on. The rule books are fairly simple to follow. Beyond lies computerland.

You may think you know better. But at least rules have a generous factor of safety, and can be followed with confidence. If you depart from them it is wise to know the way. What works on a boat of strong, curved shape may be disastrous on another with substantially flat areas – as several builders have discovered to the discomfort of their creditors and the profit of their lawyers.

While mainly of concern to production builders, the EU directive may be binding on home builders too. Selling a boat not approved could be difficult, perhaps illegal. At this time the jungle is unexplored.

Too thin

If a boat certified by a classification society proves defective pressing a claim is very difficult. The builder will scurry for shelter under the society's skirts. That means having to challenge the might of the prestigious society, whose reputation hinges on infallibility. It is easier to convince God he is wrong.

Change of use

At the moulding stage it may be possible to add extra thickness if the moulder is cooperative and the design allows. With most production yachts it is impractical because of insufficient clearance around pre-moulded or prefabricated units. Big builders cannot tolerate interference with their rigid production cycle so the cost will usually be exorbitant. Extra thickness or additional frames are more practicable when fitting out a bare shell.

Tons of extra weight are essential to cross an ocean. Up goes the waterline. Nobody remembers rule bottom thickness goes only to designed waterline. Also boats float inches deeper in fresh water.

Commercial craft and fishing boats are designed to carry heavy loads in rough conditions. But a pleasure boat is not and if used as a work boat later may not be strong enough.

Table 32.3 Glass weight for sailing yachts

L m	L ft	d mm	d in	Bottom g/m²	Side g/m²	Fin & Tuck g/m²	Keel g/m²	Keel width mm	in
5	16.4	375	15	2600	1875	3676	5200	355	14
6	19.7	380	15	3000	2150	4200	6000	380	15
7	23.0	385	15	3250	2350	4375	6200	405	16
8	26.2	390	15.5	3475	2525	4550	6400	430	17
9	29.5	395	15.5	3675	2700	4725	6575	455	18
10	32.8	400	15.5	3875	2875	4900	6775	480	19
11	36.1	405	16	4075	3050	5075	6975	505	20
12	39.3	410	16	4275	3200	5250	7175	530	21
13	42.6	415	16	4450	3375	5425	7375	555	22
14	45.9	420	16.5	4650	3525	5600	7575	580	23
15	49.2	425	16.5	4825	3675	5775	7775	605	24
16	52.5	430	17	5025	3825	5950	7975	630	25
17	55.7	435	17	5200	3975	6125	8200	655	26
18	59.0	440	17.5	5375	4125	6300	8400	680	27
19	62.3	445	17.5	5550	4275	6500	8600	705	28
20	65.6	450	18	5750	4425	6675	8800	730	29

$$L = \frac{LOA + LWL}{2} \qquad d = \text{Spacing of stringers}$$

Dimensions are metric. Imperial equivalents are approximate.
Weight of glass in g/m². 300 g/m² = 1 oz/ft² approx

Table 32.4 Approximate thickness in mm for sailing yachts

L m	L ft	d mm	d in	Bottom mm	Side mm	Fin & Tuck mm	Keel mm	Keel width mm	in
5	16.4	375	15	6.1	4.4	8.6	12.1	355	14
6	19.7	380	15	7.0	5.0	9.8	14.0	380	15
7	23.0	385	15	7.6	5.5	10.2	14.5	405	16
8	26.2	390	15.5	8.1	5.9	10.6	14.9	430	17
9	29.5	395	15.5	8.6	6.3	11.0	15.3	455	18
10	32.8	400	15.5	9.0	6.7	11.4	15.8	480	19
11	36.1	405	16	9.5	7.1	11.8	16.3	505	20
12	39.3	410	16	10.0	7.5	12.2	16.7	530	21
13	42.6	415	16	10.4	7.8	12.7	17.2	555	22
14	45.9	420	16.5	10.8	8.2	13.1	17.7	580	23
15	49.2	425	16.5	11.2	8.6	13.5	18.1	605	24
16	52.5	430	17	11.7	8.9	13.9	18.6	630	25
17	55.7	435	17	12.1	9.3	14.3	19.1	655	26
18	59.0	440	17.5	12.5	9.6	14.7	19.6	680	27
19	62.3	445	17.5	13.0	10.0	15.2	20.1	705	28
20	65.6	450	18	13.4	10.3	15.6	20.5	730	29

These thicknesses are based on an assumed average resin/glass ratio of 2.33 or Gc 30% giving 0.7 mm per unit 300 g/m², 1 oz/ft² of glass.
  The difference is less than 12% if the resin/glass ratio is reduced to 2.0 or increased to 2.5.
NB: These thicknesses do not allow for the gel coat or inside top coat. Add 0.5–1.0 mm for the overall thickness.

$$L = \frac{LOA + LWL}{2} \qquad d = \text{Spacing of stringers}$$

Dimensions are metric. Imperial equivalents are approximate.

Table 32.5   Glass weight for motor yachts

$$\frac{V}{\sqrt{LWL}} \leq 3.6 \qquad \frac{V}{\sqrt{LWL}} = 5.4 \qquad \frac{V}{\sqrt{LWL}} = 7.2 \qquad \frac{V}{\sqrt{LWL}} = 9.0 \qquad \frac{V}{\sqrt{LWL}} = 10.8$$

L m	L ft	d mm	d in	Bottom	Side	Bottom	Side	Bottom	Side	Bottom	Side	Bottom	Side
5	16.4	375	15	2300	1875	2650	1975	2925	2050	3200	2125	3400	2200
6	19.7	380	15	2625	2150	3025	2250	3325	2350	3650	2425	3875	2525
7	23.0	385	15	2875	2325	3300	2425	3650	2525	3875	2625	4225	2725
8	26.2	390	15	3075	2500	3525	2600	3925	2700	4250	2825	4525	2925
9	29.5	395	15	3300	2675	3775	2775	4200	2900	4550	3000	4825	3125
10	32.8	400	16	3500	2850	4000	2950	4450	3050	4825	3175	5125	3300
11	36.1	405	16	3700	3000	4225	3100	4700	3225	5100	3350	5400	3500
12	39.3	410	16	3875	3475	4450	3250	4950	3400	5350	3525	5700	3675
13	42.6	415	16	4075	3325	4675	3425	5200	3550	5625	3700	5975	3850
14	45.9	420	16	4250	3500	4875	3575	5425	3725	5875	3875	6250	4025
15	49.2	425	16	4450	3650	5100	3725	5650	3875	6125	4025	6525	4200
16	52.5	430	16	4625	3800	5300	3875	5900	4025	6375	4200		
17	55.7	435	17	4800	3950	5500	4025	6125	4200	6625	4350		
18	59.0	440	17	4975	4125	5700	4175	6350	4350	6975	4525		
19	62.3	445	17	5150	4275	5925	4325	6575	4500	7125	4675		
20	65.6	450	18	5350	4425	6125	4475	6800	4650	7375	4825		

$$L = \frac{LOA + LWL}{2} \qquad\qquad \mathbf{d} = \text{Spacing of stringers}$$

All dimensions are metric. Imperial equivalents are approximate.
Glass weight in g/m². 300 g/m² is approximately equivalent to 1 oz/ft².

Table 32.6 Approximate thickness in mm for motor yachts

$$\frac{V}{\sqrt{LWL}} \leq 3.6 \qquad \frac{V}{\sqrt{LWL}} = 5.4 \qquad \frac{V}{\sqrt{LWL}} = 7.2 \qquad \frac{V}{\sqrt{LWL}} = 9.0 \qquad \frac{V}{\sqrt{LWL}} = 10.8$$

L m	L ft	d mm	d in	Bottom mm	Side mm	Bottom mm	Side mm	Bottom mm	Side mm	Bottom mm	Side mm	Bottom mm	Side mm
5	16.4	375	15	5.7	4.3	6.2	4.7	6.7	4.7	7.5	5.0	8.0	5.2
6	19.7	380	15	6.1	5.0	7.0	5.3	7.7	5.5	8.4	4.7	9.0	5.9
7	23.0	385	15	6.7	5.4	7.7	5.6	8.5	5.9	9.0	6.1	9.9	6.4
8	26.2	390	15	7.1	5.8	8.2	6.1	9.1	6.2	9.8	6.7	10.5	6.8
9	29.5	395	15	7.7	6.2	8.7	6.5	9.4	6.7	10.6	7.0	11.2	7.2
10	32.8	400	16	7.3	6.6	9.4	6.9	10.4	7.1	11.2	7.4	12.0	7.7
11	36.1	405	16	8.6	7.0	9.8	7.2	11.0	7.5	11.8	7.8	12.6	8.1
12	39.3	410	16	9.0	7.3	10.4	7.6	11.5	7.8	12.5	8.2	13.2	8.5
13	42.6	415	16	9.5	7.7	10.8	8.0	12.1	8.2	13.1	8.6	14.0	9.0
14	45.9	420	16	9.8	8.1	11.3	8.4	12.6	8.8	13.6	9.0	14.6	9.4
15	49.2	425	16	10.3	8.5	11.9	8.7	13.1	9.0	14.3	9.4	15.2	9.7
16	52.5	430	16	10.7	8.8	12.4	9.0	13.7	9.4	14.8	9.7		
17	55.7	435	17	11.2	9.2	12.8	9.4	14.2	9.7	15.5	10.1		
18	59.0	440	17	11.6	9.6	13.2	9.7	14.9	10.1	16.2	10.5		
19	62.3	445	17	12.0	10.0	13.9	10.1	15.4	10.5	16.6	10.9		
20	65.6	450	18	12.5	10.4	14.2	10.5	15.9	10.9	17.2	11.2		

These thicknesses are based on an assumed average resin/glass ratio of 2.33 or Gc 30% giving 0.7 mm per unit 300 g/m², 1 oz/ft² of glass.a

The difference is less than 12% if the resin/glass ratio is reduced to 2.0 or increased to 2.5.

NB: These thicknesses do not allow for the gel coat or inside top coat. Add 0.5–1.0 mm for the overall thickness.

$$L = \frac{LOA + LWL}{2} \qquad\qquad d = \text{Spacing of stringers}$$

Dimensions are metric. Imperial equivalents are approximate.
Most displacement and semi-displacement boats will be in the first category. Higher categories are all fast planing boats.

Mechanisation

Since the very earliest days engineers have tried to mechanise moulding. Some for more output with less labour; others because they have been appalled by the apparent crudeness of 'bucket-and-brush' methods.

Spray moulding

The commonest way to speed production is spray moulding or chop. In this a string of rovings is fed into a chopper gun and sprayed on to the mould along with a stream of catalysed resin. The resin/glass ratio and catalyst are fixed at the gun which makers claim eliminates the variables. But whereas mat and woven rovings come in rolls, factory made to uniform thickness, in spray moulding the glass goes where the operator puts it, and there is no guarantee he will put it in the right place.

Thickness may vary considerably. Without elaborate testing there is no way to check. Considerable skill, experience and concentration are needed to make good, evenly distributed mouldings. Plus the forgotten factor: honesty.

Moulders use spray moulding to speed production, not improve quality. A really good operator may disprove this, but emphasises how everything depends on his skill. He may change, go sick, leave or just have a bad day. A moment's inattention or distraction, even a sneeze, can mean a thin patch.

Consequently spray moulding is generally of lower quality and reliability. Neither is it so labour saving as claimed. The fibreglass still has to be rolled by hand. Woven rovings too must be applied by hand although spraying the resin is some saving.

Sound moulding depends on the machine working properly and being set up correctly. Undetected catalyst failure has caused a host of later problems. Machines have been improved, but many older boats were moulded when they needed a mechanic standing by. Early operators were untrained and unskilled. Surprising things happened. Some boats sank!

Airless spray, where resin and catalyst are mixed in the gun and squirted under hydraulic pressure, is now reckoned the best. Mixing in an air driven jet stream can give poor results due to entrapped air and imperfect mixing, which also depends on distance. Another type uses a two drum system, one containing resin plus accelerator, the other resin plus catalyst. This does not require the accurate metering essential with separate catalyst.

All types require frequent checks to make sure the accurate metering needed is correct. Unless kept very clean faulty operation is inevitable.

The high styrene emission when spraying is a major problem now. Environmental resins do not reduce emission while actually spraying.

Void content is higher than hand lay up because of air entrapment. Humidity must be below 40% otherwise atmospheric moisture is entrapped as well and affects cure. Spray moulded boats are more likely to blister.

Some big volume builders use spray-up because they cannot get enough good hand moulders. Also their output is large enough for savings like cheaper glass and less wastage to be significant.

Press moulding

This has been a common industrial process since early days. Pressure is comparatively low, about 100 lb/in^2, much less than the tons in most press moulding. Tailored glass mat is laid over the male mould, a measured amount of resin poured over it, the female mould lowered and pressure applied. Moulding may be hot or cold. Having two matching moulds it is smooth both sides, unlike conventional fibreglass.

The cost of the stronger moulds and sheer size of the press limit this to volume production of dinghies and runabouts.

Vacuum bag

Resin suction, then called the Marco process, was used for the first fibreglass dinghies moulded in Britain in 1949, by the North East Moulding & Engineering Ltd. That was before thixotropic resins and improved materials made the familiar hand lay up possible.

Glass cloth was laid over or in the mould, covered with a flexible sheet and vacuum applied to suck in the polyester. Sometimes it worked, sometimes it didn't, and nobody was ever sure.

At intervals it is revived and hailed as the newest thing. With greater sophistication Jeremy Rogers Ltd developed it successfully for the OOD 34, using matched fibreglass moulds. Because of the care needed to tailor and butt the glass precisely there was little saving in time, but the object was to mould a class of racing yachts more identical than could be achieved by hand lay up. Rule changes soon after made the class uncompetitive and the moulds could not be altered.

The SCRIMP process uses a translucent vacuum bag which allows a visible check on resin penetration and a patent system to distribute the resin uniformly. Very high glass content is claimed, almost aircraft standard. As the mouldings are thin, vinyl resins are used to reduce brittleness. Styrene emission is very low, an important consideration with increasingly stringent controls.

This may be the way ahead for companies with sufficient production to justify the capital cost, and the technical expertise to take the leap forward.

Pre-impregnation

The largest fibreglass mouldings have been minehunters, first developed for the Royal Navy. The mould area is about half an acre and means laying up over a million square feet

or around twenty-five acres, say a dozen football pitches. The length of glass fibre can almost be measured in light years!

On time alone some mechanical pre-impregnation was thought necessary. The woven rovings used throughout was fed straight from the roll, through a bath of resin, to the mould. The idea was abandoned even before the first ship was finished. Hand lay up was found better and as quick. However, pre-impregnation is an alternative to wetting out in situ whether by hand or spray. It works only with woven material. Mat would break up as the binder dissolves.

Filament winding

So far this is limited to spars and a few experimental hulls. A string of impregnated rovings is wound round a rotating core. With computer control the angle of winding and local thickness can be controlled to make quite complicated shapes. The limit is the size of core which could be rotated.

The shape must be designed for winding, the simplest being canoe shaped, but two hulls could be wound together. Re-entrants like cabin topsides and garboards would be difficult, although claimed possible with rollers.

The hulls would be strong, production quite fast and capital cost modest as the technique is well established in other industries. The winding pattern is easily altered by re-programming the computer.

The future

There will be developments, old ideas revived in new form, breakthroughs hailed in a glare of publicity and soon forgotten. But probably nothing dramatic; as in the past just steady slow progress.

Fibreglass boatbuilding is moving towards the fourth or fifth generation. In particular a new era of production bigness, not just individual builders but whole groups, through takeovers and conglomerate piracy. Some analysts forecast boatbuilding is moving the way of the motor industry with manufacture in the hands of a few giant multinationals. Builders will be backed by money never available before and the 'City' outlook that only capital intensive production makes money.

The unemployed must pray that these boats need plenty of maintenance and repair.

References

Sail, August 1993.

Society of Boat and Yacht Designers, *Composites in Marine Applications Symposium,* 7 November 1992, William H Seeman.

Symposium on GRP ship construction, RINA, October 1972.

History of GRP, British Plastics, Brian Parkyn (Unknown date).

Yachting World, March 1978.

Inspection and quality

Quality starts at the top. Right at the top. Nowhere else. Quality does not just happen. Still less because a brochure says so. There must be continuous policy at boardroom level plus determination to achieve it.

The greatest weakness of fibreglass boatbuilding has always been lack of inspection. In most industries, inspection is a key part of production. One in ten workers in the motor industry is an inspector. On aircraft every single part is very carefully tested. Even washing machines get more testing than an expensive fibreglass boat.

Intending the boat will turn out well is not enough. Management must *know* every boat is good.

Price

Price is no guide to quality. Only to the trappings of luxury. Some cheap boats are rubbish, of course, but others, although lacking luxury, have been good honest boats. Plenty of boats do live up to their higher price tag, but even more do not and the very worst I have ever seen in forty years have been expensive yachts. Reports in yachting journals can be misleading. The reviewers are journalists and may not be qualified to judge if the fibreglass is of good quality. It probably cannot be seen.

The cost of the mouldings is a quarter or third of the total boat cost. Which means the price reflects the luxury of the accommodation, engine power and toys, far more than the quality and strength of the hull. But in a competitive field, those are what seduce buyers – and builders know it.

Management

The key to quality is good management dedicated to making a sound, honest product within their price range. But who decides policy?

Under pressure to show bigger profits, management may be forced to cut corners, use inferior materials, adopt cheaper methods of production. All companies reserve the right to 'improve' specifications, which to a buyer means a better boat but to management more profit.

Being backed by a large group with oodles of capital should mean improved methods, research and the latest techniques. Yet most of the best boats come from smaller, owner managed builders who can set their own policy.

Any company that has been rescued after bankruptcy is the same only in name. Different owners will introduce different policies. Less obvious is change through retirement or sale or takeover of a parent company.

Workers

It is common to blame the workers. But unless backed by management right down the line there is nothing those on the factory floor can do.

Throughout history men have responded to leadership, whether to follow a captain through hell or take pride in their work. *Esprit de corps*, often scorned today, is a vital quality in a regiment or naval ship, and no less in a factory. I have visited many boatbuilders. One can get a good impression from the factory floor. Workers taking a pride in their work and the firm build good boats. Uninterested workers do not.

Inspection

Most annoying minor defects can be detected easily by inspection, especially the conspicuous gel coat cavities. Yet time and again I find boats where builders did not bother.

Major moulding defects are often difficult to see later and impossible then to put right.

The only time is during moulding.

Inspection is expensive. But its real value is what it saves. Waiting for the owner to find faults is far more expensive. Every defect a new owner finds will be well publicised to the builder's detriment. To put right something minor but conspicuous may mean sending a worker hundreds of miles at high cost in time and travel. Some builders get a local agent to bodge it up as best he can.

The *only* cheap time to correct defects is before the boat goes out of the gate.

In-house inspection

Sound moulding requires an eagle eyed foreman. He is the only person on the spot all the time with authority to order a layer of bad moulding to be put right or stripped off while still wet and easy to do. Once hard, or buried under further layers of hard fibreglass, there is little anyone can do. But he must have that authority and know he has the management's backing. It should not be regarded as his own inefficiency, still less should he fear for his job.

An alternative is a full-time, qualified, in-house inspector with similar authority. Every moulder ought to have one but only large companies could afford it. Even then it would probably be a moulder with lucrative government work, not dependent on the pleasure boat market.

No visiting surveyor, who may hardly see the boat during moulding and certainly not all the time, can ever be as effective as a man on the spot. Also a surveyor has no authority. He can discuss, suggest, request but not order a worker or even management to do anything.

Each layer of glass should be passed, and recorded before the next is applied. This also checks the number of layers. It is easy to miss one.

On a speed related bonus, as was once very common, defects are more likely and there is bound to be trouble when they must be made good. Delay means loss of bonus so workers try to hide anything.

Every moulding should be weighed while still a bare shell. Trends can develop, enough to put a one-design class boat outside the rules, or attract an adverse rating, even bankrupt the company.

Building under survey

The idea that building under survey guarantees a perfect boat is wishful thinking. Some of my worst cases have been yachts built under full survey.

A fibreglass hull is moulded quickly, probably in less than a week. No surveyor can be there watching every piece of glass as it goes down. A Society surveyor may have hundreds of yachts under construction in his area. A hull can be in and out of the mould between visits. An independent surveyor will have fewer boats and can give individual attention, timing his visits for certain stages. Even so he probably sees the boat only once or twice during moulding.

My practice was a discussion with the moulders beforehand, one or more visits during moulding and a very thorough inspection of the bare hull after moulding, more detailed than a busy Society surveyor could spare the time for. This is the best time to see a boat, before everything of most interest gets covered by fitting out. The threat of this on a go/no go understanding did more than anything else to ensure a sound moulding.

Most builders are cooperative and confident in their ability. A few refuse to have a surveyor in the place. You can draw your own conclusions.

Unless really bad, poor moulding is quite hard to detect later when buried by further layers. At that stage too it is virtually impossible to correct, which is why a visiting surveyor can do so little compared with a keen foreman.

Type approval is not the same as building under survey. It means that the design has been approved and the firm are capable of building a good boat if they have a mind to. It does not guarantee they did. A lot can happen between a surveyor's routine visits. Although he may check on the general standards he does not have the time, and sometimes the ability, to examine any boat thoroughly. Some builders use approval by a classification society as a selling point, but as regards any particular boat the certificate means little.

Testing materials

Inspection must begin as soon as materials arrive. A simple laboratory should be part of every moulding department. Although material manufacturers have good inspection, mistakes have happened. A faulty batch or unannounced change of specification can affect many months of production, nearly always later after all the boats have been sold. It has put good boatbuilders out of business through no fault of their own, and seriously embarrassed some of the largest.

In law the builders are liable and cannot plead faulty materials. They may claim damages from the supplier but that is a separate case and probably limited to the cost of materials. Therefore a builder must be sure all materials are to standard before use, and remain so during storage.

Legislation in Britain is now loaded against the builder. A court can overrule their terms of business. In the American legal jungle a defective product can be worth a fortune to an owner with a sharp attorney.

Essential checks are setting time of the resin, catalyst strength and the weight and integrity of the glass fibre. More elaborate tests should include water absorption, generally by boiling, and accelerated weathering. Most can be comparative without needing expensive measuring equipment. No material or supplier should be changed until thoroughly tested to ensure there are no undesirable secondary properties, especially subtle long term effects. There should also be continuous trials under actual conditions exposed to both sea and fresh water, weather and sunshine, preferably tropical.

The laboratory should examine and keep all cut outs. These are essential reference when troubles are reported, perhaps years later after memories have faded and records are inadequate. Some moulders make sample coupons, a section of the moulding laid up at the same time for testing and reference. Routine samples are sent to a commercial laboratory, better equipped for testing strength and other properties.

Military specifications demand stringent control and testing. So do some fishing authorities when giving grants. The offshore oil industry and others have tight specifications. Various national and international quality standards require testing and as more builders boast of conforming to these (eg BSS 5750 or ISR 9001) they will have competitive advantage. It may even become a necessity.

Scrapping

What does the management do if a serious defect is not discovered until moulding is finished, perhaps by a visiting surveyor? Do they scrap the moulding, by then expensive in time and labour? Or bodge it up? Or pretend it never happened?

Scrapping an expensive hull moulding requires courage which few moulders possess. Yet it is madness to wait until far more work, equipment and three or four times more money have been poured in. The sooner the decision is made the cheaper, easier and less painful. At the latest as soon as the moulding comes out of the mould. Better still while moulding can be aborted.

Rogue boats

Even good companies can produce the occasional rogue boat. And what rogues some have been. The impossible is possible. Only a really good, foolproof inspection system can reduce the chance of the owner finding out first.

Buyers should judge a builder not just by their good boats but the chances of a bad one.

Custom moulded hull

Some builders buy hulls from a custom moulder whose business is moulding and nothing else. I have had many sad cases where a builder has taken a hull moulding on trust, spent weeks of work and a lot of money fitting it out, only to have the owner sue them because it had serious defects. The owner naturally claims the full value of the boat, plus costs, damages and anything else his lawyer can get. All the builder can recover from the moulder, whose fault it was, is the bare cost of the hull, say a quarter of the total cost.

The builders have my sympathy but it was their own stupidity. Nobody, whether professional or amateur, should pour work and equipment into fitting out a bought-in hull until satisfied the moulding is worth it.

Reliability

Specification is not enough. Every boat must be built to that specification and known to be.

Maintenance and use

'No maintenance' was the slogan that sold boats in those rosy-eyed early days. Of course it was not true. There never has been and never will be a 'no maintenance' boat. Not if one wants to stay alive.

The correct term is 'low maintenance'. That can be achieved for the first ten or even twenty years until like most durable things made by man the boat has to be painted. Even then at infrequent intervals, not every year.

We have not quite reached the stupid, wasteful concept of the 'throw away' boat. It should be assumed a fibreglass boat will last, with reasonable maintenance, at least twenty-five years. Fifty is more realistic. Good early boats show such lives should be attainable. More recent boats are questionable.

If a good fibreglass boat will not last as long as a good wooden boat we should not hail fibreglass as progress.

Design for low maintenance

Low maintenance does not happen just because boats are fibreglass. They have to be designed for low maintenance: in particular protected against wear, scuffing and foreseeable damage. With most production boats this gets little thought. Owners, mesmerised by other attractions, do not know and builders do not care.

Limits of use

At all times it is important that the boat is used within the limits for which it was designed. These limits are getting tighter and the planned lives shorter. Unlike older boats, modern ones, especially the popular cruiser/racer, cannot be taken for granted (See Chapter 37).

Damage

Damage is generally regarded as unavoidable: an Act of God, though more often of man. But the extent of damage can be greatly reduced by sensible design, perhaps a nasty scratch instead of a hole particularly difficult to repair.

Photos 35.1 **(a)** Well designed fairlead which cannot cause wear.
(b) Poor design. No protection and that short warp means severe snubbing. Few builders appreciate that in a marina warps lead downwards, over the deck edge.
(c) This catamaran is asking for wear. No fairlead and a vulnerable lip as well. Catamarans often have to moor or anchor from each bow to lie easily.
(d) Many builders do not allow for springs. This deck edge is vulnerable.

Compared with wood or steel most fibreglass boats are flimsy. But they need not be. A fibreglass boat can be as strong as any other. But under the ruthless dyarchy of performance and economics most are and getting ever more so.

Consequently it is important they are not damage prone as well. This gets little consideration. What is insurance for? is the usual attitude. Yet most popular fibreglass cruisers are so damage prone it is a wonder insurers accept them.

Running aground

As any practical sailor knows, or soon finds out, this is the commonest and most obvious mishap. Yet few designers or builders foresee that. It also seems to escape the notice of classification societies and authorities. Blame the skipper's carelessness and say boats are not meant to run aground. They may not be meant to but they certainly do! I lost count many years ago how many times I have, and the last was yesterday!

A long keel boat will ride up and over, decelerating comparatively slowly, but a modern fin keel trips and comes to an abrupt stop. This imposes a very severe stress on the hull as the keel kicks back. A strong keelson, as every wooden boat has, would prevent this but few fibreglass boats have one (Fig 17.9).

The inertia of a heavy engine aft aggravates this. Damage is significantly less when the engine is over the keel, although I doubt if that is intentional even on the charter yachts I have seen.

Boats must be strong enough to take the ground for routine haul out or beaching. After severe structural failure, when drying out for a scrub, a well known builder made the ridiculous excuse that boats were not meant to take the ground! This was no delicate racing machine but an ordinary small cruiser.

Wear

Wear causes scratches which hold dirt and are impossible to clean. Anything which moves, rubs or touches a gel coat will cause wear. Even light contact will be cumulative.

The places are predictable. The more prominent and conspicuous they are the more likely to get scratched and worn.

Prevention

Obviously if something does not touch the gel coat it cannot cause wear. Tillers must not rub; ropes lead clear; nothing allowed to swing.

Most places are easy to foresee when the boat is on an even keel. But when heeling, life is on a different plane, however crazy it looks in harbour. Feet are placed where no foot would normally go. Grooves caused by ropes pulled across a coaming or the edge of the cabin top are common, more so now many boats have halyards led aft.

It is surprising how many builders seem to assume a boat, including a motor boat, is always upright and still. That is only in a boat show, displayed like a fish on a slab.

Protection

What cannot be prevented must be protected. Fibreglass is always a thin shell; being easily abraded it cannot absorb wear (Fig 35.1). Once through the gel coat the uncoloured moulding beneath will show conspicuously. In severe cases it can be worn right through.

A vulnerable place like a coaming is part of a large, one-piece moulding and cannot be re-

Methods of protection	
Wood	Plastics extrusions
Metal	Split hose
Wear resistant putty	Extra fibreglass
Permanent rubber fenders	Rubber sheet or pads
Separate fibreglass mouldings	Paint

placed. Repair or touching up inconspicuously requires skill which may not be available locally. Exact colour match is always difficult.

Fibreglass needs to be protected with something better able to absorb the wear, easier to touch up and *designed to be replaced*. Protection is expendable. Fibreglass mouldings are not.

Wood is excellent and attractive. It can be much thicker and is easy to touch up with varnish or paint, even scarf in a piece. The skills are available worldwide, including most competent owners. It may of course require maintenance: in marketing managers' eyes suicidal for sales, and extra cost to fit which to the accountant is worse. Yet in the limited amount used maintenance is small (Chapter 20).

Metal is very wear resistant. Some owners like lots of shiny stainless steel. Aluminium is less wear resistant but more easily formed and cheaper.

Plastics extrusions are useful on sawn edges like locker openings, for fendering or protecting a 'bathtub' hull/deck join. Split hose is a cheap alternative, and makes a good dinghy fender. (If only people with stout, unfendered, old wooden boats could be persuaded to fit it!)

Photos 35.2 (a) Defenceless topsides on a popular class of production yacht. Note the crudely repaired gouges.
(b) Sensible design. This wooden rubbing strake protects the topsides.

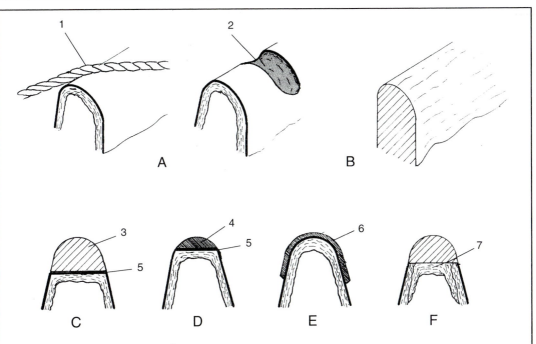

Figure 35.1   Protection against wear
A Anywhere a rope can bear, 1, will cause grooves and even wear through the gel coat, 2. Touching up is difficult and a fibreglass coaming or toe rail cannot be replaced.
B Wooden coamings wear better and are easily touched up, but more trouble for production and, perish the idea, might need maintenance. But they do look attractive and yachty.
C Wood capping, 3, is good protection and can be touched up or replaced.
D Metal or plastics strips, 4, are also good protection. Note: when planned both these require a moulded flat, 5.
E Unplanned it can be covered with metal or rubber, 6.
F To add a wood capping later means cutting away the moulding to form a flat, 7, and remoulding underneath which is sure to be difficult and probably inaccessible.

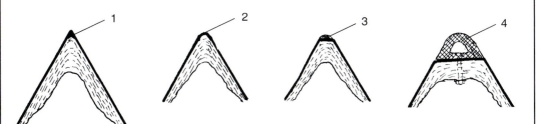

Figure 35.2 (above)   Stem protection
Although structurally strong the stem is the part most often involved in collision and contact with other objects. Consequently the gel coat is vulnerable. A sharp point, 1, will be resin rich and easily chipped. It should be as well rounded, 2, as performance permits. Few boats have the sensible precaution of a metal strip, 3. This needs to be designed as the flat must be moulded. For charter and hire boats the obvious precaution should be a rubber 'bumper', 4, not least to safeguard other boats!

Figure 35.3 (left)
Where there is danger of collision, especially ice, some boats have an expendable outer stem, 1.

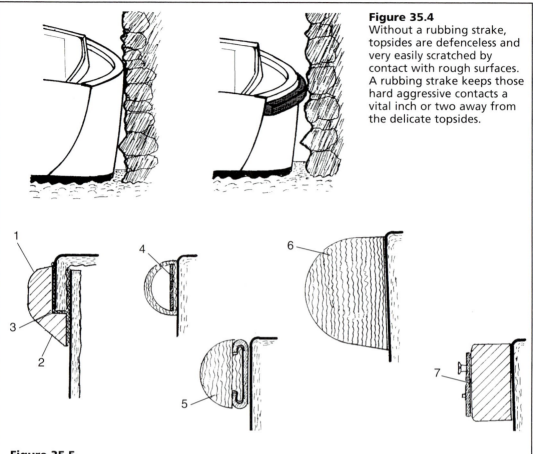

Figure 35.4
Without a rubbing strake, topsides are defenceless and very easily scratched by contact with rough surfaces. A rubbing strake keeps those hard aggressive contacts a vital inch or two away from the delicate topsides.

Figure 35.5
The rubbing strake in Fig 35.7 is not the best shape. A raked top, 1 sheds water and reduces algae stains. The sloping lower edge, 2 will slide clear of obstructions. It also protects the vulnerable and irreplaceable deck edge, 3.
Some boats have D section fendering. To prevent the flexible section moving under shear it must have a metal strip, 4. More elaborate kinds have an extruded plastics strip, 5, held in a metal channel. Pilot boats have a heavy duty solid rubber fender, 6. Fishing boats favour substantial wooden rubbing strakes, shod with metal, often with projecting screws to discourage yachts, 7. (Whatever the fishing boats are made of this is the sort of thing a smart, delicate yacht has to battle with in a fishing harbour!)

Stout rubber bumpers are fitted on hard used workboats like pilot launches.

Sometimes separate readily replaceable fibreglass mouldings are used, eg a false bow where there is risk of collision or ice (Fig 35.3). Extra thickness of fibreglass would compensate for strength but being usually on the inside would not save the gel coat. Outside it would be unsightly unless inconspicuous, eg a keel. Wear resistant putties using hard fillers (Chapter 2) have been used on keels and bilge keels.

Protection must be intended for easy replacement later. Most builders make it almost impossible. Wood is more easily replaced if made in two pieces so the outer can be removed without disturbing the inner (Fig 35.7).

Fibreglass must be properly designed where protection is to be. Capping needs a flat base not rounded like normal moulding. Consequently it is difficult to add later (Fig 35.1).

Places needing protection
This is common sense and practical boat experience. I sometimes wonder if those who build boats nowadays have either. Motor boats are as vulnerable as sailing yachts and, except for

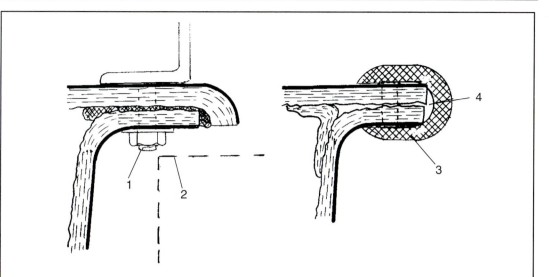

Figure 35.6   'Bathtub' flange
A projecting 'bathtub' hull/deck join is a typical victory of production convenience over common sense. Easy to assemble and bolt together, 1, but very vulnerable and impossible to protect against fouling a dock or piles, 2.
On smaller boats it has sometimes been riveted together with a plastics extrusion as a fender, 3. This can allow water to lodge in the unsealed join, 4, leading to decay and disintegration after a few years.

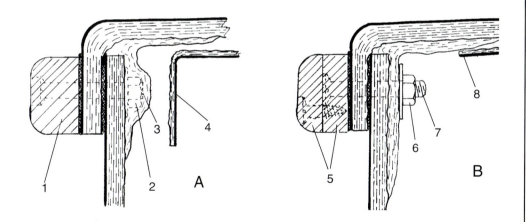

Figure 35.7   Replacing a rubbing strake
A This very common arrangement is almost designed to make replacement impossible. The wooden rubbing strake, 1, is bolted through, the nuts, 2, glassed over, and the bolts cropped, 3, so the nut is almost certain to turn. The deckhead lining, 4, prevents access for cutting away.
B Sensible design. The rubbing strake, 5, is in two parts. The outer section can be readily unscrewed to make good minor damage. If more serious the nuts, 6, are not glassed over and are accessible and the bolts, 7, have not been cropped. Finally the deckhead lining, 8, does not prevent access.
   Note how the hull/deck join has been glassed over in both cases to strengthen this important part.

Places needing protection

Hull

Topsides	Chines
Stem	Edge of raked ransoms
Keel	Bilge keels
Centreboard slots	Bottoms without keels
Corners of transoms	'Bathtub' hull/deck joins
Topsides on fishing and work boats	

Deck/cockpit

Cockpit coamings	Toe rails
Walking surfaces	Stepping points into cockpit
Cockpit floor and sides	Cockpit seats
Gangplank	Boarding areas
Companionway	Wheelhouse doorway
Mooring fairleads	Anchor stowage
Mooring cleats/bollards	Chain fairlead
Around the mast	Around anchor windlass
Working areas on fishing and work boats	

Cabin

Companionway steps	Cabin sole
Sills of doorways	Sides of doorways
Hanging lockers	Edges of lockers and cut-outs
Galley work surfaces	Corners and anywhere kicked

---

work boats, even more overlooked. Workboats are generally well protected but utility counts more than appearance. On a smart yacht appearance counts more than utility.

Hull

The most conspicuous part of the boat are those gleaming topsides (Fig 35.4). But they bear the brunt of lying alongside, whether another boat, marina berth or rough quay. One misjudgement and the topsides are deeply scratched. A wooden rubbing band saves them from all but the more severe scrunches (Fig 35.5).

No concern of theirs, claim builders yet again. Owners should buy fenders. But fenders can disappear, be forgotten in a crisis or just be in the wrong place. Certainly fenders are needed. But a good rubbing band is an invaluable back-up.

Charter yachts in particular need a rubbing band. The photograph on page 237 shows a typical modern production yacht belonging to a large company. Not only are topsides defenceless but there are protruding water outlets and window frames, which make it damage prone as well as maintenance prone.

Hirers of river cruisers think a motor boat is like driving a car, and any fool can do that. A rough sided lock shows them they can't. Topsides need wooden fendering especially aft, and a good 'bumper' at the bows, because the 'brakes' are not good either (Fig 35.3).

In many areas mooring stern to a dock or quay is customary. The fashionable raked transom and 'sugar scoop' is particularly vulnerable. Permanent protection is essential. Better still, make the sugar scoop replaceable.

Anything overhanging is vulnerable. Many motor cruisers have flaring bows. Fenders dangle uselessly. Where there is rise and fall due to swell or wash, the overhang can crash down on a pile or quay and be badly damaged. So can an outwards turning or 'bath tub' hull/deck join and it is not expendable (Fig 35.6). Wedges, moulded or added, allow it to slide clear.

Work boats come alongside every day, and crews cannot be bothered with fenders unless permanently rigged, usually dirty old tyres. All have permanent wooden fendering, stout and often iron shod for survival among other well armoured boats.

Fishing boats need good protection where pots or trawls are hauled over the side. The gear is heavy and handled roughly. Fishermen are not yachtsmen. (The worst insult!) A boat is a means to catch fish. Yet fibreglass boats

a

b

Photos 35.4 (a) Many boats spend most of their time stern-to a dock. This has a sensible rubber fender.
(b) Aqua-Star passenger ferry, licensed for 70 passengers. Note the protective wooden belting to protect the topsides when docking many times a day. (Photo: Aqua-Star Ltd, Guernsey)

have developed primarily as yachts and a yacht approach is no good for a hard used work boat with the emphasis on work. Structurally fibreglass can be as strong and tough as you like, provided the more delicate gel coat gets plenty of sensible protection against hard wear and what, on a yacht, would be gross abuse.

Keels

An iron or lead keel is a far better battering ram than fibreglass can ever be. In a serious argument with a rock or reef a fibreglass keel will be damaged. If the boat pounds even gently on the hard, jagged rock it will be ground away or pulverised. The keel may be the thickest part of the boat yet can still be battered right through. An iron keel, on the other hand, will batter holes in the reef.

The bottom of a fibreglass keel needs to be protected with a shoe of wood or steel, extending up the leading edge, the likely point of impact. This is very seldom seen. Making it renewable may be a problem as internal fastenings will be under the ballast. Wood must be durable and worm resistant because often the bottom of the keel cannot be antifouled.

In many harbours boats regularly dry out. It may be the only spot available, and far cheaper than a marina. Boats with unprotected fibreglass keels should not be left on drying sandy moorings exposed to tide or storm scour.

Iron ballast keels are often sheathed with fibreglass to prevent rusting. It seldom does. Bonding is poor unless epoxy and inevitably

the thin sheathing is porous. As the iron rusts the fibreglass becomes loose and often peels away. The sheathing is very easily damaged.

Motor cruisers need their keels and bilge keels protected even more than sailing cruisers because there is not the massive thickness. On the River Shannon many hire cruisers lose lengths of unprotected fibreglass keel due to straying from the marked channels. Most are designed for the muddy Norfolk Broads, the Shannon has rocks, a typical case of boats being used in waters for which they were not designed (Fig 35.8).

Rudder

The great yachting writer of earlier years, Claude Worth, said that the rudder was one part of a boat which should be virtually incapable of being damaged. Would that modern designers read his common sense books. Modern rudders, especially the fashionable spade rudders, are vulnerable and frequently damaged.

Nowadays it must be assumed that the rudder may have to be removed for repair or replacement. The easiest is when transom hung. Otherwise the boat must be lifted or a hole dug. Boatyards may object, especially if on concrete.

Rudder fittings must be easy to undo. As well as removal for repair, bolts need regular inspection. Stainless steel bolts through a keel or skeg can disintegrate through crevice corrosion or electrolysis. (Chapter 21).

A particularly stupid system was seen

recently on a Taiwanese boat. The heel fitting was an extension of the keel, a strong method and not unusual except that in this case it was an integral part of the hull moulding. The only way to drop the rudder was to cut off the keel extension. No easy matter as it was solid. As might be expected the shaft could not be withdrawn either without dropping the rudder.

Deck

Decks are for walking on. Most stands at a boat show look like a mosque with rows of shoes at the bottom of the ladder. The main wear is from feet. So if a deck will not stand the few days of a boat show it certainly will not stand a few years' use. Or even a night in a visitors'

berth inside six French charter yachts each with a dozen or more people packed in, and they all go ashore at least twenty times!

The common moulded pattern is poor as a non-slip surface but ideal for production as no extra work is needed. It does not wear well and being part of the basic deck moulding is impossible to renew. Stick-on treads, laid teak or even non-slip paint are more non-slip, wear better and can be renewed in whole or part when worn or damaged.

Smooth surfaces show wear more than non-slip. Some are walkways or stepping points even on an even keel. Few builders appreciate the crazy places a foot will go when heeled. Would non-slip cockpit sides really look silly?

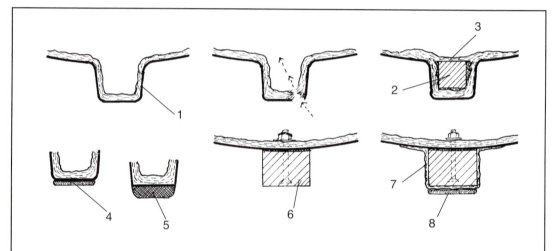

Figure 35.8   Motor boat keels
On many motor boats the keels or bilge keels are moulded integrally with the hull, 1. If damaged there is nothing to prevent a serious leak. Therefore the keel should be infilled with wood or resin putty, 2, and moulded over inside, 3. Then even if damaged it will not leak. Good practice is to protect a fibreglass keel with a metal shoe, 4, or infilling the mould first with hard, abrasion resistant resin putty, 5.

This is really a place where wood, bolted on, is more appropriate, 6. Unless a worm resistant wood it may need sheathing with fibreglass, 7, and then the sheathing itself will need a metal shoe, 8.

Figure 35.9
It is usually assumed that when aground the keel will sink into soft mud or sit on a smooth level surface. But a stone, 1 on concrete will cause very high local pressure and damage a fibreglass or fibreglass sheathed keel.

Motor cruisers often have large smooth areas, nice for appearance but suicidal to step on when wet. Motor boats may not heel, but they do roll quite wildly which is worse.

Toe rails are prominent and vulnerable. Fibreglass toe rails should be capped with wood, metal or plastics. Aluminium toe rails stand up well to wear but are easily bent. Gangplanks cause wear unless fixed at the boat end or on a pad. There is always movement. Grind the dock, not your deck.

A tiller must not rub on any part of the cockpit or coaming, including when tilted out of the way. There is still rudder movement in harbour. Winch handles must give adequate clearance for tough big fisted gorillas at every conceivable angle. Dainty hands can be worse. Rings make more scratches than almost anything else. Cleats should be high enough to make fast without fingers rubbing on the deck or coaming.

Anchors and mooring

There must be a clear, unobstructed run from the chain pipe to the roller fairlead, whether via a windlass or direct. With a deck locker it is common for the chain or rope to run out over the edge. Not only does this wreck the edge but risks injury trying to prevent it.

There must be a secure bow fairlead big enough to take any likely mooring. Despite proliferating marinas, in most areas it is still the custom for yachts to lie on moorings or at anchor. Modern yachts pitch quickly and can throw a chain or rope out of a fairlead. If during a gale, while unattended, it can literally saw through the deck edge. There are horror stories of bows being sawn off.

Some builders provide token anchoring arrangements, assuming boats now sail only from marina to marina. No matter how marina bound, any yacht may have to anchor sometimes. The less often the more likely it will be in emergency, and the more wear and damage that will result if arrangements are inadequate. A seaworthy cruising yacht must expect to anchor, often for months on end and ride out a storm or even a hurricane.

Motor cruisers and modern sailing yachts with short keels and high windage do not lie easily and sheer about or 'fishtail'. Much of the

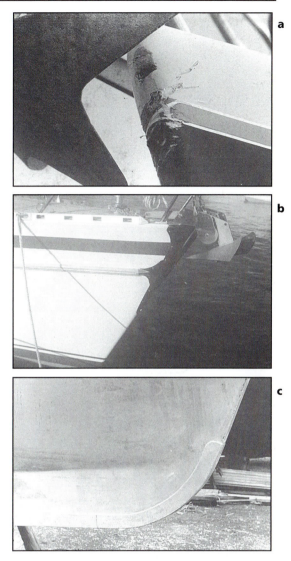

Photos 35.3 (a) Stems are often chipped by carelessly stowed anchors.
(b) Neat stainless steel stem protection. Seldom seen.
(c) This builder is one of the very few who realise boats can, and often do, run aground. Metal protection in the right place.

pull is sideways. If the chain or rope jumps out of an inadequate fairlead it can sweep the foredeck clear of pulpit and other fittings, and legs too. The same applies when being towed. Any boat may need that, probably under bad conditions.

Fairleads need a lip to protect the deck edge. Most are too far inboard. It must be assumed that mooring ropes may lead in any direction and will cause severe wear if fairleads

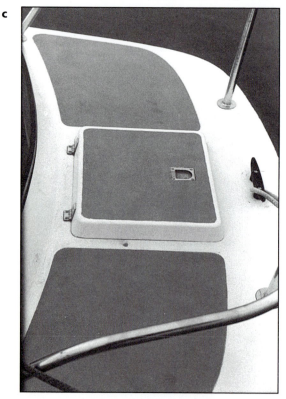

Photos 35.5 (a) The common moulded non-slip tread is an integral part of the deck moulding and cannot be replaced when damaged or worn. Convenient for production but non-slip properties have always been poor, especially when wet.
(b) Treadmaster, based on brake material. It protects the deck, is renewable and is excellent non-slip wet or dry.
(c) Trakmark, an embossed plastics sheet, is another stick-on non-slip protection.
(d) The best, nicest looking, permanent, but most expensive, is laid teak.
(e) The teak needs to be genuine planking. Inferior, teak faced plywood strips, as here, will delaminate, and hacking it away will damage the fibreglass beneath.

do not allow for this. Even in a marina there will be a lot of movement under storm conditions, with warps that are too short to prevent snubbing.

A proper cruising yacht will have permanent stowage at the stemhead for the anchor, preferably two, of any type the owner chooses. It must be secure. If allowed to swing and contact the stem it will dig deep gouges. When stowed on deck for long passages, or the second anchor, there must be proper chocks and secure lashing points. Often forgotten, any anchor below must be stowed securely.

Down below

As the crew will usually spend more time below than on deck, the cabin sole gets more wear but is easier to protect. A moulded fibreglass pattern has the same disadvantages for the user and advantages for the builder as a deck.

Especially vulnerable are the sills of doorways and openings which need protection with metal or plastics. Companionway steps get more wear than anywhere else. Angles and bunk fronts get kicked, as well as walked on when heeling.

There is always movement on a boat afloat, severe at sea of course, but even in a sheltered harbour or marina wind, waves, wash from passing boats and movement of the crew mean the boat is rarely still, including while unattended. Anything which can swing, roll, slide, bounce, move or vibrate will make marks and scratches, even soft things like curtains or a dishcloth. The ubiquitous hanging locker is a landlubberly idea. Swinging garments will make marks and shore-going clothes will get worn. If you must have one, a hanging locker needs a clamp to prevent clothes swinging.

Cleaning

Design can make cleaning easy, difficult or impossible. Scuppers should drain completely, including when laid up ashore at a different angle. Puddles cause persistent stains. Aluminium toe rail slots are generally too high for water to drain completely. Rubbing bands and toe rails should be well bedded to prevent water and mud lodging behind and the top shaped to shed water. Some grow algae, even grass.

Photo 35.6 Many boats these days have to be kept on drying moorings and need extra bottom and keel protection. Weakly fastened fin keels and spade rudders can be wrenched off.

Deck fittings can prevent a free flood of water and trap dirt like a forty-niner panning for gold. Fittings should be on smooth, rounded plinths to deflect water flow. Stanchion bases are often too close to the toe rail. Some boats have such a small gap between the cockpit coaming or cabin top and toe rail it is impossible to get a brush in. Muck collects and it becomes a garden.

The cabin is cleaned most often. Smooth fibreglass needs just a wipe with a rag but where glassed on angles are often left rough and hold dirt like a doormat. They need to be finished with plenty of resin. Food lockers too and all parts of the galley must have a smooth, easy clean surface.

Bilges

Bilge water has traditionally been foul. (When the 'heads' were wet, windy holes beside the bowsprit – hence the name – there was obvious temptation to sneak down to the bilges.) Nowadays it is more likely to be black oily scum from the engine. Bilges under the engine should always be separated from the accommodation.

Water should not seep into lockers. Porous glass angles are very common. Moulding inside is not easy and few workers would see the need to make angles watertight.

Internal mouldings often act as weirs and trap water, when the boat heels or rolls. When this reappears later it may seem like a worrying leak. All parts of the bilges need limber holes.

Engine

For production convenience the engine is usually put in early before being boxed in by the accommodation. Such builders are not concerned with how the engine will be got out again. This chapter is written, with feeling, in the midst of trying to do just that!

An engine is the principal item requiring overhaul, repair or replacement during the life of the boat. The easier to get it out the more likely the work will be done properly in a workshop. It is a big operation yet need not be made so difficult and expensive. By far the best is an engine which can be lifted easily straight out through a cockpit or wheelhouse hatch. Flexible engine mountings too need regular inspection, especially after damage to the boat, only possible by lifting the engine.

One tip, if faced with this problem, is to drill holes in the cockpit sole big enough to take a rope. The engine can then be lifted and moved forward, step by step. The holes are easily plugged or sealed afterwards.

Stern glands require easy access for tightening. Shafts get bent, especially the vulnerable P brackets. Another stupid, very common feature is a shaft which cannot be removed without dropping the rudder. That means a crane to lift the boat or digging a hole. Yet it is so simple at the design stage to allow a gap in the rudder or slightly offset the shaft. Even more stupid is a skeg which prevents the shaft being taken out at all except by removing the engine. You can bet that is one of the difficult ones.

Because the boat is new do not think this does not matter. The most serious defects are generally discovered early on. Moreover damage can occur at any time and place. Only the best behaved boats do so when convenient.

Charter yachts

Before buying a boat of well established class examine one that has been used for charter. As well as more use in one year than the average private yacht gets in five, many charterers are careless. They want their money's worth of hard sailing; it is not their boat and they do not have the loving care an owner has. Company boats are as impersonal as a hire car.

As well as indicating the points of wear, a buyer can expect to see how stupid and damage prone so many production yachts are.

Self-reliance

Old sailing ships had to be self-reliant. Storm or battle damage was repaired with their own resources. Modern yachts are increasingly difficult to repair; sophisticated equipment, let alone essential small fittings, cannot be repaired on board and often not locally either. Spares to distant places may take months and endless hassle with local customs as well as high expense. With a second-hand boat spares may not be available even at home.

Many people set off on long voyages in modern yachts which are frankly unsuitable to sail far from the comprehensive repair facilities of a large marina in their well developed home country. As well as possible repairs in mid-ocean there is often nothing on reaching land either.

Distant parts of the world are attracting yachts in increasing numbers but facilities lag by many years. Moreover you do not need to go far from home to discover that.

A crew may have to do at least temporary repairs themselves. So consider access including inspection.

Insurance underwriters in their ivory towers far inland, or perhaps the computers they worship, seem unable to comprehend that a boat may not be kept in a well serviced marina. They often reject claims based on self-help methods which would have been natural to any traditional seaman. That attitude greatly increases the cost of claims which shadier insurers then use as an excuse not to pay.

When buying a boat for the blue horizon, look very carefully at the ease of maintenance and repair for several years with no more equipment than you have or can improvise on board. As in the old days of sail a modern boat must be self-reliant. Yet never have boats been so dependent on skilled technical service ashore.

Maintenance and cleaning

This chapter is concerned only with the fibreglass, in particular the gel coat, the part most seen. Despite claims for no maintenance the finish will be preserved longer and the need for painting postponed, perhaps indefinitely, if it does get some modest maintenance.

In good condition fibreglass is easily wiped clean. It has no cracks or joints to harbour dirt and the rounded corners would delight the fussiest hospital matron.

Unlike wood and steel good fibreglass will not deteriorate seriously if never painted. The appearance suffers more than the structure.

Careful handling

Low maintenance demands careful handling: berthing carefully, scrupulous attention to fenders, making sure there are no points of wear. It does not mean never leaving the marina. On the contrary more scratches and wear are caused by rubbing in a dock than at sea!

Laying up

Fibreglass boats should not be left afloat indefinitely. Despite earlier claims it is now realised that they benefit by an occasional few months ashore to dry out. This need not be every year.

Winter covers must be well secured and not allowed to flap or they will leave thousands of scratches, especially metal cringles. Some owners secure covers with a cat's cradle of ropes. (Do please consider the poor surveyor. Some take half a day to undo!) Rick netting is fine.

Supports *must* be placed where there are strong points inside, eg bulkheads. Adjustable Acrow struts are better than traditional wedges and shores. It is common to see hulls indented where supports have been placed between bulkheads. Those cannot be made

secure because the more the wedge is hammered in the more the hull is forced inwards. While ashore the fibreglass will creep and the indentation become permanent.

The same applies to trailers. With some sophisticated mechanical handling systems, the supports cannot be moved. If the boat is badly balanced, or the powerful hydraulically operated supports are used to lift the boat, much of the weight may be taken where the hull is not strong enough. Damage is unlikely to be apparent at the time.

A sinking keel throws dangerous weight on the supports. To prevent this put wide, strong blocks under the keel. Also under supports which should be multiple in case one falls away or sinks.

It is common practice now to leave masts stepped while ashore, something never allowed in my boatyard days. The windage in a storm is terrific. Look how a boat afloat heels in a gust even under bare poles. Many modern hulls are so flexible the boat will rock on dry land, especially when not supported at strong points. Then supports fall away and over she goes. Watch thy neighbour as thyself!

Even boats in cradles have capsized. Covers can lift a modern boat like a spinnaker. At Fenit in the far west of Ireland boats are picketed down to concrete strong points.

Polish

As well as preserving the pristine gloss well polished fibreglass is easy to clean and stays cleaner. Equally important, polish sheds water and builds protection against the weather.

Topsides get most attention, yet the deck and cabin top are more exposed to the weather and sun. Polish is needed most in winter when the owner is snug at home and the poor boat is out in the open exposed to the rain, frost and snow. Not just during the summer to keep the boat smart.

Special yacht polishes are available at yacht prices, but most wax floor or car polishes are as good. The best contain carnauba wax. Silicones should be avoided despite being easy to use because they are difficult to remove when the boat needs repair or painting. Always clean the surface before polishing especially if using a power polisher. Grit will cause microscratches.

Quality

A good gel coat will be easier to keep clean than a poor one. Difficult cleaning or persistent stains may be the first indication of a bad gel coat. If so it is probably bad underwater too.

Gel coat

When new the smooth, glossy, non-absorbent surface sheds dirt and stains, and needs only a wipe with a damp rag. Once etched by the weather, or scratched and worn, the gel coat marks easily, soaks up stains and is difficult to keep clean and bright.

A gel coat may be glossy yet have patches persistently stained and difficult to clean. This is probably due to multiple microscratches, almost invisible to the eye but plain using a magnifier. Like larger scratches these hold dirt. Gritty fenders scratch like sandpaper. So can shoes, abrasive cleaners or fine sanding. Microscratches are shallow and can be burnished away.

Avoid hard scrubbing brushes. Be particularly careful where a scrubbable material adjoins fibreglass.

Never use cleaners:

- Unless certain what they are or approved for fibreglass.
- Where they can form puddles or run into inaccessible places.
- Where the moulding may be porous or have cracks or damage.
- Without removing all traces after use, preferably with water.

Topsides

One problem is how to clean them from a dinghy. Even quite small cruisers now have such high freeboard that anyone with arms of normal length cannot hang on to the rail and reach down far enough.

There are suction handles available at high prices. Equally effective are cheap rubber plungers found in any hardware store for unblocking drains. (They should be in the tool kit anyway. Because of the low head and water filled pipe, sink blockages are common.)

Decks

Decks get dirtier than any other part and also more wear. With the common moulded non-slip pattern, wear is concentrated on the peaks. Once feet and grit have caused scratches no amount of sluicing will keep the fibreglass clean. The diamond pattern is difficult to mould and usually has bubbles in the peaks which leave small craters so they are hard to clean from the start.

When non-slip paint gets worn or dirty it is easy to repaint and look like new. Stick-on treads wear well and are easily cleaned. Best of all is laid teak.

Cleaners

Most dirt can be washed off with water, fresh or salt, aided by household detergent. (The same except in name and price as expensive yacht cleaners.) Never use an abrasive cleaner, scouring powder, wire wool or pan scrubber. Although initially effective the microscratches will make the surface impossible to keep clean afterwards. They also wear away the gel coat. Kitchen sinks have harder surfaces than gel coat.

If ordinary cleaners will not shift a stain it will need an abrasive polish. Unlike a domestic scourer, these are very fine and do not leave scratches. Nevertheless they do polish away the gel coat to expose fresh material so use them only when necessary, never for routine cleaning. As well as special gel coat polishes one can use finest grade car burnishing paste, old style metal polish like Brasso or jeweller's rouge.

Beware of solvent cleaners and polishes. Polyester is attacked by many solvents. In general, household cleaners are pretty mild.

They *must* be harmless to humans. Industrial cleaners are different. 'Some good stuff we use at work' may be devastating both to the boat and user.

Cleaners and polishes, safe on fibreglass, may attack or craze other plastics, notably acrylic windows. Similarly, cleaners for metal or teak may harm adjacent fibreglass.

The boxes list approved cleaners.

Note: approval refers only to their effect on fibreglass. They may be hazardous to use. The usual warnings about keeping out of children's reach apply. What is safe to use in the open air may be toxic in a confined space. That includes a leaking can.

Some may be restricted or banned under national or local safety or environmental regulations, present or future. Most solvents emit VOCs. Ordinary prudence must be observed in use and storage when inflammable.

The cleaners have been graded for their effect on polyester, and assume short term contact. When stored on board leakages will mean much longer contact and can turn safe use into destructive. Moreover as a cleaner it may be diluted; a spillage will not be. The effect on other materials should be considered. Bleach can destroy an expensive nylon warp or sails. A wise owner will carry nothing on board which could be harmful.

Stubborn stains

Yachts, permanently berthed in a clean, well run marina, may never encounter the hazards experienced by cruising yachts. A beautiful bay may have a fishing harbour which, quoting from one of the sober sailing directions of the Royal Cruising Club, is 'covered with a dark orange detergent-like scum having a lethal effect on topsides and dinghies'. The English language lacks words for the unspeakably filthy.

Scratches and abrasion hold dirt. So does a weathered, etched gel coat. It could be the gel coat at fault not that fishing boat's oily motor tyres. White gel coats often develop brown streaks along the waterline which look like oil stains. To add worry some resemble worms or the long awaited *Fibreglassium masticus*. Actually it is probably selective leaching and means painting is due.

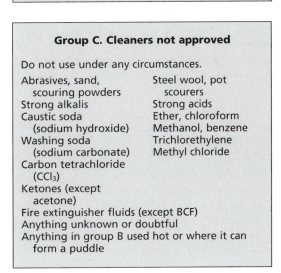

Group A. Approved cleaners

Subject to safety these may be used hot or cold, but in most cases not hotter than a hand can stand, about 110°F, 42°C.

Fresh water	Salt water
Domestic detergent	Special fibreglass
Mild industrial	cleaners
detergents	Surfactants except
Petrol, gasoline	cationic
Diesel, gas oil	Paraffin, kerosene
White spirit, turps sub	Domestic oil, fuel
Glycerine	domestique
	Linseed oil, olive oil
	BCF

Group B. Approved cleaners used cold

Use with discretion, wash off promptly, do not allow to form puddles and use cold or lukewarm up to 80°F, 26°C.

Ammonia	Bleach
Weak acids, dilute	Vinegar, citric acid
battery acid	Jet aircraft fuel
Weak disinfectants	Alcohol, alcoholic
Methylated spirits	drinks
Styrene	Acetone
Naphtha	Toluene, xylene
Polyurethane	Cellulose thinners
thinners	

Group C. Cleaners not approved

Do not use under any circumstances.

Abrasives, sand,	Steel wool, pot
scouring powders	scourers
Strong alkalis	Strong acids
Caustic soda	Ether, chloroform
(sodium hydroxide)	Methanol, benzene
Washing soda	Trichlorethylene
(sodium carbonate)	Methyl chloride
Carbon tetrachloride	
(CCl_3)	
Ketones (except	
acetone)	

Fire extinguisher fluids (except BCF)
Anything unknown or doubtful
Anything in group B used hot or where it can form a puddle

An apparently absorbent gel coat may be paint, sometimes the first the owner knows about it.

Oil stains

Polyester has an affinity for oil and it soaks in like no ordinary dirt. Light oils in harbour are worse than the filthiest sludge from a tanker. Few cleaners will chase out the oil and leave the boat behind. One mixture suggested is two parts detergent to one of paraffin (kerosene).

Oil must be prevented from soaking in by a protective film of polish which will not itself absorb oil. Otherwise the stain has to be burnished away. Inevitably this will thin the gel coat near the waterline, the most vulnerable area for blistering. Tarry sludge can be scraped off with wood or plastics. Metal will scratch.

In the political panic following an *Amoco Cadiz* or *Esso Valduz* scale disaster clean up gangs may use very powerful detergents which do more harm to sea life and boats than the oil. For miles around the water will be covered with a brown scum, like dirty washing up water, which soaks into a gel coat more than oil does. The only safe place during a major oil spill is right out of the way, ashore or in cleaner waters.

Rust

Specks from sawing or filing steel are difficult to remove. Being too heavy to be sluiced away they are not noticed until rusty and by then they have etched in. Abrasive polish may remove them but it is better to avoid doing any steel work on board, including stainless steel.

It has been reported that stubborn rust stains can be removed with the popular rust converters used on ageing cars.

Burns

Barbecues, essential equipment on charter yachts for the nightly fire up, often cause burns from cinders, sparks and hot fat. These marks cannot be removed because the gel coat is destroyed.

Distress flares too drip burning embers and sparks, but under the circumstances who

cares? Burning the boat might even speed rescue. Club firework night is a different matter.

Never, never should anyone stub out a cigarette on a fibreglass surface. Not even a galley sink. Even worse is the dangerous habit of leaving a cigarette burning on an edge.

Bilges

Domestic detergent will clean bilges. Some owners pour it in regularly to emulsify oil or diesel. It will do little harm if left but some proprietary bilge cleaners intended for wood or steel are too strong for fibreglass. So are some engine cleaners. No strong cleaner should be left in the bilges. Pump out within an hour and flush to dilute residue.

Very oily bilges can be scrubbed with paraffin (kerosene).

Metal

Abrasive cleaners may leave a halo on the gel coat. Solvent cleaners which run will stain or etch. Be careful solvent is not trapped under fittings where damage would be unseen.

Woodwork

Runs of paint remover will attack the gel coat unless it is the milder kind approved for fibreglass. Smears of teak oil, invisible at first, oxidise to a brown stain, difficult to remove.

Black mould

Uninsulated deck heads often grow black mould, especially when occupancy level is high, with cooking and a good fug below. It digs in particularly well on common emulsion paint, often used on older boats. A fungicidal wash may remove the mould but it soon returns, and will even grow through fresh paint. An effective solution is to mix 10% garden algicide into the paint.

Overloading

Sinkings in mid-ocean, now increasingly common, assume collision with some object, generally unknown. When abandoning ship in haste there is no time for analysing why. Seldom considered is catastrophic structural failure due to overloading lightly built boats not designed for it. Yet that is a serious possibility and few seem to realise the danger.

When preparing for a long cruise the boat becomes like those old fashioned coal holes in a London pavement. Car load after car load is poured in, stores, equipment, possessions. The designed waterline becomes history.

That the boat is strong enough is taken for granted. Sturdy old boats were, but they are no longer built like that. Most have a considerable weight of extra equipment and toys before they start. Owners, especially those who race, know weight reduces performance, yet until they start loading do not realise how much they must carry and the effect that will have.

Rules, regulations and codes of practice are adamant that the boat must not be used beyond its designed purpose and parameters. Earlier fibreglass boats generally followed the well established tradition of wooden boats. Some sturdy cruising yachts are still built in fibreglass. But the majority of cruiser/racers, by far the most popular and fashionable type today, are governed by the ruthless dyarchy of faster at less cost, and built no stronger than need be for their purpose. That means predominantly fun-to-sail weekend sailing and short holiday cruising. For which they are adequate.

Although frequently advertised as ideal for ocean crossing (by people who have only crossed an ocean in an aeroplane and to whom it is merely a sales gimmick), few are actually designed for that very different purpose. In particular for carrying the extra weight essential just for life support, let alone being self-contained for a year or more, often home too.

To a bureaucrat, safety means liferafts for when the boat sinks. Not a strong, seaworthy boat less likely to sink!

Seaworthiness

Technically the boat may be seaworthy. Many are used for hard offshore racing. But a race lasting only a few days, weight ruthlessly minimised, spares unnecessary, yachts in close company and every modern rescue service available, is very different from a heavily loaded, live aboard, ocean cruising yacht, alone and self-reliant.

Put a two ton load into a one ton truck and the police will have you off the road for driving a vehicle in dangerous condition. It is also dangerous with a boat. But owners are not told the safe load. Even the builder does not know. You may get away with it. The difference is that when an axle breaks or a tyre bursts you can get out and walk. If an overloaded boat cracks up the crew cannot walk home.

Strong purpose built boats cost a lot of money and more dreams than money is an endemic weakness with ocean cruisers. So they sail in what they already have or can afford, usually second-hand, perhaps already weakened by hard racing.

That crews do cross the oceans in lightly built cruiser/racers does not imply they are the right boats for the job, or that they are safe. The history of world cruising is full of long voyages in unsuitable boats. Also of disastrous voyages. Try getting insurance even for an ideal boat.

As often happens the scene is dominated by racing, where the dangers are accepted, as are the discomfort and risks of ruthless weight saving. But the casualty rate in glamorous transocean racing has been much higher than acceptable prudent seamanship. Moreover the trend is towards ever lighter, faster and less suitable boats.

Most people today start sailing on fast racing dinghies and graduate to fast cruiser/racers. Consequently they look on heavy, slower boats with contempt. The concept that a cruising yacht is a small ship has gone. Now it is an overgrown racing dinghy. When ocean crossing the overriding consideration is, or should be, not to go as fast as possible but to arrive without incident or exhausting the crew.

Factors of safety

Factors of safety with fibreglass are eroded with age and use (Chapter 8). On many modern lightly built boats they may have gone altogether after about ten years. So in theory the older the boat the potentially more dangerous to be heavily overloaded. Yet older boats were generally more strongly built with larger rule of thumb factors of safety. The dangerous ones are those newer classes where builders boast of computer analysed stresses and more exact factors of safety but based on tighter assumptions of use and a shorter life.

Effect of overloading

The merits and demerits of light and heavy displacement will be argued for years to come. Most cruiser/racers are designed by go-fast designers with a one-track mind. Builders run on the same fast track. Speed wins races, and winning races sells boats so nothing else counts. The idea that anyone may not want to sail faster than everyone else is beyond their ken.

Certainly some good strong cruisers are built. They are not the worry. The problem is the flood of lightly built race-bred cruiser/racers, more racer than cruiser, built down to a price and marketable performance in a competitive field.

Designers scream 'Keep weight out of the ends', to reduce pitching which slows the boat. Yet where else is there to put it? When heavily loaded there will be a lot of extra weight being thrown around, like a child

shaking a piggy bank, in parts of the boat not designed for it.

Extra weight imposes higher stresses on the rigging too. It can be made stronger, but that is pointless unless attachments are stronger too, including the adjacent hull and deck, a point frequently forgotten. Modern rigging is on the principle of no-redundancy to reduce cost as well as windage. Additions and upgrading to ocean standard add yet more weight.

Tons of extra weight

Tons? Very much so. An ocean crossing is far removed from weekend racing or holiday cruising. The crew have to be entirely self-contained for weeks, even months on end, carrying not only their basic life support but comfort and pleasures as well. Plus everything needed to keep a fairly complicated sailing machine working smoothly and get it safely to a distant destination.

The absolute minimum for a crew of two on a transatlantic crossing is about one ton. On most yachts the load will be two or three tons. This may sound incredible, but work it out yourself and do not forget the extra weight already added.

Certainly it is possible to reduce weight if prepared to be ruthless and take more risks. Unless racing, few owners are as ruthless, and prudent sailors do not take risks. The thirty days in the box on page 254 may seem slow for a transatlantic crossing, where the average is now about twenty, yet not unusual. You must allow a substantial reserve.

A blue water cruiser must be self-reliant with spares, tools and equipment for several years. As a rough guide the entire contents of your workshop at home! You cannot rely on finding services or spares beyond the ocean, especially in those far away islands of dreams.

As well as basic life support, masses of extra equipment will be needed. Sails, awning, electronics, refrigerator; books and charts for navigation; more and heavier anchors because anchoring is the custom and there are few marinas. Most blue water sailors are refugees from marinas anyway and boast of their massive storm anchors.

The dream may be no clothes. But you have to get there and back through waters as cold

Weight for 30 days at sea			
Assumed size of boat	25ft	30ft	35ft
Number of crew	2	3	4
Water @ 1 gall/day each	600 lb	900 lb	1200 lb
Food and drink @ 10 lb/day	600 lb	900 lb	1200 lb
Spares and tools	200 lb	400 lb	500 lb
Extra equipment/sails/anchors	200 lb	400 lb	600 lb
Dinghy/outboard	100 lb	200 lb	200 lb
Personal possessions @ 50 lb	100 lb	150 lb	200 lb
Fuel	100 lb	200 lb	500 lb
Reserve food/water @ 25%	300 lb	450 lb	600 lb
Miscellaneous	200 lb	500 lb	1000 lb
Crew	300 lb	450 lb	600 lb
Total	2700 lb	4500 lb	6600 lb
Displacement for load of 25%	10800 lb	18000 lb	26400 lb

and wet as home, and also still look respectable at times. Emergencies, let alone plans, may require going home by 'steam seagull' and emerging into the depths of winter still dressed for the tropics can be a rude shock.

Except for ruthless record breakers any cruising boat will spend more time in harbour than at sea. The weight of comforts in a variety of climates is as relevant as anything for seagoing. More dreams are ended by discomfort in harbour than poor sailing performance.

Many people seeking to escape civilisation want to bring it with them. If the boat is home too the weight will really mount up. In the family stage, the irreducibles go sky high. Modern, light weight cruiser/racers are just not designed to carry such weights. The problem becomes really acute with a 25 ft, 7.5 m, boat, and the dangers of overloading are most serious in the smaller sizes. Many experienced cruising people claim a yacht under 30 ft, 9 m, cannot carry safely enough water and stores for a crew of more than two; 35 ft, 10.5 m, if live-aboards. Consequently insurance companies' unrealistic insistence on larger crews 'in the interests of safety', and the extra weight and space they require makes the boat more dangerous not less so.

The major limitation is generally stowage. What must be carried will always exceed the space available. What you would like to carry needs a bigger boat!

Safe load

What is a safe load? A light structure can be designed to carry a heavy load. An oil tanker will carry many times its own weight. But it is designed to do so. A light weight yacht is designed to sail fast and nothing else. A realistic arbitrary figure is 25% of the displacement, but the lighter and higher performance the boat the less weight in proportion to displacement it can carry.

Therefore the absolute minimum displacement for ocean cruising is about 4 tons. In the critical small sizes an older boat like a 25 ft, 7.5 m, Vertue, nominal displacement 10,000 lb, 5,000 kg, can carry a heavier load, as well as being more strongly built, than a similar-sized modern cruiser/racer of 4,000 lb, 2,000 kg. Not until about 35 ft, 10.5 m, will a cruiser/racer have the load carrying capacity of a Vertue.

Bear in mind that one ton is the *minimum* and with most crews it will be nearer two tons. Only the more heavily built fibreglass cruisers in the 35 ft, 10.5 m, range can safely carry that. In the smallest sizes the load could exceed the displacement.

Effect on performance

Weight kills performance as every dedicated racing fanatic knows. Therefore the greater the load relative to displacement will be the greater the effect, on performance. Moreover the performance of a light cruiser/racer will be affected by overloading to a greater and sooner extent than a more heavily built pure cruiser.

Performance and seaworthiness are inseparable. A boat that does not have the designed performance because it is overloaded will be unseaworthy. On the ocean speed is not important. Seaworthiness very definitely is.

Light boats are claimed to be safer because in a storm they can use their speed to sail out of trouble (dynamic safety). That is not true when the performance has been reduced by overloading. In effect the light boat has become a heavy one yet does not handle as safely.

Catamarans have vast space for their size and make excellent mobile homes but are bad weight carriers. When overloaded they tend to wallow and if they cannot 'fly' become unseaworthy. With no ballast to offset extra weight they are the extreme example of light weight boats. Also the shape does not have the natural strength of a monohull and in many cases design and construction have been weak.

Displacement

Do not confuse displacement with registered tonnage which is based on volume, even though it did originally mean tons of best Tyne coal which could be carried, or even earlier the tuns or big barrels of wine. Thames tonnage and rating rules are also volume formulae.

Quoted displacements, generally to an accuracy only a computer would be fool enough to believe, are academic, usually the designer's figure before a boat was built. Few builders check. Moulding tolerance alone can be 10%. Normal seagoing equipment will increase displacement for a start. Allow a margin on quoted figures. The crew's weight may also be significant.

What is the structural effect?

Every time the boat pitches when close-hauled the bows must lift that heavy extra weight and then crash down with extra force behind it. These are forces for which the boat was not designed.

Unlike an afternoon race, on an ocean passage this can go on for days or weeks. Before reaching the fair trade winds there may be several thousand miles of rough, close-hauled sailing. The number of times that bow lifts and crashes will get towards a million. Well into critical fatigue cycles. Some peculiar people even sail round the world that way.

Fibreglass fails progressively (Chapter 5). Fatigue and overstrain are both cumulative

and the boat has probably had some years of hard use already. The effect of bashing close-hauled for days on end when heavily overloaded would be progressive weakening. Final failure would be sudden and catastrophic, and the bang could well be mistaken for collision. There should be some warning like movement or noise, probably building up over a time, but it could be overlooked or considered normal.

Motor cruisers

Few motor cruisers make ocean crossings, mostly only the sturdier displacement or trawler type. However, because the dynamic stresses are greater overloading the popular fast cruiser will be dangerous, even for short distances. So too would be increasing the speed or engine power.

Recommendations

Unless a racing fanatic, and prepared to accept the risks to yourself, family and crew, do not go ocean cruising in the modern cruiser/racer where the emphasis is on speed and light displacement.

Look cynically at the claims in a brochure. Use your own judgement and the class record.

A slow boat is safer than a fast one. This will be hotly disputed and it depends on the boat. There is a very important difference between a good seaworthy cruiser designed to sail relatively slowly *by racing standards* and a light race-bred boat slowed by being overloaded. Under those conditions the heavier cruiser will probably be faster because its speed is less affected.

Someone to whom sailing means racing may not bear the thought of a slow boat. Yet a good cruising yacht is no sluggard. Many were once good handicap or ocean racers. With nobody to compete against, the marginal difference between fast and fastest, what a racing man means by a 'slow' boat, is unimportant.

Tropical waters expose deficiencies in manufacture and materials which one would get away with for many years longer in home waters. Sophisticated factors of safety will become more critical and exhausted sooner. The fact that an overloaded boat has got there is no assurance it will be safe a few years later for the tougher sail back.

If you must go ocean cruising in a light boat add extra stiffening, especially in the forward sections. Because a boat of the same class has made an outstanding voyage do not assume yours will. That boat may have been strengthened. Some builders have made special boats for well publicised stunt voyages.

Sail with the smallest crew possible. Carrying less weight the boat will be much safer than when heavily overloaded with stores and water for the larger crew demanded by insurers 'in the interests of safety'.

Look out for and do not disregard warning signs. If you hear noises or notice structural movement abandon the voyage if still practicable. If not, sail gently.

Do not race in an overloaded boat, or try record breaking or even to make par for the course. Sail the boat's pace always, regardless of what others may do, or what you think they may think of you.

There is an irreducible minimum below which one cannot reduce the weight of stores and water, spares and equipment to cross the ocean in safety, comfort (a decidedly relative term) and with an adequate margin for emergencies. Moreover only a cruising skipper of rare ruthlessness will manage to keep the weight anywhere near that minimum. Boats may get lighter but not crews and their needs. Whether designed for it or not, that weight is what the boat has to carry in all weathers and all sea conditions without being unseaworthy or breaking up.

Trailering

Too often trailer sailer, whether sail or power, just means small and light enough without considering the special requirements when travelling on land at speeds unheard of at sea. The motion can be worse than a storm afloat. Everything loose will vibrate, roll, slide or fall out. Heavy items like outboard motor or anchor need well fastened and padded lashing points. At sea anything adrift would be spotted at once, but in the towing vehicle you cannot hear what chaos is happening behind.

A heavy duty four wheel trailer rides easily but speed is impossible. A two wheel trailer bounces and pitches much more. As the boat is lighter and can be towed at full legal speed the motion is more violent. In most countries once off the main highways roads are not as smooth as in Britain.

The boat must be designed for the trailer and reinforced where supports will be. Alternatively the trailer supports must be positioned at strong points of the hull. Numerous lashing points are needed, all well reinforced. A towing eye, commoner on motor boats than sailing cruisers, makes loading easier. The stem should be reinforced strongly enough to take the full weight of the boat. There must be secure restraint against movement fore and aft. Lashings alone are not enough. Most boats tend to 'walk' forwards which may become a steeplechase on emergency braking.

If the boat is allowed to bounce there may be broken stiffeners and fatigue damage. Some hulls are so flexible the boat sways or cannot be bowsed tight. Inspect for cracks on arrival. A light racing boat can distort and be disqualified on arrival at a distant regatta.

Know the exact air height. Pulpit, pushpit, stanchions and everything else including a wheelhouse should be easily removable down to cabin top level and reduce the risk of unexpectedly finding too small a hole. They are sometimes difficult to remove in a hurry while holding up traffic.

Know the boat weight too, not just the brochure weight, probably wrong anyway, but loaded with equipment plus everything needed for the cruise. Include the trailer and car as well. It is easy to run out of steam on a mountain pass.

Have drain holes to prevent collecting a weight of rainwater and a cover to protect the hull from exhaust fumes, tar and chips from stones.

Greater precautions are needed on deliveries by trailer or lowloader not designed for the boat.

Painting

Fibreglass boats became popular largely because they did not need to be painted. It was still the era of the wooden boat which had to be painted every year. Faced with large annual yard bills and memories of pre-war wage rates, many owners found it had become an unendurable expense. The idea of a boat which did not need to be painted was very attractive indeed.

One important aspect was never mentioned. A wooden boat reappears every spring freshly painted and varnished, as smart as ever, for a hundred years. The never painted fibreglass boat just gets dingier with nothing to hide the accumulated scars of earlier years.

It is now accepted that 'no painting' is another myth. After a time fibreglass boats do need to be painted to restore their appearance, or make good damage. Ten, perhaps fifteen, years is the average 'no painting' holiday.

Having no seams to open, a common reason for painting a wooden boat, paint will last until it fades and modern paints last longer. Consequently fibreglass does not need repainting every year. Just as well. For the cost of a present day spray paint one could have bought the whole boat in the bad old days of annual painting!

Spray painting

To serve the ageing fleet of middle aged yachts special clinics have been set up where a professional spray painting job can be done under the proper conditions necessary for superior modern paints. Coupled with handling and transport this is expensive yet reckoned to last only five years or so. Averaged out, the cost of spraying a fibreglass boat every five years is probably more than having a wooden boat hand painted professionally every year.

Despite the claims very few of those spray painters can produce a finish as good as original gel coat. This will be hotly disputed not least by the proud owners who have just paid through the nose for it. Do not be misled by that bright shiny finish. Look closely and critically. It will generally have orange peel as bad as brush marks. I have yet to see a spray painted yacht that could compare with a car, and some are more like a shiny gravel path.

The only way to get a finish as good as original gel coat is by repeated rubbing down and burnishing. That original gel coat finish was obtained from the mould after weeks of hard work getting the perfect finish on the pattern. Worthwhile when hundreds of boats will come out of the mould; totally uneconomic for an individual boat.

Certainly spraying, if done well, gives a good enough finish to delight most non-critical owners. But it does need to be done inside in a properly equipped, draught free paint shop. That means a biggish building plus equipment to handle large, heavy boats. The right conditions cannot be obtained outside.

Spraying is messy. All parts of the boat must be masked. As overspray can travel a long way, especially in a wind; every other boat in range must be masked or screened too. Nearby owners sometimes object to their boats looking as if they had measles. This adds to the time and expense.

Hand painting

The idea that fibreglass boats must always be sprayed professionally is another myth. They can be painted by hand, often just as well. Brush marks may show, but no worse than average orange peel when spray painted. They were acceptable on the very finest wooden yachts. Traditionalists might prefer them!

As boats age they go down the social scale.

Long before their useful life is over they will not be worth the expense of professional respraying. But an owner can still paint by brush.

Although scorned by professionals, paint rollers can be used with all paints except polyurethane and are much faster. Cheap ones may be dissolved by the solvents in certain antifoulings.

Polyurethane

This is the best and longest lasting. It is tough and hard with a good finish, but needs skill to apply by spray or brush and perfect conditions normally indoors.

Although usually sprayed it is feasible to apply by brush but difficult. It must be put on quickly with even strokes. Picking up an edge or going over what has just been applied will raise lumps. The recommended method is by two people, one putting on with a brush, the other smoothing out with a paint pad close behind. Paint rollers cause horrible orange peel.

Conditions are critical. In hot sunshine polyurethane will harden almost as soon as applied. In damp, high humidity or cold it will not harden properly at all. Minimum temperature is 50°F, 10°C. If mistakes are made or it turns out to have unacceptable orange peel the paint is so hard that rubbing down is a long and laborious job.

True polyurethane is a chemically curing, two part paint. The one part polyurethanes rely on atmospheric moisture for setting and are not as good. They are ordinary paints modified with polyurethane.

Alkyd paints

These are the modern yacht enamels, longer lasting than traditional oil based paints. Being more tolerant of conditions they are much easier to apply by brush or roller than polyurethanes. The finish is as good as on wood or steel yachts, and nobody complains about that. They are certainly better than badly applied polyurethane.

Enamel does not last as long. But if polyurethane means the complications and expense of putting the boat into a distant spray clinic for weeks, whereas enamel can be applied in a day without moving the boat, by the owner using a brush or roller, it has strong advantages. On a good seamfree substrate like fibreglass it should last at least three years, and is the obvious answer as the boat gets older and into the hands of more practical but impecunious owners.

A second class paint applied well is better than a superior one like polyurethane in unsuitable conditions.

Epoxy

In recent years epoxy has been favoured as a less permeable coating underwater than polyester gel coat (Chapter 27). The reason, lost among the extravagant claims for low and even zero permeability, is because the modern solventless epoxies can be applied as much thicker coats than paint and comparable to original gel coat thickness. At best, seldom achieved under practical conditions, it is only three times less permeable, useful but not dramatic and certainly not zero.

Above water the finish and gloss are poor and choice of colours limited. Epoxy does not weather well.

Antifouling

The early claims that nothing would grow on the smooth surface of fibreglass were very soon proved wrong. One cannot beat Nature so easily. Fibreglass boats do still need painting with antifouling, and that generally means every year. (An old tip is not to paint until June. From March to May little weed grows and expensive antifouling goes to waste, or, as some say, pollutes the seas unnecessarily.)

A thick build up from repeated antifouling is considered undesirable because the weight is marginally 'speed stealing', or something. Yet the thicker the paint, the greater the protection against permeation (Chapter 26) and hence blistering. Thick paint is as effective as expensive epoxy. This is shown by the way boats blister along the unpainted waterline earlier than under the antifouling.

Primer

Few paints adhere well to a shiny, smooth surface. The special primers for fibreglass chemically attack and etch the surface. This is suspected of being a possible cause of blistering, especially on a sensitive, marginal quality gel coat. As few gel coats are perfect, primers are discouraged underwater and in the vulnerable splash zone.

Preparation

Paint manuals give instructions for preparation and use, and of course nobody should open a tin of paint without reading the instructions.

Regardless of whether a primer is used, key the surface by rubbing down to remove the gloss. Ordinary sanding may seem to dull the surface, but seen under a magnifier or highlighted scratches are still separated by glossy surface. Better keying is with steel wool or kitchen scouring powder, the only time an abrasive scourer should be allowed within sight of fibreglass.

Residual release agent can remain for many years, not just on new boats. Use a proprietary degreasing agent; alternatively white spirit, methylated spirits or denatured alcohol. These also remove hydrocarbons which have soaked into the gel coat. Spillages from a fuel dock or boat are more penetrating than a tanker disaster and far more common.

The surface must be free of polish. Degreasing agents are effective on most kinds except silicone. This is difficult to remove because it smears. Wiping just moves it somewhere else. The recommended technique, seldom mentioned in instructions, is to find a supermarket offering a special deal on kitchen rolls. Armed with a dozen or more and a tin of degreaser, work on the basis of one wipe and throw away. Do not use the same piece twice. Newspaper, also suggested, may leave black marks.

A sensible owner will never use silicone polish despite the attractions of no hard rubbing. But there is no knowing what previous owners have used. Silicone is persistent.

Removing paint

Enamel and antifouling can be taken off using *approved* paint remover without attacking the fibreglass. Unapproved paint remover will etch and damage the gel coat, even destroy it. Polyurethane and epoxy, however, are a lot tougher and more chemical resistant than the gel coat. You may be left with the paint but no boat.

If the paint is the same colour as the gel coat, it is very easy to go too far when sanding. Undercoat, if not the paint itself, should be a contrasting colour.

Repair

Moderate structural damage to a fibreglass boat is easier to repair than wood, and within the ability of an owner. The problem is usually to match the finish and probably means premature painting. However, major damage requires a high degree of skill. Few boatyards really have the experience, equipment or premises, although plenty try.

Replacing damaged equipment, engines and much else is generally more expensive than the fibreglass repair.

A seldom appreciated feature with fibreglass is that although still structurally intact, and often showing no signs, hidden damage will extend over a considerably wider area (Chapter 5).

Many instructions, articles and other books have been written about repairs to fibreglass. This section is mainly concerned with practical points commonly overlooked. Those who write instructions have seldom done repairs.

CHAPTER

Temporary repair

This chapter assumes no facilities other than likely to be on board a reasonably well equipped boat.

Unlike steel, fibreglass does not need special equipment, an important point when a boat is aground in an inaccessible place. Indeed fibreglass can be used for temporary repairs to steel or wooden boats.

Temporary repairs too often become permanent. They must be replaced by proper permanent repair at the first opportunity. Temporary repairs should be to get you home or, if not serious, no longer than the end of the season.

However, repair facilities may be far away. Temporary repairs may have to last days, even months, and withstand hard sailing. As with old sailing ships the most important thing is being resourceful and self-reliant.

Materials
Glass mat is the most versatile and easily formed. Stronger woven rovings are not necessary for temporary repairs. Glass tape is invaluable for binding broken oars, boathooks or spars, and not just temporarily. My garden spade was mended with glass tape forty years ago! But throw away the useless open weave

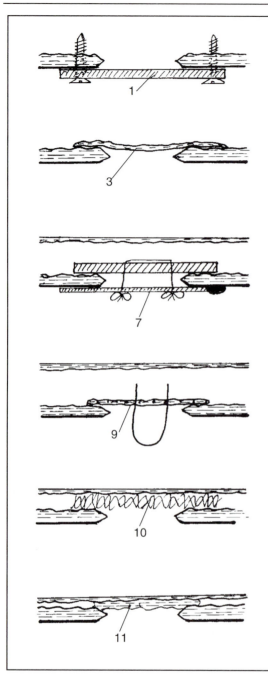

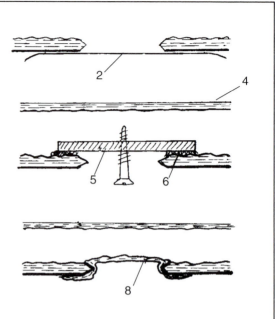

Figure 39.1
Fibreglass cannot be moulded in the air. There has to be backing of some sort, easiest when there is access both sides. Cardboard, plywood, tin can lid, 1, can be secured temporarily with self-tapping screws, or use sticky tape, 2. Or lay in one layer of pre-wetted mat, 3, which must be allowed to set. It will be poorly moulded and porous but firm enough to act as backing for further layers.

When an inner lining or woodwork, 4, prevents access repair is more difficult. As damage is usually a split the backing can be wriggled in and turned. Cardboard, 5, can be held manually by a screw until resin has set, 6, or tied to matchsticks, 7. Pre-wetted mat, 8, can be speared on wire, or pushed in, 9. Cloth holds together better than mat. If the inner lining is close the space can be packed with newspaper or plastics foam, 10, or, if closer still, moulded solid, 11.

scrim cloth and tape, commonly included in multi-use repair kits.

Polyester, the usual resin in repair kits, is adequate provided the surface can be made reasonably dry, cleaned of weed, slime, mud and loose paint, and well sanded. A doubtful bond can be supplemented with self-tapping screws. No repair should be put to test until the resin has set.

Nowadays some prefer epoxy because it is a better adhesive but the surface has to be just as dry and clean. It is also more tolerant of bad conditions but there is little control over setting time, generally longer than polyester. Speed is often critical. The tide waits for no resin.

Temperature

Instructions say polyester resin should not be used at a temperature below about 60°F, 15°C. That is little help when up the creek. But this is not an arbitrary go/no go limit. At progressively lower temperatures polyester will set more slowly and not be as strong or cure properly. Damp too will delay setting and prevent proper cure. But if it sets at all in the time available it will do. Increasing catalyst will speed setting time. The normal 2% can be increased to 7% without harm. An amine booster is useful when likely to be wrecked in cold climates. In hot conditions the catalyst should be reduced to prevent resin setting too quickly.

Heat from any source will speed setting. A blow torch is risky. It may set fire to the resin – and the boat. **Note: In the liquid state polyester is inflammable** (Chapter 10). A safer way is to warm the surface first. Try simpler methods like a hot water bottle wrapped in polythene to prevent sticking. Sitting on it has also been suggested. Again polythene to prevent sticking is advisable.

Epoxy is less affected by temperature. With special hardeners some can be used at low temperature but setting time will be very slow and it will not cure properly. As the proportion of hardener cannot be altered there is no control as with polyester; only heat.

All resins become thick and difficult to use at lower temperatures. They become thinner if warmed which is also the best way to speed setting. Being inflammable this must be done with caution (Chapter 20).

Above water

The outside will be accessible and being unpainted is easy to make dry. But the topsides may be underwater for prolonged periods later as the boat rolls or heels.

Sandwich mouldings

Even a small puncture must be sealed at once to keep water out of the core. Only in laboratory samples is the claim that water is confined to the point of entry true. Most sandwich mouldings have long internal waterways, especially older ones. Damage will break the bond anyway.

Small holes

Fill small holes with polyester or epoxy putty. Other sealants can also be used. Sticky tape is a good standby, especially strong fabric tape, duct tape or parcel tape.

Some epoxy putties will set in damp, cold conditions, but as they will not bond to a wet surface, underwater setting epoxies are overrated. Few other sealants will bond to a wet surface either.

Larger holes

A fibreglass patch cannot be moulded over nothing. A firm backing must be improvised somehow using ingenuity and whatever is to hand (Fig 39.1).

Underwater

With a sufficient tidal range to dry out, perhaps careening as in olden days, a fibreglass patch can be applied. The surface must be dry because no resin will stick to a wet surface. If the tide rises before the resin has set the outside will be soft and tacky, although it will still harden after a fashion underneath. Covering with polythene will keep the water off.

With no fibreglass available or conditions impossible you can still use the old fashioned tingle using plywood, a can lid, fabric, even strong polythene, with plenty of sealant. One cannot hammer nails into fibreglass but it can be secured with self-tapping screws, or at a pinch, steel wood screws. Brass screws tend to break. Through bolting assumes access behind.

Do not scorn old fashioned methods. No fibreglass boat should be without caulking cotton (if you can find it today!). There may be no seams to caulk but plenty of leaking skin fittings, stern tubes, rudder trunks, even small holes. Sealant cannot be applied to a wet surface or against a pressure of water, but caulking cotton can be packed in.

Emergency action

At sea little more than emergency action to keep the boat afloat is possible. A diver might apply a patch but would need calm conditions: a sheltered lagoon, not mid-ocean.

From outside the only practical thing is still the old idea of a collision mat: a sail or awning pulled tight against the hull. Old sailing ships however did not have fin keels. From inside one can stuff something into the hole if (and a very big if) it is possible to locate the leak and get access before the boat sinks.

A collision mat is held in place by the pressure of water, but anything inside will be against a considerable inrush which will wash away anything not firmly backed. Various methods have been tried or suggested: wooden struts; expanding *in situ* foam inside a polythene bag; inflating a dinghy seat inside a locker; with crew to spare having someone sit on it. (That kept a yacht afloat during a Sydney–Hobart race.) Even releasing the liferaft below, although that smacks of Russian roulette if it does not work!

Access

This is the biggest problem with any repair. You cannot stuff a sock in the hole unless you can see and reach where the water is pouring in. Yet ready access to the inside of the hull with a large inside or pan moulding is impossible.

Therefore a lot of experienced sailors declare modern fibreglass yachts are unsafe to go to sea. That is a sweeping statement, which every builder and designer will hotly deny and try to suppress. Certainly it is absolutely wrong to condemn fibreglass boats as a whole. The danger is the way in which so many are designed and built, with common sense and seaworthiness being subordinated to production convenience.

It is claimed that the lining is bonded on in so many places any leak would be contained in a small area. That is rubbish. Even if bonded perfectly when built, which it seldom is and there is no way to check, damage will break the bond. Many are splodge bonded and there are usually holes for wires and pipes. The chances are the inner moulding will be split too.

The probable situation is for the crew to find water pouring from an edge of that moulding with no idea where it is coming in and little time to find out before water rises so high work is impossible.

Even if located how do they hack away that inner lining? Few yachts carry a comprehensive tool kit. Sawing will be too slow and with the hull close behind more blades will be broken than are likely to be on board.

This will be very different from the way builders assume access would be gained for repair: carefully planned, unobtrusive cuts; a skilful boatyard operation using power tools; boat steady ashore, good lighting, absolute safety. Not in a seasick panic, thrown around by violent motion in the dim light of a torch and water already up to one's knees; destructive, brutal butchery by desperate, frightened people with anything they can lay hands on. Few these days even carry an axe.

In contrast, if the inside of the hull is accessible through lockers or under floorboards, there is a good chance of locating and controlling the leak before it becomes too late. That is how *safe* fibreglass boats are designed.

No classification society or national authority overconcerned with safety equipment seems to have considered this. Yet if a crew have to take to the mandatory liferaft, or Mayday for the lifeboat, simply because they cannot reach a modest leak to stuff in a sock, can such a boat really be classified seaworthy?

It is no exaggeration to say access can mean the difference between staying afloat and sinking – life or death. No wonder yachts nowadays have to carry liferafts!

Repair kit

Polyester has a limited shelf life, quoted as 6–12 months, but usually good for two years. (Remember: it may have been on the supplier's shelf for months.) After a few years stowed away in a locker it can be solid or too thick to use when needed in emergency. Catalyst too can lose strength. Then the resin, although usable, does not set or sets too slowly. Polyester and catalyst should be replaced at least every two years.

Epoxy has indefinite shelf life although the hardener is hygroscopic and can solidify after opening.

The binder of glass mat can be hydrolysed by damp air and although still usable it gets fluffy and is best replaced with the resin. It should be kept well sealed.

The quantities depend on the size of boat and distance from repair facilities. The resin and catalyst or hardener should be selected according to the climate and likely temperature under which the repair may be needed.

Hints

Some hints are contrary to good moulding practice. But who cares if they keep you afloat.

- A polythene bag over a slow setting resin will keep off water if caught by a rising tide or rain.
- If polyester has not set in time try brushing catalyst on the surface.
- Avoid general purpose repair kits which usually contain non-marine materials despite their claims to mend anything. Better to make up your own.
- Obtain at least four times the usual quantity of catalyst so polyester can be boosted in cold conditions.
- Carefully warming resin will speed setting and also make it easier to use (Chapter 20). Warning: this is hazardous. **Temperature should not be more than finger painful**.
- Warming the surface will also speed setting.
- Measure catalyst or hardener accurately. An eye dropper or dropper bottle is a convenient way to measure the small quantities. 10 drops per 1 oz, 25 g, is about 1%.
- The resin quantity can be guessed. Baked beans and resin weigh about the same. A half full, small 6 oz tin is roughly 3 oz, 150 g.
- Mix small quantities at a time, 1–3 oz, 25–75 g. *Never* all the resin at once. If it sets sooner than expected (as it probably will) you will be caught with the job half finished and no more resin.
- Practise using the repair kit. Do not wait until an emergency to find out. Read the instructions when stowing away. Even if there is time when needed the light may be too bad or your glasses lost.
- Keep containers well closed. Put polythene under the lids of resin tins after opening otherwise the drips may set hard and make it impossible to reopen.
- Store glass fibre in well sealed bags to keep it dry. If practicable, warm before use to drive off condensation.
- Replace polyester resin and catalyst every two years whether used or not. Glass mat too if no longer crisp. If polyester pours it is usable. Old crystallised epoxy will become clear if warmed.

Repair kit

Tin of polyester resin with catalyst,
or
Tin of epoxy resin with hardener
Amine booster for polyester (cold climates only)
Chopped strand glass mat
Woven rovings (optional)
Close weave glass fibre tape
Acetone for cleaning
'Wet and dry' sandpaper
Touch-up kit for gel coat in appropriate colours
Measure for resin
Measure for catalyst or hardener (must be separate)
Mixing cartons (or clean and save a few food tins)
Stirrers (or save wooden ice cream spatulas)
Cheap disposable brushes
Marine quality resin putty, polyester or epoxy
Strong sticky tape, eg reinforced PVC, or duct tape
Self-tapping screws (plus drills)
Polythene (never a shortage of polybags)
Caulking cotton

Minor repair

This covers cosmetic repair and minor structural damage which an average owner might tackle himself. Such people are generally resourceful and ingenious, which is more important than detailed and often inappropriate instructions.

Cosmetic repair

All boats are vulnerable to cosmetic damage regardless of size and sturdiness of construction. This is shallow surface damage, mostly no deeper than the gel coat, ranging from an isolated scratch or chip to a wide area of abrasion. It is unsightly rather than structural but to fussy owners that can be greater agony.

Scratches and chafe show because the roughness holds dirt. Also, regardless of colour, scratched fibreglass goes a light grey, more conspicuous on a coloured moulding than white. Cleaning and smoothing the roughness with acetone using a fine paint brush may blend in a scratch.

Colour matching

The chief problem is to match the colour. Gel coat changes colour due to exposure so even original supplied by the moulder will be subtly different. White changes least, yet there are still half a million shades. No hand mixed colours will be exactly the same.

To avoid conspicuous mismatch confine the filling very strictly to the scratch or chip. The technique which many bodgers, professional as well as amateur, have yet to learn is to fill and then scrape, sand and burnish away all excess. It will then hardly show. A narrow line of contrasting colour is less conspicuous than the wide smear of closer matching shade so often seen.

A repair and gel coat will weather differently. Moulders' defects made good skilfully

enough to be almost invisible, often become noticeable some years later.

Texture is as important as colour. A dull patch on a well polished surface will stand out. So will a well polished repair on a dull, weathered surface. Pinholes may be a clue to past repair.

Some gel coat touch-up kits are not densely coloured and dirty scratches show through. Shallow scratches and microscratches are more easily burnished out with fine abrasive polish but this wears away gel coat and should not be repeated.

Deep scratches

Scratches through the gel coat must be treated more seriously because they expose the structural moulding. They should be filled with polyester or epoxy putty without delay. It must be marine grade. Alternatively make your own (Chapter 2).

Deep gouges or abrasion need to be built up with mat, after chiselling away the edges to get back to sound material.

Access

Repair is usually simple. The problem is access to do it. The proper way is from behind (Fig 40.1). This allows a wide overlap on to surrounding sound material. It is a feature of fibreglass that damage always extends beyond the obvious. From inside it is easy to reinforce margins but from outside repair is restricted to the immediate damage leaving the surrounding area still weakened. Also the bonding area is far smaller.

From outside mostly mat will be used because of practical moulding difficulties and the repair will not be as strong as the original. If inside the moulding can be thicker to compensate for lower strength and uncertain lay

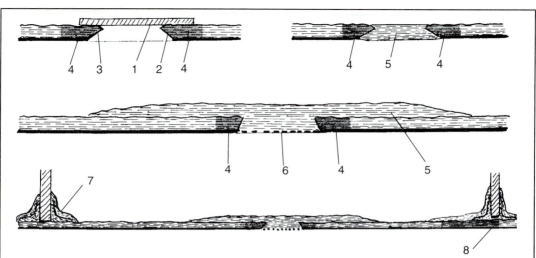

Figure 40.1
The common method of repair is to work from outside by inserting a backing piece, 1, chamfering the edges, 2, with a slight V, 3, then moulding over the hole, 5. This leaves a weak area with hidden damage around the edge, 4.

The better method is to work from inside with the backing outside. The new moulding, 5, can then extend well beyond known or suspected hidden damage and repair is much stronger, also thicker. Any repair is unlikely to match the original lay up, generally unknown, and for mouldability contain mostly mat. Extra thickness compensates. This method can also replace the gel coat, 6. By working inside bulkhead angles, 7, can be inspected and doubled and the hull reinforced if there are cracks on the gel coat, 8 indicating hidden damage.

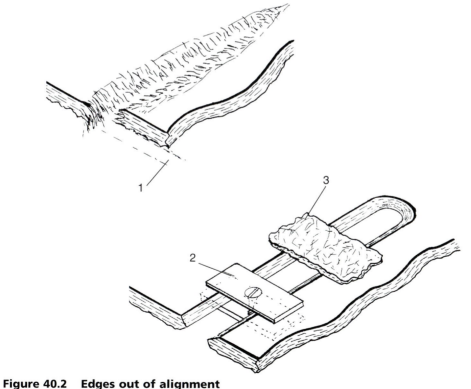

Figure 40.2   Edges out of alignment
Often edges must be brought back into line, 1. After shaping the edges, simple clamps, 2, will hold them in position while tacking pieces, 3, are moulded.

up, and because of the easier shape can include woven rovings.

Splits

Like torn trousers, fibreglass splits rather than forming a hole. Not until battered into multiple splits does a hole appear. Do not allow helpful friends to tear away pieces. Although shattered they can often be held together to form the essential backing and original shape. A split should never be repaired simply with putty, as often recommended. Putty has little strength.

Edges may be out of alignment. Simple clamps will hold them in position while being 'tacked' (Fig 40.2).

Repair of small holes and splits

Assuming a sensible design with reasonably easy access, clean the inside surface, sand it free of paint and to key the surface. Be sure it is paint, not finishing resin which will need keying only. Because of the uneven and possibly fibrous surface it is difficult to clean paint from all the hollows. More harm will be done by sanding or grinding down to the lowest level than leaving deeper patches of paint as long as it is substantially clean and oil-free. A wire brush in an electric drill is more effective at getting into the hollows than a grinder and does not destroy so much boat.

Attach a smooth backing piece to the outside with sticky tape and mould inside to more than hull thickness with a generous, well tapered overlap. With strength restored fill the gap and finish cosmetically.

If access behind is not possible the repair gets a lot more difficult despite the glib instructions often supplied. Also it cannot be nearly as strong. Clean up and trim the edges, then chamfer and V them so the repair will hold with a rivet action. Do not, as often recommended, rely on bonding alone.

Larger holes

The larger the hole the more important that the repair is done properly from inside, even if it means cutting away inner mouldings to do so. The greater the damage the wider the extent of hidden damage and weakness, a point seldom considered.

Pre-wetted mat tends to sag if more than a few inches. On wider holes use a backing of plywood or metal covered with polythene to prevent sticking.

Inspection

Make sure that what seems a minor repair really is. With anything more than superficial cosmetic damage there may be hidden damage. Inspect carefully for gel coat cracks beyond the obvious damage and at nearby hardspots. Also check angles inside for breaking away or white lines showing weakening from bending. Behind deep gouges the inner laminates have often split especially after sharp pointed impact.

What appears at first to be merely cosmetic often turns out on closer examination to be structural damage. With good access behind this can be repaired simply and minds set at rest. Without access there must always be nagging doubt, despite glib and generally ignorant assurances.

Major repair

For the amateur this is in the realm of 'Don't'. Major repair is for the professionals. However, they do vary very widely, from the highly skilled, with proper working conditions and facilities, who have achieved miracles on yachts declared beyond repair, to the over-confident boatyard or moonlighter with little experience of fibreglass and no proper facilities.

For many years few people knew how to repair fibreglass. A lot of inadequate work was done under primitive conditions. Beware of an old boat that was repaired in earlier years; and sometimes recently too.

Any major repair will involve a great deal of other work. If sunk, almost everything else on board. The fibreglass is often the simplest and cheapest.

The saddest sight on a boat is the appalling mess inside after being wrecked. Everything nice in a sodden heap mixed with broken glass, mud, seaweed, and saturated with engine oil and diesel. Who can blame an owner for weeping?

Hidden damage
Hidden damage extending well beyond the obvious (Chapter 5) must always be assumed even if there are no obvious signs and the surrounding area should be strongly reinforced to at least half thickness. If there is any doubt, over- repair is safer than theory. Or more often ignorance.

Access
No major repair should be attempted without cutting away inside if need be to gain access to allow work behind. Only if quite impossible,

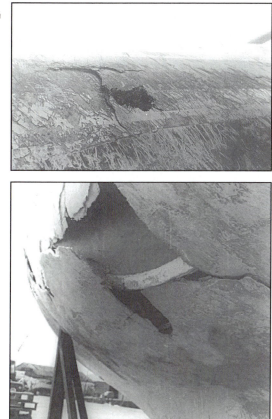

a

b

Photos 41.1 (a) Most damage takes the form of splits. Only when these link under multiple impact will a hole appear. Most damage when aground on rocks or reefs is accompanied by pounding and very severe abrasion. The cosmetic repairs are often more difficult than modest structural damage and invariably mean painting. **(b)** Severe damage to a Nicholson 35. (Note how the support has sunk in.) I declared the yacht beyond repair, but she was repaired, and very well too, by scarfing in a large, newly moulded section of the hull. But the insurers barely ended on the right side, especially as the only firm capable of doing so were a thousand miles away and overseas. It shows what can be done, although only by very skilled specialists. Whether economic is another matter.

eg a ballast keel, should major repair be attempted from outside.

Survey

The first essential is to establish the full extent of the damage. For this it is far better to employ your own surveyor, someone who really understands fibreglass and can look for the fainter signs of that hidden damage. The insurance surveyor's duty is to minimise the cost to his principals and many do not look beyond what is obvious and undeniable. Moreover outside a yachting area even a Society appointed surveyor is more likely to be a steel ship man than a fibreglass specialist.

An important part of repair is reinforcing areas that are still intact but have been weakened or are suspected of having been. Do not accept any assessment of damage that does not include inspection of the inside, despite extra expense and difficulty cutting away an inner moulding. In particular never accept that damage is limited to the obvious holes. If not satisfied get a second opinion.

Abrasion

Major damage is generally complex. When grounding on a reef or grinding against a wall there is bound to be movement and pounding. Fibreglass is vulnerable to abrasion and quite quickly ground away or pulverised. Consequently most major damage includes severe abrasion over a wide area, much of it gouging deep, sometimes right through even on the thickness of the keel.

Deep abrasion should be built up by moulding. Small or shallow areas can be faired with resin putty. Painting is inevitable: a significant loss of value on a newish boat.

Restoring shape

Major damage may cause distortion. This must be checked and corrected before repair starts. Also if bulkheads or stiffeners need cutting away for access, the hull must be braced first to maintain the shape. Temporary repairs are often done hurriedly and lock in distortion.

One problem is knowing what shape the hull was. A 45 ft ocean racer had distorted after keel damage had broken all the floors. The designer supplied the lines but despite pushing and pulling that bottom could not be forced back into the shape it was supposed to be. Then someone thought of checking against an undamaged sister ship. Her lines were even further out!

Few fibreglass boats are exactly the shape the designer intended. Even from the same mould there will be subtle differences. It is better to fair by eye or a batten.

As much of the original moulding should be left as possible. Although shattered and lacking strength it will still form much of the backing and the important shape. That is the hardest thing to recreate.

However, the hull is often battered away leaving a substantial hole as well as splits. Backing is relatively easy on flattish or gently curved surfaces. Cardboard, plywood, sheet metal, plastics and similar materials can be taped on or screwed temporarily. Compound curves are difficult. Sometimes the shape can be reformed with battens and plaster or crudely moulded fibreglass. Small complicated parts like a coaming or toe rail can be built up solid and ground to shape.

Scarfing

Extensive damage, where a large part of the shape has been lost, must usually be considered beyond repair. However, miracles have been done (Photo 41.1).

It is more feasible when the original mould is available in which to mould a new section, but this is likely only on a newish boat. Even when the builders are still in business, old moulds get dumped carelessly outside and are often distorted or damaged by then. Sometimes a mould can be taken off a sister ship although the owner may need his arm twisted pretty hard to allow his precious boat to be used and there is risk of some damage.

Arranging the join in exactly the right place on both parts is a tricky job. Old and new must be well and accurately chamfered. Scarfing without obvious discontinuity of line in the smooth, glossy surface requires craftsmanship of the highest order. A great deal easier in theory than practice.

I have seen a few cases where this has been done expertly, and others where it was plainly obvious. One yacht I declared beyond repair

Photo 41.2 Glass tape can be used for many repairs. Here it has been used to bind my broken oar.

and was proved wrong, although the insurers barely ended on the right side. On another if I had not been told I would have been deceived. I am not deceived easily, and know only one company in the world which might do so.

Sandwich mouldings

Material suppliers gloss over the difficulties of repairing sandwich or cored hulls. They are far more difficult than single skin. The core will delaminate or shear over the whole area of bending. Gap filling, if any, will break away. It is seldom realised this will extend well beyond obvious damage. One skin must be cut away over the whole of this wide area to rebond or replace the core. Even discovering the extent is difficult and doubtful.

Most damage is in wet conditions. A major problem is the inevitable water in the core. In theory, the material suppliers' theory, water cannot migrate through the core. They assume the moulding is made perfectly and there are no waterways. Even if so perfect there were none before, there certainly will be after a good bump, even when there are no external signs.

This book is concerned largely with how boats were made in earlier years. Nearly all older sandwich mouldings were like a chess-board with gaps between every square. Water can filter from one end of the boat to the other.

How to detect this water, beyond the range of average moisture meters, let alone get it out

and dry the core, must be left to the repairer's ingenuity. At best it will prolong repair. Many repairers will not bother or even realise it is there, still less appreciate the serious implications (Chapter 19).

Be cautious about buying a sandwich or cored hull that has been damaged, especially an older one or with damage underwater.

Finish

To get a fair surface needs considerable skill and much tedious work. Most repairs are given away by unevenness on the glossy painted surface.

Conditions

Major repair is tantamount to original moulding and demands the same controlled conditions of temperature and humidity maintained day and night. This is structural work on which the integrity and safety of the boat depend.

Work done in the open or under unsuitable conditions, even by repairers who claim to be professionals, should be regarded as temporary repair. While a moulding shop may be impracticable, not least because moulders are unlikely to have equipment to handle a boat now fitted with a heavy keel and engines or even a door high enough, it should at least be indoors. A tented enclosure within the building may be sufficient. Inside the boat proper conditions are easily achieved with heaters, another good reason for working from inside.

Without proper conditions major repair cannot be as strong as the original and that means the boat will not be safe. Major repair is not a job for a boatyard who think they will have a go, and work in the open under a sheet of draughty, leaking polythene exposed to wet winter winds or tropical showers and high humidity. If conditions are not suitable they must be made suitable or the job not attempted on a permanent basis.

The owner may know nothing about repairing fibreglass. But he can see the conditions under which the work will be done. Do not be misled by assurances. Insist on proper conditions. It is your life and your crew's at stake.

Every crack tells a story

Cracks in the gel coat are very common. In themselves they are not serious but they are very important signs of more serious damage. Often the *only* signs.

Do not ignore cracks. Never believe an expert however well qualified who says they are unimportant, or 'Every fibreglass boat has them'. That means he has never learned to read them. What caused the cracks? What is the story they tell?

How serious?

Because gel coat has greater flexibility than moulding resins, cracks do not appear until at least 50% failure level in the moulding (Chapter 5). Cracks are not the first indication, as widely assumed, but show *structural failure has already reached an advanced stage*. With the more flexible gel coats now recommended cracks may not appear until failure is imminent.

A few earlier gel coats, although higher quality and longer lasting than modern ones, lacked resilience and cracked sooner. It was a time when development was proceeding faster than experience, and no one really knew what compromise of properties was needed.

Cracks always extend the full depth of the gel coat but cannot go further because they are stopped by fibres beneath. However, as cracks do not appear until the moulding beneath is already damaged there will be shattered resin and capillary paths beyond. Cracks are an entry for water which will penetrate deeper via these paths.

Sealing may keep water out but does nothing to repair the damage they indicate.

Crack or scratch?

A nervous person, reading about the meaning of cracks, will see every mark, scratch or red herring as a sign of imminent disaster. So look calmly and carefully to see if it really is a crack. The difference is easy to see with a magnifier. The pattern, too, is a clue (Fig 42.1).

It is very easy to be confused. One owner worried because there seemed to be a crack from top to bottom amidships. It really did look as if the boat was breaking in half. But it was only a scratch.

What do cracks tell?

A lot of information can be gathered from the pattern (Fig 42.2). They are always associated with damage of some kind, seldom limited to the gel coat and very often at a distance from the cause.

The commonest are star cracks caused by external impact. Generally there will be a shattered centre because most impact has projections. If no definite centre it may indicate impact from inside. Boats have been holed by badly stowed anchors.

Some second class moulders in earlier days hit the inside of mouldings with a rubber

Crack or scratch?

Cracks	Scratches
Very narrow	Comparatively wide and variable
Full depth of gel coat	Shallow
Bottom cannot be seen	Bottom rough
Edges sharp	Edges ragged
Branch and have crow feet	Never branch or have crow feet
Do not crisscross	Multiple scratches crisscross
May run in parallel lines	Lines seldom parallel
Star or crazing patterns	Never form stars or crazing
Seldom single	May be isolated
Can emanate from a feature	Seldom associated with a feature

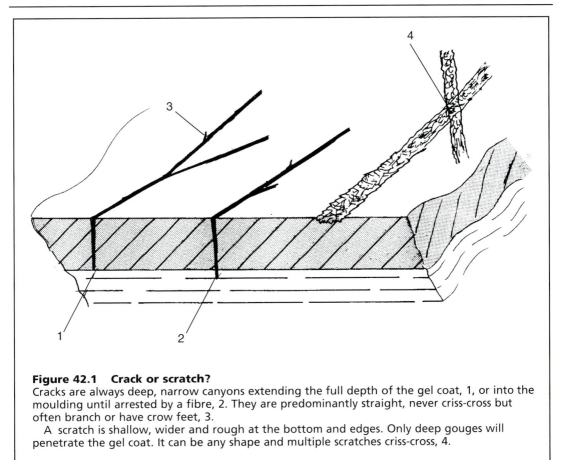

Figure 42.1   Crack or scratch?
Cracks are always deep, narrow canyons extending the full depth of the gel coat, 1, or into the moulding until arrested by a fibre, 2. They are predominantly straight, never criss-cross but often branch or have crow feet, 3.
   A scratch is shallow, wider and rough at the bottom and edges. Only deep gouges will penetrate the gel coat. It can be any shape and multiple scratches criss-cross, 4.

hammer to initiate release, a bad practice which left star cracks in the gel coat. Nowadays it probably indicates the moulding stuck. Look out for other trouble.

Inexperienced surveyors hit boats with a hammer. This can leave fine star cracks which do not become visible until months later. I have seen hulls with close spaced stars all over, the marks of a brutal surveyor who did not understand fibreglass.

Stars emanating from a fastening show it was overtightened. On a sandwich deck it means there was no insert, or it was in the wrong place.

Parallel lines are common along hardspots like bulkheads or deck edge and indicate damage there from bending. Generally there is obvious damage too and the cracks confirm hidden damage goes further. If the impact or pressure was well padded there may be no obvious damage or marks at all (Fig 17.8). Cracks can be a clue to unsuspected or incom-

plete repair, especially by repairers who did not know, or bother about hidden damage. As many still do not.

Often they are curved like tramlines roughly enclosing an area. On flat topsides forward these indicate panting or oil canning; amidships more likely crushing, commonly between fenders with no obvious damage.

Cracks along angles like a cabin top are usually stress relief and show the mouldings were forced to fit. Near a highly stressed fitting they suggest the boat needs strengthening. I have found them on the topsides below a genoa turning block, and around rudder attachments.

Forward or aft of a fin keel cracks are a sure sign the keel has hit something and kicked back. Look for serious damage inside.

A pattern like the lines of force of a magnet shows how bending was constrained by a hardspot (Chapter 17).

General crazing, not unusual on very early

Testing

At first surveyors, even the most prestigious, went round tapping with no more than a penny, and looking as knowledgeable as a medieval physician. Survey methods have not greatly improved since, and are still pretty medieval. The art of testing fibreglass boats in a practical, economic manner has lagged far behind their development. Certainly more sophisticated testing methods have been developed, but are expensive and more suitable for aerospace budgets at the taxpayers' expense than surveying boats at the owner's.

Interpretation generally depends on the surveyor's experience. In any doubt get a second opinion, particularly when incurring a lot of expense and *before* irreversible damage has been done.

Surveyors are by no means infallible. The more self-confident the less infallible. Despite impressive qualifications, many know much more about steel ships than fibreglass. Very few have qualifications or training in plastics or organic chemistry which is more relevant.

Tapping

This is still the standard method. Good fibreglass is resonant. Bad sounds dull. Voids sound hollow. Or so most people believe. But that is much too simple. Fibreglass boats make many different sounds. Red herrings swim in shoals.

Sounds are difficult to describe. A lot of

experience is needed to distinguish good from bad, almost a piano tuner's ear. It is very easy to be misled. Note how a lot of the significant sounds listed in the box overleaf also have normal explanations, and what seems sound may not be.

Do not jump to conclusions. Cross check suspicions by other means. In particular, investigate behind.

Everyone has their own choice of tapper, whether a coin from their pocket or a special tool. The early favourite, the old Britannia penny, was a substantial coin.

Some surveyors use a hammer. Heaven help the poor gel coat. Banging with a hard hammer will cause cracks and as these will not show until later may be mistaken then for crazing or a defective gel coat. Some advocate a softer, phenolic hammer on the topsides and a hard one on the bottom. Yet even a phenolic hammer is too hard, and it is muddled thinking to assume the bottom matters less.

Whatever is used must be used gently. One can sound as effectively with a gentle tap as a hard one. My own tapper, also used for rubbing along angles to check for cavities, is a short brass rod, rounded at one end and blunt pointed at the other. This will pinpoint faults more precisely than the wide face of a hammer. The 'wig-wag', described below, is less precise but gives a rapid rat-a-tat, and reaches further.

Tapping will test one side only of a sandwich or cored moulding. The core effectively insulates the other face. Lack of access usually means it is impossible to test the inner face. There is no way to test a sandwich deck covered with non-slip tread or teak.

Rubbing

Tapping is hit-or-miss. Mainly miss. Moreover it is difficult to keep track of where, on the

---

Misleading sounds

Hollow stiffeners	Bulkhead padding
Glass angles	Sandwich cores
Ballast keel	Fairing compounds
Fibreglass lining	Soft lining
Embedded wood	Embedded pipes or wires
Tanks	Locker contents

large expanse of boat, has been tested. Tapping is slow, tedious, and requires prolonged concentration.

Many years ago I found rubbing covers a wider area more thoroughly and much faster. It is a better way to detect small flaws which can then be pinpointed by tapping. For this I devised the 'wig-wag', a rounded knob on a length of springy wire. The rough surface of antifouling and non-slip on a deck makes a good sounding board, but with experience it can be used on smooth topsides too.

Interference

A major problem with all audible testing is the need for quiet. Machinery, power tools and nearby workers can make testing impossible. Sometimes one must wait until dinner hour or after work. My worst case was a few miles from an American air force base. Nearly as bad was in the depths of the country, at a farmyard, and the boat was next to the pigsty!

Ultrasonic testing

This is the best of the sophisticated methods but has serious limitations. To appreciate these one needs a very good knowledge of both the nature of fibreglass and the transmission of sound. Fibreglass is not a homogeneous material like steel for which these instruments are intended. Glass and resin have different transmission characteristics so every fibre will return an echo (the principle is the same as a depth sounder). So will each of the millions of tiny voids in even the best mouldings. Specular reflection is very high and attenuation massive compared with steel. However, the thickness is not great and by understanding the limitations it can work, just as many depth sounders fire through a fibreglass hull.

Sound transmission through air is poor (despite what one might think when within a mile of a disco!). So flaws, which in effect are air pockets, and major discontinuities, can be detected.

The instrument should have an analogue display, not digital, so the whole scan can be seen and interpreted. There may be multiple flaws at different depths. Also the amount of specular reflection and attenuation shows the quality of moulding. Cheaper instruments give a digital read-out only. This shows the thickness, or depth of the first flaw, but not deeper flaws or quality.

Significant Sounds

Sound	Meaning	Alternative meaning
Good or normal		
Resonant, medium pitch	Sound moulding with nothing behind	Moulding with high void content, spotty bond, thin, deep flaws, putty filling, undercure – and most moulding faults!
Resonant, higher pitch	Bulkheads, stiffeners, glassed on accommodation engine bearers, increased thickness etc	Something in contact
Solid, higher pitch	Encapsulated ballast	
Metallic	Metal tank inside	Bilge water
Rattling	Locker contents (Don't hit so hard!)	Can in a locker
Bad		
Dull	Bad moulding, unset resin, soggy fibreglass	Stiffener core, sandwich, soft lining, locker contents
Hollow, small area	Voids, blisters, bad bonding, broken away glass angles	Stiffener core, inserts, spaced bulkhead roots, embedded cable duct
Hollow, large area	Delamination, breakaway of encapsulated ballast	Some sandwich cores, embedded wood or foam, built-in tank, empty locker, moulded lining

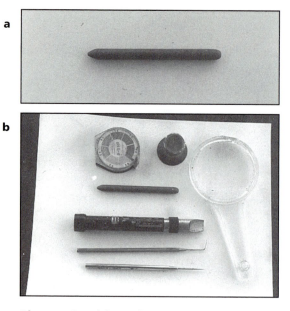

Photos 43.1 (a) My favourite tapper, a simple brass bar, 4 in, 100 mm long, rounded at one end for search, pointed at the other for pin-pointing.
(b) Surveyor's tool kit. Litmus paper for testing blisters, watchmaker's eye glass (essential for close examination), ordinary magnifier, tapper, pocket microscope, dental probes. Note: no brutal hammer.
Not shown, 'wig-wag', extension handles, moisture meter, thickness tester and penetrant staining kit.

Interpretation is the critical factor. What do the 'blips' and 'grass' on the display really mean in terms of fibreglass? I had the advantage that before the days of fibreglass I worked on sonar development.

Other tests

An old test was shining a light through the moulding, bright patches being assumed thin. As the main opacity is the gel coat, all it shows is an uneven gel coat, like paint on a window. It does not mean a thin moulding, although still advocated in some misguided circles. However, with a gel coat removed it does help to reveal deep dry areas and white spots.

For thickness, the easiest parameter to measure, see Chapter 32.

The standard test for cure is Barcol hardness. But gel coats very greatly in hardness so as an arbitrary test it is ambiguous. It is more use as a comparative test on production always using a known gel coat. In any case only the gel coat surface can be tested. Barcol hardness tells absolutely nothing about the far more important cure of the structural moulding beneath.

A simpler hardness test is rubbing with pencils of increasing hardness until one scratches. This is quite effective on a personal basis using roughly the same pressure each time.

Fibreglass 'talks' under stress, as fibres debond and break. This is supersonic and requires special listening equipment: more use in a quiet laboratory than noisily bashing about at sea. Nevertheless if you do hear the boat 'talking', and are not drunk or suffering the hallucinations common when sailing, it could be a warning of impending catastrophe.

Unlike cracks in metal, flaws in fibreglass are laminar and do not show well when X-rayed.

There is a chemical test for weathering but the chemicals are nasty to handle. As weathering etches the gel coat a simple test is the red stain used for crack detection. Good gel coat sheds stain, weathered absorbs it like a sponge which can be embarrassing.

Testing for material strength and glass content is destructive. On a boat cutting out large enough samples for testing is usually done only to prove defective manufacture in court and nobody wants what is left of the boat.

Do not despise crude methods. Like pressing the hull to see how flexible. Or that boat show favourite, a hefty thump.

Moisture meters

Moisture meters are now standard instruments for surveyors (belatedly, I have been using them since 1958), and often bought by owners too. Few instruments can give such misleading information. They have been described as the most dangerous instruments to use on a fibreglass boat! In ignorant hands this is certainly true and emphasises that it is absolutely essential to know their limitations. Even most professionals do not. The construction, material, age and use of the boat are relevant yet generally unknown. Consequently the *interpretation of the reading*, not the value, is what matters, and needs an intimate knowledge of both

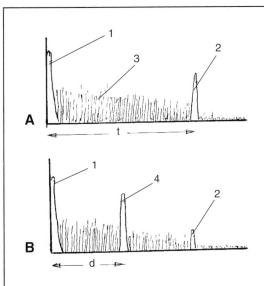

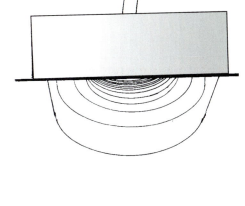

Figure 43.1
Typical display on an ultrasonic tester with a time base display. (Sometimes called A scan. Familiar to those who remember early radar.)
A Sound moulding. 1, is the transmitted pulse. The blip, 2, is the echo from the back face, therefore t, is thickness. 3 is specular reflection or 'grass' from fibres and normal small voids, an indication of moulding quality.
B Unsound moulding. An intermediate blip, 4, indicates a flaw at depth d. Note how it masks signals beyond. A clue if too close to the surface to show separately, eg gel coat.

Figure 43.2
Electronic moisture meters work on a field effect. The closeness of the lines are an indication of sensitivity and show how this decreases quickly with depth.

fibreglass and the operating principles of the instrument. They can give valuable information. But you must know what you are doing.

The surface resistance kind with probes, used on timber, is useless. Unlike wood, polyester resin, even when damp, is still a good insulator. That is what it was originally developed for; electrical insulation, not boatbuilding! Water collects principally in the innumerable voids. Being discrete these do not form a continuous conductive path. Therefore the meter must be an electronic kind, usually working on capacitance, able to detect and average sub-surface moisture (Fig 43.2).

A very common mistake is assuming a moisture meter can detect moisture at any depth. Sensitivity falls off quickly with depth, as is to be expected with a field effect. Fig 43.3 shows a typical calibration curve based on several popular meters, including the early model Sovereign and Nomex. Note how quickly sensitivity and hence accuracy decrease with depth. Beyond about 1/4 in, 6 mm, they hardly detect anything.

The later model Sovereign meter is the best I have found. It has a more useful pattern, being accurate to approx 5/32 in, 4 mm, but thereafter sensitivity falls rapidly, and again 1/4 in, 6 mm, is the effective limit.

These figures have been disputed, mainly by those who do not know because they have never bothered to check. But they are based on my own repeated calibration tests over a wet rag which, being wetter than any fibreglass moulding, are conservative. Before use the effective working range of *your* meter must be discovered by practical test, not assumed. Otherwise readings will be misleading. (Credit cards are about 1 mm and make convenient

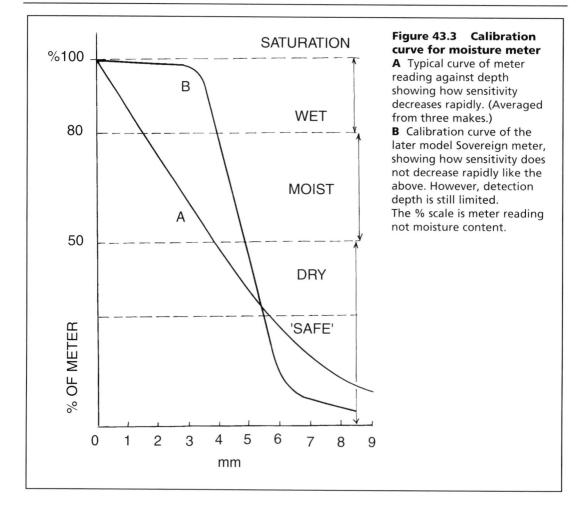

Figure 43.3   Calibration curve for moisture meter
A Typical curve of meter reading against depth showing how sensitivity decreases rapidly. (Averaged from three makes.)
B Calibration curve of the later model Sovereign meter, showing how sensitivity does not decrease rapidly like the above. However, detection depth is still limited.
The % scale is meter reading not moisture content.

spacers over a wet rag. Use them each side, not in the line of fire because of the magnetic strip.)

A very simple test is to hold the detector over your hand and note how quickly the reading decreases as it is moved away. You have a higher moisture content than any fibreglass!

In practical terms only the very smallest cruiser hulls would be ¼ in, 6 mm, thick on the bottom. Most would be more than ³⁄₈ in, 10 mm, and double that in the keel area. The outer skin of most sandwich mouldings would be thick enough to put the core and its waterways beyond detection.

It is important to realise that a 'dry' reading does *not* mean 'safe' beyond effective detection range.

Meter scales are not calibrated for fibreglass, impossible anyway because of its very

variable nature. A moulding with few but saturated voids, ie a 'wet' hull, will give a drier, 'safer', reading than one with more numerous but only part filled voids even though the latter is in better condition. The value of a moisture meter is not in arbitrary measurement but relative readings as a hull dries.

Moisture meters must be used on a dry surface which may sound a contradiction. They are very sensitive to a thin film of surface moisture or condensation, often too slight to notice, and also to high humidity. Some days they cannot be used. When newly out of the water, antifouling and weed take days to dry. Condensation on the surface will also mask the true reading beneath. Recalibration will give false readings unless done against a test piece or something known to be dry.

Forced drying will create a moisture gradient. The surface may read dry, yet the fibre-

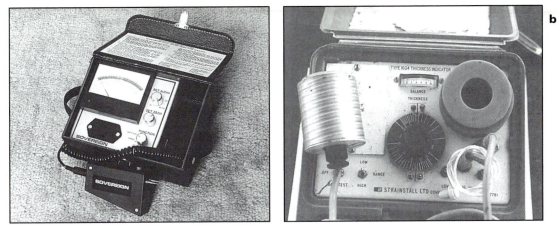

a

b

Photos 43.2 (a) Mark II Sovereign moisture meter. A considerable improvement over the earlier model (Sovereign Chemicals Ltd).
(b) du Plessis thickness tester. The detection head is on the left. Round doughnuts are calibration discs. Adjust for minimum meter reading and read thickness off the dial.

glass out of range still have high moisture.

Depending on the principle of operation, other materials especially metal, some fillers and carbon fibre can give spurious readings. So can hydrocarbons, even as a thin film. In one case a highly qualified New York surveyor, flown in at great expense, misinterpreted the effect of a metallic filler and caused the owner massive and quite unnecessary expense. You cannot dry out what is not wet! However, sensitivity to metals and most other materials is less than to water. Suspect claims to detect internal wiring. It could mean water has penetrated.

One might expect to detect bilge water, but I have always found it beyond the meter range. To prove this, see how close you can detect a bucket of water, and bilges are much thicker. If bilge water is detected it is more likely because it has permeated through the moulding. Or a nastier reason, a clue perhaps to generally bad moulding.

Close fitting metal tanks would be beyond detection range. But by preventing moisture which permeates through from outside from evaporating inside as it normally would, may give an apparent reading which is actually a high moisture level in the fibreglass.

If a hull reads high scrape away antifouling to test the hull itself. The topsides well above

Causes of spurious readings	
Metallic filler	High metallic content
Embedded metal	antifouling
Metal ballast	Internal tanks
Condensation	High humidity
Bilge water	Pipes and wires
Carbon fibre	Built-in tanks
	Hydrocarbons

the splash zone will give a base reference, and should normally be near zero. No amount of drying will get the bottom below the natural topsides level. If a high reading does not decrease on drying suspect some other possibility. Moisture meters can lie or, more likely, you are not interpreting the readings correctly.

Finally if you find a high reading be sure the boat really is fibreglass and not wood or steel. Yes it sounds ridiculous but even experts make mistakes!

References

How much use are moisture meters? Hugo du Plessis, *Practical Boat Owner*, 1990.

Moisture Meters. Trials on test pieces. Southampton Institute of Higher Education, October 1992.

Plastics & Rubber Weekly, 1975.

Technical terms & equivalents

Units of measurement

Imperial		*Metric*	
Length			
'thou' 'mil' }	thousandth of inch	µm or µ	micron
			(one thousandth of a millimetre)
in	inch	mm	millimetre
ft	foot	cm	centimetre
yd	yard	m	metre
Area			
in^2	square inch	mm^2	square millimetre
ft^2	square foot	cm^2	square centimetre
yd^2	square yard	m^2	square metre
Volume			
fl oz	fluid ounce	cc	cubic centimetre
Imp gall	Imperial gallon	ml	millilitre
US gall	US gallon	l	litre
Weight			
oz	ounce	g	gram
lb	pound	kg	kilogram
Weight per unit area			
oz/ft^2	ounces per sq ft	g/m^2	grams/sq metre
oz/yd^2	ounces per sq yard		
Force			
lbf	pound force	N	Newton
Pressure or stress			
lbs/in^2	pounds/sq inch (psi)	N/m^2	Newtons/sq metre
		Pa	Pascal

Technical abbreviations expressed in either units

E	Elasticity or Young's Modulus (Material stiffness)		
	lbs/in^2	kN/M^2	
I	Moment of inertia (Stiffness of shape)		
	in^4	mm^4	

UTS   Ultimate tensile strength = breaking point
           lbs/in^2 kN/m^2

Dimensionless terms

SG   Specific gravity (density relative to water)
g_c Glass content
R/g   Resin/glass ratio

Equivalents

Imperial			*Metric*	

Length

1 'thou'	= 25.4 microns		1 micron	= 0.04 'thou'
1 in	= 25.4 mm		1 mm	= 0.039 in
1 ft	= 0.304 m		1 m	= 39.37 in
1 yd	= 0.91 m			= 3.28 ft
				= 1.09 yd

Area

1 in^2	= 645 mm^2		1 mm^2	= 0.0015 in^2
1 ft^2	= 0.093 m^2		1 m^2	= 10.8 ft^2
1 yd^2	= 0.84 m^2			= 1.2 yd^2

Volume

1 cu in	= 16.4 cc		1 cc/1 ml	= 0.06 cu.in
1 Imp gall	= 4.54 litres		1 litre	= 0.22 Imp gall
1 US gall	= 3.78 litres		1 litre	= 0.26 US gall

Weight

1 oz	= 28.35 g		1 g	= 0.035 oz
1 lb	= 0.45 kg		1 kg	= 2.2 lb
1 ton	= 1016 kg		1000 kg	= 2204 lbs
1 ton	= 1.02 tonnes		1 tonne	= 0.98 tons

Weight/unit area

1 oz/ft^2	= 305 g/m^2		100 g/m^2	= 3.2 oz/ft^2
1 oz/yd^2	= 34 g/m^2			= 0.35 oz/yd^2

Force

1 lbf	= 0.14 N		1 N	= 7.23 lbf

Pressure and stress

1 lb/in^2	= 6.89 kN/m^2		1 kN/m^2	= 0.15 lbs/in^2
	= 6.89 kPa		1 kPa	= 0.15 lb/in^2

Weight of glass reinforcement

1 oz/ft^2	= 9 oz/yd^2	= approx 300 g/m^2		

Multiples

μ	= 10^{-6}		micro-	one millionth
m	= 10^{-3}		milli-	one thousandth
k	= 10^3		killo-	one thousand
M	= 10^6		Mega-	one million

Weight/volume of resins

Polyester	1 Imp gallon	= 12.5 lbs	= 5.7 kg
	1 US gallon	= 9.2 lbs	= 4.2 kg
	1 litre	= 2.75 lbs	= 1.25 kg
Vinyl ester	1 Imp gallon	= 11.4 lbs	= 5.2 kg
	1 US gallon	= 8.6 lbs	= 3.9 kg
	1 litre	= 2.5 lbs	= 1.14 kg
MEKP	1 Imp gallon	= 9.0 lbs	= 4.1 kg
	1 US gallon	= 6.6 lbs	= 3.0 kg
	1 litre	= 2.0 lbs	= 0.9 kg
Epoxy	1 Imp gallon	= 12.1 lbs	= 5.5 kg
	1 US gallon	= 9.1 lbs	= 4.1 kg
	1 litre	= 2.7 lbs	= 1.2 kg
Hardener (average)	1 Imp gallon	= 10.8 lbs	= 4.9 kg
	1 US gallon	= 8.1 lbs	= 3.7 kg
	1 litre	= 2.4 lbs	= 1.1 kg

Gel coat coverage

Wet thickness		Coverage	
0.010 in	0.25 mm	0.9 oz/ft^2	0.27 kg/m^2
0.012	0.30	1.1	0.33
0.014	0.35	1.28	0.37
0.016	0.41	1.46	0.44
0.018	0.46	1.55	0.49
0.020	0.51	1.82	0.56
0.022	0.56	2.0	0.60
0.024	0.61	2.2	0.66
0.026	0.66	2.4	0.72

Cured thickness is about 0.7 wet thickness
(By courtesy of RP Associates)

Index

'A' glass 18
abrasion 35, 36, 39, 237, 264, 268
abrasive cleaners 249, 259
abrasive polish 167, 249, 251, 264
abrasion resistance 13, 22, 145, 147, 155, 159
accelerator 11, 16, 30, 203
access Ch23, 65, 67, 68, 73, 84, 86, 100–8, 112, 121, 124, 220, 247, 263, 268
acetone 25, 26, 30, 31, 67, 146, 164, 190
accommodation 14, 81, 84, 88, 114–21, 145, 148, 157, 158, 223, 247
age 35–9, 49–53
air inhibition 13, 173
Airex 131
allergies 30, 31
amateur building 12, 29, 32, 84, 145, 203, 217, 223
amine hardener (see hardeners)
amine booster 182, 203, 262
anchoring 105, 244, 256
antifouling 34, 191, 193, 196–202, 258, 276–80
antimony 32, 58

ballast 149, 150
balsa 129, 133, 148
Barcol hardness tester 276
barnacles 183, 193
barrier coat 160
barrier cream 25, 31, 192
bathtub flange 84, 141, 237, 241
beading 84, 87, 154, 155
bends, bending 39, 68, 75, 110–6, 127
benzoyl peroxide 15
bigheads 99, 100, 102
bilges 82, 87, 88, 104, 206, 231, 246
bilge keels 77, 147, 237, 242
bilge water 173, 246, 279
binder 16, 18, 172, 192, 209, 228, 263
biphenol polyester 160
blind stars 273, 274
blistering Ch26, 8, 13, 18, 32, 42, 46, 54, 59, 128, 141, 163, 203–11, 226, 251, 258, 259
blister juice Ch26, 32, 33, 43, 45, 138, 162, 173, 178, 190, 193, 211
'boat pox' Ch26, 8
bolting 95–106, 124, 139, 149, 262
bond burn 40, 67
bond – gel coat Ch26, 160, 163, 165
resin/glass 14, 15, 17, 35–54, 154, 179
bonding 15, 63–78, 84, 94, 97, 100, 109, 112, 119, 121–56, 203, 204, 212, 216, 242, 263

buckling 82, 96
bulkheads Ch14, 39, 45, 78, 81, 91, 92, 114–19, 136, 139
buoyancy 144
burnishing 249, 251, 257, 264
butt strap 63, 65, 73, 206, 213, 215

capillary paths 138, 163, 173, 179, 183, 189, 190, 199
capital cost 2, 6, 29, 145, 228
carbon fibre 3, 21, 22, 59, 92, 279
carcinogens 25, 28, 30, 31
catalyst 4, 15, 16, 26–31, 57, 191, 192, 202, 208, 231, 263
cement 150
chalk 14, 23
change of thickness 65, 68
charter 14, 55, 241–3, 247
chemistry 10, 54
chemical bond 5, 15, 63, 65, 67, 165
chips 24, 99, 264
cleaning Ch36, 25, 30, 67, 167, 192, 212, 237
clinker 77, 151, 152
clogging 24, 139, 153, 196
coaming 77, 146, 231
cobalt napthanate 11, 147
cold conditions 35, 40, 42, 54, 102, 111, 112, 129, 138, 144, 150, 162, 167, 168, 180, 194, 203, 211, 258, 262, 272
collision 51, 97, 255
collision bulkhead 97
colour 13, 16, 42, 53, 58, 73, 111, 145, 159, 160–8, 180, 193, 203, 212, 258, 262, 272
colour matching 73, 237, 264
composite fabrics 21, 35, 92
compression 48, 50, 108, 109
condensation 129, 161–79, 192, 200–12, 279
conditions for moulding Ch28, 50, 63, 111, 112, 139, 152, 162, 163, 171, 182, 189, 190, 194–9, 210–14, 257–62, 270
conductivity 15, 22, 23, 40, 53, 54, 59
contamination 40, 67, 160–5, 173, 192, 197, 212
contraction 14, 15, 39, 40, 54, 67, 123, 168, 273
copper 17
copperclad 162
cores Ch19, 45, 78, 85, 88, 102, 125
cored moulding (see sandwich)
corrugation 77, 82, 96
cosmetic problems Ch24, Ch40, 160–7, 203, 210, 229, 264–7

cost 17–22, 51, 57, 58, 77, 78, 92, 109–17, 121, 125, 131, 136, 139, 151–4, 160–3, 188–201, 213, 218, 230, 234, 237, 252, 257
countersinking 99, 105
coupling agent 17, 35, 39, 172, 175, 192, 203, 212
coupons 231
covers 167, 168, 198, 248, 256
cracks Ch42, 13, 24, 35–48, 113–19, 154, 159–67, 256, 267, 275
crazing 13, 42, 54, 59, 159–65
creep 22, 35, 40, 248
crushing 71, 102, 106, 139, 155
cure 12–17, 28, 32, 39, 40, 54, 73, 91, 111, 112, 132, 135, 152–71, 183, 203, 204, 212, 227, 233, 262, 277
cut outs 81–7, 117, 141, 220, 222, 232
cyclohexanane peroxide (CHP) 15

damage 15, 16, 25, 35–62, 73, 81, 84, 88, 97–103, 113, 116, 122–38, 144, 147, 150, 155–9, 197–200, 235, 244–8
damp 12, 17, 138, 162, 202, 210, 212, 258, 262, 278
decay 35, 42–46, 99, 112, 138, 144, 207
decks 42, 53, 54, 74, 88, 91, 107, 117, 125, 133–58, 168, 178, 220, 243, 249
deckhead lining Ch18, Ch19, 59, 84, 103, 104, 112, 158
decorative dents 77
delamination Ch19, 24, 25, 35, 39, 40, 53, 54, 59, 69, 81, 98, 136, 165, 176, 190, 198, 200, 207, 216, 270, 272
dermatitis 30
design Ch35, 73, 77, 93, 96, 104–19, 127, 157, 180, 188, 211, 218, 225, 254
diagnosis 171, 194
difficult moulding Ch11, Ch19, Ch22, 68, 189, 197, 204–13, 247, 269
disposal 10, 32, 33
distortion 14, 15, 40, 71, 73, 88, 92, 101–3, 116–24, 144, 146
Di-Vinyl 131
double gel coat 161
drying Ch27, 169, 180, 184, 190, 193, 248, 270, 279, 280
dry moulding 174, 176, 188, 191, 192, 207–12, 219, 220, 277
ductility 22, 38, 40, 70
du Plessis thickness tester 221, 222
durability 22, 128–32, 148, 161, 242
dust 26, 31–3, 60, 67, 165, 166, 171, 193, 197, 204, 210, 212
dyneema fibre 3, 22

'E' glass 3, 18
E – Young's modulus 3, 50, 150
early boats 2, 10, 16, 18, 50, 104, 105, 125, 135, 136, 139, 146, 151, 160, 164, 166, 169, 170, 175, 195, 196, 207, 208, 213, 217, 218, 227–9, 234, 268, 270, 271
early conditions 12, 14, 16, 22, 23, 27, 30, 42, 53, 61, 104, 105, 151, 152, 162, 169, 172, 175, 180, 202–9, 212–15, 221, 233, 234, 240, 258, 271
edges 24, 43, 84, 96, 105, 110, 117, 122, 124, 136, 141, 144, 148, 154, 155, 220, 237, 244, 267, 272
eggcrate 81, 84, 88
elastomers 108, 111
electrolysis 22, 103, 162
elongation 3, 12, 23, 163
embedding 44, 45, 98–106, 146, 150
emulsion binder 18, 179, 182, 209, 211
engine 58, 157, 236, 247
engine bearers 84, 124, 139, 146
environmental resins 12, 14, 29, 40, 132, 173, 192, 227
Environmental Protection Agency (EPA) 28
erosion 18, 24, 35, 41–3, 172–6
exhaust pipes 60, 164
exotherm 15, 17, 149, 175, 182, 207
explosion Ch4, 30, 33, 58–60
eye protection 30, 31

fabrication cost 7, 22
factor of safety Ch8, 48, 108, 113, 253, 255
Factory Acts (see regulations)
failure Ch5, Ch6, 22, 48, 254, 271
failure to set 17, 263
fairing Ch27, 23, 73, 167
fastenings Ch15, 70, 71, 81, 104–14, 139, 158
fatigue Ch7, 22, 38, 40, 49, 51, 109, 139, 144, 255, 256
fibreglassium masticus 46, 250
fillets 88, 141
fillers 16, 23, 132, 193, 200, 201, 217, 264, 280
fin keel 88, 114, 116, 236, 272
finishing resin 13, 32, 44, 45, 138, 144, 153, 217, 267
fire Ch10, 30–3, 164, 252, 273
fire barrier 55, 58
fire extinguishers 60, 61
fire retardant resins (see self-extinguishing)
first aid Ch4, 27, 31
fishing boats 9, 139, 241
fit 14, 63, 71, 73, 198, 121, 132
flammability 53, 58
flash point 13, 17, 31, 57
flexibility 17, 48, 75, 92, 116, 123, 160, 223, 248, 251, 271
floors 88, 116
foam Ch19, 29, 30, 55, 58, 94, 103, 111, 124–31, 138
forcing to fit 24, 73, 88, 116–19, 272
fresh water 32, 45, 167, 178, 180, 188, 191, 193, 231
fuel tanks 58, 60
fumes Ch4, 24, 57, 58, 121

gauze 19, 154, 156, 163, 179, 209, 273
gel coat Ch24, Ch25, Ch26, Ch27, Ch35, Ch36, Ch42, 7, 8, 13, 16, 41–4, 54–7, 65, 73, 74, 101, 106, 138, 153, 207–17, 259, 264, 274, 276
gel coat defects (See cosmetic problems)
glass angles 63, 64, 94, 96, 119, 123, 223, 246, 267
glass content, 5, 48, 55, 57, 218–28
glass cloth 19, 40, 58, 60, 151–6, 172, 175, 220, 272
glass fibre 3, 18, 31, 43, 55, 68, 73, 92, 154, 172, 173, 218
glass mat 4, 17, 18, 38, 55, 64, 81, 88, 151–5, 164, 172, 205, 218–28
glass tape 19, 21, 78, 149, 216, 260, 264
glassing in Ch11, 121, 124, 158
gloss 8, 167, 248, 249, 257–9, 269–74
glueing 71, 73, 132, 147, 158
green stage 13, 14, 24, 39, 65, 73, 132, 216
gribble 45, 147
grinding 24, 32, 67, 190, 196, 197, 267
grit blasting 196
grounding 116, 117, 236, 242

halogens 58, 61
hand cleaner 26
hardener 17, 31, 53, 57, 152, 203, 262
hard spots Ch17, 39, 48, 75, 85, 94, 267, 271, 273
hazards 27
health Ch4
heat Ch9, 35, 42, 128, 196, 262, 273
heat distortion temperature, (HDT) 16, 53, 128, 179, 200
heat resistance temperature, (HRT) 16, 24, 35, 42, 53, 128–31
het acid resins 58, 60
hidden damage Ch5, Ch9, Ch39, Ch40, Ch41, Ch42, 40, 45, 53, 116, 128, 158, 163, 168, 178, 181
high tech mouldings 17, 21, 51, 116, 119, 125, 136, 160, 179, 201, 216–20
history 1, 169, 171, 192, 204, 209, 210, 218, 223, 228, 233
humidity Ch28, 15, 111, 165, 199, 203, 227, 258
hydrolysis Ch26, 36, 39, 48–50, 138, 172–9, 183, 188, 189, 196, 203, 212

Moment of Inertia Ch13, 126, 222
ice 42, 239
impact 22, 116, 119, 124–34, 270–2
inhibiter 12, 16, 207
inflammable materials Ch10, 58–60, 146, 250
inflammability 55, 58, 146
inserts 45, 78, 84, 88, 98–103, 114, 136, 139, 141
inside appearance 8, 55, 60, 68, 73, 141, 144, 207
inspection Ch34, 21, 100, 104, 124, 134, 158, 194, 198, 211, 247, 267
interlamina bond Ch26, 15–19, 188, 198, 212
internal damage (see hidden damage)
intumescant coatings 58

isophthalic polyester 13, 131, 160, 179, 188, 198, 209

jig 14, 88, 232

keel 45, 73, 88, 100, 103, 116, 139, 141, 200, 207, 214, 220, 236, 239, 242, 248, 269
Kevlar 3, 21, 22, 25, 93, 125, 131, 179, 234
king plank 104
kits 30
knitted fabrics 19, 207

laboratory test 15, 38, 48–58, 172, 210, 212, 220, 232
labour cost 7, 21, 219, 233, 234
laminations 4, 189
leaching 50, 51, 54, 58, 165, 167, 183, 198, 250
leaks 45, 107, 123, 124, 139, 144, 151–8, 207, 250, 263
limber holes 87, 88, 93, 246
lightning 22, 59
lockers 84, 121, 246
locked-in stress 14, 39, 42
LPG 58, 62, 158

maintenance Ch35, Ch36, Ch38, 8, 41, 45, 157, 166–8
management Ch34, 50, 105, 208
marinas 104
MARPOL 33
material cost 9, 117
measurement 15, 16, 28, 68, 222
Methylethylketone Peroxide, (MEKP) (see catalyst)
microballons 23, 88, 136
microscratches 249, 264
middle age 9, 10, 12, 34, 49, 51, 169, 170, 193, 209, 210, 257, 268
moisture meters 138, 189, 200, 277, 278
monocoque 75, 116, 119, 125
mould 5, 6, 23, 73, 88, 94, 121, 159–66, 173, 183, 202–7, 216, 257, 268, 273
  black 251
mouldless construction Ch31, 6, 125, 136, 166

needles 32, 152
neopentyl glycol-isophthalic 160
neoprene 106, 110
newspaper boat 217
'No Maintenance' 145, 168, 248
no smoking 29
non-destructive testing Ch43
non-slip surface 136, 154, 243, 249, 274, 275
notch effect 3, 18, 43, 117

oil Ch36, 57, 167, 200, 246, 250, 251
oil canning 116, 119, 272
oil spills 251, 259
oil stains 249, 250

older boats Ch24, Ch30, 1, 9, 10, 34, 39, 42, 46, 49, 50, 55, 58, 113, 123, 125, 132–8, 146, 151, 152, 160, 166–80, 190, 195–204, 215–19, 227, 233–6, 262, 270

opaque resins 16, 161, 207

openings 96, 97, 117, 121, 122, 141, 246

orange peel 257, 258

orientation 20, 21, 78

orthophthalic polyester Ch24, 13, 131, 160, 179, 188, 209

osmosis theoretical Ch26, 42, 170, 177, 178, 198, 199

'osmosis' (see blistering)

overlaps 68, 152, 219, 220, 264, 267

overstrain Ch5, Ch7, Ch37, 47, 49, 163, 255

paint Ch38, 41, 159–68, 183, 235, 237, 248, 249, 267, 269

paint stripper 190, 197, 249

pan moulding 85, 121, 145, 158, 263, 267

panting (see oil canning)

pattern 5, 6, 23, 123, 259, 274

penny washers 71, 98, 101, 102

permeability Ch26, 17, 39, 41, 42, 125, 136, 141, 144, 150, 152, 161, 162, 165, 199, 258, 279

phenol 17, 23, 95, 132, 146, 148, 153, 154, 204, 212

phenolic resin 17, 131

pinholes 19, 32, 152, 165, 204, 214, 264

plasticiser 15, 161, 192, 193

plywood 17, 75, 84, 94, 97, 114, 135, 145–8, 151, 204, 212

poisoning 17, 18, 23, 94, 149, 154

polish Ch36, 26, 41, 65, 166, 168, 248, 264

pollution 28–33, 45, 179, 212

polythene fibre, (Spectra) 22

polythene tent 12, 201, 205, 270

pop rivets 99, 103

porosity 32, 81, 88, 102, 104, 160, 182, 193, 203

postcure 15, 17, 32, 50–3, 60, 162, 163, 179, 201

pounding 116, 241, 268

powder bound mat 179

pre-accelerated resin 30, 203

prestressing 40, 73, 88, 117

prefabrication 88

pre-wetting 267

primer 258, 259

properties 34, 41, 49, 50, 109, 111, 128, 129, 167

protection 22, 43, 58, 60, 74, 99, 102, 138, 145, 159, 166, 168, 237, 248

'pushing-in-with-a-stick' 73, 102–4, 207

putties 14, 22, 23, 88, 94, 110, 111, 122, 132, 141, 167, 198, 239, 261–8

quality Ch34, 10, 12, 16, 34, 35, 38, 41, 45, 46, 49, 50, 54, 155, 162, 167, 171–9, 182, 188, 193, 199, 203, 205, 208, 213, 214, 219, 227, 249, 259, 270, 276

radiant heat 59

reactivity 206

regulations 13, 25, 28, 29, 32, 33, 52, 55–62, 197, 223, 250, 252, 263

red herrings 119, 136, 168, 171, 271, 275

red penetrant stain 167, 174, 277

rehydration 200

release 23, 173, 136, 163, 165, 207, 270, 271

release agent 23, 65, 166, 259

repairs Ch39, Ch40, Ch41, 12, 13, 17, 26, 28, 29, 38, 40, 51, 57, 59, 73, 81, 84, 97, 157–68, 179, 181, 183, 204, 235, 237, 242, 247, 249, 272

repair kit 261, 263

research 41, 49, 160, 162, 169, 171, 233

residual stress 14, 39, 40, 42, 272

resilience 42, 53, 127, 131, 139, 144, 165, 167, 270, 272

resin/glass ratio (see glass content, Gc)

resorcinol 32, 153

rovings 4, 19, 227

rollers, moulding 25

rollers, paint 258

rot 43, 45, 138, 148, 154, 171

rubbing band 77, 238, 241, 266

rudder 45, 88, 92, 102, 104, 116, 117, 144, 147, 149, 200, 242

rules Ch32, 2, 52, 57, 78, 194, 207, 214, 218, 222, 228, 236, 252, 263

rust 24, 45, 150, 183, 242

rust stains 24, 183, 251

'S' glass 3, 18, 22

safety precautions Ch4, Ch37, 57, 104, 124, 146, 156, 158, 197, 250, 263, 270

sail training ship regulations 55–60

sanding 24, 31, 32, 60, 153, 191, 201, 217, 249, 259

sandwich moulding Ch19, 24, 102

sawdust 17, 23, 33, 49, 67

scarfed join 73, 268

scrapping 34, 210, 231

scratches 24, 71, 116, 154, 168, 235–50, 259, 264, 270

scuppers 88

SCRIMP vacuum process 134, 175, 227

sealants Ch16, 102, 162

sea water Ch26, 178, 179, 191, 193, 231

self-extinguishing resin Ch10, 13, 22, 32

self-tapping screws 99, 103, 262

setting time 11, 71, 111, 123, 132, 134, 149, 152, 159, 161, 164, 165, 173, 193, 232, 261–3

shape 14, 24, 73, 75, 77, 88, 94, 119, 121, 144, 207, 211, 216, 218, 223, 255, 267, 268

sheathing Ch22, 19, 45, 217, 242

shroud plates 94, 99, 100, 101, 106, 108, 116, 117, 149

silane 39, 175, 178, 179, 182

silica 14, 163, 172, 192, 193, 209

silicone polish 249

sisal 22
skeg 88, 102, 116, 117
skill 5, 9, 21, 22, 34, 68, 73, 111, 121, 124, 139, 145, 158, 163, 164, 187, 208, 209, 227, 268
skimping 65, 67, 139, 152, 154, 198, 201, 212, 217, 219
smell 12, 27, 53, 173, 182, 193
smoke 58–60
solvents 17, 26, 29, 30, 33, 133, 152, 199, 249, 251
speed of moulding Ch33, 10, 65, 141, 144, 172, 205, 206, 212, 213, 219, 231
spillages 33
splash zone 173, 192, 194, 202, 259, 279
split mould 6, 73
splits Ch5, 117, 124, 144, 167, 269
spray moulding 19, 27, 28, 160, 164, 165, 179, 191, 202, 212, 221
spray painting 257
staining test 274
star cracks 24, 273
stem 97, 238, 241
stern tube 157, 247
stiffening Ch13, Ch14, Ch19, 14, 53, 118–24, 256
stiffness Ch13, 18, 21, 22, 48, 51, 92, 121, 125, 127, 138, 212, 218, 223
stitching 94, 95, 217
storage 29, 31, 250
storage life 12, 16, 202, 263
strength 3, 12, 16, 19–21, 34, 37, 38, 48–50, 58, 68, 75, 129, 146, 151, 152, 172, 203, 218, 256
stress concentration Ch17, 96, 97
stress relief 35, 37, 49–51, 70, 271
styrene 12, 14, 17, 27, 29, 32, 57, 65, 128, 133, 144, 146, 154, 160, 203, 204, 227, 228
sun 16, 17, 22, 31, 35, 40, 42, 53, 54, 132, 138, 144, 150, 160, 167, 188, 191, 232, 248
support 73, 88, 91, 116, 248, 256
survey 16, 40, 59, 157, 163, 167, 171, 208, 222, 231, 232, 269, 272, 274, 275, 277
swelling 40, 45, 138, 146, 150, 173
syntactic foam 88, 132, 141, 216

tanks 32, 58, 60, 119, 158, 280
taped joint 216
tapping, (screw thread) 99, 103
tapping, (testing) 136, 141, 164, 191, 275
teak 136, 141, 146–148, 153, 249, 274
telegraphing 14, 19, 40, 67
temperature 11, 14–17, 53, 54, 111, 144, 152, 167, 178, 193, 202, 203, 258, 262, 263
tension 48, 50, 75, 98, 109, 111, 127, 128
terredo 45, 147, 155, 242
testing Ch43, 21, 122, 125, 133, 136, 160, 167, 220, 227, 231, 275–80
thermal expansion/contraction 22, 40, 42, 53, 102, 110, 111, 144, 150
threshold limit value (TLV) 27
thickness Ch32, 68, 78, 98, 109, 113, 114, 123–128, 138, 141, 145, 160–3, 179, 190, 192, 197, 201, 212, 217, 239, 267, 268, 275, 276
testing 190, 192, 197, 220, 221, 276
thixotropic resins 13, 14, 23, 132, 146, 149, 191
threshold of damage Ch5, 17, 47, 49, 54
toe rail 88, 100, 244, 246, 270
tolerance 19, 49, 50, 68, 81, 217, 219, 255
tools Ch3, 141, 251
top hat stiffeners Ch13
toxic fumes 57, 58, 60
trailering 116, 248, 256
transport 14, 17, 31, 57
trimming 25, 32, 33
tropical conditions 51, 53, 111, 132, 150, 153, 155, 167, 175–180, 188, 192, 193, 199–203, 232, 255, 262
twin keels 116, 117

ultrasonic testing 277
undercure 15, 28, 42, 67, 160, 163, 179, 182, 191, 202, 211, 262
underwater 8, 16, 22, 41, 58, 97, 112, 149, 152, 161–4, 187, 207, 249, 258, 259, 262
underwater setting 112, 152, 262
uni-directional materials 4, 21, 78, 92, 95, 129

vacuum bag 123, 134, 175, 193, 228
veneers 45, 95, 145–148
ventilation 29, 148, 203, 212
vinyl lining 103, 112
vinyl ester 13, 21, 28, 60, 116, 152, 160, 163, 179, 180, 191, 192, 209
V.O.C. 25–9, 250
voids Ch26, Ch27, 19, 41, 59, 81, 125, 139, 141, 205–9, 277–9

washers 71, 98–103
waste disposal 32, 33, 198
water absorption Ch26, 13, 21, 35, 40, 45–9, 51, 136, 138, 139, 232
water resistance Ch26, 12–24, 58, 128, 131, 138, 152, 159, 162, 165, 203
water soluble molecules, (WSMs) Ch26, 41–5, 50, 101, 197
water tanks 32, 119, 158, 280
watertight doors 96, 97
waterways Ch19, 44, 45, 88, 112, 126, 131, 135, 138, 207, 262, 270, 279
wax 13, 23, 153, 165, 173, 249
weathering Ch25, 12, 22, 29, 40, 51, 58, 99, 131, 159–165, 232, 248–50, 264, 274, 277
wear Ch35, 39, 84, 99, 145, 159, 168, 248, 249
weave 19, 20, 218, 220
webs Ch13, 82, 84, 96
wet mat 71, 109, 123, 132, 138
wet strength 12, 21, 22, 48–51, 58
wicking 42, 138, 182, 189
wig-wag 276

wire brush 67, 267
wiring 59, 60, 158, 280
wood Ch20, Ch22, 145-8
wood preservative 17, 148, 152
wood primer 146, 152
work boats 9, 241
workers 34, 68, 105, 157, 172, 175, 189–219, 241
working conditions Ch3, 12, 25–9

woven rovings 8, 19, 55, 58, 60, 64, 65, 81, 88, 141, 152, 164, 175, 197, 204, 208, 213, 317, 319, 221, 226, 227, 273

yellow pigment 161
yellow penetrant stain 274

Z angle 82